Tourism in Post-Communist States

This book addresses tourism and its development in the post-communist context of Central and Eastern Europe (CEE). Although it has been over 30 years since many countries of Central and Eastern Europe embarked on the path of transition from state socialism to capitalism and liberal democracy, the ongoing atrocious events in Ukraine bluntly remind us that the perception of CEE as a 'transition' region may have been done away with too early and that the legacies of communism continue to influence the reality of the region. Tourism is no exception here. On the one hand, tourism has significantly contributed to the post-communist restructuring of CEE, and on the other, the communist heritage has played (and still plays) an important role in shaping the tourism geographies of the CEE region.

This book consists of 14 chapters (divided into two sections), a new introduction and a reflective concluding section. All 14 main chapters in this book were originally published in the *Tourism Geographies* journal. The aim of the book is two-fold. First, it summarises, distils, and highlights the important and often ground-breaking contributions *Tourism Geographies* has made over the years to the debate on tourism in CEE. Second, it lays foundations for further research on tourism in the post-communist states of CEE. This book will be of great interest to upper-level students, researchers, and academics in various disciplines – human geography, politics, sociology, and tourism studies in general.

Piotr Niewiadomski is an Economic Geographer interested in the worldwide development of the tourism production system and uneven impacts of tourism on economic development, with a particular interest in Central and Eastern Europe. Piotr is a Senior Lecturer in Human Geography at the University of Aberdeen, Scotland, UK.

Tourism in Post-Communist States

Central and Eastern Europe

Edited by
Piotr Niewiadomski

Routledge
Taylor & Francis Group

LONDON AND NEW YORK

First published 2023
by Routledge
4 Park Square, Milton Park, Abingdon, Oxon, OX14 4RN

and by Routledge
605 Third Avenue, New York, NY 10158

Routledge is an imprint of the Taylor & Francis Group, an informa business

Foreword © 2023 Jarkko Saarinen
Introduction, Conclusion © 2023 Piotr Niewiadomski
Chapters 1–14 © 2023 Taylor & Francis

British Library Cataloguing-in-Publication Data
A catalogue record for this book is available from the British Library

ISBN13: 978-1-032-42355-5 (hbk)
ISBN13: 978-1-032-42356-2 (pbk)
ISBN13: 978-1-003-36241-8 (ebk)

DOI: 10.4324/9781003362418

Typeset in Minion Pro
by codeMantra

Publisher's Note
The publisher accepts responsibility for any inconsistencies that may have arisen during the conversion of this book from journal articles to book chapters, namely the inclusion of journal terminology.

Disclaimer
Every effort has been made to contact copyright holders for their permission to reprint material in this book. The publishers would be grateful to hear from any copyright holder who is not here acknowledged and will undertake to rectify any errors or omissions in future editions of this book.

To my beloved wife Karolina

Contents

Part I

Tourism in transition: From problems and challenges to success and prosperity?   11

Part II

Advancing post-communist change: Tourism as a transformative force

Citation Information

The chapters in this book were originally published in various volumes and issues of the journal *Tourism Geographies*. When citing this material, please use the original page numbering for each article, as follows:

Chapter 1
Tourism patterns and problems in East Central Europe
Russell L. Ivy and Charles B. Copp
Tourism Geographies, volume 1, issue 4 (1999) pp. 425–442

Chapter 2
Troubled sustainability: Bulgarian seaside resorts
Marin Bachvarov
Tourism Geographies, volume 1, issue 2 (1999) pp. 192–203

Chapter 3
Gazing on communism: Heritage tourism and post-communist identities in Germany, Hungary and Romania
Duncan Light
Tourism Geographies, volume 2, issue 2 (2000) pp. 157–176

Chapter 4
Unpacking the local: A cultural analysis of tourism entrepreneurship in Murter, Croatia
Irena Ateljevic and Stephen Doorne
Tourism Geographies, volume 5, issue 2 (2003) pp. 123–150

Chapter 5
Ecotourism in post-communist Poland: An examination of tourists, sustainability and institutions
Agnes M.K. Nowaczek and David A. Fennell
Tourism Geographies, volume 4, issue 4 (2002) pp. 372–395

Chapter 6
Relationships between international tourism and migration in Hungary: Tourism flows and foreign property ownership
Sándor Illés and Gábor Michalkó
Tourism Geographies, volume 10, issue 1 (2008) pp. 98–118

For any permission-related enquiries please visit:
http://www.tandfonline.com/page/help/permissions

Notes on Contributors

Irena Ateljevic did her PhD in Human Geography at the University of Auckland, New Zealand. She taught at many Universities worldwide but has recently returned back to her home country of Croatia. She currently teaches at Aspira College in Split and Zagreb, Croatia. In order to walk her talk, she has also established a Center for Regeneration and Human Potential – Terra Meera.

Marin Bachvarov has been a Professor in the Department of Geography in the Sofia St. Kliment Ohridski University, Bulgaria, since 1990. His fields of interest include the regional geography of tourism, heritage as tourist attractions, and social and political geography.

Charles B. Copp, MAI, is a commercial fee appraiser and partner with Appraisal & Consulting Group LLC of Portland, USA. Bryan graduated from Florida Atlantic University, Boca Raton, USA, with a Bachelor's and Master's degree in Geography with an emphasis on economic and tourism geographies.

Adrienne Csizmady is the Director of the Institute for Sociology of the Hungarian Academy of Sciences. Her research interests include social problems of large housing estates, social segregation, urban poverty, social consequences of urban renewal, culture and heritage, and sustainable social environments.

Stephen Doorne is a Lecturer in Tourism Studies at the School of Social and Economic Development at the University of the South Pacific, Suva, Fiji. His academic research includes the cultural context of entrepreneurship, tourism and community development, backpacker tourism, and heritage interpretation.

Tamás Egedy (PhD) is an Urban Geographer. He is an Associate Professor at the Budapest Business School and a Senior Research Fellow at the Geographical Institute of the Research Centre for Astronomy and Earth Sciences. His research activities are in the field of urban regeneration, housing estates, and creative economy in Hungary.

David A. Fennell researches and teaches in the areas of ecotourism, tourism ethics, animal ethics, and sustainability ethics. His research involves the use of theory from other disciplines (e.g., biology, philosophy) to gain traction on many of tourism's most persistent issues. Fennell is the founding Editor-in-Chief of the *Journal of Ecotourism*.

Dana Fialová works as an Assistant Professor of Geography at the Faculty of Science at Charles University, Prague, Czech Republic. She focuses on the geography of tourism and leisure, specialising on the research of second homes. At the same time, she is the Vice President of the Czech Geographical Society.

Derek Hall, BA PhD PGDipLing, is a Partner in Seabank Associates, Ayrshire, Scotland; a formerly Professor of Regional Development at the Scottish Agricultural College; and a Visiting Professor at the HAMK University of Applied Sciences, Finland. His research interests have included Arctic tourism, climate change and geopolitics, Tourism and post-socialist development, Tourism and rural development, Mobilities and transport policy.

Sándor Illés is the Director of Active Society Foundation, Budapest, Hungary. He is a Geo-Demographer combining with migration studies expertise. His major research interest is the multidisciplinary themes of international migration in which he deals with retirement migration, migration-tourism nexus, circular migration, and migration politics.

Russell L. Ivy, PhD, currently serves as a Vice Provost for Academic Affairs and Professor of Geosciences at Florida Atlantic University, Boca Raton, USA. His research focuses on the spatial analysis and modelling of flows, specifically as applied to the impacts of both governmental and corporate policy changes in transportation and tourism.

András Jancsik is a Vice Rector for Education at the Budapest Business School, Hungary. His research interests include tourism policy and planning, tourism marketing, destination competitiveness, and tourism and technology.

Jeff Jarvis has an industry background and has developed an international research reputation in the high yielding segment of independent travellers. He has delivered keynote presentations at the national tourism conferences of Australia, Estonia, Fiji, and Kenya. He has presented on behalf of the UNWTO at ITB Berlin on the role independent travellers play in the development of emerging economies.

Bálint Kádár is an Associate Professor at the Budapest University of Technology and Economics, Hungary. An Architect, Urban Scholar and Planner, his research focuses on the spatial development of tourism in cities and regions based on the analysis of user generated digital content. He also leads a professional NGO and international projects focusing on the rehabilitation of historic urban centres and stakeholder involvement in such processes.

Piret Kallas graduated from the Tallinn University of Technology in International Economics and Business Administration in 1997 and received Graduate Certificate of Tourism from Monash University, Australia, in 2003. Since 1995, she has been responsible for market research and analysis at the Estonian Tourist Board (now part of Enterprise Estonia).

Tiit Kask (MSc in Human Geography) is a Freelance Researcher, Consultant and Lecturer, and Development Manager of the Pärnu Museum, Estonia. He also serves as a Visiting Lecturer at the Estonian University of Life Sciences, Tartu, Estonia. His research interests include tourism and development, historical geography and regional studies, and history of seaside resorts.

Duncan Light is a Principal Lecturer in Tourism Management at Bournemouth University, UK. A Human Geographer by background, he has long-standing research interests in heritage tourism, particularly in Romania (a country he has visited regularly). He is the author of *The Dracula Dilemma: Tourism, Identity and the State in Romania* (Routledge, 2016).

Gábor Michalkó is a Scientific Advisor at the CSFK Geographical Institute and Professor of Tourism at Corvinus University of Budapest, Hungary. He is a Steering Committee's Member of IGU Commission on Global Change and Human Mobility. His research interests include both principles of tourism and problems focusing on tourism geography.

Piotr Niewiadomski is an Economic Geographer interested in the worldwide development of the tourism production system and uneven impacts of tourism on economic development, with a particular interest in Central and Eastern Europe. Piotr is a Senior Lecturer in Human Geography at the University of Aberdeen, Scotland, UK.

Agnes M.K. Nowaczek is a Professor at the School of Hospitality and Tourism at Niagara College Canada. Her academic interests focus on visitor behaviour and management, transformational visitor experiences, and program design and evaluation. Dr. Nowaczek is the Associate Editor for the *Journal of Ecotourism* and a Board Member of the North American Ecotourism Network.

Gergély Olt is an Assistant Researcher at the ELKH Institute for Sociology. His research interest is how different empirical experiences of urban transformations can be theorised by the revision of universally claimed political economic narratives. His publications are about locally appearing social conflicts (i.e. gentrification, touristification, and mega-projects) and how grassroots movements can be involved in them.

Tamara Rátz is a Professor of Tourism and the Head of Tourism Department at Kodolányi János University, Hungary. She is the author or co-author of more than 190 publications, including 12 books. Her current research projects include the role of Art Nouveau heritage in tourism and responsible tourism in the post-covid era.

Jarkko Saarinen is a Professor of Human Geography at the University of Oulu, Finland. His research interests include tourism and development, sustainability, adaptation and resilience, tourism-community relations, and nature conservation. He has been a Visiting Lecturer at Pärnu College at the University of Tartu, Estonia, with research and lecturing interests on tourism planning and development.

Melanie Smith is an Associate Professor at the Budapest Metropolitan University, Hungary, and a Researcher whose work focuses on urban planning, cultural tourism, and well-being. She has been an Invited Lecturer and Speaker in many countries worldwide. She was the Chair of ATLAS for seven years and has undertaken consultancy work for UNWTO and ETC.

Jana Spilková worked as an Associate Professor of Human Geography at the Department of Social Geography and Regional Development at Charles University, Prague, Czech Republic, before joining the European Research Council as a Project Adviser. Her research interests include geography of consumption, alternative food networks, and urban agriculture.

Foreword

Many disciplines and research fields have their own understandings of what makes specific topics essential and timely to study and discuss. Some political geographers, for example, have a continuous tendency to justify their research interest on borders as more relevant and topical than ever before. This persistent relevance seems to be independent of whether borders are built up or torn down as both cases demonstrate the need understand what is happening at and for specific borders or the idea of border. On a certain level, this prolific book *Tourism in Post-communist States: Central and Eastern Europe* resonates with the notion of changing borders and the impacts of de/bordering processes. However, the approach adopted is more comprehensive, focusing beyond borders on states, regions, and their transformations and contexts. Furthermore, an emphasis is placed upon how tourism development and tourists in the select region have played their agency and shaped different complex, often difficult, and uneven transition processes from state socialism to (neo)liberal market economies.

The region under scrutiny, Central and Eastern Europe (CEE), has been in a major state of flux politically, socially, and economically over the past three decades. This versatile collection sheds light on the role of tourism in post-communist states and their transition characterised by emphases on neoliberally driven economic development and contextual structural problems from past communism. However, although the CEE region may have been externally perceived as uniform with some widely shared connecting elements, this book rightfully demonstrates the internal complexities of the region and the diversified ways in which tourism has been used as a vehicle of change. These internal intricacies and pluralities are well explored in the excellent introduction by Piotr Niewiadomski. He points out, for example, that in the CEE transition process, the original bloc of nine communist countries eventually transformed into 21 sovereign states in the new Europe. These 'new' states not only share some similarities but also exhibit significant differences in terms of their economic and political connections to the rest of Europe and the global economy.

After the collapse of state socialism and the rise of new CEE nation-states, there have been some calmer periods in the region's economic and political restructuring. This 'normalizing' phase has seen the rise in tourism development and consumption as well as related research on tourism geographies. That said, the Russian attack in 2022 and the resulting war in Ukraine has reignited and re-intensified territorial thinking, bordering, and research interests on the wider CEE region and its internal and external mobility questions.

As Niewiadomski notes, the post-communist restructuring after 1989 involved tourism development aspects, but geographical research interests in the region's tourism were still limited and somewhat undervalued, partly because tourism was not fully considered a serious subject in geographical scholarship. Interestingly, this hierarchical division on relevant and irrelevant research topics was (probably) primarily based on Marxist geography thinking from the 1960s and 1970s, indicating that instead of focusing on wealthy individuals' free time, geographers should have more serious research interests on uneven power relations, inequalities, and global capitalism, for example. Against this backdrop, it is surprising to read some Marxist geographers' recent analyses of neoliberalism and global inequalities. For example, David Harvey mentions the role of tourism in the global neoliberal agenda and its uneven development in his book *A Brief History of Neoliberalism* from 2005. In a more recent work, *The Anti-capitalist Chronicles* from 2020, Harvey goes further by underscoring the role of global tourism as a neoliberal tool for spatial fix aiming to resolve the problems of the overaccumulation of capital.

However, based on the book at hand, the critical and severe nature of tourism for regional (uneven) development, politics, and identities in the post-communist states is unsurprising, on the contrary. As Niewiadomski flags in the introduction, the determined work of tourism geographers from the 1990s onwards has demonstrated that tourism offers a beneficial lens through which the transition of CEE states from top-down manufacturing entities to market-driven and service-orientated economies can be understood and analyzed in more depth. In this respect, Niewiadomski highlights two fruitful research avenues for tourism geographies in post-communist states. Firstly, there has been a strong focus on the role of communist legacies in shaping tourism patterns and new developments in the region. Secondly, tourism geographers have assessed the role of tourism in post-communist transformations and how tourism has served as an agent of change in regional transformation in the CEE states. These perspectives are both timely and relevant within the context of the current situation.

This book is based on a selected collection of research papers published in the journal of *Tourism Geographies* on tourism in the CEE region. The individual chapters are aptly described and contextualized in the introduction by Niewiadomski who also concludes this book in a chapter that discusses and speculates, as carefully as an academic can, about the impacts of the war in Ukraine on the future of tourism and tourism geographies in the CEE. While it is challenging to form conjectures on these matters, as history has not yet defined the outcome of the war nor closed the period during which time the war took place, the invasion of Ukraine has revived the 'ghost of communism' and has served as a reminder of how the communist legacies continue to shape the contemporary reality of the region. As Niewiadomski states, "post-communism is not yet over."

Furthermore, Niewiadomski points out that despite the great tragedy and impact of the war in Ukraine, it is not the only element that defines the influence of the past communism on the present or the future of the region and its tourism. In this respect, he stresses the role of emerging semi-authoritarian regimes in CEE, for example, differentiating parts of CEE away from democratic policies and state governance in political, economic, social, and geopolitical terms. For Niewiadomski, this stands in contradiction to bringing post-communism thinking to an end. Rather, the recent populist political agenda has ushered the CEE region into a bizarre era that he refers to as "post-post-communism" where the future development paths of CEE countries are much more diversified than after the collapse of state socialism in 1989.

With its fresh introduction and conclusions, this collection is interesting, essential, and timely. Through its exploration of the state-of-art but also a lacuna in tourism geographies focusing on CEE, this book informs us and points us towards a new research agenda that acknowledges past research contributions and evolving new research questions and needs. I truly hope that this excellent collection prompts critical engagement and invites the reader to contribute towards future scholarship on tourism geographies in Central and Eastern Europe.

Jarkko Saarinen

Acknowledgements

This volume builds on the online collection of papers on tourism in the post-communist countries of Central and Eastern Europe (CEE) that have been published in *Tourism Geographies* (TG) since the onset of the journal. The collection was compiled in June 2022 on the Taylor & Francis / *Tourism Geographies* website. I am grateful to both Editors-in-Chief of *Tourism Geographies* – Professor Joseph Cheer (Wakayama University) and Professor Mary Mostafanezhad (the University of Hawai'i at Mānoa) – for starting the series of online collections of *TG* papers, supporting my idea to develop the collection on tourism in CEE, and, subsequently, facilitating the development of this volume.

I would also like to thank all contributors to this volume. This volume would not have been possible without their valuable, often ground-breaking research over the last 20-30 years. In this respect, this book is a testimony to their important contributions to the 'tourism in post-communist states' research agenda. Connected to this, I want to acknowledge the crucial role played over the years by Professor Alan Lew (Northern Arizona University) – the founder and the former Editor-in-Chief of the *Tourism Geographies* journal, whose excellent editorial decisions helped the *TG* journal make a significant contribution to this important research field. This acknowledgment also needs to be extended to all current and former members of the *Tourism Geographies* Editorial Board who also facilitated and encouraged these advancements.

I am also grateful to Professor Jarkko Saarinen (University of Oulu) for writing an inspiring foreword for this book and for peer-reviewing my new contributions to this volume – the introductory chapter and the reflective chapter at the end.

This book would also have not been developed without the help and support offered by Routledge – particularly Ms Anveshi Gupta, Commissioning Editor, whose professional advice throughout the whole process was truly invaluable.

On a more personal level, I am grateful to my MA supervisor – Professor Alison Stenning (Newcastle University), and my PhD supervisors – Dr Martin Hess (The University of Manchester) and Professor Neil Coe (currently the National University of Singapore, formerly The University of Manchester) for helping me develop academic curiosity in my home region and for equipping me with the skills and knowledge to pursue my research interests.

Piotr Niewiadomski
University of Aberdeen
October 2022

Introduction: Tourism development and post-communist transformations in Central and Eastern Europe

PIOTR NIEWIADOMSKI

30 years of research on tourism in post-communist states

The fall of communism in Central and Eastern Europe (CEE) over three decades ago was one of the most significant events in the post-WWII history. As the majority of formerly communist states in CEE rejected state socialism and opted to free themselves from Soviet hegemony, the world witnessed a major reorientation of CEE and the onset of complex political, economic, and social changes that transformed not only the CEE region but the whole Europe (Smith, 1997; Sokol, 2001). While East Germany reunited with West Germany (with the fall of the Berlin Wall becoming a symbol not only of the German re-unification but of the whole demise of communism), the Soviet Union disintegrated into 15 independent states, Czechoslovakia into two, and Yugoslavia into seven. As a result, the CEE communist bloc, which consisted of nine countries bundled together by Soviet control and authority (i.e. the Soviet Union, Czechoslovakia, Poland, Hungary, Bulgaria, Romania, East Germany, Albania, and Yugoslavia), transmuted into 21 sovereign states (not including former Soviet republics outside Europe), most of which adopted an objective to establish a form of capitalism and liberal democracy and (re-)connect with the global economy (Amsden et al., 1994; Gowan, 1995; Kołodko, 2000).

Inspired by the neoliberal doctrine and guided by a range of Western multilateral organisations, most CEE countries hoped for a smooth transition from state socialism to a market economy and a quick and painless re-integration with the West (Bradshaw and Stenning, 2004; Smith and Pickles, 1998). The transitional project orchestrated by Western advisors envisaged a swift implementation of a stock set of policies, mechanisms, reforms, and other relevant structural adjustments to kick-start economic liberalisation, internationalisation, marketisation, and privatisation; dismantle central planning; and help replace former socialist institutions with new ones (Bradshaw and Stenning, 2004; Smith, 1997; Smith and Pickles, 1998; Sokol, 2001). However, the post-communist reality proved different than expected. Given that each state had different historical experiences, a different earlier path of growth, and a different capacity to accommodate the suggested changes (despite sharing a communist past for a few decades), the transition assumed different forms in different countries and fostered (or exposed) different economic and social problems (Smith and Pickles, 1998, Sokol 2001). Moreover, due to the fact that the legacies of institutional frameworks and social relations derived from communism proved to play a critical role in determining the pace, depth, and direction of the post-communist restructuring (Bradshaw and Stenning, 2004; Smith, 1997; Smith and Pickles, 1998; Sokol, 2001), instead of 'a smooth transition', CEE experienced a diversity of complex and asynchronous transformations – "a plurality of transitions (...), a multiplicity of distinctive strategies, (...) not one transition but many occurring in different domains – political, economic and social" (Stark, 1992, p. 301).

Thus, further to the fall of communism in 1989, the CEE region entered a period of post-communism characterised by a complex interplay between the universal neoliberal project and the variety of post-socialist contexts. Given that the communist past and its incessant influence on further development were the common differences from the West which CEE states shared (despite following different paths of post-communist growth), the category of post-communism became a defining attribute of the CEE region for many years to come (Stenning and Bradshaw, 2004). Although the admission of as many as eleven formerly communist countries to the European Union (Estonia, Latvia, Lithuania, Hungary, Poland, Czechia, Slovakia, and Slovenia in 2004, Romania and Bulgaria in 2007, and Croatia in 2013) was anticipated by many observers to bring an end to post-communism, the traces of the communist past remained apparent in the geographies and space economies of CEE also after the EU expansion (Smith and Timar, 2010).

Quite naturally, and rather inevitably, the post-communist restructuring after 1989 also encompassed tourism. The disintegration of the Council for Mutual Economic Assistance (the communist economic organisation that kept the CEE bloc isolated from the global economy), followed by the processes of internationalisation which opened the region to import competition and foreign direct investment and fostered the development of competitive export industries (Bradshaw and Swain, 2004; Dunford and Smith, 2004), sparked a re-evaluation of tourism in the economies of CEE (Franck, 1990; Johnson and Vanetti, 2004). Given that in the Marxist philosophy services were considered non-productive and that communist authorities were ideologically pre-occupied with manufacturing and other heavy industries (Hall, 1992; Johnson and Vanetti, 2004; Williams and Balaž, 2002), the transition which tourism in CEE had to embark on was exceptionally challenging. The vast range of problems deriving from the communist era which the sector had to overcome to find a place in the new reality not only determined the complexity of tourism development in CEE but also attested to the unprecedented and unique nature of this process. It should not be therefore surprising that the multi-dimensional relations between post-communist transformations and tourism growth in the CEE region after 1989 sparked a lot of scholarly interest and became an important research theme in its own right.

Although initially tourism was not a primary focus in research on post-communist changes (e.g. the seminal volumes edited by Pickles and Smith, 1998, and Bradshaw and Stenning, 2004, do not include chapters on tourism, while Turnock's edited volume, 2001, includes only one contribution), tourism researchers quickly addressed this gap. While economists, sociologists, and business and management scholars made an important contribution to this process (e.g. Buckley and Witt, 1990; Burns, 1998; Harrison, 1993; Pearlman, 1990; Scott and Renaghan, 1991; Smeral, 1993), tourism geographers, who still had to fight at that time for a better recognition of tourism as a valid topic of research within geography (as opposed to a mere fun activity not worthy scholarly attention) (see Butler, 2004; Hall and Page, 2014; Ioannides and Debbage, 1998; Williams, 2009), played a central role in enhancing the general understanding of tourism in transition and bridging the gap between tourism studies and the wider scholarship on the post-communist restructuring in CEE. The pioneer work of Derek Hall (1990, 1991, 1992, 1995, 1998a, 1998b, 2000a, 2000b, including a chapter in the aforementioned volume edited by Turnock, – see Hall, 2001) laid essential foundations for further studies of tourism development in CEE. The work of Turnock (1990, 1999), Light (2000, 2001) and Light and Dumbrăveanu (1999) on Romania; Unwin (1996) and Jaakson (1996) on Estonia; Bachvarov (1997) on Bulgaria; Johnson (1995, 1997) on the Czech

Republic and Slovakia, and on Hungary, respectively; and Balaž (1995) and Williams and Balaž (2000, 2001, 2002) on the Czech Republic and Slovakia also deserves special credits here for delivering a number of in-depth geographical and sectoral case studies that exposed and examined a wide variety of issues associated with tourism (re-)development in CEE.

By means of unpacking the place-specific nature of tourism growth in the post-communist context, geographical research on tourism not only helped examine tourism (re-) development in CEE *per se* but, given that customer services in CEE had been previously underdeveloped, also helped explore various important aspects of post-communist transformations which research on other sectors could not always address (Niewiadomski, 2018). As such, tourism proved to be a useful (and in many ways unique!) lens through which the transition from a system based on manufacturing to a more service-orientated economy could be understood in more depth. Although geographical research on tourism in CEE took many different directions over the 1990s and later, two broad themes could be identified in this scholarship. First, a considerable amount of research focused on the impacts of post-communist restructuring on tourism (re-)development and the role of communist legacies in shaping the tourism geographies of the CEE region. In this respect, by examining the various problems which tourism in CEE grappled with, geographical research on tourism helped unravel the chaotic and contested nature of post-communist restructuring, thus further challenging the neoliberal idea of a painless and smooth shift from communism to capitalism (Niewiadomski, 2018). Second, the work of tourism geographers also explored the contribution of tourism to post-communist transformations and its role in driving economic and social upgrading at different spatial scales – from local to national. As such, tourism was recognised as a significant transformative force and an important agent of regional change across different contexts – urban, rural, coastal, remote, etc. (Niewiadomski, 2018).

A particularly important role in promoting geographical research on tourism in CEE and facilitating the debate on the interdependencies between tourism and post-communist change has been played by *Tourism Geographies – An International Journal of Tourism Place, Space and Environment* (TG). Since its outset in 1999, the journal has served as a perfect outlet for tourism geographers interested in CEE and looking to connect tourism studies with the wider literature on the CEE region after 1989. The journal's special issue "Tourism in Transition Economies" (vol. 10, issue 4, 2008), guest-edited by Saarinen (2008), deserves special recognition here, although many other TG papers have addressed tourism in CEE in the meantime too.

The primary aim of this volume is to bring all these papers together and thus distil the contribution to the debate on tourism development in CEE made by the *Tourism Geographies* journal over the years. As such, this volume builds upon the online collection of TG papers compiled and published in June 2022 under the same title on the Taylor & Francis / *Tourism Geographies* website (Niewiadomski, 2022). However, this volume also has a secondary aim. Given that the legacies of the previous system continue to shape the reality of the CEE region (thus showing that the transition is not yet over despite the significant progress which many CEE states have made to date), this collection of papers aims to serve as a basis for further research on tourism in the post-communist context of CEE. Although the economic and political success of various formerly communist states in CEE allowed many scholars to forget about the region's communist past and stop looking at it through the lens of what the previous period may have left behind, the atrocious invasion of Ukraine in February 2022, driven by a desire to restore the pre-1989 political order, is a blunt reminder that the category of post-communism is still 'alive' and that the perception of CEE as a 'transition' region may have been done away with too early. More research will be therefore needed

on tourism in CEE as a formerly communist region, as opposed to CEE as a mere geographical location. The story which the essays included in this volume tell will therefore require a
continuation. The final chapter of this volume builds upon these papers' contributions, and,
with reference to the recent events in CEE, it outlines a new research agenda on tourism in
the post-communist states of CEE.

Structure of the book

Following this introduction, this book is divided into two main parts, with each part representing one of the two aforementioned broad themes in geographical research on tourism in
CEE. Part I consists of eight papers that analyse, explore, and reflect on how the legacies of
communism and the chaotic, turbulent processes of post-communist restructuring shaped
the tourism geographies of CEE further to the fall of communism. As the title of this part
implies, this group of papers illustrates the progress which the national and regional tourism industries as well as various tourist destinations across CEE made in the first 20 years
of transition – from the challenges inherited from the past and the dilemmas associated
with the political, social, and economic re-orientation of the region to a range of successes
which post-communist transformations catalysed. Altogether, Part I paints a picture of the
'bumpy' and 'rocky' journey which tourism in CEE embarked on after 1989 for the years to
come – a journey that is not yet fully concluded.

Chapter 1 (the paper by **Ivy and Copp, 1999**) provides a discussion of the different problems that hampered tourism development in CEE in the 1990s and that could be directly
attributed to the neglect of services under communism and the strong centralisation of
tourism planning and management in the communist system. Shortages of trained staff, a
low quantity and a poor quality of accommodation facilities, under-developed tourist infrastructure, non-existent or slowly evolving tourism marketing, and low levels of entrepreneurship amongst CEE citizens are some of the key issues identified in the paper. **Ivy and
Copp** also utilise the case studies of Slovakia, Hungary, and Slovenia to demonstrate how
the controlled concentration of international tourism in selected geographical areas before
1989 determined the patterns of international visitation at the onset of the transition, thus
reinforcing (or causing) vast regional disparities in the distribution of foreign tourists and
slowing down the potential contribution of tourism to regional upgrading.

In a similar vein, **Bachvarov (1999) (Chapter 2)** discusses a range of challenges which
Bulgarian resorts had to face during the restructuring of Bulgarian tourism after 1989. This
paper focuses on the peculiar case of large Bulgarian resorts on the Black Sea coast (e.g.
Sunny Beach and Golden Sands) – major infrastructural projects that were purposefully
developed by communist authorities as mono-culture summer destinations and that faced
a serious decline after 1989 due to the discontinuation of central management. The gradual
deterioration of accommodation facilities (and the accompanying infrastructure), which the
withdrawal of central funding caused, combined with numerous economic problems such
as high inflation and the difficulties with evaluating the market value of hotels, made the
privatisation of individual accommodation establishments much slower and more selective
than expected, thus hampering the introduction of market activities, values, and principles
to those resorts. Moreover, because of the fact that many of those resorts had no separate
settlement status (and no or little permanent population), deciding on the direction which
tourism development on the Bulgarian coast should take proved to be more difficult than
expected and, as such, it became another challenge which the tourism industry had to face
to survive.

By contrast to **Chapters 1 and 2**, both of which focus on concrete and material issues, the following two papers address various cultural dimensions of tourism in transition – no less important sources of problems and dilemmas which tourist destinations across CEE experienced at the onset of post-communist transformations. Thus, **Light (2000) (Chapter 3)** explores the clash between the efforts of CEE states to deny (or erase) the legacies of communism, re-appraise the past, and construct a new post-communist national identity, and the strong interest in communist heritage which international tourists coming to CEE exhibited in the 1990s. Due to the fact that communist legacies (and sites associated with the fall of communism) proved to be an important force attracting foreign visitors to CEE, many destinations faced the challenge how to promote those tourist 'assets' (and capture the economic value which communist heritage tourism could bring) without celebrating or glorifying the communist past and compromising the construction of a post-communist identity. This paper discusses three specific objects – the Berlin Wall (Germany), Statuepark in Budapest (Hungary), and the House of the People in Bucharest (Romania) – to exemplify the various ways in which this dilemma was tackled and the conflicting interests of tourists and tourist destinations were negotiated. In turn, the paper by **Ateljevic and Doorne (2003) (Chapter 4)** draws from the 'cultural turn' in geography to analyse the influence of local cultural values on tourism entrepreneurship in the village of Murter (Croatia). Relying on the assumption that culture and economy are mutually constituted, this paper demonstrates how various cultural attributes of the local community (e.g. family and social relations) steered the re-development of tourism in the village after the fall of communism and the atrocious war that shook the Balkans in the 1990s. While local cultural values ensured the continuity, security, and stability of both the local community and the local tourism industry, tourism was simultaneously found to serve as a carrier of these values. In this respect, by paying attention to the role of non-economic, lifestyle-related values in shaping entrepreneurship (as opposed to business-related factors), **Ateljevic and Doorne (2003)** make a noteworthy theoretical contribution to the literature on tourism entrepreneurship and the wider culture-economy debate in the social sciences.

Chapter 5 (the paper by **Nowaczek and Fennell, 2002**) focuses on ecotourism in Poland – one of those categories of tourism that were largely underdeveloped during communism and which started gaining in popularity in CEE only in the 1990s, thus largely diversifying the tourism product inherited from the communist past. On the one hand, this paper identifies a vast array of factors hindering the development of ecotourism in Poland in the first decade of transition (e.g. a shortage of funding, poor planning, low environmental awareness of domestic tourists, negligible cooperation between different levels of government, a shortage of social leadership in the area of environmentalism, and different institutional constraints), all of which could be directly or indirectly attributed to the communist past. On the other, it optimistically recognises the role of ecotourism in 'greening' Polish tourism and lists various conditions (e.g. a stronger commitment to the management of protected areas, appropriate environmental education, and more investment in the related infrastructure) that had to be met for ecotourism to help solve some of the related social, economic, and environmental problems.

The last three papers of Part I **(Chapters 6-8)** were written and published after some of the formerly communist countries joined the EU, and, as such, amongst a few other things, they address the impacts which the admission to the EU – a significant milestone in the post-communist transitions of all those states and a symbolic confirmation that the transition had started bringing expected results – proved to have on tourism in the CEE region. **Chapter 6** (the paper by **Illés and Michalkó, 2008**) focuses on various forms of international mobility to and from Hungary and how the interrelations between tourism and migration in Hungary evolved after the fall of communism and, later, after the country joined the EU. Apart from recognising an increase in shopping tourism to Hungary after 1989 and an inflow of foreign workers seeking employment in the Hungarian tourism industry, this paper pays attention to the VF&R (visiting friends and relatives) tourism by Hungarian emigrants – both those who had fled the country before 1989 for political reasons and those who moved abroad after 2004 to seek better economic opportunities elsewhere in the EU. Importantly, **Illés and Michalkó** also discuss the involvement of those emigrants in property acquisition in Hungary and their influence on the real estate market in the country.

Rather than offering a single case study, the paper by **Hall (2008) (Chapter 7)** provides a review of some of the key literature on tourism development in CEE to discuss a range of contemporary issues in the aftermath of the EU enlargement and to identify further research directions. This paper groups the reviewed literature into two broad themes: (1) 'the mobility turn' and the links between tourism and other forms of transnational mobility and cross-border activity and (2) the interrelations between tourism and the process of identity building in CEE states – both as new post-communist democracies and as new tourist markets. Importantly, by making a distinction between 'bricklaying' (defined as gradual development through consolidation and integration) and 'bricolage' (a term that captures the fragmented nature of post-communist changes), **Hall**'s paper offers a useful framework for analysing tourism development in the region, thus also enhancing the general theoretical understanding of post-communist transformations. In the same vein, this paper emphasises the difference between the notion of 'transition', defined as a smooth shift between two points and used in relation to the prescriptive, neoliberal-inspired forms of post-communist restructuring, and the notion of 'transformation', which recognises the diverse, asynchronous, and open-ended nature of changes in CEE (see also Bradshaw and Stenning, 2004; Smith, 1997; Sokol, 2001; Stark, 1992). Although these terms are often used interchangeably (also in this volume!), **Hall**'s paper introduces conceptual clarity to the scholarship on tourism in CEE. As such, this paper serves as a helpful 'bridge' between the work on the problems which tourism in CEE faced after 1989 and the research on the future development of tourism in the CEE region.

Part I ends with the paper by **Jarvis and Kallas (2008) (Chapter 8)** who discuss the development of the Estonian tourism industry from the Soviet era to the first few years after Estonia joined the EU and outline the effects of the accession to the EU on the Estonian tourism industry and the country's position as an attractive and safe international tourist destination. As such, this paper exemplifies the progress which some of the formerly communist countries made in the first 15–20 years after the fall of communism. This paper shows that the accession to the EU not only improved the business climate in Estonia (thus stimulating inward investment in tourist infrastructure) but also facilitated access to this relatively remote market by removing border controls, inserting Estonia into the networks of low-cost carriers, and securing positive coverage for the country in the international media. Although **Jarvis and Kallas** also reflect on some negative effects of the EU accession (e.g. the popularisation of stag parties and their potentially detrimental impact on the reputation of Tallinn), this paper ends Part I on a positive note. In other words, it counterbalances the critical (albeit fully justified) accounts that dominated the literature on tourism development in CEE in the first years of transition and with which Part I inevitably started.

While Part I concentrates on the impacts of the communist past and the processes of post-communist restructuring on tourism development in CEE after 1989, Part II addresses the other side of the coin and, recognising that tourism is a powerful transformative force, it explores its various contributions to the post-communist development of CEE countries, cities, and regions. Altogether, the six papers included in this part **(Chapters 9–14)** provide an array of sectoral and geographical case studies that picture tourism as an important agent of regional and urban change in the post-communist reality and reflect on its positive and negative impacts. Given that all these papers were published in the end of the second and during the third decade after the fall of communism, they also illustrate the important place which tourism secured for itself in the post-communist context.

Part II starts with the paper by **Rátz, Smith, and Michalkó (2008) (Chapter 9)** who critically reflect on the role of tourism in the post-communist urban regeneration of Budapest. **Rátz et al.** discuss the emergence of new, more modern tourism spaces in the city and how they clash with the regenerated and re-packaged sites of pre-communist (and communist) heritage that are key to the city's new post-communist identity. By highlighting the conflicting objectives of urban regeneration in the city, i.e. to preserve its unique character based on heritage on the one hand and to become a cosmopolitan and dynamic European city in a competitive market environment on the other, this paper touches upon the same dilemma as **Light** in **Chapter 3** – how to shake off the shackles of the communist past while preserving its heritage for tourism purposes. In their detailed discussion, **Rátz et al.** unpack this clash by paying attention to numerous specific processes and factors, including the multiplicity of tourism strategies within the city and a lack of consensus on the direction of tourist development, the rising significance of market forces (epitomised by real estate investors looking for short-term profits), the emergence of relatively new forms of tourism (e.g. business tourism and MICE), the development of new shopping and leisure areas, and the role of tourism in regenerating less attractive parts of the city.

In a similar vein, **Chapter 10** (the paper by **Saarinen and Kask, 2008**) analyses the transformation of Pärnu (a historic town and beach resort in Estonia), with a special emphasis on the contribution of tourism to the post-communist re-development of the city. Drawing from the work of Williams and Baláž (2002), **Saarinen and Kask** adopt the notions of path-dependence and path-creation to explore the role of historical legacies (both pre-communist and communist) in shaping the post-communist trajectory of tourism growth in the city on the one hand (path-dependence) and the active influence of various tourism actors on this trajectory on the other (i.e. path-creation). This paper argues that the evolution of a tourist destination cannot be fully understood without paying attention to wider socio-political changes. As such, by means of utilising the ideas associated with the so-called 'alternative approach' to post-communist transformations (e.g. Stark 1992, 1994, 1996; Sokol, 2001), **Saarinen and Kask** not only help connect the work on tourism with the wider scholarship on post-communist changes in CEE but also make an important theoretical contribution to the literature on tourist destination evolution. In this respect, this paper helped lay important foundations for the subsequent popularisation of evolutionary perspectives in tourism studies, which culminated in the publication of the special issue of *Tourism Geographies* entitled "Evolutionary Economic Geography and the Economies of Tourism Destinations" (vol. 16, 2014), and the volume edited by Brouder et al. (2017) – "Tourism Destination Evolution".

Chapter 11 (the paper by **Spilková and Fialová, 2013**) discusses the emergence of culinary tourism in Czechia in the post-communist era and the role of culinary tourism packages in fostering regional rural development in the country. Although this paper identifies a number of obstacles which culinary tourism needed to overcome to bring desired results (e.g. poor links between local entrepreneurs and other tourism stakeholders), special attention is paid to the (potentially) productive interrelationships between culinary products and regional branding, i.e. how culinary products rooted in local traditions contribute to the creation of regional brands, and how such brands market respective regions, promote their culinary traditions, and encourage culinary tourism. As such, this paper counterbalances the focus on urban tourism represented by **Chapters 9 and 10**, thus adding an important empirical example to the diversity of ways in which tourism helped advance post-communist changes in CEE.

Similarly to the paper by **Saarinen and Kask**, **Chapter 12** (the paper by **Niewiadomski, 2015**) also utilises theoretical advancements made in economic geography to further analysis of tourism and its development in CEE. However, rather than concentrating on a particular destination, **Niewiadomski** takes on board a particular sub-sector of tourism – the international hotel industry. This paper adopts the global production networks (GPN) framework (particularly the concept of strategic coupling) and combines it with selected assumptions of evolutionary economic geography (EEG) (mainly the ideas of path-dependence, path-creation, and lock-in) to explore the impacts of international hotel groups on regional upgrading in CEE on the basis of Poland, Bulgaria, and Estonia. This paper discusses three main categories of impact (direct investment and infrastructure upgrading, job creation, and know-how transfer) and highlights their potential to help de-lock the tourism economies of CEE from the post-communist path-dependence. The analysis demonstrates that the impact of international hotel groups on regional development hinges upon the business model which a given group adopts (i.e. a kind of GPN which it develops and relies on) and that it is also largely influenced by local factors. Alongside **Chapters 4 and 10**, **Niewiadomski**'s paper is another key example in this volume of how concepts and ideas imported from elsewhere in geography can enhance the general understanding of tourism and how tourism can serve as a useful sectoral case through which various issues debated in geography and, more widely, in the social sciences (in this case: post-communist transformations in CEE and their complex and diverse nature) can be explored in more depth.

Back to urban environments, the last two chapters of Part II **(Chapters 13 and 14)** address the issue of urban transformation, regeneration, and gentrification in post-socialist cities. While the paper by **Smith, Egedy, Csizmady, Jancsik, Olt, and Michalkó (2018) (Chapter 13)** utilises the example of Budapest, the paper by **Kádár (2018) (Chapter 14)** focuses mainly on Prague, although informative comparisons to Budapest and Vienna are also made. Highlighting that the regeneration of urban cores in CEE after 1989 unfolded in a different way than in Western cities, **Smith et al.** discuss the role of 'party tourism' in transforming District VII in Budapest – a neighbourhood known for the so-called 'ruin bars' established in old, neglected buildings, and for multiple Airbnb services that mushroomed in the area in the recent period. While both positive and negative consequences of these processes are explored, **Smith et al.** attribute these developments to the absence of coordinated urban planning in the city – a side-effect of the peculiar structure of governance in Budapest and the division of the city into 23 districts, each with a high level of autonomy. The paper by **Kádár**, in turn, concentrates on hotel development in Prague and discusses how the centralised urban planning of the communist era and the processes of restitution and (re-) privatisation in the newly liberalised Czech economy after 1989 (and after the disintegration of Czechoslovakia) determined hotel development in Prague from the 1990s onwards, leading to a high concentration of hotels in the city centre and, subsequently, to an intense and uncoordinated 'touristification' of the urban core. Similarly to **Smith et al.**, **Kádár** identifies a source of these problems in a shortage of balanced planning in the first years of transition. As such, both papers highlight that, although tourism has the potential to bring substantial economic upgrading, positive effects of its development cannot be guaranteed, and careful planning is required if this potential is to be realised.

As the above review demonstrates, the papers in this volume vary widely both in terms of the focus and the approach, thus highlighting the diversity of issues which geographical research on tourism in CEE has addressed (and continues to address) and attesting to the heterogeneity and richness of the field. While some papers have a predominantly empirical character (e.g. **Chapters 1, 2, and 8**), some others draw from key advancements made elsewhere in geography to offer a theoretically informed analysis of a given issue (e.g. **Chapters 4, 10, and 12**). Importantly, the papers also differ in terms of their geographical focus, drawing case studies from an array of formerly communist countries in CEE (although some states such as Latvia, Lithuania, Moldova, Ukraine, and various Balkan countries are not represented in this collection). Since the papers are compiled in chronological order (albeit with exceptions), they altogether tell a consistent story of tourism development in CEE and its complex interdependencies with the post-communist restructuring in the CEE region after 1989 – a story that has yet to be concluded. In this spirit, the final chapter of this volume provides a set of reflections on tourism development in CEE in the period of post-communism and identifies a few future research avenues to provide this story with a necessary continuation.

References

Amsden, A., Kochanowicz, J,. Taylor, L. (1994) *The Market Meets Its Match: Restructuring the Economics of Eastern Europe*, Cambridge, MA: Harvard University Press

Bachvarov, M. (1997) End of the model? Tourism in post-communist Bulgaria, *Tourism Management*, 18(1), pp. 43–50

Balaž, V. (1995) Five years of economic transition in Slovak tourism: successes and shortcomings, *Tourism Management*, 16(2), pp. 143–150

Bradshaw, M., Stenning, A. (2004) Introduction: transformation and development, in: M. Bradshaw, and A. Stenning (eds) *East Central Europe and the Former Soviet Union*, Harlow: Pearson, pp. 1–32

Bradshaw, M., Swain, A. (2004) Foreign investment and regional development, in: M. Bradshaw, and A. Stenning (eds) *East Central Europe and the Former Soviet Union*, Harlow: Pearson, pp. 59–86

Brouder, P., S.A. Clave, A. Gill and D. Ioannides (eds) (2017), *Tourism Destination Evolution*, London and New York: Routledge.

Buckley, P.J., Witt, S.F. (19910) Tourism in the centrally-planned economies of Europe, *Annals of Tourism Research*, 17(1), pp. 7–18

Burns, P. (1998) Tourism in Russia: background and structure, *Tourism Management*, 19(6), pp. 555–565

Butler, R. (2004) Geographical research on tourism, recreation and leisure: Origins, eras and directions, *Tourism Geographies*, 6(2), pp. 143–162

Dunford, M., Smith, A. (2000) Catching up or falling behind? Economic performance and regional trajectories in the new Europe, *Economic Geography*, 76, pp. 169–195

Franck, C. (1990) Tourism investment in Central and Eastern Europe, *Tourism Management*, 11(4), pp. 333–338

Gowan, P. (1995) Neo-liberal theory and practice for Eastern Europe, *New Left Review*, 213, pp. 3–60

Hall, C., Page, S. (2014) *The Geography of Tourism & Recreation: Environment, Place and Space* (4th edition), London: Routledge

Hall, D. (1990) The changing face of tourism in Eastern Europe, *Town and Country Planning*, 59(12), pp. 348–351

Hall, D. (ed.) (1991) *Tourism and Economic Development in Eastern Europe and the Soviet Union*, London: Belhaven Press

Hall, D. (1992) The challenge of international tourism in Eastern Europe, *Tourism Management*, 13(1), pp. 41–44

Hall, D. (1995) Tourism change in Central and Eastern Europe, in: A. Montanari and A. Williams (eds), *European Tourism: Regions, Spaces and Restructuring*, Chichester: Wiley, pp. 221–224

Hall, D. (1998a) Central and Eastern Europe, in: A. Williams and G. Shaw (eds), *Tourism and Economic Development in Europe*, Chichester: Wiley, pp. 345–373

Hall, D. (1998b) Tourism development and sustainability issues in Central and South-Eastern Europe, *Tourism Management*, 9(5), pp. 423–431

Hall, D. (2000a) Evaluating the tourism-environment relationship: Central and East European experiences, *Environment and Planning B: Planning and Design*, 27(3), pp. 411–421

Hall, D. (2000b) Sustainable tourism development and transformation in Central and Eastern Europe, *Journal of Sustainable Tourism*, 8(6), pp. 441–457

Hall, D. (2001) Transport and tourism, in: D. Turnock (ed.) *East Central Europe and the former Soviet Union – Environment and Society*, New York: Oxford University Press, pp. 140–151

Harrison, D. (1993) Bulgarian tourism: A state of uncertainty, *Annals of Tourism Research*, 20(3), pp. 519–534

Ioannides, D., Debbage, K. (eds) (1998) *The Economic Geography of the Tourist Industry: A Supply Side Analysis*, London: Routledge

Jaakson, R. (1996) Tourism in transition in post-Soviet Estonia, *Annals of Tourism Research*, 23(3), 617–634

Johnson, M. (1995) Czech and Slovak tourism: patterns, problems and prospects, *Tourism Management*, 16(1), pp. 21–28

Johnson, M. (1997) Hungary's hotel industry in transition 1960–1996, *Tourism Management*, 18(7), 441–452

Johnson, C., Vanetti, M. (2004) Market developments in the hotel sector in Eastern Central Europe, *Advances in Hospitality and Leisure*, 1, pp. 153–175

Kołodko, G. (2000) *From Shock to Therapy: The Political Economy of Post-socialist Transformation*, Oxford: Oxford University Press

Light, D. (2000) An unwanted past: contemporary tourism and the heritage of communism in Romania, *International Journal of Heritage Studies*, 6(2), pp. 145–160

Light, D. (2001) 'Facing the future': tourism and identity-building in post-socialist Romania, *Political Geography*, 20(8), pp. 1053–1074

Light, D., Dumbrăveanu, D. (1999) Romanian tourism in the post-communist period, *Annals of Tourism Research*, 26(4), pp. 898–927

Niewiadomski, P. (2018) Geography, tourism studies and post-communist transformations in Central and Eastern Europe – 20th Anniversary Volume Commentary, *Tourism Geographies*, 20(1), pp. 182–184

Niewiadomski, P. (2022) (ed.) *Tourism in Post-communist States: Central and Eastern Europe*, an online collection available at: https://www.tandfonline.com/journals/rtxg20/collections/Tourism-in-post-communist-states

Pearlman, M.V. (1990) Conflicts and constraints in Bulgaria's tourism sector, *Annals of Tourism Research*, 19(1), pp. 103–122

Pickles, J., Smith, A. (1998) (eds) *Theorising Transition: The Political Economy of Post-communist Transformations*, London & New York: Routledge

Saarinen, J. (2008) Special Issue: Tourism in transition economies, *Tourism Geographies*, 10(4), p.409

Scott, J., Renaghan, L. (1991) Hotel development in Eastern Germany: opportunities and obstacles, *The Cornell Hotel and Restaurant Administration Quarterly*, 32, pp. 44–51

Smeral, E. (1993) Emerging Eastern European tourism markets, *Tourism Management*, 14(6), pp. 411–418

Smith, A. (1997) Breaking the old and constructing the new? Geographies of uneven development in Central and Eastern Europe, in: R. Lee, and J. Wills (eds) *Geographies of Economies*, London: Edward Arnold

Smith, A., Pickles, J. (1998) Theorising transition and the political economy of transformation, in: J., Pickles and A. Smith (eds) *Theorising Transition: The Political Economy of Post-communist Transformations*, London & New York: Routledge, pp. 1–22

Smith, A., Timar, J. (2010) Uneven transformations: space, economy and society 20 years after the collapse of state socialism, *European Urban and Regional Studies*, 17, pp. 115–125

Sokol, M. (2001) Central and Eastern Europe a decade after the fall of state-socialism: regional dimensions of transition processes, *Regional Studies*, 35, pp. 645–655

Stark, D. (1992) The great transformation? Social change in Eastern Europe, *Contemporary Sociology*, 21, pp. 299–304

Stark, D. (1994) Path dependency and privatisation strategies in East-Cenral Europe, in: E. Milov (Ed.) *Changing Political Economies – Privatisation in Post-Communist and Reforming Communist States*, pp. 115–146 (New York: Lynne Reinner Publishers).

Stenning, A., Bradshaw, M. (2004) Conclusions: facing the future?, in: M. Bradshaw, and A. Stenning (eds) *East Central Europe and the Former Soviet Union*, Harlow: Pearson, pp. 247–256

Turnock, D. (1990) Tourism in Romania, *Annals of Tourism Research*, 17(1), pp. 79–102

Turnock, D. (1999) Sustainable rural tourism in the Romanian Carpathians, *Geographical Journal*, 165(2), pp. 192–199

Unwin, T. (1996) Tourist development in Estonia: images, sustainability, and integrated rural development, *Tourism Management*, 17(4), pp. 265–276

Williams, A., Balaž, V. (2000) *Tourism in Transition: Economic Change in Central Europe*, London: I.B. Tauris

Williams, A., Balaž, V. (2001) From collective provision to commodification of tourism?, *Annals of Tourism Research*, 28(1), pp. 27–49

Williams, A., Balaž, V. (2002). The Czech and Slovak Republics: conceptual issues in the economic analysis of tourism in transition, *Tourism Management*, 23, pp. 37–45

Williams, S. (2009) *Tourism Geography: A New Synthesis* (2nd edition), London: Routledge

Part I

Tourism in transition: From problems and challenges to success and prosperity?

Tourism patterns and problems in East Central Europe

RUSSELL L. IVY AND CHARLES B. COPP

Abstract

Tourism development in post-communist East Central Europe is characterized by growing numbers of international visitors. The region, however, has inherited infrastructural and policy limitations that perpetuate two distinct tourism spaces within most nations. International tourists remain very concentrated in the capital cities and a few resort locations, while domestic tourists display a much more diffused pattern of travel. The infrastructure that international tourists demand, and the information they require in making holiday decisions, is still quite geographically limited in East Central Europe.

Introduction

As East Central Europe makes the transition to a liberal market economy, socioeconomic and political upheavals have become the norm. In particular, many of the Eastern bloc countries are finding that the tremendous buildup of heavy industrial infrastructure that was favoured in their centrally-planned economy of the past is often not competitive in today's global marketplace. Thus, the restructuring of the economy has witnessed a decline in industrial importance for many of these nations, and a rise in the service sector, which had never really been promoted to anywhere near the same degree as was industry during the communist era. A 1991 report from the Organization for Economic Cooperation and Development (OECD) argues that the service sector in general has been underdeveloped in East Central Europe, and that its growth is necessary to assist these countries in surviving in their new economic environment.

This article describes the development of tourism in post-communist East Central Europe (i.e. that area of Central Europe that was formerly governed by communist regimes). Tourism is currently receiving a great deal of attention from regional governments and the private enterprise alike. A discussion of the importance and development of tourism in the communist era will show that the patterns and problems of tourism in this region (both past and present) largely resemble those of developing nations, and that a discrete, 'two-track' economy (foreign versus domestic) exists in the tourism sector, thus creating discrete tourism spaces. Urry (1990), among others, argues that tourism has greatly changed with the movement towards capitalism, but such change is not without difficulty. A review of the literature along with the mapping of tourism patterns for selected countries is used to describe the problems that the region faces today in developing tourism. Finally, the results of a tourist survey in Bratislava, Slovakia are presented to help highlight some additional problems in marketing tourism in East Central Europe.

Tourism planning in communist Europe

Even though much of East Central Europe has favourable natural and cultural conditions for tourism and recreation development, tourism has not typically been as major a source of income in comparison to the region's Western European neighbours (OECD 1991). An abundance of natural and cultural attractions alone are not enough to ensure successful tourism development (Bachvarov 1997). During the communist years the region placed less emphasis on developing the service sector, as the main goal was to increase the output of industrial commodities. Adequate infrastructure for transport, food, lodging and entertainment facilities, as well as travel agencies and tour operators was lacking in both quality (at least by Western European standards) and quantity (Bacharov 1997).

Just as in the USSR, the planning and management of tourism throughout the region was given low priority, and was typically assigned to a state planning office that delegated the organization of such activity to a national tourist agency such as Cedok in Czechoslovakia, IBUSZ in Hungary and Balkantourist in Bulgaria (Arefyev & Mieczkowski 1991; Carter 1991; Compton 1991; Vodenska 1992; Jaakson 1996; Kreck 1998).

These agencies played a strong role, in particular, in guiding and directing tourists from outside the Iron Curtain to 'low security risk' areas and higher priced accommodation facilities (Arefyev & Mieczkowski 1991; Shaw 1991). Typically, tourism development was one small part in the long-term economic plans of central government agencies. As reported by Allcock (1991: 257), there was a 'tendency of central planners in socialist systems to think in terms of the expansion of aggregate "production" targets without giving adequate attention to questions of the integration of services, the standards achieved and the need to market the product properly'.

Thus, in the centrally-planned economies of post-World War II Europe, tourism development took a very different path from that in Western Europe (Hall 1991; Williams & Shaw 1991; Mihalik 1992; Pearce 1992; Rafferty 1993; Davidoff *et al.* 1995; Borocsz 1996; Hollier 1997). Tourism in Eastern Europe was planned with the goal of achieving a high return, in the form of foreign hard currencies, on selected investments. As such, minimal tourist marketing and modest infrastructure was put in place in a limited number of potentially lucrative geographic areas. Buckley and Witt (1990) showed that comparing such measures as arrivals and receipts, as well as proportion of national product and total exports, the centrally planned economies of Europe lagged far behind their Western counterparts, as illustrated in Table 1.

International versus domestic tourists in communist Europe

Prior to the 1960s, international tourism was given much less focus than domestic tourism throughout much of Eastern Europe. Buckley and Witt (1990: 12) argued that this led 'to a predominately inward looking industry not geared to international standards and foreign tastes'. International tourism in these earlier years was focused on coastal Yugoslavia (largely present-day Croatia and Slovenia) and a few urban centres (such as Budapest and Prague) and health spas (such as Karlovy Vary in the present-day Czech Republic). Increasing numbers of Western tourists to other areas of the Eastern bloc came about as a result of targeted planning starting in the 1960s as the region sought to obtain increasingly needed hard currency (Matley 1976; Carter 1991; Compton 1991).

According to Bachvarov (1997: 43), Bulgaria, for example, was developed to be 'the most prominent foreign tourism receiving country' of the Eastern bloc, and indeed functioned as

Table 1 International tourist arrivals and receipts for Europe and the world, 1986-1994

Year	International arrivals			International receipts		
	World total (000s)	European share (%)	CEE* share (%)	World total (US$ mill.)	European share (%)	CEE* share (%)
1986	330746	65.42	9.85	140019	54.99	1.37
1987	356440	64.90	10.58	171319	56.26	1.39
1988	381824	63.04	12.32	197692	54.15	1.31
1989	415376	64.35	11.74	211366	52.01	1.24
1990	459233	62.43	10.17	264708	54.39	1.83
1991	466044	61.77	11.87	271827	52.73	2.75
1992	503617	61.02	12.23	308596	52.71	3.08
1993	518258	60.54	13.36	313963	50.16	3.88
1994	546260	60.38	13.60	346674	50.43	4.15

CEE = Former Communist Nations of Central and Eastern Europe excluding Albania and the former Yugoslavia.
Source: World Tourism Organization.

such from the 1960s until the end of the 1980s. Rapid growth in international tourist flows (at least by Eastern bloc standards) to Bulgaria began with the selected development of large tourist complexes along the Black Sea Coast, such as Golden Sands (18,500 beds) and Sunny Beach (24,500 beds). As reported by Vodenska (1992), however, the lodging infrastructure was often accompanied by inadequate development of restaurants, bars and entertainment facilities.

While international, especially Western, tourism developed in a halting manner, throughout much of the Eastern bloc domestic tourism flourished (Borocz 1990; Carter 1991; Hall 1991). Trade unions, state industrial enterprises and youth organizations sponsored large numbers of holidays as part of the social development of the people. The spas, which had traditionally served the luxury market, were now oriented towards maintaining the health of the working class. Borocz (1990) has noted that the difficulty in getting exit visas for international travel also restricted holidays to domestic locations. As tourism was no longer a privilege of the rich, but a 'right' of the people, a tremendous rise in the domestic market occurred which put great pressure on the accommodation facilities in most resort areas.

Even as late as the 1980s, domestic tourists comprised the overwhelming majority of visitors to tourist regions outside of the capital cities, as most foreign visitor flows were centred on the capital cities only. Moreover, the foreign tourists who did come were largely from neighbouring socialist countries (Carter 1991). In the late 1970s, almost 95% of the foreign visitors to Czechoslovakia, for example, were from Eastern bloc countries. It should be noted, however, that the number of Western tourists to Hungary climbed significantly during the 1980s from 1.2 million in 1980 to 2.2 million in 1988 (Compton 1991) due largely to a liberalization of exchange rate policies and greater ease of entry (AESEI 1989; Borocsz 1990; Compton 1991). Hungary's international tourists, however, were still largely concentrated in Budapest and the Lake Balaton area (Buckley & Witt 1990).

Thus, what developed in most of the Eastern bloc nations were two highly discrete tourism spaces. The international, especially Western, tourist flow was highly concentrated in most countries to the capital city and sometimes one or two other districts, while the domestic tourist flow was much more expansive geographically. Even in the few areas of geographic overlap (i.e. those areas popular with both international and domestic tourists), such as capital cities, the domestic and international tourists were often in 'isolation' or spatial separation from one another, particularly with respect to accommodations. This was directly planned by the national tourism development agencies.

Problems for international tourism development

Although the number and share of international visitors to East Central Europe has grown in the post-communist 1990s (Tables 1 and 2), problems still exist that limit the ability of these nations to market themselves and to live up to their touristic potential. Many of these problems result from the planning and development schemes of the earlier communist era. Hall (1991), for example, cites infrastructural constraints related to the quality and quantity of accommodation facilities, poor quality staff training, discouragement of entrepreneurial activity, and poor marketing and promotion of tourism. His work also discusses the problems associated with the high concentration ratio (percentage of international visitors from a country's top three markets) of the Eastern bloc countries entering the 1990s, ranging from 51.7% in Romania to 83.6% in the former Czechoslovakia.

The need for diversification extends beyond the problem of highly concentrated source markets. For example, the lack of diversification of the tourist product in Bulgaria has created regional economic disparity (due to the overly concentrated buildup along the Black Sea), severe seasonality problems and a strain on resources (Vodenska 1992). Balkantourist has attempted to diversify the nation's tourism product by promoting mountain and spa tourism in the Bulgarian interior, but the distribution of existing facilities and infrastructure does not coincide with the variety and location of these alternative tourism and recreation resources. The quality, quantity and distribution of accommodation facilities remains a primary issue. By the late 1980s, almost half Bulgaria's bed capacity consisted of rooms in private homes, and most hotels that had been built by that time were poor in quality and often without heating facilities (as they were planned and developed for the summer season only). Another issue for Bulgaria, as well as many other East Central European nations, is the high degree of transit traffic (tourists quickly passing through enroute to another destination), which comprised 63.5 percent of international visits to Bulgaria in 1991 (Vodenska 1992). Such travel patterns shorten the average stay and reduce the average tourist spending within the country.

Similar to Bulgaria, Allcock (1991) reported that in the former Yugoslavia, more than half of the tourist overnight stays were generated during a two month period (July and August). The focus on the shortduration, high tourist season was the norm throughout the communist controlled portion of Europe. Even though the former Yugoslavia had a variety of

Table 2 International tourist arrivals for Europe by sub-region, 1990–1994

(% of European Total)	1990	1991	1992	1993	1994
Western Europe	39.71	39.71	39.03	37.47	35.91
Southern Europe	32.11	29.52	28.61	28.21	29.01
E/Central Europe	16.30	19.21	20.05	22.07	22.54
Northern Europe	9.29	8.96	9.03	9.25	9.53
E. Mediterranean	2.59	2.60	3.27	3.00	3.01

Source: World Tourism Organization

tourist options, only coastal resort locations were marketed aggressively. The other regions had serious problems with quality of accommodations and other tourist infrastructure that resulted from a failure to modernize over time. Additionally, there were serious shortages of trained staff, particularly senior managers, and local entrepreneurs. Oppermann (1993) argues that much of post-communist Eastern Europe exhibited tourism development patterns similar to Third World nations, with international visitors being overwhelmingly concentrated in the capital city, due to their greater ties to the global economic system, leaving the rest of the region underdeveloped and remote from international tourism.

Regional tourism patterns in Hungary, Slovakia and Slovenia

Figures 1 to 4 identify basic tourism patterns for Hungary, Slovakia and Slovenia, three countries in post-communist East Central Europe, in 1995 and 1996. To assess the concentration issue, the importance of the capital city in the tourism economy of each country was measured using Mergard's Index, which is a ratio of the capital's percentage of total accommodations to that city's share of the nation's population (Oppermann 1993). A value greater than 1 indicates an overconcentration of tourism infrastructure on the capital city, and is typical for most developing countries. For Hungary (Figure 1), tourism was clearly concentrated in 1995 in two main regions, Budapest and the Lake Balaton area (the cluster of three administrative districts in the southwest). Both of these areas were the favoured destinations of international visitors (as well as domestic) to Hungary in the past, and this trend continues. Because of Lake Balaton, the Mergard's Index for Hungary was a somewhat modest 0.64, indicating that not all tourism is concentrated in the capital city. However, international arrivals are still almost exclusively concentrated in these two major destinations, as is evidenced by the domestic/foreign (D/F) ratio given in the bottom map in Figure 1 (values below 1 indicate areas dominated with foreign visitors). The average length of stay (centre map) is only differentiated strongly in the resort region of Lake Balaton which tends to be more associated with family vacations.

The 1996 data for Slovakia (Figure 2) also yielded a concentrated pattern, with a very high Mergard's Index of 1.45 indicating the dominance of the capital city of Bratislava in the nation's tourism economy. A high proportion of overnight stays was found in the capital city and the skiing region in the High Tatras (not shown in the figures); however, districts with high average lengths of stay were somewhat dispersed. Of interest is the fairly strong relationship between the districts with a low percentage of the nation's total overnight stays and high D/F ratios (indicating that few foreign visitors frequented these areas).

In Slovenia (Figure 3), the capital of Ljubljana (identified by the smallest polygon at the centre of the map) had a Mergard's Index value of a mere 0.23, indicating that it was not a dominant tourist destination in the country. The coastal region in the southeast (centring on resort cities like Portoroz) and the skiing areas to the north (with quaint tourist villages like Kranjska Gora) captured a large share of both domestic and international visitors. These areas, plus other spa regions in eastern Slovenia, showed up stronger than the capital for average length of stay. The smaller concentration of Slovenia's tourism economy in the nation's capital was largely a combination of the smaller size of Ljubljana (pop. 276,000) compared to the other capitals discussed, the high emphasis placed on 'spot' tourism planning of selected resort areas during the years that Slovenia was part of communist Yugoslavia, the attractive coastal environment (not available in Hungary or Slovakia), and the reputation of northern Slovenia as a low-cost alternative to alpine skiing in nearby Austria and Switzerland. The

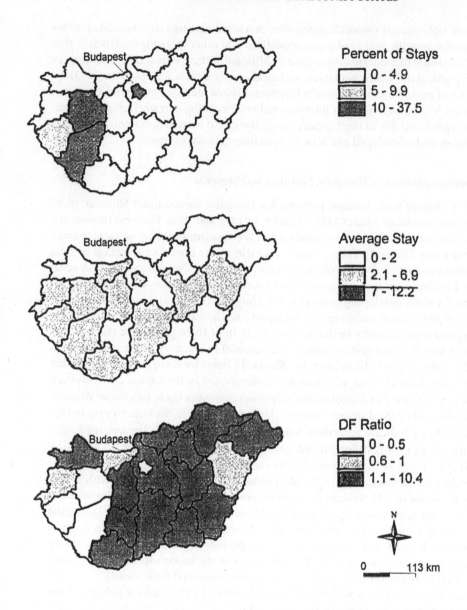

Figure 1   Selected tourism statistics: Hungary, 1995.

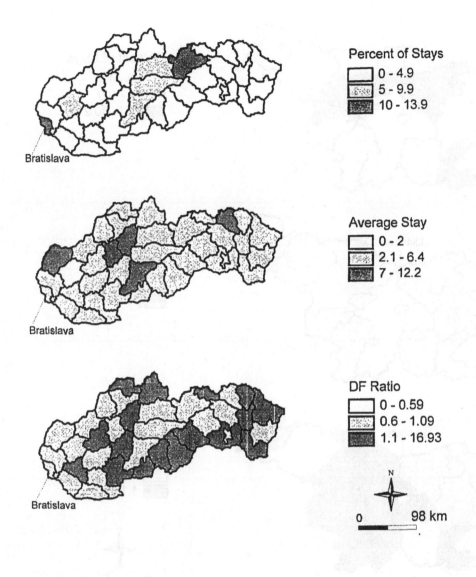

Figure 2 Selected tourism statistics: Slovakia, 1996.

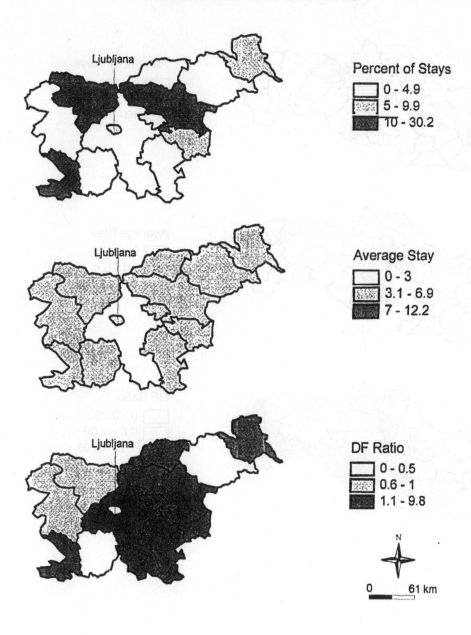

Figure 3 Selected tourism statistics: Slovenia, 1995.

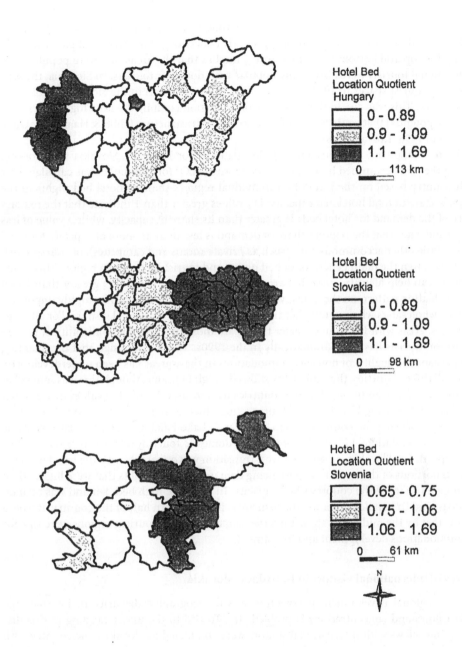

Figure 4 Hotel accommodation patterns.

D/F ratio for Slovenia showed that foreigners strongly outnumber domestic visitors only in Ljubljana and two other areas, indicating a fairly concentrated international pattern. Comparing the top and bottom maps in Figure 3 implies that the areas that were popular with international tourists were also highly popular with domestic tourists. In Slovenia, the separation of tourist spaces in 1995 was, therefore, less severe than in the Slovak Republic and in Hungary. This was due to the small size of the nation combined with a high diversity of touristic potential that could be built upon existing infrastructure (Gibb & Haas 1996; Gulic 1996; Hall 1998; Koscak 1998).

Figure 4 maps out hotel accommodation patterns for Hungary, Slovakia and Slovenia during the years examined here. A location quotient (LQ) for bed nights was calculated for each country based on the ratio of an individual region's share of hotel bed nights to the region's share of total hotel bed capacity. LQ values greater than 1 indicate that the region's share of the demand for hotel beds is greater than its share of capacity, while a value of less than 1 indicates that the region's share of demand is less than its share of capacity for hotel beds. While other accommodations (such as private rooms and campsites), of course, exist, hotels are often the main generator of bed nights and tourist income in a region. This crude measure can help identify areas that are potentially undersupplied (LQ greater than 1 and darker shading pattern on the maps) with hotel beds, an issue that can be highly important for tour wholesalers who put together travel packages for international visitors. For all three countries, areas with LQ values greater than 1 are those in which the availability of private rooms for tourists has risen dramatically in the 1990s. This is also a sign that the quantity, and perhaps the quality, of hotel accommodations in these areas has been underdeveloped.

For all three countries, the capital city showed a high LQ value, though this was somewhat less in Slovenia. In addition, all three countries tend to show higher LQ values in areas that were largely frequented by domestic tourists and which were not well developed as tourist destinations during the communist era. Hungary's Lake Balaton area was relatively stable in its accommodations LQ, while some of the domestic tourism regions were seen as undersupplied. For Slovakia, a clear east-west transition was apparent, with the less developed eastern portions of the country experiencing demands for bed nights that were higher than the region's share of the country's bed capacity. In Slovenia, high bed demand was seen on the coast and in popular domestic tourism areas in the eastern half of the country. It would appear that by the mid-1990s these underdeveloped domestic tourism regions were ripe for accommodations development and investment.

Survey of international visitors to Bratislava, Slovakia

From a regional development perspective, a wide geographic disparity in international tourist flows and concentrations is problematic. To add to the understanding of this disparity, interviews with international visitors were conducted in Slovakia (the country with the highest concentration pattern). On-site, personal interviews with tourists in Bratislava's Old Town Square and the Bratislava Castle district were conducted during the middle of August 1996 and the first week of March 1997 to capture both a peak tourist period and an off-peak period. The interviews were conducted in the English or German languages due to the limitations of the interviewers. However, very few visitors that were stopped were unable to communicate in one of these languages, at least at the level required to answer the basic questions from the survey.

For each survey period, one weekend day (Saturday) and one weekday (Thursday) were selected to interview international tourists and excursionists (stays of less than 24 hours).

No domestic tourists were interviewed. The August 1996 round of surveying yielded 87 responses (54% of whom were excursionists), while the March 1997 round yielded only 39 responses (41% excursionists). It should be noted that there were fewer tourists at the Old Town Square in March as this was an off-season month, and though the weather was sunny it was unseasonably cold during that particular week. Moreover, the problem of being restricted to the German and English languages, which was almost a non-issue in August, was slightly more pronounced in March as more of the visitors were from the former communist block countries (about 15% of whom could not be communicated with) than from Western Europe or elsewhere. Table 3 gives a summary of selected trip characteristics of the respondents. It should also be noted that the ski areas in the central and northern sections of the country attract a fair number of international visitors during the winter months who bypass the capital, though the purpose of the interviews was specifically to address the tourism concentration factor in Bratislava.

Most of the respondents fell into one of two categories. Many were on a short stop in the Slovak Republic as part of a package tour that included multiple countries. For these travellers, the stop in Bratislava was either scheduled as part of the package, or a 'free day' on a planned stop in Vienna, which is a short distance across the border. The second main category of respondents consisted of Austrians on day trips across the border to take advantage of lower prices for food, retail and even service items. The short average length of stay of the respondents in both periods was brought down, of course, by the inclusion of excursionists in the survey. However, it is worth restating that even those staying overnight in Slovakia were largely passing through the nation *en route* to other destinations. If a nation does not seem to draw tourists on its own (i.e. it is with other countries), then it is likely that the flows would be highly concentrated in select destinations due to tight trip itineraries.

A few interesting, but perhaps expected, seasonal differences were brought out by the responses. The length of stay was shorter among the March visitors, and fewer visited other sites in Slovakia outside of the capital. This may be a reflection of the behavioural differences of winter travellers versus summer travellers to Europe, but could also be a reflection of a smaller number of package tours during the winter that include the capital of the Slovak

Table 3 Selected trip characteristics of foreign visitors to Bratislava, Slovakia

	August 1996	*March 1997*
Length of stay in Slovakia	1.75 days	1.22 days
Percentage visiting places other than the capital city	28%	14%
Package tour:	69%	32%
Independent	25%	64%
Other	6%	4%
Business	47%	61%
Pleasure	53%	39%
Main tourist activity:		
Shopping	42%	59%
Sightseeing	39%	27%
Other	19%	14%
Respondents (*n*)	87	39

Table 4   Respondents' reasons for visiting Bratislava only

(1) Package holiday only included the capital	48%
(2) Lack of time in travel itinerary	44%
(3) Lack of knowledge/information about additional destinations	40%
(4) Concern about quality of food/lodging	29%
(5) Concern about language barriers	16%
(6) Lack of interest in the rest of Slovakia	12%
(7) Poor public transport infrastructure	5%

Republic. It is important to point out that many (49%) of the respondents visiting Bratislava mentioned that they probably would not have visited Slovakia at all, had it not been either attached to a tour package with a variety of other destinations that piqued their travel interest, or was along the route to their final travel destination. Note also the higher percentage of business travellers during the March survey period, which is typical of an off-season pattern.

For respondents who were visiting the capital only (76% overall), the survey allowed them to list as many reasons as necessary to explain their concentrated travel behaviour in Slovakia. Table 4 is a summary of the responses that were given by at least 5% of the interviewees. The top two responses again show the dominance of visitors who were in the country on short stops as part of a travel package, or merely across the border from Austria for a quick weekend trip. A perusal of the remaining responses on the list, however, helps identify some potentially important regional problems.

Perhaps Slovakia gets a light treatment by tour wholesalers who put travel packages together due to marketing and quality problems (perceived or real). Certainly if tour wholesalers have difficulty assessing the travel potential of an area, then it is even less likely that individuals will be able to do so. In the case of Slovakia a marketing problem exists. Most of the respondents surveyed knew very little about the touristic potential of Bratislava, and much less information about anywhere else in the nation.

At most, the interviewees gave vague answers about 'thinking that maybe one could ski in some parts of the country'. The food and lodging quality issue, whether merely perceived or a reality, is probably related to quantity as well. Certainly from the perspective of tour operators, a lack of quality and quantity of accommodations (particularly facilities that can accommodate large groups) could be a hindrance. Additionally, the lower levels of education often associated with rural areas may indeed mean that fewer people are available to speak English, German or other languages. It should be noted here that concern over the language issue was strongest among American and British respondents from the survey.

Conclusions

As Buckley and Witt (1990) have argued, the upgrading of the total tourist product (perhaps through foreign joint ventures which can help assure product quality), as well as improved marketing techniques, is of crucial importance for equitable tourism development in the East Central Europe region. The former Eastern bloc countries are in the position of having to upgrade, and to some degree 'reinvent', themselves as tourist destinations, but not because of reaching the end of their product life cycle (market saturation and exhaustion), as is the situation for many of their Western European neighbours (Zimmermann 1991; Formica & Uysal 1996). The former lack of concern over international tourist standards for quality and quantity is probably the more serious issue. Thus, these countries are having to deal with vast regional disparities in the distribution of international (particularly Western European) tourists, with significant economic consequences. The survey conducted in Bratislava confirms the lack of proper tourist infrastucture and adequate tourist information on other potential destinations in Slovakia.

As noted earlier, many of the East Central European nations really have two discrete tourism spaces: international and domestic. Much of this pattern is tied to accommodation space and their associated amenities. As reported by Johnson (1997: 444), Western tourists generally spend more on their vacations, especially on accommodations, and as such 'require high quality accommodation of an international standard'. The internationalization of Eastern Europe's tourism should include the international lodging industry. This would establish a known quality in hotel accommodations (along with the power of their worldwide computer reservation systems) which would be valued by tour wholesalers. A tremendous amount of privatization of formerly state-owned hotels has been occurring throughout the region, but the highest quality facilities still tend to be concentrated in the capital cities and a few other high-volume international tourist resorts. In Hungary, for example, all of the five-star hotels and nearly two-thirds of the four-star properties are located in Budapest, with the Lake Balaton area also an important clustering of the nation's high-quality lodging facilities (Johnson 1997).

Tourism as a regional development tool, particularly for lagging rural areas, has been promoted throughout Europe (and elsewhere) with mixed results (Kariel 1989; Unwin 1996). Eastern Europe's transition to a market economy has left some areas in dire straits, particularly as many of the region's large industrial complexes have failed to compete effectively in the new economic environment. This has led to a debate over the effective realities of creating spatial equity in the region's standard of living (Barta 1992; Zaniewski 1992). Some politicians and economists see the expansion of tourism (particularly international) as a potential solution. As the new federal governments seem to continue their focus on known, tried-and-true tourism products, perhaps marketing and planning policy at the subnational level (where the level of concern and stakes are higher), as is done by neighbouring Austria (Zimmermann 1990; Downes 1995), would be an answer to help diffuse the international visitors and their money more equitably.

References

Allcock, J. 1991. Yugoslavia. In *Tourism and Economic Development in Eastern Europe and the Soviet Union*, ed. D.R. Hall, pp. 236–58. London: Belhaven Press.

Arefyev, V. and Mieczkowski, Z. 1991. International tourism in the Soviet Union in the era of glasnost and perestroyka. *Journal of Travel Research* **29**: 2–6. Austrian Eastern and Southeastern European Institute (AESEI). 1989. *The Expansion of Tourism from Western Countries to Hungary in the Eighties: An Atlas of Eastern and Southeastern Europe*. Vienna: AESEI.

Bachvarov, M. 1997. End of the model? Tourism in post-communist Bulgaria. *Tourism Management* **18**: 43–50.

Barta, G. 1992. The changing role of industry in regional development and regional development policy in Hungary. *Tijdschrift voor Economische en Sociale Geografie* **83**: 372–89.

Borocz, J. 1990. Hungary as a destination: 1960–1984. *Annals of Tourism Research* **17**: 19–35.

Borocz, J 1996. *Leisure Migration: A Sociological Study on Tourism*. Oxford: Elsevier Science.

Buckley, P. and Witt, S. 1990. Tourism in the centrally-planned economies of Europe. *Annals of Tourism Research* **17**: 7–18.

Carter, F. 1991. Czechoslovakia. In *Tourism and Economic Development in Eastern Europe and the Soviet Union*, ed. D.R. Hall, pp. 154–72. London: Belhaven Press.

Compton, P. 1991. Hungary. In *Tourism and Economic Development in Eastern Europe and the Soviet Union*, ed. D.R. Hall, pp. 173–89. London: Belhaven Press.

Davidoff, P., Davidoff, D. and Eyre, J. 1995. *Tourism Geography*, 2nd edn. Englewood Cliffs, NJ: Prentice Hall.

Downes, R. 1995. Regional policy in Austria: what is its role? *Regions: Newsletter of the Regional Science Association* **195**: 5–8.

Formica, S. and Uysal, M. 1996. The revitalization of Italy as a tourist destination. *Tourism Management* **17**: 323–31.

Gibb, A. and Haas, Z. 1996. Developing local support services for small business development in central and eastern Europe: the donor challenge. *Entrepreneurship and Regional Development* **8**: 197–216.

Gulic, A. 1996. Regional development in Slovenia: dilemmas of transportation network construction. *European Planning Studies* **4**: 99–109.

Hall, D.R., ed. 1991. *Tourism and Economic Development in Eastern Europe and the Soviet Union*. London: Belhaven Press.

Hall, D.R. 1998. Tourism development and sustainability issues in central and south-eastern Europe. *Tourism Management* **19**: 423–31.

Hollier, R. 1997. Marketing Europe as a tourist destination: trends and achievements. *Tourism Management* **18**: 195–8.

Jaakson, R. 1996. Tourism in transition in post-soviet Estonia. *Annals of Tourism Research* **23**: 617–34.

Johnson, M. 1997. Hungary's hotel industry in transition, 1960–1996. *Tourism Management* **18**: 441–52.

Kariel, H. 1989. Tourism and development: perplexity or panacea? *Journal of Travel Research* **28**: 2–6.

Koscak, M. 1998. Integral development of rural areas, tourism and village renovation: Trebjne, Slovenia. *Tourism Management* **19**: 81–6.

Kreck, L. 1998. Tourism in former eastern European societies: ideology in conflict with requisites. *Journal of Travel Research* **36**: 62–7.

Matley, I. 1976. *The Geography of International Tourism*. Washington, DC: Association of American Geographers (resource paper no. 76-1).

Mihalik, B. 1992. Tourism impacts related to EC 92: a look ahead. *Journal of Travel Research* **31**: 27–33.

Organization for Economic Cooperation and Development (OECD). 1991. *Services in Central and Eastern European Countries*. Paris: OECD.

Oppermann, M. 1993. Tourism space in developing countries. *Annals of Tourism Research* **20**: 535–56.

Pearce, D. 1992. Tourism and the European regional development fund: the first fourteen years. *Journal of Travel Research* **30**: 44–51.

Rafferty, M. 1993. *A Geography of World Tourism*. Englewood Cliffs, NJ: Prentice Hall.

Shaw, D. 1991. The Soviet Union. In *Tourism and Economic Development in Eastern Europe and the Soviet Union*, ed. D.R. Hall, pp. 119–41. London: Belhaven Press.

Unwin, T. 1996. Tourist development in Estonia: images, sustainability, and integrated rural development. *Tourism Management* **17**: 265–76.

Urry, J. 1990. *The Tourist Gaze: Leisure and Travel in Contemporary Societies*. London: Sage.

Vodenska, M. 1992. International tourism in Bulgaria: problems and perspectives. *Tijdschrift voor Economische en Sociale Geografie* **83**: 409–17.

Williams, A. and Shaw, G. 1991. Western European tourism in perspective. In *Tourism and Economic Development: Western European Experiences*, 2nd edn, ed. A. Williams and G. Shaw, pp. 13–39. London: Belhaven Press.

Zaniewski, K. 1992. Regional inequalities in social wellbeing in central and eastern Europe. *Tijdschrift voor Economische en Sociale Geografie* **83**: 342–52.

Zimmermann, F. 1990. The organization of tourism in Austria: marketing at the provincial level. In *Marketing Tourism Places*, ed. G. Ashworth and B. Goodall, pp. 199–208. London: Routledge.

Zimmermann, F. 1991. Austria: contrasting tourist seasons and contrasting regions. In *Tourism and Economic Development: Western European Experiences*, 2nd edn, ed. A. Williams and G. Shaw, pp. 153–72. London: Belhaven Press.

Submitted July 1998; Revised January 1999

Troubled sustainability: Bulgarian seaside resorts

MARIN BACHVAROV

Abstract

This article describes changes in the tourism settlement network of a highly developed travel destination in Eastern Europe - the Bulgarian Black Sea Coast - against the background of regional tourism development efforts during the severe economic crisis that accompanied Bulgaria's transition from a centralized economy to a market economy. Two levels of tourism and recreation settlement networks are identified: (1) a narrow group of 178 specialized resort communities and (2) a broader group embracing all other settlements hosting tourism-related activities, including recreation in second homes. The specialized resort communities can further be divided into three types of settlements: large multifunction cities (Varna and Bourgas); new tourist resorts (so-called 'resort complexes', of which there are two subdivisions); and small coastal towns and villages, usually of ancient origin, and in which tourism development has marginalized the older functions. Sustainable forms of tourism development are more successful in the smaller towns, largely irrelevant in the large cities, and a major problem for the large, mono-cultural resort complexes.

Introduction

Bulgaria, until recently the 'Riviera' of the Soviet bloc, has a network of 178 resorts and other settlements that specialize in tourism and recreation for both foreign and domestic visitors (Table 1 and Figure 1). These settlements are primarily located along the country's Black Sea Coast, where they provide about 150,000 beds in legally established resorts and tourism centres (*Tourism* 1995). However, while most foreign tourists frequent the major resort developments that are included in this official network, most domestic tourism and recreation is centred in facilities associated with a less expensive auxiliary or secondary recreational network. This secondary network is comprised of over 400,000 second homes and rural houses that are mostly located outside the major resorts. While an important subject in their own right, this paper focuses primarily on the officially designated tourism and recreation settlement network, and does not address issues related to the secondary tourism network beyond these communities.

The Black Sea region of Bulgaria is the most developed tourism area in the country, receiving almost 80 percent of foreign visitor nights and 40 percent of domestic holiday nights in registered hotels. Of the country's 507 registered hotels in 1995, 297 (58.6%) were in the coastal region (*Tourism* 1995). The coast is a major international summer holiday destination with a high level of 'touristification' (Dewailly & Flament 1993). The height of the region's development, however, was reached at the end of the 1980s, and there has been a steady decline since then.

Since 1989, when the communists were removed from office, Bulgaria (and the rest of Eastern Europe) has been undergoing an economic and social crisis. This has made it difficult for both foreign and domestic tourism development in the country. Since 1990, the Bulgarian Black Sea Coast has become a dramatic example of a highly developed destination that has experienced serious decline. The situation, however, has not been as serious as in some other places where tourism has experienced stagnation and even total disappearance over the past couple of decades, such as the Caucasus, former Yugoslavia, Lebanon, Cuba and some Mediterranean resorts. The difference is that in these other instances it has been hostilities, embargos or ecological deterioration that have caused the decline. The Bulgarian coast is neither a battlefield nor an ecologically damaged destination. Here, the decline is primarily a result of the collapse of the centrally planned economy and an accumulation of problems caused by poor planning and mismanagement.

A western market economy was introduced to a good start in Bulgaria in 1990 after the overthrow of the communist regime. However, this trend was effectively halted after the 1994 elections when a backlash against the hardships of a western-style economic system resulted in a return to power by former communist officials. This caused a drastic deterioration in the economic crisis, since the communist economy had been destroyed but not effectively replaced by a new economic environment. As for the Black Sea region, the existing tourism infrastructure was poorly suited to the demands of the new economy. Here one could observe a major tourist area in a critical stage of its development, where decisions being made would either lead to its further decline or to rejuvenation (Butler 1980). The region could no longer rely upon its previous development model, which was based on government-owned and managed tourism. It needed to form a new concept of tourism that could both restructure and revitalize the region by attracting investments and guests to experience the area's natural and cultural heritage.

Table 1   Structure of the tourism and recreational settlement network in Bulgaria: number of resorts in 1995 by population of settlements

Type of resort	Population of settlements				
	<1000	1000-5000	5000-10,000	10,000-30,000	>30,000
Seaside (n =28)	9	12	2	3	2
Balneotherapy (n = 41)[a]	5	24	6	5	1
Mountain (n =44)	18	16	5	5	
Heritage (n = 65)	14	11	5	11	24
Total (n = 178)	46	63	18	24	27

[a]Balneotherapy refers to therapeutic and curative mineral baths.

Both Butler's (1980) resort cycle development model and the broader concepts associated with sustainable development indicate that the development and management of tourism destinations is more successful when approached from a regional and comprehensive basis, rather than a sectoral basis. A regionally based tourism system requires strong links between local communities and the tourism industry. Considering the pattern of past development, the strategic, long-term objective of restructuring on the Bulgarian Black Sea Coast should be to make it a more sustainable tourism destination. Some successes have already been achieved in this respect, including having several resorts recognized for their ecologically sound practices by the European Commission for Tourism.

Bulgaria's tourism settlement network

One of the most distinct aspects of tourism development on the Bulgarian Black Sea Coast is its association with both existing communities and with specially created tourism settlements (Barbaza 1970; De Kadt 1979). At the end of the 1980s, 70 percent of Bulgaria's tourist beds and 80 percent of its tourist nights were associated with the specially created tourism settlements (Bachvarov 1997). This spatial distribution is even more pronounced in the Black Sea region. The Bulgarian Black Sea Coast stretches for 387 km (240 miles) and includes two major urban and port centres (Varna and Bourgas), 10 smaller towns and 20 villages. Within and outside these settlements there are about 1600 separate tourist facilities (accommodations and catering establishments). They tend to cluster in two zones around the cities of Varna and Bourgas (Figure 1). Tourism has played a major role in shaping the form and function of these areas, although the impact has mostly been on the sea-facing side of each city. The designated tourism and recreational settlement network can further be divided into three types of communities: (1) small towns and villages, (2) large cities and (3) resort complexes.

Small towns and villages

Smaller communities combine relatively pristine seaside environments with opportunities for recreation in the local vicinity. Most of these settlements are very old, often of ancient origin, in which the tourism functions, although relatively new (since the 1950s), have marginalized older activities such as agriculture, fishing, sea trade and forestry. At the same time, tourism development has enhanced the development of surface transportation, as well as recreation-related service and industrial activities. The tourism infrastructure in most of these small towns and villages is focused on social tourism and recreation opportunities of modest quality. Except for the sand and sea recreation in towns such as Nessebar, Balchik and Sozopol, the historic architecture and heritage is the primary tourist attraction. With the rise of the holiday clubs, rural tourism and ecotourism, smaller coastal towns and villages have new opportunities to expand their tourism product, provided the technical and ecological infrastructure is improved and a proper system for their promotion and marketing is developed. At present, the state of the infrastructure, especially the supply of drinking water, sanitation and sewage, is a major limiting factor for small coastal resorts, while the natural and architectonic attractions, as well as the lack of air and water pollution, are their primary strengths.

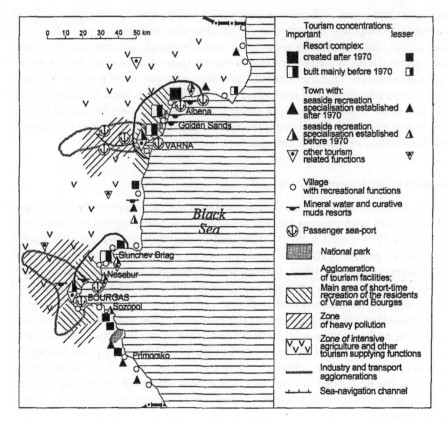

Figure 1   Spatial organization of the Bulgarian Black Sea region.

Large cities

There are two large urban and administrative centres on the Bulgarian Black Sea Coast: Varna (population 304,000) and Bourgas (population 200,000). Both are important ports serving extensive hinterlands (see Figure 1). The entire urban population of the Black Sea coastal region exceeds 600,000, which is 70 percent of the area's total population (SYB 1996). Tourist functions are concentrated on the coastal side of the agglomerations, but extend inland along the major transportation axes as well. As the centre of the tourist region, and a major resort in itself, Varna is the more important city of the two. Bourgas specializes in heavy industry and seaport activities, creating serious pollution in the town and the adjacent area.

Historically, Varna was Bulgaria's first officially recognized resort (in 1909) and it still attracts large numbers of tourists. In 1990, the town provided 28,000 tourist beds, of which 8000 were in hotels. Foreign overnight stays in 1995 reached 1.5 million, but most of these were spent in the 'resort complexes' of Zlatni Piasatsi and St. Constantin, which belong administratively to the Varna County ('resort complexes' are discussed in more detail in the next section). Considering the urban municipality proper, tourism, although important, is not a priority economic sector. On the level of the larger regional agglomeration, however, tourism is of primary importance. This paradox is due to the administrative and distributive functions of the city, which serve the surrounding hinterland. Both tourists and goods for resorts and accommodations of all sizes are funnelled through Varna to the larger destination region around it.

The Bourgas agglomeration is smaller and newer, although its industrial and seaport activities now exceed those of Varna (SYB 1996). As mentioned above, largely because of its economic success, Bourgas, although situated on the coast and surrounded by lakes, is not a major tourist destination. The high levels of air and water pollution in the Bourgas Bay are caused by the largest industrial and petrochemical complex in Bulgaria. In 1990, Bourgas had 11,000 tourist beds, less than 2000 of which were in hotels. The rest were in private rooms used by visitors to the mineral waters and mud baths of the nearby lakes. Only one percent of Bulgaria's foreign visitor nights were registered in Bourgas in 1990.

Although tourism to the Bulgarian coast was first seen in these large cities, its importance to each is now less significant than in the resort complexes and smaller seaside towns and villages. The main weakness of the larger cities, in terms of tourism development, has been their deteriorating environmental situation, while their basic strength has been their highly developed infrastructure and well-organized system of supply and distribution. A major difference for the larger cities, compared with the other types of tourism settlement, is the massive recreational demands of their local populations. Interestingly, the vacations of large, coastal city residents are typically directed to the interior of the country and not to the coastal region. Varna has a relatively well-developed suburban recreational zone, while Bourgas weekenders tend to visit more distant localities due again to the poorer environmental conditions in the vicinity of this industrial city.

For residents of most large cities in Bulgaria, however, leisure time is more likely to be spent in their home city rather than taking a distant holiday trip. A 1989 survey of 400 inhabitants of Sofia, Pleven and Bourgas found that the home town is the most likely recreational venue in both winter and summer, indicating a passive character in the use of free time. The residential quarters of the cities were of less significance, while the downtown areas attracted much local recreation. In Bourgas, urban recreation usually takes place within walking distance of one's residence, while weekend trips are mostly to places 30-90 minutes away by car. The recreational flows from Varna and Bourgas to the major coastal resort complexes are less numerous than one might expect due mainly to the lower purchasing power of the Bulgarians as compared to foreign visitors, who book in advance and pay in hard, international currencies.

Resort complexes

Resort complexes consist of groups of large and medium-sized hotels in specially designed areas. They were planned and constructed according to communist state investment policies in several undeveloped (except for agriculture) coastal regions between the 1960s and 1980s. Over this relatively short period of time, the Bulgarian Government concentrated its investment to create a series of major international holiday resort centres. These resort complexes were not settlements or communities in the conventional sense, as they had an insignificant permanent population and have never been granted settlement status by the government. They represent an intensive sectoral infrastructure development on land that was used extensively rather than intensively prior to their existence. Today, these resort complexes comprise built-up areas occupied by different types of tourism facilities owned and operated by a mix of state and newly privatized enterprises. According to the intensity of their infrastructure and activities, there are two types of resort complexes: large tourist complexes and holiday centres.

The large tourist complexes include Slunchev Briag (Sunny Beach) with 25,000 hotel beds, Zlatni Piasatsi (Golden Sands), Sveti Constantin and Alhena. Most of these facilities are relatively new, although portions of them date back to the early 1960s and are in need of serious renovation and upgrading. One of their technical problems is the small size of the hotel rooms, which are below minimum international standards. The facilities in the large complexes are still mostly state property. In 1991, the state properties were reorganized into 130 smaller holdings, divided on a geographical basis. Within each holding, restaurants, cafeterias, practically all shops, a large part of the services and some smaller hotels were leased to private managers. The total accommodation capacity of the large coastal complexes is about 60,000 beds, generally in two- and three-star hotels situated within walking distance of the seafront. The large seaside resort complexes in Bulgaria are monocultural summer-time recreation destinations. Efforts to extend the season by providing mineral baths and the related curative facilities, as well as holding conferences and other events, have produced very limited results.

The holiday centres consist of smaller groups of two- and three-star hotels and bungalows amounting to 2000–3000 beds each (e.g. in Roussalka, Beli Briag, Eleni, Duni, Primorsko, Kiten, Lozenets). They are generally more modern than the large resort complexes and provide better recreation and sporting facilities. The oldest holiday centre is Roussalka, which was built in the 1970s as a model village and leased to Club Med. The total share that holiday centres have of the accommodation capacity of the Black Sea region is relatively modest - no more than 9000 beds.

Originally, the resort complexes of Bulgaria and Romania were seen as innovative approaches to enhancing people's relationship with the coastal environment (Barbaza 1970). Today, however, they represent out-of-fashion hotels, what De Kadt (1979) has termed 'tourist ghettos'. The strengths of the tourism complexes were their quick construction, on largely vacant land, and with a comprehensive town plan. This enabled them to avoid problems with conflicting sectoral functions that might also want the same site, as well as problems with the reclamation of land and changes in the local labour force. The new complexes were not thought of as separate settlements with respect to their legal and administrative status, but as units belonging to the nearest (sometimes quite distant) towns or villages.

In practice, the resort complexes were managed, at least until 1991, by the local branches of the Bulgarian state tourism organization, Balkantourist. This conflicting identity, being under the jurisdiction of both the nearby town and the state, resulted in administrative confusion and interference. In addition, the absence of a significant resident population within the resort complex intensified the degree of commuting for workers from more distant communities. This required the development of regular transportation systems between the complexes and the communities. The lack of residential quarters for workers made the complexes even more dependent on the neighbouring settlements and on extended infrastructure. They were, therefore, clearly sectoral units with no special legal status, and without the characteristics of a typical 'community'.

Problems and transformations of resort complexes

Considering their character, planning and infrastructure, the resort complexes could be considered a form of a tourism enterprise, with expansive facilities providing a variety of accommodation and recreation opportunities. In fact, the public infrastructure in the resort complexes (e.g. roads, utilities, public beaches) were built with investments made directly from either the national budget or the budget of the state enter prise, Balkantourist. When, in 1991, state-held properties were put out for lease, market competition was created among the large number of independent holdings that resulted. Unfortunately, little government financial support was left for the continued maintenance and upgrading of the public infrastructure, which became marginalized in the priorities of the now private tourist enterprises. The deterioration of these public facilities is a serious problem in all of the resort complexes today.

The resort complexes still require and receive some non-tourism services. These include the physical infrastructure (e.g. electricity, water, sewage, communications, street lighting, solid waste disposal, street cleaning and parks maintenance) and the social infrastructure (e.g. health services, security, sporting facilities and cinemas). These non-tourism activities, however, are almost exclusively offered to support tourism operations and the tourist population of the resort. As a rule, non-tourism services in the resort complexes are organizationally bound and subordinated to tourism enter prises. In addition, the future of the public infrastructures of the resort complexes is a major question, since these public goods cannot be split among newly privatized firms.

The development model that was originally applied to Bulgaria's resort complexes resulted in their having an important role in national development, but a far lesser significance for the socio-economic life of the places in which they were located. This paradox was due to the relatively limited cooperation that existed between the resorts and nearby settlements, with the exception of commuting and transportation development (Bachvarov 1984).

If the resort complexes were able to achieve a separate community status, then they would be able to create their own governments to better manage their public infrastructure and redevelopment. But, according to Bulgarian habitat law, this would require the existence of an autochthonous population. In addition, the existing local governments would strongly object to the separation of the resort complexes from their juris diction. During the communist regime, the adjacent settlements received little benefit from the giant complexes put up on their land. However, they now receive a considerable portion of the profits (from taxes) without having to make significant capital allocation to them (since, without people, the resorts have limited local voting power). This 'parasitic attitude', typical in Bulgaria after 1989, is another paradox of the country's post-communist development.

Generally speaking, the resort complexes do possess a number of positive features deriving from the master planning of each complex as an enterprise in a locality reserved only for tourism activities. This includes, in principle, stricter environmental protection. Over time, however, it has become increasingly evident that this development model has suffered from several weaknesses, including isolation from the regional settlement network, absence of local resident population, and serious off-season inactivity. Furthermore, until recently, the state monopoly stifled diversification, which resulted in an over-reliance on sea, sun and sand recreational products.

Bulgaria's tourism infrastructure has been designated for privatization, although only about 20 hotels (including four luxury hotels) had been sold by the end of 1997. The privatization programme has been undertaken in cooperation with the State Committee for Tourism. One of the reasons for the serious delay in the privatization of resorts in the Black Sea region has been the difficulty in assessing the market value of the facilities. In addition, inflation of the national currency has been very high (over 100% in the first half of 1996). There is widespread suspicion that one of the sources of the rampant inflation has been an artificial devaluation of the currency (the 'lev') so that industrial plants, transportation facilities and tourist facilities could be bought at cheaper prices by the Bulgarian nouveaux

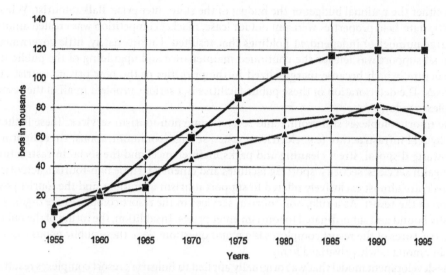

Figure 2 Number of beds in the three types of specialized tourist settlements in the Bulgarian Black Sea region. ◆, resort complexes; ▲, the large town of Varna and Bourgas; ■, small settlements.

rich. Privatization has been more rapid for profitable enterprises, while less profitable hotels and other risky investments remain dependent on state support.

With privatization, the promotion of the resorts as integrated destinations has either disappeared or been greatly reduced, as individual firms market only their products and often in a less effective manner than in the past. The fracturing of the resort complexes into separate entities has also allowed an increase in delinquency and criminal activity (Bachvarov 1997). Usually, this has been against properties, owners and staff through different forms of racketeering, rather than directly against tourists. All of these problems generate little interest from foreign business groups in purchasing or investing in the Black Sea Coast resort complexes, despite the fact that the government has designated tourism as a priority sector for development.

With the progress of privatization it is expected that owners, managers and their families will prefer to settle in the resort complexes, and thereby create a local population. Considering the seasonality of coastal tourism, a more permanent population will require alternative, non-tourism jobs and the provision of year-round services. This will end the tourism monoculture of the past, as more varied economic activities are introduced and urbanization of the complexes intensifies. The latter is in direct conflict with the initial objectives and definition of the resort complex model, especially its ecological prerequisites. From a sustainable development standpoint, the further expansion of the complexes should be carefully limited and trends towards urbanization should be placed under strict control.

Conclusion

A comparison of the three types of specialized tourist settlements in the Black Sea region (see Figure 2 and Table 1) points to differential dynamics, with the smaller settlements showing the most dynamic tourism development. The least stable have been the large resort complexes, due to their monocultural tourism profile. The bigger cities are displaying stable growth, not bound exclusively to tourism, which has been less significant in their socio-economic spectrum.

Tourism development is in an advanced and critical state in the Black Sea region. Only four of 32 coastal communities do not have some type of resort status. The development model of the past, based mainly on creating large resort complexes, has been exhausted. New ways to rejuvenate and rehabilitate the resort complexes must be a priority. The large resort complexes should be linked with the smaller tourism settlements and holiday club centres through the marketing experience and personnel skills that the larger complexes can offer. Such a scheme would benefit both smaller tourism settlements and holiday club centres, as well as help to diversify the monoculture of the large resort complexes. One addition to the current product mix could be the provision of a wider range of recreation and sporting opportunities in existing ecological clearings.

Despite their early potential as ecologically designed, high-quality destinations, the large resort complexes are no longer a model of sustainable tourism, whether from an economic, social or environmental perspective. Curiously, the decline in tourism activity on the Black Sea Coast (and throughout Eastern Europe due to the region's economic crisis) has lessened impending issues of tourism saturation and carrying capacity. The ecological problems persist, however, due in part to the increasing pollution of the Black Sea by the countries that bound it and the Danube River. Truly long-term tourism sustainability will require a level of international cooperation beyond the capabilities of the Bulgarian coastal region alone.

References

Bachvarov, Marin. 1984. Les relations tourisme 'arriere-pays dans le littoral Bulgare du Mer Noire. *Mediterranee* **2**: 3–10.

Bachvarov, Marin. 1997. End of the model? Tourism in post-communist Bulgaria. *Tourism Management* **18(1)**: 43–50.

Barbaza, Y. 1970. Trois types d'intervention du tourisme dans l'organisation de l'espace littoral. *Annales de Geographie* **434**: 80-9.

Butler, R. 1980. The concept of a tourist area cycle of evolution: Implications for management of the resources. *Canadian Geographer* **24(1)**: 5–12.

De Kadt, E. 1979. *Tourism: Passport to Development*. New York: WTO and World Bank.

Dewailly, J.-M. and Flament, E. 1993. *Geographie du tourisme et des loisirs*. Paris: Cedes.

Statistical Yearbook of Bulgaria (SYB). 1996. Sofia: Institute of Statistics, Government of Bulgaria.

Tourism (annual statistical bulletin). 1995. Sofia: Institute of Statistics, Government of Bulgaria.

Submitted: January 1997; Revised: January 1998

Gazing on communism: heritage tourism and post-communist identities in Germany, Hungary and Romania

Duncan Light

Abstract

This paper considers 'communist heritage' tourism (that is, the consumption of sites and sights associated with the former communist regimes) in contemporary Central and Eastern Europe. As one form of special interest tourism, this phenomenon is an illustration of the ever-diversifying tourist gaze. However, such tourism also raises wider issues concerning the relationship between tourism and the politics of identity in the region. While the former communist countries of Central and Eastern Europe are seeking to construct new, post-communist identities (a process in which tourism can play a significant part), this project is frustrated by tourists' interest in the 'heritage' of communism. Through consideration of three case studies of communist heritage tourism (the Berlin Wall, Budapest's Statuepark, and Bucharest's 'House of the People') the paper examines the strategies which different countries (Germany, Hungary and Romania) have adopted to negotiate and accommodate such tourism without compromising post-communist identities.

Introduction

Since the collapse of communist hegemony in 1989, the countries of Central and Eastern Europe (CEE) have been attempting to redefine senses of national identity. This project involves first, the rejection of identities

created during four decades of state socialism, including the desire to deny
– even to erase – memories of the recent communist past. The former
communist regimes enjoyed little popular support due to their failure to
deliver economic prosperity, and the widespread suppression of freedom
and basic human rights. Second, is the desire to construct new post-
communist national identities, characterized by a democratic, pluralist,
capitalist and largely Westward-looking orientation: this in itself involves
'de-constructing' identities created during the socialist period. This process
of remaking national identities in the post-communist period is complex
and contested, not least because in some countries – Russia is perhaps
the best example – there remains considerable nostalgia for the 'certain-
ties' of the former regime.

Although such questions of identity may initially seem to be unrelated
to tourism, Lanfant (1995) argues that the theme of identity is omnipresent
within tourism discourse. In particular, one means by which a country
presents 'itself' to 'others' is through international tourism, particularly
by encouraging visits by foreign tourists as a way of increasing their
knowledge and understanding of the country (Hall 1995a). Each country
will seek to present its own unique character and identity to its visitors
and to promote itself in a way which emphasizes and flatters its sense of
national identity (Lanfant 1995). Identities are thus, in part, produced
and affirmed by the images and representations of a country constructed
(or reproduced) for foreign tourists (O'Connor 1994; Urry 1994). One
way in which a country can present itself to its visitors is through the
promotion and interpretation of its national heritage. Through museums
and other heritage sites foreign tourists can be told the 'national story',
presented so as to affirm and reinforce national identity and self-image.
As such, the presentation of national heritage is an ideological process:
as Allcock (1995: 101) argues 'to speak of heritage is to speak of politics' (cf. Ashworth 1994; Tunbridge and Ashworth 1996; Morgan and
Pritchard 1998).

In post-communist CEE concepts of national heritage and the national
past are unstable, contested and in a state of flux. The reappraisal of the
past is an integral part of the process of constructing post-communist
identities (indeed Azaryahu and Kellerman (1999) note the importance of
national history and memory at times of national revival). Consequently,
history is being re-written and re-worked to forge and reinforce new
national identities (Hall 1994; Tunbridge and Ashworth 1996). The legitimacy of communist interpretations of national pasts are being consciously
rejected, whilst pre-communist interpretations – themselves rejected by
communist authorities – are being revived. As Morgan and Pritchard
(1998) observe, the construction and promotion of new post-communist
national pasts is as ideologically driven as the production of national
history by the former communist governments.

However, the process of redefining national pasts in the post-communist period is frustrated by the enduring presence of the material legacy of communism. Certainly, some symbols of the former regimes – such as public statuary – can be rapidly erased. However, other elements of the built heritage of communism – whether monumental public buildings or the plethora of tower blocks built for industrial workers – will persist for much longer, representing highly visible symbols of a period of history which many people want to forget.

Moreover, any attempts to consign the communist period to history are frustrated by the growing interest among tourists in the material legacy of communism. Western Europeans have visited CEE in large numbers since 1989 (Hall 1995b). Such visitors will vary considerably in their motives and interests, and while many may have no interest at all in the communist past of the region, others may visit specifically to gaze upon such heritage (a group which could be labelled as 'communist heritage tourists'). Another group of heritage tourists, whilst having less of a specific interest in the legacy of communism, will find themselves encountering this legacy whilst visiting the region. The outcome is that many of the key sights associated with communism – for example Warsaw's Palace of Culture or the remains of the Berlin Wall – are being constructed as 'attractions' for the gaze of Western tourists. The promotion of such resources for the tourist gaze is rarely initiated by the countries themselves. Instead, it is largely promoted by those actors and organizations that influence tourists' decision-making, particularly travel brochures and guidebooks. These are primarily external influences for external consumers, and the CEE countries themselves are able to exercise little influence on the ways in which their communist past is promoted to tourists.

This situation creates a dilemma which Tunbridge (1994) has described (in a related context) as 'identity versus economy'. For the CEE countries the priority is to place the communist period – now widely regarded as a historical aberration – firmly behind them. The heritage of communism is a symbol of the former regime which is discordant (or dissonant) with the identity politics of the post-communist period. Yet this heritage is also a source of revenue as a resource which attracts tourists, some of whom have a particular interest in seeing the legacy of the political economy which dominated the post-war history of this region. To discourage or deny tourist interest in the legacy of communism is both to miss out on a valuable source of foreign revenue, and to miss the opportunity to present an important part of the 'national story' (the processes which shaped a country's development in the second half of the twentieth century) to foreign visitors. Yet, to celebrate or preserve such a legacy may challenge or compromise efforts to construct post-communist national identities. This is an illustration of how the promotion of a resource for global heritage tourism can have the effect of 'disembedding' local or nationally produced senses of identity (Edensor 1997).

This paper explores this uneasy relationship between tourism and the 'heritage' of communism in post-communist CEE. Tourists' interest in communism is not a post-1989 phenemonon and to contextualize this activity the discussion initially considers the nature of communism as a tourist attraction. Subsequently, the production and consumption of 'communist heritage' is examined with reference to case studies in Berlin (Germany), Budapest (Hungary) and Bucharest (Romania). On one level this can be taken as an exploration of one form of special interest tourism. However, this paper is also concerned with the wider relationship between tourism and the politics of identity in post-communist CEE, with reference to the ways in which three countries have responded to, and negotiated, tourist interest in their communist pasts.

At this point, the term 'heritage' needs clarification. Heritage is frequently defined as material practice considered to be 'old' and of a certain value (Pearce 1998). However, defining the legacy of communism in such terms is highly problematic, not least because few people in CEE would regard the legacy of four decades of state socialism as of value. Instead, this paper employs a definition of heritage as 'the contemporary uses of the past' (Ashworth and Graham 1997: 381), the uses being in this case for tourism. The communist heritage of CEE is therefore defined in terms of contemporary consumption.

Communism and the tourist gaze

As Urry (1990) notes, tourism is constructed on the basis of difference. All tourists seek experiences which are in some way differentiated from their everyday lives and work: tourism results from a distinction between the ordinary and the extraordinary. In recent decades the ways in which tourists encounter difference has diversified considerably with the emergence of post-modern (or post-mass) tourists. Such individuals – in particular the new middle class and independent travellers – have increasingly rejected mass tourism in favour of more specialized and small-scale tourism experiences. A key requirement of this group is an experience of 'otherness', particularly minority and non-Western cultures (Munt 1994): consequently such tourists seek out places spatially removed from traditional tourist circuits. These post-modern tourists also tend to intellectualize their leisure activities, so that tourism is increasingly linked with learning and discovery (Munt 1994).

For Western European tourists who desired an experience of the 'other', the communist states to the east offered particular opportunities: a political, economic and social system which was the antithesis of 'Western' countries. Hence, during the 1980s there was increasing interest among Western tourists in visiting communist countries, particularly Czechoslovakia and Hungary (cf. Carter 1991; Compton 1991). Ironically, while attributes such as poor-quality accommodation, protracted entry formalities, and the prospect of surveillance and possible harassment by the security services were enough to deter many tourists, they were accepted as an integral part of the experience by others. While not all of these tourists may have visited specifically to experience a communist state, the nature of the political/economic system would have under-pinned all aspects of those visits. In other countries – such as Stalinist Albania – tourism was tightly regulated and controlled, and foreign visitors were taken on prescribed itineraries which promoted the achievements of the communist state (Hall 1990, 1991a). In such countries, communism was the context for the tourist's entire experience.

East Berlin provided the most celebrated focus of tourist curiosity in communism. The Berlin Wall was itself one of the city's biggest attractions, and the level of interest in the Wall – and the country which lay beyond it – led the West Berlin authorities to construct several observation posts around the city to allow tourists to gaze into East Berlin. Day-trips from West to East Berlin became a central component of a visit to the city (see, for example, Stratenschulte 1988), allowing many tourists an easy – and brief – opportunity to experience directly an 'other' form of political system.

In a similar manner, the events which brought about the collapse of communism in 1989 were also constructed as tourist attractions (Hall 1991b). In the early 1990s several holiday companies arranged tours of key sites (in various countries) associated with the collapse of communism (Greenberg 1990). Following the opening of the Berlin Wall in November 1989 numerous tourists visited Berlin to obtain a souvenir piece of the Wall: in the following week British Airways carried 30% more passengers to Berlin than at the same time in the previous year (Smith 1990). In Romania, arrivals of foreign visitors in 1990 increased by 1.6 million on the previous year (Light and Dumbrăveanu 1999). Although many visitors were certainly not tourists, the sights and sites of the overthrow of Nicolae Ceauçescu and Eastern Europe's most violent revolution did have a particular tourist appeal. This is another example of a long-established trend – the consumption of sites associated with death and disaster – termed 'dark tourism' (Foley and Lennon 1996) or 'thanatourism' (Seaton 1999).

Although the huge initial wave of tourist interest in CEE has now ebbed somewhat, heritage tourists continue to visit the region in large numbers, and many are drawn to the heritage of communism. In the following section this form of tourism is examined in more detail with reference to three case studies: the remains of the former Berlin Wall in Germany, an open-air museum of communist-era public statuary in Budapest (Hungary), and the 'House of the People', a vast monumental building in Bucharest (Romania). These case studies were selected to illustrate some of the ways in which the heritage of communism is being presented to, and consumed by, tourists, but also the different strategies which have been adopted locally to negotiate this interest without challenging post-communist identities. The material presented draws upon a combination of critical and contextual fieldwork observations, and conversations with local people undertaken at the three sites in the summer and autumn of 1998.

Germany: the Berlin Wall

After the Second World War, Berlin was partitioned between Britain, France, the USA and the Soviet Union. The Soviet Sector later became East Berlin, the capital of the socialist German Democratic Republic (GDR), while the remaining sectors combined to form West Berlin, itself an enclave of the Federal Republic of Germany (FRG) within the GDR. In August 1961 a barbed wire barrier was built by the GDR authorities around West Berlin to stem the widespread migration from the GDR. This was later replaced by a permanent 'wall' of 155 km. In fact, as Baker (1993) observes, 'wall' was something of a misnomer. First, over a third of the barrier was a metal fence; second, there were two parallel walls (of which only the outer wall facing West Berlin was decorated with graffiti). Between the walls was a 'death strip' containing 300 observation towers. Although, the GDR claimed that the purpose of the Wall was to deter a Western occupation of East Berlin, its purpose was generally regarded as being to prevent the exodus of GDR citizens. In this context the Berlin Wall was widely interpreted as a grotesque demonstration of the failure of the GDR to provide economic prosperity and gain popular support. Over time it came to be regarded as the defining symbol of the post-war division of Europe, and of the Cold War itself.

The Berlin Wall ceased to be a barrier for GDR citizens on 9 November 1989. Faced with rising popular unrest and the mass exodus of its citizens through Hungary, the communist regime announced that its citizens could travel freely to the FRG. In the following two days over 2.7 million exit visas were issued to East Berliners (Smith 1990), and some parts of the Wall were removed or demolished to create new border crossings. Following elections in March 1990 the government announced that the wall was to be demolished completely. The final section (apart from parts preserved as memorials) was removed on 13 November 1991: the demolition was so complete that less now remains of the Berlin Wall than of Hadrian's Wall (Baker 1993). Unification between the two Germanies took place at midnight on 2 October 1990.

Since 1989/90 the city of Berlin has had to reconcile a number of conflicting demands concerning the future of the Wall. On one hand, the city is actively recreating itself: not only is it attempting to construct a new identity as a united democratic city but, having been declared the capital of reunited Germany in 1991, it is preparing for the relocation of the government to the city in this new millennium (Cochrane and Jonas 1999). In this context the city's legacy of division is anachronistic and unwelcome: it represents the very antithesis of the city which Berlin is in the process of becoming. Similarly, the discourse of German reunification – an agenda largely dictated by the FRG on its own terms – demands that the Wall should be forgotten. In promoting its post-war democratic traditions the powerful FRG has been eager to deny the legitimacy of the GDR and, as a result, there has been a concerted effort to rid the centre of the city (the designated government district) of symbolic references to the GDR past (Azaryahu 1997). This is achieved in a multitude of ways including the renaming of GDR street names (Azaryahu 1997), and the re-writing of GDR history as presented in museums (Penny 1995). Priority has also been given to the physical reconstruction of the former Wall zone in the centre of the city and large areas of formerly derelict land adjacent to the Wall – most notably around Potsdamer Platz – are now huge building sites.

However, other voices demand that the Wall should not be completely forgotten. Among these are Berliners who have called for the preservation of parts of the Wall as a memorial to the forced division of Berlin and as a key to understanding the post-war history of the city (cf. Sikorski and Laabs 1997). Indeed, in the early 1990s many Berliners were reported to feel some degree of nostalgia for the Wall (Baker 1993). Moreover, any attempts to consign the Wall to history are frustrated by the enduring tourist interest in its remains. Tourism is booming in Berlin and in 1997 the city received 3.4 million visitors (Berlin Tourismus Marketing 1998). The few remaining sections of the Wall continue to be firmly established as tourist 'attractions' and are included in many organized tourist itineraries in the city. Although the level of interest in the former Wall is difficult to quantify, an indication can be gained from the popularity of Berlin's privately run Wall-museum (*Haus am Checkpoint Charlie*) which attracts over half a million visitors annually (Schulte-Peevers and Peevers 1998).

The city authorities have carefully negotiated these competing demands. Representative fragments of the Wall have been retained, both as memorials and to satisfy tourist interest. Foremost among these is the 'East Side Gallery', a 1.3 km stretch of the Wall, located about 4 km from the centre of the city. In September 1990 this was designated as an open-air art gallery to which 118 artists contributed 106 paintings (Maclean 1991). The popularity of the gallery prevented its demolition at the end of 1990 and became a permanent attraction when it was declared a historic monument in 1991 (Kusdas 1998). It is now the main focus of tourist interest in the Wall. As a largely intact and brightly painted section of the Wall, the East Side Gallery contains all the sights required by Wall-tourists: in effect it is a visual soundbite of the Berlin Wall. The gallery attracts a steady stream of visitors, either strolling along its length or gazing at it from nearby coach stops. A souvenir complex has been established at one end. This is, in fact, a highly atypical section of the Wall: first, this is the inner Wall (facing East Berlin) which was rarely seen by tourists and which East Berliners were not allowed to paint; second, the painting of the wall was carefully structured and organized, unlike the anarchic wall art on the western face before 1989. Despite its popularity, the gallery is in a deteriorating state, since many paintings have not weathered well, and souvenir-hunters have also taken their toll.

Other short sections of the Wall have been retained elsewhere in the city and are equally popular tourist sights. In the city centre a short section has been retained as a memorial at Niederkirchnerstrasse (adjacent to the former Gestapo headquarters) with interpretative panels (in German) at either end. Despite enjoying protection as a historic monument this section is in a poor state and is now protected by a metal fence. Further from the city centre a section of the Wall running through a cemetery at Invalidenstrasse has been preserved (again with interpretative panels). Yet another section remains at Bernauer Strasse (again several kilometres from the city centre).

Since 1996 the Wall has also been memorialized through the permanent marking of its course in the centre of the city (Kusdas 1998). This is a further indication of how the process of forgetting the Wall is itself contested, and testifies to the concern that the division of the city should not be completely forgotten. The marking of the Wall's course takes a variety of forms including stone setts or a metal strip embedded in the road surface, or a painted red line. For tourists interested in the Wall this marking effectively 'signposts' their gaze as well as offering a ready-made self-guided trail along the Wall's former course. Indeed, several trail guides along the Wall's route have been published (for example Haus am Checkpoint Charlie 1997; Gympel and Wernicke 1998).

Elsewhere in the city distinct spaces of memory have been created on the former Wall complex. One of these is at the former 'Checkpoint Charlie' border crossing on Friedrichstrasse, itself one of the defining sites and sights of the division of Berlin. Before the fall of the Wall this area was one of Berlin's main attractions, and the city's Wall museum (*Haus am Checkpoint Charlie*) located here in 1963 (Hildebrandt undated). The site has changed considerably since 1989. The checkpoint guard house on the West Berlin side was removed in June 1990 (it now stands in the *Allierten Museum* (Allied Museum) in the suburbs of West Berlin). Similarly, the extensive GDR border complex was demolished in 1991.

Large areas of the former border crossing have subsequently been redeveloped. However, the Checkpoint Charlie area remains a powerful draw for tourists and has become a distinct focus of 'Wall-nostalgia' tourism (at the time of my visit in October 1998 it attracted a steady flow of visitors, both on foot and in coaches, throughout the day). Along with the East Side Gallery and the Brandenburg Gate (now the symbol of reunification), this is also the focus of a thriving business of 'GDR-nostalgia tourism': street vendors sell a range of GDR memorabilia including the inevitable Wall fragments, army hats and uniforms, and model Trabants.

The city authorities have acknowledged the significance and interest to tourists of the Checkpoint Charlie area but have negotiated it through the subtle heritagization of this area. Checkpoint Charlie has become a 'Memoryscape', a piece of urban space organized around social remembering through the assemblage of key icongraphic forms (Edensor 1997). Selected structures have been retained: on the former GDR side of the border a guardhouse (now designated a historical monument) has been preserved, while on the West Berlin side a replica of the Allied Sector signpost (declaiming in four languages 'You are now leaving the American sector') stands in its original position. A unique memorial has recently been installed on the former border demarcation line in the form of an elevated illuminated portrait in the centre of the road. On one side, facing the former West Berlin, is the portrait of a GDR border guard, whilst on the other side is the portrait of an American soldier. The former line of the Wall is also clearly marked by stone setts in the road surface. This is now a distinct piece of heritage space, organized for tourist consumption (an effect reinforced by recently laid cobbles on nearby streets newly created on the border complex). What is being remembered here is just over a decade old, yet through the 'heritagizing' of this area Berlin has attempted to consign the Wall firmly to distant history.

A similar memoryscape has been constructed elsewhere in the city at Bernauer Strasse. Here a 50 m section of the double Wall with death strip was restored in 1998 to form a 'Memorial of German Separation'. Since it is more reconstruction than original this section of the Wall is as yet undamaged by souvenir-hunters. Again, newly laid cobbles around the memorial confirm this as a piece of heritage space and reinforce the narrative that the Wall is firmly part of Berlin's past. Opposite, a documentation centre and exhibition are due to open which will no doubt join the Wall tourist trail.

Although little of the Wall remains physically intact, it retains its iconographic significance in other ways: a Wall fragment has become the defining souvenir of a visit to Berlin. Indeed, within hours of the opening of the border, sections of the Wall were on sale in West Berlin's main shopping street (Baker 1993). A decade later Wall souvenirs remain ubiquitous, and numerous outlets in the city – including Tourist Information Centres – sell the Wall in a variety of forms. Prices range from DM1.5 (£0.57/$0.9) for a tiny sliver set into a postcard to upwards of DM130 (£50/$80) for a more substantial chunk of concrete. Almost all Wall fragments sold to tourists are decorated with graffiti: what tourists want to buy is the graffiti-covered outer Wall with West Berlin. Yet, demand for such sections has exceeded supply: there are widespread reports of sections of the (unpainted) inner wall being hastily spray-painted and broken off to be sold to tourists (Baker 1993). Ultimately, the authenticity of much of what is now sold as the Wall is unverifiable (and there are many reports of complete fakes being sold to tourists), yet tourists continue to purchase it. This is perhaps another example of staged authenticity in tourism (cf. MacCannell 1989).

In a variety of ways Berlin has attempted to satisfy calls to both forget and remember the Wall. The desire to forget the division of the city has been achieved through the demolition of most of the Wall, and the rebuilding of much of the former Wall zone. Elsewhere, the Wall is selectively preserved, but in such a way as to blunt its symbolic impacts. One section has been turned into an open-air art gallery. Another has been reconstructed and enjoys the self-conscious status of a memorial. The one remaining section in the city centre is so badly damaged as to be virtually unrecognizable. Similarly, perhaps the most famous location associated with the Wall – Checkpoint Charlie – has been turned into a deliberately contrived heritage space. What remains of the Wall are isolated fragments which are long-divorced from their original context as part of a fearsome barrier: their status as designated monuments further emphasizes that they are part of Berlin's past. Moreover, the commemoration of the Wall is clearly spatialized. In the centre of the city almost all traces have disappeared with only its former course being unobtrusively marked on road surfaces. All but one of the remaining Wall segments are located several kilometres from the city centre, so that tourists need to make a purposeful visit to see them.

Hungary: Statuepark

Following the Second World War Hungary experienced a hard-line Stalinist regime (which was re-imposed after the 1956 uprising). However, during the late 1960s the Communist Party leader János Kádár introduced gradual liberalization to reform central planning, introduce market forces and permit the existence of a small private sector. Although Hungary emerged as the most prosperous of the Eastern Bloc countries, the economy was experiencing stagnation by the mid 1980s. The Communist Party became increasingly divided between conservatives and those advocating that only further reform could solve Hungary's problems. Kádár was ousted in 1988, opposition parties were formed, and in 1989 the government met with opposition parties to negotiate a new political system. At its congress in October 1989 the Communist Party agreed to abolish the Party's leading role. Democratic elections followed in March 1990. Thus, Hungary's transition to economic liberalization was a gradual process, while the final collapse of the communist party was entirely peaceful (Henderson and Robinson 1997).

Budapest's post-communist city authorities faced the problem of what to do with some of the most visible symbols of the former regime: the numerous statues and monuments erected to celebrate communist heroes (both Soviet and Hungarian). Opinions were divided, again illustrating how the significance of the communist period is contested. One group campaigned vigorously for the removal of all such traces of the communist past (and some extremists threatened to dynamite them if they were not removed). Another group wanted the city's statues to remain in place as a reminder of Hungary's experience of communism, while many Budapesters were apparently indifferent to their fate (Dent 1992; Nash 1993). In December 1991 a compromise was reached: the choice of which statues were to be removed and which were to be kept was assigned to the individual districts of the city (Anon 1995). Those statues which were designated for removal were to be gathered together for public display on the edge of Budapest. The cost of their relocation was estimated at 50 million forints (c. £385 000/$61 6000) (Dent 1992). Budapest experienced a tourist boom in the immediate post-communist period (Hall 1995b) and the city authorities were no doubt aware that such a park would have considerable tourist appeal.

The architect Árkos Eleőd was given responsibility for the design of the statue park. His stated intention was to create something which was politically and artistically neutral, neither celebrating nor ridiculing the communist era, whilst acknowledging that the statues were a part of Hungary's history (Nash 1993). In particular he aimed to avoid creating an anti-propaganda park from these propagandist statues (Anon 1995). The park represents a serious attempt to present and interpret Hungary's recent past, describing itself as an open-air museum: Western commentators have inevitably labelled it a theme park.

The statue park (Szoborpark) opened to visitors in 1993 on a half-acre site in southern Budapest. Despite its name the park contains a wide variety of public monuments from the communist period, most dating from after the 1956 uprising (Dent 1996). Seventeen of the 41 exhibits are statues or busts, 13 are memorial plaques and the remainder are metal or stone monuments. Considerable attention was paid to the layout of the park in providing an appropriate context for the statues and monuments inside (Anon 1995). In typically post-modern style the very design and layout of the park include metaphors for state socialism (cf. Jencks 1991). Visitors are greeted by statues of Lenin and Marx, set within an imposing red-brick neo-classical facade which mimics and parodies 'socialist realism' architecture, a style which as the guidebook claims, 'wishes to create the illusion that it is a natural successor to classical architecture but on its own legitimate terms' (Anon 1995). The park is arranged in the form of a straight path, from which 'figure-of-eight' walkways lead off (so that the wandering visitor will always return to the true path!), around which statues and monuments are displayed. In the centre of the park is a flower bed in the form of a Soviet Star. Eventually, the path ends abruptly in a brick wall, representing the 'dead end' which state socialism represented for Hungary: visitors have no choice but to walk back the way they have previously come.

Statue Park is a museum unique in Central and Eastern Europe and has rapidly established itself as one of Budapest's most unusual tourist attractions. There is some irony in that statues and monuments which have been largely rejected in the civic landscape of Budapest are now used to generate revenue from foreign tourists (Johnson 1995). Despite being a 20-minute bus ride from the city centre, many foreign tourists are prepared to make a special visit to the park (although inevitably the museum has a selective appeal to those tourists with a more focused interest in understanding Budapest's history). The park offers a range of souvenirs, largely aimed at Western tourists, which gleefully mock the communist era.

Statue Park can be initially interpreted as an indication of the sense of confidence of post-communist Hungary. It suggests that the country is sufficiently relaxed about its experience of communism to have few reservations about remembering it (there seems to have been little protest from Hungarians about the construction of the park). In many ways this sense of making a clean break with the past is mirrored in the National History Museum in Budapest (itself another of Budapest's main tourist attractions). In 1996 the museum opened a gallery interpreting the post-war period up to 1990. This includes portraits of Rákosi (Hungary's post-war Stalinist leader), patriotic posters, a statue of Stalin, and displays on the gradual collapse of the communist state in 1988–9. The communist period is presented as just another era in Hungary's history, an era which is closed, and to which there will be no return. For Hungary, communism is history.

However, Statue Park, is also a way of remembering the communist period within tightly defined parameters. Its statues are sufficiently impressive to have been of interest to tourists had they been left *in situ* in the urban landscape of Budapest. However, as Johnson (1995) observes, a statue in a civic square inscribes that square with a particular meaning (cf. Withers 1996). This meaning is incompatible with the post-communist identity which Hungary is seeking to construct. In particular, Hungary is eager to rebuild its former links with Central and Western Europe (often described as a 'return' to Europe) and to turn its back on the post-war period of Russian influence. Statue Park represents an ingenious solution to the problem of overcoming a heritage of essentially Soviet influence, without denying it completely. Like Checkpoint Charlie in Berlin, Statue Park has been constructed as a carefully self-contained 'memoryscape' which satisfies both the interest of tourists, and the demands of those wanting to remember the communist period. It also ensures that while the statues are preserved, they are stripped of their original meanings through removal from their original contexts. Furthermore, the location of the park on the very edge of Budapest means that there is a strong element of 'out of sight, out of mind' in the treatment of the statues.

Hungarians sometimes express disappointment and even bewilderment that foreign tourists should want to visit *Szoborpark*. However, the museum is not just a resource for foreign tourists: indeed it attracts as many Hungarians as it does foreigners (Anon 1995). Many Hungarians feel a certain amount of nostalgia for the communist period since the statues, regardless of their political meanings, were part of their everyday lives (Nash 1993). Perhaps the clearest indication of this nostalgia is a CD of patriotic and propagandist songs from the communist period which was released by Statue Park. Although intended as a satirical memento of communism in Hungary, the CD proved to be a runaway success reaching number one in Hungary's music charts (Roddy 1997). Hence, while Hungary's national and local governments strive to consign the communist period firmly to history, there is some ambivalence regarding this period among Hungarians. Similarly, the significance and meaning of the monuments and statues in *Szoborpark* remain contested.

Romania: the 'House of the People'

Whereas Hungary pursued a course of gradual liberalization in the 1980s Romania took exactly the opposite course. Romania's president, Nicolae Ceaușescu was an ardent believer in Marxist–Leninist central planning, and state control over Romanian society was progressively extended during the 1980s. In addition, political and economic power was increasingly concentrated in the hands of Ceaușescu and his family, around whom a grand personality cult developed. Internal dissent was suppressed by an all-pervasive security service and by the late 1980s Romania was, after Albania, the most repressive of the Eastern European countries. In a decision illustrative of the leader's isolation from the population Ceaușescu introduced draconian austerity measures designed to eliminate Romania's foreign debt which caused living standards to plummet for his own citizens.

As part of his Marxist–Leninist ideology which stressed the creation of the 'new socialist man' Ceauşescu was convinced of the need to modernize Romania's cities (Cavalcanti 1997). During the 1980s he embarked on a grandiose scheme to re-create central Bucharest as a modern socialist capital. Almost five square kilometres (a quarter of the historic city centre), mostly composed of one-family houses was razed and the population moved to the suburbs. In its place arose Ceauşescu's 'Centru Civic', the central piece of which was Casa Poporului – the 'house of the people' – an immense building where all Presidential, State and Communist Party activities were to be centralized. Built in an eclectic neo-classical style, with 12 storeys and over 1100 rooms, and covering an area of 6.3 hectares, this was designed to be one of the world's largest buildings. Casa Poporului represents Ceauşescu's efforts to shape society through the symbolic control of space: the building was intended to demonstrate to Romanians the authority and power of the communist state, and of Ceauşescu himself. In many ways it is the defining monument of totalitarianism in Central and Eastern Europe.

At the time of Ceauşescu's violent overthrow and execution in 1989 the building was uncompleted. Romania's post-communist administration (itself dominated by former communists) was faced with the problem of finding a future for the building. Romanians are extremely ambivalent about the building. Since it is so closely associated with Ceauşescu, and since so much damage was caused to Bucharest in its construction, many Romanians would willingly have seen it torn down. Others are more circumspect, pointing out that the building was built entirely by Romanians (over 400 architects and 200 000 workers were involved in its construction (Williams 1998)) and represents the best of Romanian craftsmanship. The post-communist government eventually decided that the building should house the Romanian Parliament. Part is also used as an international conference centre which opened in 1994.

However, in the post-communist period Casa Poporului – later renamed Palatul Parlamentului (the Parliament Palace) – has also become the city's biggest tourist attraction. To some extent this may reflect the relative absence of more conventional attractions in the central area of the city – indeed it has been described as 'the main tourist site of a pretty drab city (Burford 1998). However, the sheer size of this unique building, along with its role as perhaps the defining symbol of the tragedy of totalitarianism, make it the focus of tourist curiosity. In a context where Romanian tourism has experienced relentless decline since 1989 (Light and Dumbrăveanu 1999) Romania has had little choice but to respond – albeit with reluctance – to the tourist appeal of the building. Guided tours of a small part of the palace were introduced in mid-1997 (which, according to a spokesman for the building, attract approximately 25 000 visitors annually). In addition, images of the building feature increasingly in promotional material for holidays in Romania: in the process the building is becoming a 'sign' which represents Romania itself.

However, Romania's dilemma over how to come to terms with the legacy of communism is clearly reflected in the presentation of *Palatul Parlamentului* to tourists. During the guided tour visitors are told virtually nothing about the building's history, Ceauşescu's role in its construction, or the context in which it was built. Instead guides focus on other themes. First, the tour draws attention to the physical dimensions and scale of the building, including the number of floors and rooms and the dimensions of some of the largest rooms. Second, the materials and craftsmanship of the building are stressed. In particular the building is presented as being built almost entirely of Romanian materials, and containing the finest examples of Romanian craftsmanship. Third, the tour emphasizes that this is a working political building, and the seat of the Romanian parliament. To reinforce this theme a small museum has recently opened in the building which traces the origins of parliamentary democracy in Romania in the nineteenth century. Finally, the tour includes some of the rooms used for international conferences including the vast *Sala Unirii* (Unity Hall).

Palatul Parlamentului again illustrates the ambivalent and contested nature of heritage in Central and Eastern Europe. Presenting this building to tourists represents a considerable challenge since there is considerable dissonance between what the building means to Romanians, what it represents to foreign visitors, and what Romanians would like it to mean to foreign visitors. Many Romanians find it simply incomprehensible that foreigners should want to visit such a despised building, and are irritated when visitors miss the other attractions that Bucharest offers. No doubt aware that many visitors associate the building with Ceauşescu, the building's managers have attempted to create a new narrative for it, one which attempts to deny its connections with the former regime, and Ceauşescu in particular. Hence, while visitors may wish to consume the building as a monument to totalitarianism, the managers of the building are attempting to present an entirely different message: the building is presented as a remarkable piece of Romanian-built architecture. Moreover, by emphasizing the role of the building as the seat of the legislature Romania is eager to emphasize that it is a post-communist, pluralist democracy.

Given its harsh experience of totalitarianism Romania has compelling reasons for wanting to forget its experience of communism. Romania, like Hungary, is eager to emphasize its post-communist credentials, and is seeking to renew links with Central and Western Europe. However, Romania has been less successful than Hungary in making a decisive break with the former regime. The presence of many of the former *nomenklatura* in government between 1990 and 1996, and the slow pace in reforming the economic structures inherited from the super-centralized economy of Ceauşescu means that Romania still has some way to go before it can be said to have put communism truly behind it. The opening of *Palatul Parlamentului* to tourists may represent a step along this road: it is probably no coincidence that the building opened properly for visitors only after elections of November 1996 had returned a centre-right government, marking a genuine break with the former administration.

Conclusion

As contemporary tourists seek an ever-widening range of experiences and destinations, there has been a rapid growth in 'special interest' and 'alternative' forms of tourism. Underpinning these are motives common to many types of post-modern tourism: a search for difference and the 'other' in destinations and experiences. In Central and Eastern Europe parts of the material heritage of communism offer such experiences and sights, whether for those with a focused interest in communism (a subset of special interest tourists who might perhaps be labelled as 'communist heritage tourists') or more 'general' heritage tourists. This paper has examined ways in which selected parts of the heritage of communism – the remains of part of the 'iron curtain', public statuary and a monumental building – have become the focus of the tourist gaze.

However, for the CEE countries this tourist interest in their communist past is far from welcome. Although in all these countries the significance of the communist past – as well as their future direction – is contested, 'official' policy is to draw a line under the communist period and seek to construct a new, post-communist future. In Berlin's case this involves creating a unified city as the capital of a united Germany; in the case of Hungary and Romania this involves a 'return' to Europe. Tourism is one way in which these countries can affirm their self-image and aspirations both to themselves and to the wider world. As such there are particular pieces of the national story which are considered acceptable – and unacceptable – for the tourist gaze. Visitors' interest in the heritage of communism can be a problematic challenge to this project.

As the case studies presented in this paper have illustrated, each country has responded to the tourist interest in its communist past in different ways. In Berlin and Budapest there has been a cautious or reluctant acknowledgement of tourist interest in communism. In Berlin some sections of the Wall itself have been retained, and distinct heritage spaces have been created around Checkpoint Charlie and at the Memorial of German Separation on Bernauer Strasse. In Budapest there has been a frank – even ironic – engagement with the public monuments of state socialism. The construction of Statuepark is recognition of the revenue-generating potential of this heritage, but it is also a careful attempt to reinterpret the communist period, for post-communist visitors. In Romania a different strategy – of attempted denial – has been adopted. The presentation of the 'House of the People' is silent on the building's associations with the communist past, and attempts instead to inscribe it with new meanings appropriate to Romania's self-image as a post-communist democracy.

In all three case studies there has been an attempt to negate the meanings of the heritage of communism by decontextualizing it. In Berlin, only short segments of the former Wall remain, long divorced from the context – a complete double Wall with 'death strip' – in which they once stood. In Statuepark, the statues lose their original meanings through removal from their original settings. In Bucharest, the *Palatul Parlamentului* has attempted to construct a narrative which denies all connections with Ceauşescu, emphasizing instead the contemporary uses of the building. Moreover, in Berlin and Budapest, the presentation of communist heritage takes place within spatially prescribed parameters. The retention of the legacy of communism in the city centre was deemed inappropriate: hence, the significance of this heritage is further blunted by removing it from the centre of the city. In Berlin, all but one of the remaining Wall segments are several kilometres from the city centre. Similarly, in Budapest, communist statuary has been removed to a designated heritage space on the city's perimeter.

The relationship between tourism and politics is one which is frequently overlooked in tourism studies (Hall 1994). However, through an exploration of the management and presentation of the heritage of communism in post-communist Central and Eastern Europe, this paper has illustrated that tourism cannot be divorced from its political context. In a region where identities are fluid, unstable and sometimes fragile, tourism is one means through which a country can present itself to the world as a credible and legitimate post-communist democracy. But, 'communist heritage' tourism challenges this entire project, although such tourists are probably oblivious to the fact. As the case studies discussed in this paper have illustrated, the presentation of the recent past for tourists is a politically mediated process, circumscribed by wider debates in the post-communist period concerning the politics of memory and identity.

Acknowledgements

I wish to thank David Phinnemore (for German translations) and Teresa Ploszajska (for her comments on an earlier draft of this paper). I am also grateful to Liverpool Hope University College for financial support which enabled me to visit Berlin.

References

Allcock, J.B. 1995. International tourism and the appropriation of history in the Balkans. In *International Tourism: Identity and Change*, ed. Marie-Françoise Lanfant, John B. Allcock and E. M. Bruner, pp. 101–12. London: Sage.

Anon. 1995. *Statue Park* (guidebook). Budapest: Szoborpark. See also *http://www.szoborpark.hu*.

Ashworth, G.J. 1994. From history to heritage – from heritage to identity: in search of concepts and models. In *Building a New Heritage: Tourism, Culture and Identity in the New Europe*, ed. G.J. Ashworth and P.J. Larkham, pp. 13–30. London: Routledge.

Ashworth, G.J. and Graham, B. 1997. Heritage, identity and Europe. *Tijdschrift voor Economische en Sociale Geografie* 88 (4): 381–8.

Azaryahu, M. 1997. German reunification and the politics of street names: the case of East Berlin. *Political Geography* 16 (6): 479–93.

Azaryahu, M. and Kellerman, A. 1999. Symbolic places of national history and revival: a study in Zionist mythical geography. *Transactions of the Institute of British Geographers* 24 (1): 109–23.

Baker, F. 1993. The Berlin Wall: production, preservation and consumption of a 20th century monument. *Antiquity* 67: 709–33.

Berlin Tourism's Marketing. 1998. *Destination Berlin* (factsheet). Berlin: Berlin Tourismus Marketing GmbH.

Burford, T. 1998. New socialist man meets Vlad the impaler. *The Independent on Sunday*, Travel Section (April 5): 8.

Carter, F.W. 1991. Czechoslovakia. In *Tourism and Economic Development in Eastern Europe and the Soviet Union*, ed. Derek R. Hall, pp. 154–72. London: Belhaven.

Cavalcanti, M.B.U. 1997. Urban reconstruction and autocratic regimes: Ceausescu's Bucharest in its historic context. *Planning Perspectives* 12: 71–109

Cochrane, A. and Jonas, A. 1999. Reimagining Berlin: World city, national capital or ordinary place? *European Urban and Regional Studies* 6 (2): 145–64.

Compton, P. A. 1991 Hungary. In *Tourism and Economic Development in Eastern Europe and the Soviet Union*, ed. Derek R. Hall, pp. 173–89. London: Belhaven.

Dent, R. 1992. The hiss in history. *The Guardian*, 13 November: Section 2, p. 18

Dent, R. 1996. *Budapest*. London: A and C Black.

Edensor, T. 1997. National identity and the politics of memory: remembering Bruce and Wallace in symbolic space. *Environment and Planning D: Society and Space* 29: 175–94.

Foley, M, and Lennon, J. J. 1996. JFK and dark tourism: A fascination with assassination. *International Journal of Heritage Studies* 2 (4): 198–211.

Greenberg, S.H. 1990. Freedom trail. *Newsweek*, 14 May: 12–17.

Gympel, J. and Wernicke, I. 1998. *The Berlin Wall*. Berlin: Jaron Verlag GmbH.

Hall, C. M. 1994. *Tourism and Politics: Policy, Power and Place*. Chichester: Wiley.

Hall, D.R. 1990. Stalinism and tourism: A study of Albania and North Korea. *Annals of Tourism Research* 17 (1): 36–54.

Hall, D.R. 1991a. Albania. In *Tourism and Economic Development in Eastern Europe and the Soviet Union*, ed. Derek R. Hall, pp. 259–77. London: Belhaven.

Hall, D.R. 1991b. Contemporary Challenges. In *Tourism and Economic Development in Eastern Europe and the Soviet Union*, ed. Derek R. Hall, pp. 281–9. London: Belhaven.

Hall, D.R. 1995a. Eastern Europe: Tourism/leisure perspectives – an introduction. *Tourism and Leisure – Culture, Heritage and Participation*, ed. David Leslie, pp. 3–10. Brighton: Leisure Studies Association.

Hall, D.R. 1995b. Tourism change in Central and Eastern Europe. In *European Tourism: Regions, Spaces and Restructuring*, ed. A. Montanari and Allen M. Williams, pp. 221–44. London: Wiley..

Haus am Checkpoint Charlie. 1997. *Walk the Wall*. Berlin: Pharus-Verlag.

Henderson, K. and Robinson, N. 1997. *Post-Communist Politics: An Introduction*. Hemel Hempstead: Prentice Hall.

Hildebrandt, R. undated. *Museum Haus am Checkpoint Charlie*. Berlin: Verlag Haus am Checkpoint Charlie.

Jencks, C. 1991. *The Language of Post-modern Architecture* (5th edition). London: Academy Editions.

Johnson, N. 1995. Cast in stone: monuments, geography and nationalism. *Environment and Planning D: Society and Space* 13: 51–65.

Kuzdas, H.J. 1998. *Berliner Mauer Kunst*. Berglin: Elefanten Press Verlag.

Lanfant, M.-F. 1995. International tourism, internationalization and the challenge to identity. In *International Tourism: Identity and Change*, ed. Marie-Françoise Lanfant, John B. Allcock and E. M. Bruner, pp. 24–43. London: Sage.

Light, D. and Dumbrăveanu, D. 1999. Romanian tourism in the post-communist period. *Annals of Tourism Research* 26 (4): 898–927.

MacCannell, D. 1989. *The Tourist: A New Theory of the Leisure Class* (2nd edition). New York: Shocken Books.

Maclean, C. 1991. *East Side Gallery*. Berlin: Wuva GmbH.

Morgan, N. and Pritchard, A. 1998. *Tourism Promotion and Power: Creating Images, Creating Identities*. Chichester: Wiley.

Munt, I. 1994. The 'other' postmodern tourism: culture, travel and the new middle classes. *Theory, Culture and Society* 11: 101–23.

Nash, E. 1993. Communism: the theme park. *The Independent on Sunday*, 12 September: 40–1.

O'Connor, B. 1993. Myths and mirrors: tourism images and national identity. In *Tourism in Ireland: A Critical Analysis*, ed. Barbara O'Connor and M. Cronin, pp.68–85. Cork: Cork University Press.

Pearce, S. M. 1998. The construction of heritage: the domestic context and its implications. *International Journal of Heritage Studies* 4: 86–102.

Penny, H. G. 1995. The Museum für Deutsche Geschichte and German national identity. *Central European History* 28: 343–72.

Roddy, M. 1997. Communist songs head to top of charts in Hungary. *Nouvelles: Information-Archives-Bib. Http://www.fas.umontreal.ca/EBSI/ebsi-l/1997/msg00663.html*; 21 September.

Schulte-Peevers, A. and Peevers, D. 1998. *Berlin*. Hawthorn, Australia: Lonely Planet.

Seaton, A. V. 1999. War and thanatourism: Waterloo 1815–1914. *Annals of Tourism Research* 26: 130–58.

Sikorski, W. and Laabs, R. 1997. *Checkpoint Charlie and the Wall*. Berlin: Ullstein.

Smith, K. 1990. *Berlin: Coming in from the Cold*. Harmondsworth: Penguin.

Stratenschulte, E. D. 1988. *East Berlin*. Berlin: Informationszentrum Berlin.

Tunbridge, J. E. 1994. Whose heritage? Global problem, European Nightmare. In *Building a New Heritage: Tourism, Culture and Identity in the New Europe*, ed. G.J. Ashworth and P.J. Larkham, pp.123–34. London: Routledge.

Tunbridge, J.E. and Ashworth, G.J. 1996. *Dissonant Heritage: The Management of the Past as a Resource in Conflict*. Chichester: Wiley.

Urry, J. 1990. *The Tourist Gaze: Leisure and Travel in Contemporary Societies*. London: Sage.

Urry, J. 1994. Europe, tourism and the nation-state. In *Progress in Tourism, Recreation and Hospitality Management Volume 6*, ed. Chris P. Cooper and Andrew Lockwood, pp. 89–98. Wiley: Chichester.

Williams, N. 1998. *Romania and Moldova*. Hawthorn, Australia: Lonely Planet.

Withers, C.W.J. 1996. Place, memory, monument: Memorializing the past in contemporary highland Scotland. *Ecumene* 3 (3): 325–44.

Unpacking the local: a cultural analysis of tourism entrepreneurship in Murter, Croatia

Irena Ateljevic

Stephen Doorne

Abstract

In recent years, there has been a paradigmatic shift articulated by the 'cultural' turn of tourism geography. Within the cultural analysis of economic relations the embrace of complexity and diversity has become essential to broadening our understanding of tourism development processes. This paper seeks to engage with local cultural perspectives, which inform these 'new' ways of theorizing tourism. This study focuses on small-scale tourism entrepreneurship in the village of Murter in the Balkans set against the backdrop of economic transition in a post-war environment. It is argued that the role of local values is critical in the re-emergence of tourism as a key economic sector and the shaping of small enterprise culture. The analysis utilizes an 'insider' perspective as a key positioning element in the discussion.

Introduction

The reconceptualization of geographical subdisciplines and the embrace of 'de-differentiation of the economy and culture' (Crang & Malbon 1996; Amin & Thrift 2000; Sayer 2000) are central to the emergence of a 'new' theorization of tourism. Within *'the economic'*, contemporary cultural and social geography attempts to account for both the material condition and the experience of individuals, as well as the place of the individual within the structures of power and economy. Within '*the cultural*', contemporary economic geography embraces the economy as a cultural and social formation, opening up, as Thrift (2000) suggests, a Pandora's box of complexity. These processes have seen the integration of cultural politics in a more inclusive human geography, in which the challenge to transgress boundaries has produced a 'new' discourse of tourism geography through which the interface between geography and tourism studies has begun to be re-examined (Squire 1994a; 1994b; Iaonnides & Debbage 1998; Ringer 1998; Ateljevic 2000; Pritchard & Morgan 2000; Milne & Ateljevic 2001).

The process of overcoming the separation of the economic, cultural and social necessarily demands the reconciliation of structure and agency. Rather than the re-creation of still further tangential directions, crossing these traditional boundaries requires the internalization of the structure–agency dialectic. Differences and pluralities of places and social groups have been identified in opposition to 'structuralist/reductionist' generalization. The process of articulating difference has been driven by the 'crisis of representation' in broader social sciences, whereby social researchers are increasingly being asked to identify their position within their writings, as texts are revealed as epistemological representations (Marcus & Fisher 1986).

In response to these concerns new strategies have been developed in which the researcher's desire to advance an argument is enhanced by the integration of traditional methods of inquiry, reshaped by a transgression of boundaries. In this paper, we pursue this strategy by drawing on the established literature on tourism entrepreneurship and small business development, seeking to unpack the cultural complexities of economic dynamics. The traditionally economic concepts of tourism entrepreneurship have been predominantly interpreted from a 'structuralist/reductionist' perspective in isolation of tourism economy. Following the argument of Crang & Malbon (1996) we examine our case study of tourism entrepreneurship, pursuing the de-differentiation between culture and economy in terms of both: (1) the cultural regulation of the economic; and (2) the 'cultural materialization of the economic' (see also du Gay 1996).

In this theoretical context this study explores tourism entrepreneurship in Croatia (a former republic of Yugoslavia), with particular focus on the village of Murter on the Adriatic coast. The paper analyses the cultural context surrounding the decision-making of small business entrepreneurs in the village with respect to economy and lifestyle, the role of family and the intergenerational nature of tourism businesses, gender issues and relations of politics and the black-market. The paper reveals the benefit of a cultural analysis of tourism entrepreneurship that goes beyond the consideration of purely economic criteria. The study illustrates the extent to which the 'insider' perspective informed by local values has the capacity to unpack the complexities of social, economic and political relations which underlie tourism entrepreneurship and development.

The discussion begins with an overview of the study of entrepreneurship and small business development in general, identifying the range of perspectives and theoretical constructs that inform contemporary understanding. In doing so, we discuss the extent to which economic factors have remained central to the analyses and concurrently point to emerging studies of tourism entrepreneurship and small tourism businesses that have begun to integrate the cultural with the economic. Drawing on this foundation we argue that socio-cultural contingencies of the local, which shape tourism entrepreneurship provide opportunities to rejuvenate our theoretical gaze. Given that our research context is characterized by an economy in transition and a post-war environment it is important to detail the issues relevant to our discussion. Following this, the case study is introduced first by outlining the study approach, followed by a description of the background to tourism in Croatia and the village of Murter. The case study presents a description of the industry structure–agency dynamic and from this proceeds to discuss the key issues which emerged during the research. The paper concludes by arguing that an appreciation of the local cultural perspective enhances the conceptualization of entrepreneurship in tourism. This argument reaffirms the value of emerging theoretical perspectives which conceptualize economy and culture in terms of their mutual constitution.

Theorizing tourism entrepreneurship: traditions and ways forward

Historically the conceptualization of entrepreneurship emerged within classical economic theory and was concerned with entrepreneurial activity as a key factor and dynamic element in economic performance (Hawley 1907; Schumpeter 1934; 1965; Cole 1942; 1954). In general terms, the concept can be unravelled in terms of the entrepreneur and the structural conditions surrounding his or her activity. Whilst often used to designate the formation of new businesses, economic perspectives have sought to define the qualities that characterize entrepreneurial acts as being different from those of other 'ordinary' managers (see for example, Porter 1980; Drucker 1985; McMullan & Long 1990; Cunnigham & Lischeron 1991).

Social science perspectives have concentrated on identifying various issues that condition the level of entrepreneurial activity yet perpetuate the economic theoretical premise around which issues of entrepreneurship are discussed. For example, psychological theory has attempted to identify personality traits of the entrepreneur (Chell, *et al.* 1991) and sociological perspectives have sought to define the 'entrepreneurial middle class' (Scase & Goffee 1982). On the subject of small business initiation, an extensive interdisciplinary body of literature has discussed entrepreneurship in the context of small firm development (see for example; Deakings, *et al.* 1997; Legge & Hindle 1997). This body of literature draws attention to significant differences between small and large enterprises, and has been predominantly informed by conceptual lenses derived from general management and business studies, henceforth perpetuating an economic view of the small business sector. Storey (1994) for example, in his highly regarded review of small business research, points to polemic discussions of small enterprises and their economic (in)capacities.

Dewhurst & Horobin (1998) note the difficulty of applying a similar economic perspective to the tourism and hospitality context. Despite fairly limited research on tourism entrepreneurship and small firms, they note that a picture is emerging of entrepreneurs 'who are not motivated by a desire to maximize economic gain, who operate businesses often with very low levels of employment, and in which managerial decisions are often based on highly personalized criteria' (p. 25). In light of this, they argue there is a need to move beyond purely economic definitions to conceptualize the entrepreneur in wider terms. In an attempt to provide a new perspective they propose a continuum for small business owner-managers stretching between commercial and lifestyle goals and strategies. For those business owners who are lifestyle-orientated 'their business success might best be measured in terms of a continuing ability to perpetuate their chosen lifestyle' (Dewhurst & Horobin 1998: 30). This conceptual thinking is revolutionary in a sense that it moves our approach towards a concept of entrepreneurship that comprises social and cultural values as 'success' factors, rather than just 'development and business growth'.

It was Williams, *et al.* (1989) who initially observed the phenomenon of lifestyle aspirations in small-scale businesses as blurring the boundaries between consumption and production. They argued that lifestyle entrepreneurs are generally motivated by non-economic goals and, by accepting suboptimal profits, seriously constrain the economic and tourism development of the region (Shaw & Williams 1987; 1990; 1998). Throughout their work, mainly with reference to British seaside resorts, they reiterate the issue of small business survival (particularly in the context of peripheral regions of developed economies) and urge for more research to explore the nature of small-scale tourism entrepreneurship and its role in local economies.

Similarly, Morrison, *et al.* (1999) provide a range of typologies and contexts surrounding tourism entrepreneurship in which they identify lifestyle small firms as significant elements. They note that these businesses are often initiated by the need to create a chosen lifestyle in which the needs of family, income and a way-of-life are balanced. A key issue surrounding these businesses, they also argue, is related to economic survival and viability. Ateljevic & Doorne's (2000) discussion of lifestyle entrepreneurship in New Zealand illustrates the extent to which 'non-economic' values are key elements in entrepreneurial decision-making and the extent to which these perspectives are often instrumental in the creation of new products and simultaneously in providing a niche opportunity to engage with that market on their own terms and to sustain their businesses.

This work in the Western context of developed economies illustrates what can be identified as the integration of the cultural with the more traditional and economic concepts. This merging of traditional and contemporary perspectives on entrepreneurship has been paralleled by discussions in a developing world context. Traditional development theory has often sought to apply and reproduce the Western development model across the cultural mosaic of the developing world (for example, Berstein 1973; Todaro 1997). The balance between external and local entrepreneurs has lain at the heart of a debate over ownership and control of the tourism economy and, in turn, who benefits from subsequent economic growth. Against this back-drop, the structuralist perspectives sought to explore and intervene with the conditions that constrain and facilitate local entrepreneurial activity (see, for example, Michaud 1991; Din 1992; Archer 1995; Echtner 1995; Thompson, *et al.* 1995). These studies have been, however, primarily concerned with economic factors in which the considerations of the local culture was regarded as the 'Other' (Said 1988; Chambers 1993; 1997). Consequently, the socio-cultural barriers and local contingencies shaping entrepreneurship have been traditionally overlooked in the process.

In recent years, there have been notable responses to the development model, which sought to impose a set of foreign values upon local ways of life (Hettne 1990; Cowen & Shenton 1996; Rist & Camiller 1997). With respect to tourism entrepreneurship the work of Dahles (1997) and Dahles and Bras (1999) in SE Asia reveals the extent to which the indigenous cultural fabric is woven into the economic life. Their case studies of indi-vidual entrepreneurs illustrate 'alternative' value systems, which shape dynamics of their personal economies. Similarly, Gartner's (1999) study of tourism small-scale enterprises in Ghana looks at the influence of culture on economic dynamics of local entrepreneurship. Identifying socio-cultural obligations rather than economic factors as prime drives behind business decisions, Gartner effectively reveals the limitations of the overtly economic reductionist approach of 'Western development models', whereas 'inter-jecting cultural conditions into the equation' (1999: 171) helps more fully to understand local development issues. Hitchcock's (2000) case study of ethnicity and entrepreneurship in Java and Bali identifies the value of what he terms a 'situational approach' that 'rejects simplistic conceptions of culture as bounded entities and places emphasis on ethnicity as a set of social relationships and processes by which cultural differences are commu-nicated' (Hitchcock 1999: 21).

The geopolitical shift over the last decades has, however, blurred the distinction between the former First, Second and Third Worlds introducing still further regions in 'need of development', particularly the 'economies in transition' in Central and SE Europe. Despite a proliferation of studies on issues of tourism and economic development in these regions (see, for example, Harrison 1993; Airey 1994; Balaz 1995; Hall 1995; Johnson 1995; 1997; Jaakson 1996; Unwin 1996; Bacharov 1997), Hall (1998: 423) argues that countries of SE Europe, particular the Balkan states, remain 'very much the "Other" with respect not only to research but also to their cultural peripherality in the regional tourism mosaic'. This paper explores a cultural 'interior' of the Balkan's 'Otherness' in the context of socio-cultural issues surrounding tourism entrepreneurship in post-Communist and post-conflict era in Croatia through an examination of the case study of the village of Murter. In doing so, it is important to note that the paper aims to make a broader theoretical contribution to the previously discussed 'economic/cultural' debate, rather than the literature on the economies in transition *per se*. An overview of the broader regional economy-in-transition context of Murter is given below.

Research context: the economies in transition and the Balkans

The transition from a centrally planned to a market economy in the former 'socialist bloc' of Europe region has been widely documented and explored (for example, Blanchard, *et al.* 1991; East 1992). The processes of political, economic and social restructuring have resulted in the loosening of constraints on personal mobility, enhanced and reorientated foreign trade and investment, and encouraged entrepreneurial activity through programmes of large- and small-scale privatization, deregulation, price liberalization, divestment and internal currency convertibility. Economic restructuring has, however, proved to be a long-term and painful process. The individual distinctiveness of nations and the social diversity in the region have further perplexed the prospect of applying the 'general success formula' to regional development (see, for example, Jeffries 1993).

Despite numerous case studies of tourism development in Central and Eastern Europe as noted earlier, the role of tourism in the Balkan states remains relatively unexplored largely due to the domino effect of ethnic conflicts in the former Yugoslavia (Hall & Danta 1996; Hall 1998). At the heart of this conflict have been the articulation of cultural difference and the establishment of national, and regional identities. However, over the last five years tourism has re-emerged as a key agent in the post-war environment, and the economic transition has been underpinned by a broader policy focus encouraging tourism entrepreneurship and a small enterprise culture (Horvat 1999; Hitrec 2000). Gosar (2000), for example, observes the rejuvenation of tourism in the Balkan post-socialist era (Albania, Bosnia and Herzegovina, Bulgaria, Croatia, Macedonia, Romania, Slovenia, Yugoslavia, Serbia and Montenegro). He notes that, despite the intense disruptions of social and intercultural relations, touristic activity has recovered and continues to grow. In the process, newly emerged states have sought to redefine their national identities and state-building processes based on their historical and cultural population distribution, reflecting what Hall (1998: 429) describes as the 'potentially dangerous forces (cultural) of inclusion and exclusion, most forcibly expressed in the former Yugoslavia'. It is in this context that tourism continues to play a significant role in the constitution of cultural identity as well as the productive capacity of the economy, particularly driven by the small firms sector (Hitrec 2000). It is in this multidimensional context that this study proceeds to explore the role of culture in tourism entrepreneurship in the village of Murter, Croatia.

Research approach

Accompanying the previously discussed theoretical shift has being significant progress in the methodological sophistication of research, particularly with respect to the role of the researcher and the multiplicity of research methods. It follows that this more complex research approach necessarily reveals a more complex world. Although such an approach may lead to theoretical and methodological eclecticism, Eyles (1988: 5) asserts that is 'a useful if difficult to control characteristic of much human geography'. In these circumstances, the field researcher is seen as a 'methodological pragmatist' who 'sees any method of inquiry as a system of strategies and operations designed – at any time – for getting answers to certain questions about events which interest him (sic)' (Shatzman & Strauss 1973: 7, as quoted by Eyles 1988: 6). Moreover, the reflexivity of the researcher is a critical dimension of the whole research process that involves the evolution of research from its conceptual foundation through trust-building to the interpretation and analysis of 'data' (Harding & Hintikka 1983; Evans 1988; Smith 1988; Denzin 1997).

The proposition of using diverse methods to tackle a research problem has been advocated by many social scientists in order to overcome the limitations of single method studies (Campbell & Fiske 1959; Stacey 1969; Douglas 1976; Denzin 1989). The combination of methodologies in the study of the same phenomenon is usually described as one of convergent methodology, multi-method/multi-trait (Campbell & Fiske 1959), 'mixed strategies' (Douglas 1976) or what has been called **triangulation** (Webb, *et al.* 1966). It is this strategy, which allows us to view qualitative and quantitative methods as complementary. Adorno (1957: 246) claims that qualitative and quantitative exploration (often mistakenly imagined as a dichotomy) form a continuum where one always involves a component of the other:

> The opposition of quantitative and qualitative analysis is not an absolute one: it finds no ultimate support in the subject-matter itself. It is well-known that, in order to quantify, one has always to begin by ignoring qualitative difference between various elements; and every individual social phenomenon bears within itself the general determinisms to which the quantitative generalizations apply. But the categories of the latter are themselves of course qualitative (as quoted by Pile 1991: 459).

There are different forms of multiple research strategies (see Burgess 1982). For this paper we have employed the strategy of multiple sets of data, requiring different methods of investigation, as conditioned by different phases of the research process (Denzin 1989). This approach has generated what anthropologists call 'holistic work' or thick description (Geertz 1973). It was indeed the early anthropologists who advocated and practised such strategies. Eyles (1988) refers to Malinowski's work (1922), who indicated that the goal of ethnographic fieldwork had to be approached in three ways: first, by the method of concrete statistical documentation of the 'units of observation'; second, by observation of the behaviour of individuals and collectivity; and third, ethnographic description based on conversation and interviews. In this light, 'statistical surveys and quantitative analysis remain relevant for interpretative research' (Eyles 1988: 5).

The methodology used here draws on a triangulation of participant observation, in-depth interviewing, and a quantitative analysis of demographic and historical characteristics of entrepreneurs and their enterprises. The village of Murter, which features as the case study for this research, is the birthplace of one of the authors. We draw heavily on her knowledge and understanding of the local and cultural environment and her capacity to interpret meanings from the insider perspective. A total of 62 interviews were conducted during the shoulder season of summer 2000 with a range of tourism operators in the village including accommodation, local/tour operators, travel agencies, restaurants and cafés. The interviews were accompanied by a survey instrument gathering quantitative data on the personal and business characteristics of entrepreneurs. In the paper, most of the respondents' views are integrated into the interpretation and only a few statements are quoted to illustrate the key issues of the analysis. Participant observation drew on six weeks of (re)immersion in the life of the village, which was facilitated by one of the author's status as a returned village 'local'. The author's own experience of living in the village for twenty years facilitated considerable ethnographic depth and insight. Her position of being a Croatian who worked in the local tourism industry during the socialist period for several years, provided an important insight into the cultural context and facilitated reflexive interpretation of value structures informing the dynamics of tourism entrepreneurship.

Tourism development in Croatia: a historical perspective

The former Yugoslavia within the socialist bloc of Central Eastern Europe used its political independence to introduce a unique type of market socialism based on the self-management by workers councils of 'socially owned' enterprises. Agriculture was predominantly privately managed and private sector development elsewhere was encouraged, particularly in tourism. One of the republics most developed in terms of tourism was Croatia (Figure 1).

Figure 1 Map of Croatia (source: Croatian National Tourist Board brochure, 2001).

Being part of the traditional '4S' market, and attracting predominantly Western Europeans seeking Mediterranean summer holidays, tourism development in Croatia and Yugoslavia since 1965 was erratic, yet became (in the 1980s) one of the top ten international destinations of the world (Pearce 1991: 224). In 1990 Yugoslavia received 88 million bed-nights; 43 million of which were foreign visitors and 45 million domestic. In the same year Croatia achieved almost 60 percent of the entire regis-tered tourist turnover in the former Yugoslavian state, that is, 79 percent of foreign and 41 percent of domestic visitation (Hall 1995). The tourism demand has been built around two major market segments: package groups and independent travellers exemplified by the 'young automobile society' (Gosar 1999: 67). Given the nature of demand, the industry has been structured primarily around the accommodation sector. There have been two main categories of accommodation: large publicly owned hotels catering to group bookings and representing 60 percent of tourism assets, with an average of 300 beds per facility (Hitrec 2000: 10–11); and accommodation in the form of small-scale, family-run home-stay rental accommodation often on a room-by-room basis, locally known as 'izna-jmljivaci' (private accommodation providers).

This latter sector has been an extremely dynamic area of entrepreneurship, with the emergence of purpose-built tourist flats, apartments and bungalows, built on the proceeds of families renting their own residential space. These purpose-built facilities have been aligned with upgraded modern standards of hygiene and technical specifications, catering to the perceived needs of Western consumers. In the 'golden times of tourism development' these investments were primarily local and appeared to be 'largely a self generating process and one not heavily dependant on external involvement' (Pearce 1991: 229). Another group of significant entrepreneurs were returning immigrants of 'guest-workers, particularly Yugo-Germans' who perceived tourism on the Adriatic coast as a lucrative business opportunity to capitalize on their contacts and experiences acquired working abroad. These individuals were involved in acquiring land from local landowners, which then provided further capital impetus for locals to invest in their properties and tourism businesses (Pearce 1991: 229).

Supplementing the accommodation sector has been a plethora of cafés and restaurants, mostly small scale and under private ownership, displaying the second most dynamic domain of local tourism entrepreneurship. The integration of tourism in the economy of the region occurs, for example, through fishing boats being used for touristic tours during summer months. Other than these activities there have been only a few commercial attractions and activities – a situation that again reflects the nature of the tourism '4S' product.

Contemporary conditions: structuring tourism entrepreneurship in the post-war environment

The last decade has produced some dramatic changes to tourism demand and the structure and ownership of the industry. Following the disintegration of Yugoslavia, Croatia emerged as a newly independent state. The impact of the war from 1991 to 1995 and the continuing Bosnian and Kosovo crises significantly reduced international tourist demand. Gosar (2000) suggests that, at some point between 1991 and 1995, tourism collapsed completely. Whilst the tourism trade suffered badly during the civil war, tourism has experienced a significant rejuvenation in the past few years. In 1996 foreign visitor nights increased by 94 percent in comparison to 1995 (Gosar 2000).

In this process of rejuvenation, the structure of international tourism markets has also significantly shifted. Contemporary markets are less dependent on Western Europe and are more responsive to the growing

Table 1 Overnight stays of international tourist markets to Croatia (1990–2000)

Country	1990 (%)	2000 (%)
Czech Republic	–	13.3
Slovakia	–	3.4
Poland	–	3.2
Slovenia (former domestic market)	–	19.8
Germany	36.0	21.1
Austria	8.7	11.1
Italy	15.8	12.1
Hungary	1.5	3.8
Holland	7.2	2.8
France	2.2	0.4
UK	13.3	1.3

Source: Ministry of Tourism (1997) and Institute for Tourism (2000).

consumer awareness of Eastern Europe. The current demand of the former Eastern Bloc countries reflects characteristics typically associated with the early stages of the Western consumption of the '4S' product in the 1960s and 1970s (Smeral 1993). Table 1 shows the emergence of visitors from Eastern Europe in the late 1990s paralleled by a fairly dramatic decline of Western markets (with the exception of Austria).

The changing structure of the tourism industry is reflective of a wider structural shift associated with the overall process of economic transition. In the accommodation sector many former state-run hotels have now come under a variety of ownership structures, including cooperative ventures whereby employees have become collective owners and/or shareholders. This structure has facilitated the privatization of a number of larger businesses as individuals sell their interests. By early 1997, 71 companies out of 227 became completely transformed and privatized. In economic terms, this represents 443 million DEM (German Deutsche Mark) or 8.3 percent of the total estimated tourism portfolio of 5.2 billion DEM being transferred to private ownership (Ministry of Tourism 1997).

The economic transition can also be seen to reflect prevailing cultural changes and socio-political structures. Notably, Horvat (1999) identifies the Croatian entrepreneurial culture as suffering from post-war stress, yet grounded in traditional values and orientations. She suggests that these provide stability yet also to some extent provide initiative and motivation for entrepreneurs at the micro-level. Whilst Horvat (1999) frames the analysis in terms of a psychological map of attitudes to work and lifestyle, the diversity of the cultural environment in the region cautions these authors against broad generalizations about cultural characteristics, and underlines the value of place-specific case studies grounded in ethnographic detail.

The general re-emergence of tourism in the post-war period has been facilitated by a central government initiative aimed at transforming the concept of Croatia as a cheap, mass destination through the development of a layer of 'value-added' attractions and infrastructure. This layer is based on the 'stimulation and acceleration of privatization process with general emphasis on the development of entrepreneurship, particularly in the area of the so-called economy of small scale' (Ministry of Tourism 1997: 14). Reflecting this initiative, the Ministry of Tourism published 'Guidelines for Entrepreneurs in Tourism' in 1999, in conjunction with the state budget to secure funding for promoting tourism amongst small- and medium-sized enterprises (Ministarstvo Turizma RH 1999). Changes to the structural environment of tourism have been aligned with broader policy initiatives facilitating the economic transition within the European Union's Agenda 2000 supporting small- to medium-sized enterprises in 'candidate countries' (Middleton 1998). As such, tourism entrepreneurs at the micro-level have a strategic role in the macro-integration of Croatia as a developed Western allied nation.

The case study of the 'Mjesto' (village) of Murter

The village of Murter (Figure 2) is located in the historically recognized region of Dalmatia, on the island of Murter which is connected by a bridge over the 'Tisno' straits between the town of Sibenik (30 km away) and Zadar (50 km away). There are another three villages on the island (Tisno, Betina and Jezera), notable for the presence of olive-oil producers, fishermen, farmers and shipbuilders. The village of Murter is the main visitor area of the island and has a residential population averaging around 2,000, which would in pre-war times normally receive a visitor population averaging around 10,000 and concentrated over the peak summer period of two months. With property rights over the National Park of Kornati Islands, the village serves as main point of departure for this attraction of more than 180 uninhabited islands, islets and reefs scattered over some 300 km². The area is the largest uninhabited – or only seasonally inhabited – land mass in the Adriatic (69 km²).

Reached in a few hours by powerboat, the Kornati islands traditionally served as a focal point for agricultural and fishing activities in the village of Murter. With no power and limited water resources (rain water in wells), a small number of simple stone huts (around 300) were built around isolated bays of the islets to provide shelter for seafarers, shepherds and fishermen. In the last few decades, however, since tourism became a significant element in the regional economy and the greater part of the area has become a National Park, these huts were upgraded into tourist bungalows and today are generally promoted as an island romance for 'Robinson Crusoe' holidays. In the course of this rapidly growing tourism, the area has also become

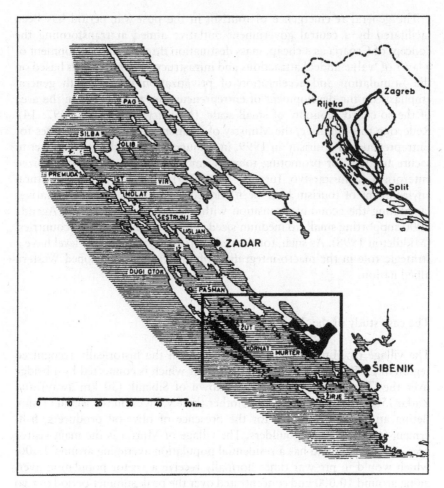

Figure 2 The study area (source: Erak 2000).

a very popular destination for maritime tourists who are attracted by safe sailing around numerous islands and bays.

Consequently, in the 1980s two main marinas with the capacity for approximately 120 boats (with shops, restaurant and boat servicing) were built in the area by the public/state-owned company the Adriatic Yacht Club of Yugoslavia (since renamed, Adriatic Croatia International Club), also involved in the development of another 20 marinas along the Adriatic coast since its foundation in 1983. Local entrepreneurs from the village of Murter followed this development and turned some of their huts into small-scale restaurants, catering for visitors who sail around on their boats. Given that the area is easy accessible to and from the Italian coast, this form of tourism continued even during the Croatian war.

Within the village itself the tourist trade is mainly organized around 'typical' Mediterranean tourist activities, such as staying in tourist bungalows or private houses, lying on beaches, interacting with locals, taking one-day excursions to Kornati Islands and going out to local bars/restaurants/cafés at night. Generally, local businesses are concentrated in the accommodation sector, with one private (former publicly owned) hotel of 200 units; private houses/tourist apartments with a capacity for around 2,000 visitors; two campsites of another 1,000 units, and a marina that can accommodate around 600 boats (fieldwork 2000).

Many accommodation providers are not formally registered and still exist as 'informal, black-market' operations, which originate from the 'pioneering' stage of tourism development, where local industry has reflected developments at the national level discussed earlier. In its early years, during the late 1960s, the accommodation sector developed from a stock of locally owned houses for the provision of commercial accommodation. More intensive developments, including building tourist flats and bungalows, flourished in the 'golden times' of the late 1970s and 1980s. Most importantly, these development were exclusively local initiatives, as the 'black-market' practice of avoiding taxes enabled the people of the village to earn sufficient profit not only for living costs but also for capital accumulation, the proceeds of which were subsequently invested into the building of new apartments and/or the further upgrading of existing private houses.

This 'black-market' practice was paradoxically underpinned by the socialist system of public ownership, which ensured the absence of individual accountability, provided political protectionism and privileges, and consequently eroded any sense of public good. In this context, many local tourism businesses flourished in the absence of strict tax control, enabling locals to generate capital over a short period of time. The extent to which tourism sustained the local economy of Murter is illustrated in the fact that many families in the village generated sufficient tourism income over the two months of peak summer business to sustain themselves for the rest of the year (additionally supported by fishing and their own subsistence agriculture). Furthermore, the savings accumulated over two decades of the tourism 'golden age' were so significant that they helped people to 'survive' the war years and the complete cessation of the tourist trade in the mid-1990s. In the last years of tourism rejuvenation, locals expressed a desire to return to 'business as usual'.

The characteristics and structure of tourism in the area is very much a microcosm of the Croatian coastal tourism outlined above with respect to visitor markets and business scale and is representative of the infrastructurally, spatially and economically peripheral region of Dalmatia within which it is located. Given the high dependence on tourism the economic effects of the war were the most heavily felt in this region, yet in the period of tourism rejuvenation the process of tourism entrepreneurship is highly dynamic. Entrepreneurship has continued to be dominant in the accommodation sector as the number of units in 2000 almost reached the 1990 pre-war figure. Table 2 shows a comparison over the respective years of the overall regional accommodation capacity (today politically identified as a territorial unit of Sibenik-Knin county), reaching 5.5 percent of the country's tourism accommodation capacity.

The importance of small operators is clearly illustrated by the fact that 40.4 percent of visitor nights in the region in 2000 took place in homestays of private accommodation providers (Erak 2000). Figure 3 shows the scale of 'private accommodation providers' where more than 50 percent can accommodate less than six visitors.

Table 2 Accommodation capacity in the region of Sibenik and Knin county

Form of accommodation	1990 (units)	2000 (units)
Hotels	7,450	5,130
Private apartment units	520	820
Campsites	16,000	11,700
'Private accommodation' providers	20,000	19,679
Odmaralista*	4,080	1,330
Total	48,050	39,803

*The former socialist concept of working class holiday hostels.
Source: Erak (2000).

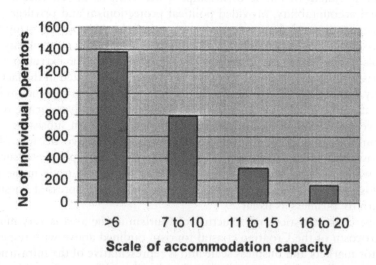

Figure 3 Small-scale accommodation providers in the Sibenik and Knin county (source: Erak 2000).

The following discussion seeks to illustrate the elements of the cultural context behind dynamics of rejuvenating tourism entrepreneurship and small business development.

Unravelling the cultural context of tourism entrepreneurship: localism, values and traditions

The results of quantitative data relating to the personal characteristics of respondents revealed entrenched and stable patterns of involvement in tourism activities. For example, 93 percent of those interviewed could be classified as locals, that is, born, bred and currently living in the village. Only 7 percent of respondents were from outside the village, most of these from the capital city of Zagreb and/or migrant workers from Western Europe. A common characteristic of this ownership pattern stems from a period in which urban dwellers purchased holiday accommodation in the village that has now been upgraded to return tourist income. Nevertheless, the overwhelming characteristic of entrepreneurs is a long-term association with the place. The traditional role of tourism in the economy and long life of small businesses is also reflected in the fact that for 90 percent of respondents their business had been their first business venture. This is clearly illustrated in Table 3 which shows significantly long periods of operation for the majority of respondent's businesses.

The dominance of local ownership in the tourism economy and the obvious consistency of the ownership structure is very much a reflection of the cultural context in which tourism is enmeshed. Interviewees expressed largely conservative values towards the village and the Dalmatian region, in general, to the extent that an obvious emotional attachment underlay their personal and business commitment. This commitment was articulated as a nostalgic affection for the physical characteristics of the area, together with its climate and pace of life. This 'traditional' lifestyle of Dalmatia is very much expressed as a relaxed, carefree approach to social relations and business activities. These integrated economic and social rituals overtly revolve around drinking coffee and enjoying conversation in public areas

Table 3 Operation period ($n = 62$)

Period (years)	Percentage
Less than 4	14
5–9	11
10–15	19
16–20	34
21–25	13
More than 26	9

and cafés. One respondent typically identified the significance of these cultural practices as follows: 'Our place is all about us Dalmatians and our culture of going easy about life, cruising around with our friends, helping each other, having coffee and drinks in our local café for hours, having siesta after lunch . . .'

These activities reflect not only the desire to engage in the active reaffirmation of the local, but also a rejection of what are perceived to be more stressful, high-paced lifestyles in other parts of the country, as one of respondents stated: 'This is *my* place, where I was born, where my family has lived for generations . . . and tourism has been ideal to maintain this lifestyle and make a living at the same time'.

Whilst these lived practices of cultural identity reflect common tourist perceptions of Dalmatian culture the ability of 'outside entrepreneurs' to integrate themselves with local culture is, however, confined to summer. Most of the social activities in the off-peak period draw heavily on the vernacular associations of the indigenous people. Comparatively cold winter months repress the public life on the street during this time and long-standing intergenerational social networks become the basis for the articulation of personal and economic life. These markers of local belonging serve to differentiate and distance outsiders and subsequently reinforce the social dynamics of the local tourism economy. These values are particularly strongly expressed on issues of land ownership and development where locals are frequently reluctant to sell to 'outsiders' for fear that land would be inappropriately developed, that is, reflecting cultural values inconsistent with those expressed locally, as one respondent stated:

> In 1960s we lost a lot of good land by selling sections to tourists from the city and now they turn their holiday homes into tourist apartments and make more money than most of us . . . now that whole area is overbuilt and crowded with all sorts of building styles, there is not space for parking and it doesn't feel like a local place any more . . . we just don't want to sell land to them any more.

This polarization of 'us' and 'them' is commonly expressed across generations. Intergenerational family ties significantly structure relationships and economic ties in the village. Some 75 percent of respondents were solo trade operations and 23 percent partnerships, commonly between individuals and, by extension, their families. It should be noted these figures reflect the lineage of the intergenerational family business rather than current management, as one respondent expressed:

> I always worked in this business and I grew up with this activity and a lifestyle . . . since I've been married, there was no other option to support my family, and as my parents are getting older it's me and my wife who are looking after them and taking care of the business.

The nature of family businesses normally includes the wide involvement of family members but rarely is this manifest as formal, taxable employment. Given the widespread use of family members, nearly 76 percent of businesses did not employ people from outside of the family. Formal employment in tourism normally occurs in the restaurant/café, tours and travel agency sectors. Accommodation, however, represents by far the most widespread touristic activity and is representative of the regional and national structure of the industry. Table 4 illustrates the dominance of the accommodation sector, gain illustrative of the '4S' markets discussed earlier.

The intergenerational nature of businesses is also reflected in the financial structure of entrepreneurship. Of those businesses studied, 80 percent were financed from within the family and 17 percent were financed from private loans from friends and relatives. None were financed by bank loans or business development loans (see Table 5).

It is common for family assets and property to be passed down through the male line of families, producing extended family homes in which several generations live under one roof. The home is also the basis for the family's economy being used as tourist accommodation during the peak summer period. All family members are often involved in the business; their roles are often informal, with the main business responsibility falling on the younger to middle-aged family members. Whilst the senior members of the family

Table 4 Structure of tourism industry ($n = 62$)

Tourism sector	Percentage
Accommodation	80
Travel agency	2
Restaurant	3
Café	6
Local tours	2
Transport	None
Retail/souvenir shop	3
Other	4

Table 5 Major sources of financial support ($n = 62$)

Sources	Percentage
Family heritage	80
Private loan	17
Bank loan	None
Local business development board	None
Other	3

hand over the financial responsibility to younger, more able-bodied family members, their role within the household remains significant in terms of providing mentoring for business activities and playing a socially active role with guests, as one of respondents expressed:

> Even though my son now takes care of most of the business it is still my duty as his mother to help him . . . so I am the one who very often greets the guests, makes beds, cooks dinner . . . young couples these days need to go out, I can help looking after the children.

These strong family ties stem from the traditional practice of financially supporting children and assuming a nurturing responsibility for them throughout one's life. The relationships also reflect a deep-seated suspicion and mistrust of socialist state institutions and banks, to the extent that the extended family remains a financial, emotional and socially discrete unit.

Given the patriarchal nature of society there are strong gender divisions within the businesses as regards the financial control and day-to-day management of the business. Tourism businesses are predominantly small in scale, where 90 percent of respondents were both owners and managers. However, it should be noted that strong gender divisions characterize issues of ownership and control where owners and managers are considered a couple under the male line. Table 6 shows the age structure of business owners and managers, illustrating the predominance of ownership in younger and middle-aged groups, nearly 90 percent of whom were couples with children at home.

It should be noted with respect to the above discussion that women's empowerment in tourism development in the Balkans is very much characterized by a 'double burden' (see also Hall 1998), in which their involvement in tourism is regarded as a 'natural' extension of their domestic role, whilst their husbands maintain financial control. Activities such as making beds and cooking for guests is traditionally regarded as a woman's domain, whereas the male role involves the broader orientation of the business based around male social networks, and any technical and maintenance requirements. Despite the appearance of more gender equity in public and social life, gender divisions characterized by a strong machismo culture remain

Table 6 Age groups of respondents ($n = 62$)

Age groups	Percentage
19–24	4
25–34	27
35–44	26
45–54	31
55–64	8
65+	3

characteristic of social interactions. As one of the women noted: 'My husband would never dream of making a bed or pushing a pram . . . this is typically considered as women's work . . .' Issues of women's empowerment are exemplified either in the context of financial control or social norms and expectations. Although women assume most of the responsibility for the day-to-day activities of the business and the household, their economic and social independence is still controlled by their husbands. As one of the respondents stated:

> I am the one who manages and works in our shop, looks after the children and takes care of my mother in law . . . we always have enough to pay for business and household costs, but not for myself to travel abroad as my husband does fairly often. He goes away on his own and it's never even considered that I can do that as well.

These gendered roles have been traditionally entrenched in Dalmatian culture, where women are traditionally perceived as hard working, providing the backbone of the business whether in a rural environment or in a touristic setting such as Murter. As well as this domestic role women are also involved in promoting their businesses to agents, as mediators, arranging bookings and other day-to-day networking. Men are rarely involved in directly promoting their businesses to tourists, instead choosing to use intermediaries (wives or children who receive commission). In the intensely patriarchal culture of Murter, dealing directly with tourists is often regarded as beneath male dignity.

As noted earlier, the networks of patriarchal society very much underpin the economic structure of the tourism industry. The patriarchy of business ownership is also expressed in a general cynicism towards state structures and bureaucracy. This is not only apparent in local attitudes but also materializes in the economic culture of the black market. Here, social values and economic resourcefulness are inseparable from one another and form the heart of a cultural, political and economic life. The legacy of being a socialist state for 45 years and frequent shifting political boundaries has undermined local trust in the public sector, particularly with respect to benefits received from collective taxation and public good. As a result, the informal nature of businesses operating within the black market has been based on the more direct relationships and benefits of personal economies and social networks. Although businesses, whether formal or informal, choose to distance themselves from formal taxation by disguising income, a more transparent form of taxation flourishes within the broader practice of 'mito' (baksheesh). This form of exchange has been normally in the form of gift-giving in return for favours or preferential treatment for not only services but all facets of social, political and economic interaction.

As well as local and personal politics the structure of the industry and economy is very much enmeshed in the wider dynamics of party politics.

During the socialist era, membership of the Communist Party would secure power for individuals and, similarly, the significance of the Nationalist Party during the 1990s prevailed. Currently, the re-emergence of the left wing within party politics continues to perpetuate the structural environment of economy. It should be noted that despite the oscillations of politics the relationships and often the role of individuals within political structures have remained relatively consistent. Although party politics rarely affects businesses at the local level, the relationships through which they operate are far more significant on its day-to-day operations. The social skills and resourcefulness required for economic survival in this environment is a key characteristic of the cultural context of entrepreneurship, and is not only apparent in political dealings but prevails in most managerial and operational activities. In this context, more rigorous government regulation, privatization and the shift towards 'Western' systems of free trade and taxation are widely perceived as a potential threat, the economic 'Other'.

Conclusions

The description and interpretation of tourism and its entrepreneurial characteristics given above reveals a complex web of structural and social–agency elements, which condition and shape the nature of the industry. The paper illustrates the role of culture in Murter as the principal regulator of the economic, yet simultaneously reveals elements and practises in which the cultural manifest as materialization of the economic (see Crang & Malbon 1996). The cultural context described here through the use of insider perspectives reveals a rationality through which social structures, politics and economy are maintained and advanced despite the last decade of political instability, upheaval and war. The social and cultural identity has persevered through the deliberate practice of perpetuating its traditional form, and has enhanced the social stability of the village. A solely economic interpretation of entrepreneurship in tourism in this region is clearly insufficient to fully appreciate the cultural complexities surrounding the place as an economy in transition.

The cultural regulation of the economic has been identified through a number of elements. For example, the intergenerational nature of tourism businesses requires that the conceptualization of entrepreneurship move beyond its traditional focus on new business development, but also incorporate strategic considerations, which seek to express values of continuity, stability and entrenchment. The primary entrepreneurial characteristics can be conceptualized in terms of resourcefulness, adaptability and cultural integrity in the face of turmoil and perpetual change.

The discussion further illustrates the way in which the entrepreneurs of Murter construct and articulate their preferred lifestyle and nostalgic associations of place. Extended family structures have been revealed as the primary units around which businesses are financed and employment roles based. One of the most persistent characteristics of the cultural environment remains gender division in terms of work roles and machismo, which simultaneously provide references against which patriarchal and social relations are reaffirmed within a culture. It is these cultural attributes closely associated with place, landscape and its people, which simultaneously form the principal elements of the tourism product. Despite decades of change with respect to national and regional affiliations at the political level, the persistence of tourism and its representation has provided a continuity of local and regional identity.

These values play a critical role in the emergence, persistence and stability of tourism as a key economic sector. Indeed, given that these values are not exclusive to the tourism sector it can be suggested that they are also instrumental in shaping the broader small enterprise culture of the place. The culture of the black market, for example, illustrates the way the structural conditions of the wider political economy are enmeshed within it, particularly with respect to the perception of social, political and economic fortune. This 'informality' of social networks, whilst an expression of cynicism of state bureaucratic structures, provide stability at the business level which promises more continuity and security than the inevitable 'efficiencies' accompanying the process of transition to the market economy. This activity can be seen as direct cultural materialization of 'the economic'.

In a broader sense, the arguments presented above contribute to the further transgression of boundaries within the geographical study of tourism. In doing so, the discussion further unravels the structure–agency dialectic within a place-specific reference. Our articulation of the local is necessarily founded on a reflexive understanding of insider perspectives. In doing so the text also reveals its epistemological representation through which the authors' perspectives and subjectivities serve to position the paper. Together with these voices and observations, more traditional methods of inquiry have served to triangulate and authenticate the 'data' in empirical terms. The integration of these more 'traditional' elements of the study of entrepreneurship, together with their cultural context, also serves to inform our appreciation of tourism processes generally and to provide an objective quality to what are inherently and necessarily subjective research processes. Our emphasis on the local naturally presents difficulties for extrapolation to a broader national or regional context, a problem reminiscent of the difficulties of asserting particular cultural values across broader human geographies. Instead, it is important to reiterate the contribution local cultural perspectives, and application of new theoretical gazes, lend to the analysis of economic relations and the complex, contradictory and diverse dynamics of tourism entrepreneurship.

Acknowledgements

The authors gratefully acknowledge the Faculty of Commerce at the Victoria University of Wellington for supporting this research. A special thanks goes to Sanda Weber at the Institute of Tourism, Zagreb and Neda Livljanic at the Tourism Office in Sibenik for providing necessary secondary sources of data.

References

Adorno, T. W. 1957. Sociology and empirical research. In *Critical Sociology*, ed. P. Connerton, pp. 78–95. Harmonsdworth: Penguin.

Airey, D. 1994. Education for tourism in Poland: The PHARE programme. *Tourism Management* 15(4): 467–71.

Amin, A. and Thrift, N. 2000. What kind of economic theory for what kind of economic geography? *Antipode* 32(1): 4–9.

Archer, B. H. 1995 Importance of tourism for the economy of Bermuda. *Annals of Tourism Research* 22(4): 918–30.

Ateljevic, I. 2000. Circuits of tourism: stepping beyond a production–consumption dichotomy. *Tourism Geographies* 2(4): 369–88.

Ateljevic, I. and Doorne, S. 2000. 'Staying within the fence' Lifestyle entrepreneurship. *Journal of Sustainable Tourism* 8(5): 378–92.

Bacharov, M. 1997. End of the model? Tourism in post-communist Bulgaria. *Tourism Management* 18(1): 43–50.

Balaz, V. 1995. Five years of economic transition in Slovak Tourism: Successes and shortcomings. *Tourism Management* 16(2): 143–59.

Berstein, G. 1973. *Underdevelopment and Development: The Third World Today*. Harmondsworth: Penguin.

Blanchard, O., Dornbusch, R., Krugman, P., Layard, R. and Summers, L. 1991. *Reform in Eastern Europe*. Cambridge, Mass: MIT Press.

Burgess, R. G. 1982. Multiple strategies in field research. In *Field Research*, ed. R. G. Burgess, pp. 38–49. London: George Allen and Unwin.

Campbell, D. T. and Fiske, D. W. 1959. Convergent and discriminant validation by the multitrait-multimethod matrix. *Psychological Bulletin* 60: 81–105.

Chambers, R. 1993. *Challenging the Professions: Frontiers for Rural Development*. Exeter: Intermediate Technology Publications.

Chambers, R. 1997. *Whose Reality Counts: Putting the First Last*. London: Intermediate Technology Publications.

Chell, E., Haworth, J. and Brearly, S. 1991. *The Entrepreneurial Personality*. London: Routledge.

Cole, A. H. 1942. Entrepreneurship as an area of research. *The Tasks of Economic History: Supplement to Journal of Economic History* 2: 118–26.

Cole, A. H. 1954. An appraisal of economic change: Twentieth-century entrepreneurship in the United States and economic growth. *American Economic Review* 40: 35–50.

Cowen, M. and Shenton, R. 1996. *Doctrines of Development*. London: Routledge.

Crang, P. and Malbon, B. 1996. Consuming geographies: a review essay. *Transactions of the Institute of British Geographers* 21(4): 704–11.

Cunningham, J. B. and Lischeron, J. 1991. Defining entrepreneurship. *Journal of Small Business Management* 29(1): 45–61.

Dahles, H. (ed.). 1997. *Tourism, Small Entrepreneurs and Sustainable Development: Cases from Developing Countries.* Tilburg University: ATLAS.

Dahles, H and Bras, K. (eds) 1999. *Tourism and Small Entrepreneurs: Development, National policy and Entrepreneurial Culture: Indonesian Cases.* London: Cognizant Communications.

Deakings, D., Jennings, P. and Mason, C. (eds) 1997. *Small Firms: Entrepreneurship in the Nineties.* London: Paul Chapman Publishing.

Denzin, N. K. 1989. *The Research Act: A Theoretical Introduction to Sociological Methods* (third edition). New Jersey: Prentice Hall.

Denzin, N. 1997. *Interpretative Ethnography: Ethnographic Practises for the 21st Century.* Thousand Oaks: Sage.

Dewhurst, P. and Horobin, H. 1998. Small business owners. In *The Management of Small Tourism and Hospitality Firms,* ed. R. Thomas, pp. 19–38. London: Cassell.

Din, K. M. 1992. The 'involvement' stage in the evolution of a tourist destination. *Tourism Recreational Research* 17: 10–20.

Douglas, J. D. 1976. *Investigation in Social Research: Individual and Team Field Research.* Beverly Hills: Sage.

Drucker, P. 1985. *Innovation and Entrepreneurship.* New York: Harper and Row.

du Gay, P. 1996. *Consumption and Identity at Work.* London: Sage.

East, R. 1992. *Revolutions in Eastern Europe.* London: Pinter.

Echtner, C. M. 1995. Entrepreneurial training in developing countries. *Annals of Tourism Research* 22(2): 119–34.

Erak, B. 2000. *Stanje i Problemi Turisticke Ponude Sibensko-Kninske Zupanije* (State and Problems of Tourism Supply in the Region of Sibenik–Knin County). Sibenik: Ured Za Turizam Sibensko-Kninska Zupanija, Republika Hrvatska.

Evans, M. 1988. Participant observation: The researcher as research tool. In *Qualitative Methods in Human Geography,* ed. J. Eyles and D. Smith, pp. 197–218. Cambridge: Polity Press.

Eyles, J. 1988. Interpreting the geographical world. In *Qualitative Methods in Human Geography,* ed. J. Eyles, and D. M. Smith, pp. 1–16. Cambridge: Polity Press.

Gartner, W. 1999. Small scale enterprises in the tourism industry in Ghana's central region. In *Contemporary Issues in Tourism Development,* ed. D. G. Pearce and R. W. Butler, pp. 158–75. London: Routledge.

Geertz, C. 1973. *The Interpretation of Cultures: Selected Essays.* New York: Basic Books.

Gosar, A. 1999. Reconsidering tourism strategy as a consequence of the disintegration of Yugoslavia – The case of Slovenia. *Turizam, Special issue 'Tourism and Violence: Crisis and Recovery'* 47(1): 67–73.

Gosar, A. 2000. The recovering of tourism in the Balkans. *Tourism Recreation Research* 25(2): 23–34.

Hall, D. R. 1995. Tourism change in Central and Eastern Europe. *In European Tourism: Regions, Spaces and Restructuring,* ed. A. Montanari and A. M. Williams, pp. 221–44. Chichester: Wiley.

Hall, D. R. 1998. Tourism development and sustainability issues in Central and South-Eastern Europe. *Tourism Management* 19(4): 423–31.

Hall, D. and Danta, D. (eds)1996. *Reconstructing Balkans.* Chichester: Wiley.

Harding, S. and Hintikka, M. (eds) 1983. *Discovering Reality: Feminist Perspectives on Epistemology, Metaphysics, Methodology and Philosophy of Science.* Dordrecht: Reidel.

Harrison, D. 1993. Bulgarian tourism: A sate of uncertainty. *Annals of Tourism Research* 20(4): 519–34.

Hawley, F. B. 1907. *Enterprise and the Productive Process*. New York: G. P. Putnam's Sons.

Hettne, B. 1990. *Development Theory and the Three Worlds*. Harlow: Longman Development Studies.

Hitchcock, M. 1999. Tourism and ethnicity: Situational perspectives. *International Journal of Tourism Research* 1(1): 17–32.

Hitchcock, M. 2000. Ethnicity and tourism entrepreneurship in Java and Bali. *Current Issues in Tourism* 3(3): 204–25.

Hitrec, T. 2000. Small and medium-sized enterprises in the hospitality industry: Some European trends and Croatian experiences. *Tourism* 48(1): 5–12.

Horvat, B. 1999. The role of culture during the period of recovery and the development of tourism. *Turizam, Special issue 'Tourism and Violence: Crisis and Recovery'* 47(1): 55–60.

Iaonnides, D. and Debbage, K. G. (eds) 1998. *The Economic Geography of the Tourism Industry: A Supply-Side Analysis*. London: Routledge.

Institute for Tourism, 2000. *Osnovna Obiljezja Turisticke Potraznje u Hrvatskoj za 1998–2000* (Visitor Characteristics of Croatia for years 1998–2000). Zagreb: Institute for Tourism.

Jeffries, I. 1993. *Socialist Economies and the Transition to the Market*. London: Routledge.

Jaakson, R. 1996. Tourism in transition in Post-Soviet Estonia. *Annals of Tourism Research* 23(3): 617–34.

Johnson, M. 1995. Czech and Slovak Tourism. *Tourism Management* 16(1): 21–8.

Johnson, M. 1997. Hungary's hotel industry in transition, 1960–1996. *Tourism Management* 18(4): 441–52.

Legge, J. and Hindle, K. 1997. *Entrepreneurship: How Innovators Create the Future*. Melbourne: Macmillan Education Australia.

Malinowski, B. 1922. *Argonauts of the Western Pacific*. London: Routledge & Kegan Paul.

Marcus, G. and Fisher, M. (eds) 1986. *Anthropology and Cultural Critique: The Experimental Moment in the Human Sciences*. Chicago: University of Chicago Press.

McMullan, W. and Long, W. A. 1990. *Developing New Ventures: The Entrepreneurial Option*. San Diego: Harcourt Brace Jovanovich.

Michaud, J. 1991. A Social Anthropology of tourism in Ladakh, India. *Annals of Tourism Research* 18(4): 605–21.

Middleton, V. 1998. Agenda 2010: SMEs in European tourism: The context and a proposed framework for European action. *Revue de Tourisme* 53(4): 29–37.

Milne, S. and Ateljevic, I. 2001. Tourism, economic development and the global–local nexus: Theory embracing complexity. *Tourism Geographies* 3(4): 369–93.

Ministry of Tourism, 1997. *Tourism: Guide for Investors and Business Partners*. Zagreb: Ministry of Tourism, Republic of Croatia.

Ministarstvo Turizma RH, 1999. *Vodic za Poduzetnike u Turizmu* (Guideline for Entrepreneurs in Tourism). Zagreb: Ministarstvo Turizma RH.

Morrison, A., Rimmington, M. and Williams, C. 1999. *Entrepreneurship in the Hospitality, Tourism and Leisure Industries*. Oxford: Butterworth & Heinemann.

Pearce, D. 1991. Challenge and change in East European tourism: A Yugoslav example. In *The Tourism Industry: An International Analysis*, ed. M. T. Sinclair and M. J. Stabler, pp. 223–40. Wallingford: CAB International.

Pile, S. 1991. Practising interpretative geography. *Transactions of the Institute of British Geographers* 16: 458–69.

Porter, M. 1980. *Competitive Strategies*. New York: Free Press.

Pritchard, A. and Morgan, N. 2000. Privileging the male gaze: Gendered tourism landscapes. *Annals of Tourism Research* **27**(4): 884–905.

Ringer, G. (ed). 1998. *Destinations: Cultural Landscapes of Tourism*. London: Routledge.

Rist, G. and Camiller, P. 1997. *The History of Development: From Western Origins to Global Faith*. London: Zed Books.

Said, E. 1988. *Orientalism*. Harmondsworth: Peregrine.

Sayer, A. 2000. Critical and uncritical cultural turns. In *Cultural Turns/Geographical Turns*, ed. I. Cook, D. Crouch, S. Naylor and J. R. Ryan, pp. 166–82. Harlow: Prentice Hall.

Scase, R. and Goffee, R. 1982. *The Entrepreneurial Middle Class*. London: Croom Helm.

Shatzman, L. and Strauss, A. L. 1973. *Field Research: Strategies for a Natural Sociology*. Englewood Cliffs: Prentice Hall.

Shaw, G. and Williams, A. M. 1987. Firm formation and operating characteristics in the Cornish tourism industry – the Case of Looe. *Tourism Management* **8**(3): 344–8.

Shaw, G. and Williams, A. M. 1990. Tourism, economic development and the role of entrepreneurial activity. In *Progress in Tourism, Recreation and Hospitality Management* (Volume 2), ed. C. Cooper, pp. 67–81. London: Bellhaven.

Shaw, G. and Williams, A. M. 1998. Entrepreneurship, small business culture and tourism development. In *Economic Geography of Tourism*, ed. K. Debbage and D. Ioannides, pp. 235–55. London: Routledge.

Schumpeter, J. A. 1934. *The Theory of Economic Development*. Cambridge: Harvard University Press.

Schumpeter, J. A. 1965. Economic theory and entrepreneurial history. In *Explorations in Enterprise*. ed. H. G. J. Aitken, pp. 45–64. Cambridge: Harvard University Press.

Smeral, E. 1993. Emerging Eastern European markets. *Tourism Management* **14**(4): 411–18.

Smith, S. 1988. Constructing local knowledge: The analysis of self in everyday life. In *Qualitative Methods in Human Geography*, ed. J. Eyles and D. Smith, pp. 17–38. Cambridge: Polity Press.

Squire, S. J. 1994a. Accounting for cultural meanings: the interface between geography and tourism studies re-examined. *Progress in Human Geography* **18**(1): 1–16.

Squire, S. J. 1994b. The cultural values of literary tourism. *Annals of Tourism Research* **21**(1): 103–21.

Stacey, M. 1969. *Methods of Social Research*. Oxford: Pergamon.

Storey, D. J. 1994. *Understanding the Small Business Sector*. London: Routledge.

Thompson, G., O'Hare, G. and Evans, K. 1995. Tourism in the Gambia: Problems and proposals. *Tourism Management* **16**(4): 571–81.

Thrift, N. 2000. Pandora's box? Cultural geographies of economies. In *The Oxford Handbook of Economic Geography*, ed. G. L. Clark, M. P. Feldman and M. S. Gertler, pp. 689–704. Oxford: Oxford University Press.

Todaro, M. 1997. *Economic Development* (sixth edition). Longman: Harlow.

Unwin, T. 1996. Tourism development in Estonia: Images, sustainability, and integrated rural development. *Tourism Management* **17**(2): 265–76.

Webb, E. J., Campbell, D. T., Schwartz, R. D. and Sechrest, L. 1966: *Unobtrusive Measures: Nonreactive Research in the Social Science*. Chicago: Rand McNally.

Williams, A. M., Shaw, G. and Greenwood, J. 1989. From tourist to tourism entrepreneur, from consumption to production: Evidence from Cornwall, England. *Environment and Planning A* **21**: 1639–53.

Submitted: month year; Revised: month year

Ecotourism in post-communist Poland: an examination of tourists, sustainability and institutions

Agnes M. K. Nowaczek

and

David A. Fennell

Abstract

In the present study, a sample of Polish ecotourists is compared to a sample of mainstream or conventional Polish tourists, with the purpose of examining differences between these groups on the basis of attractions and benefits sought. It replicates a study conducted by D. A. Fennell and B. J. A. Smale in 1992 on Canadian ecotourists. Contrary to this latter study, the present study found that both Polish groups were similar on many aspects relating to the importance of attractions and benefits, their demographic characteristics, and their trip expenditures. Implications for ecotourism development in Poland are discussed, along with the many constraints and opportunities confronting the region.

Introduction: tourism in Poland

Poland is located in Eastern Europe, bordered in the north by the Baltic Sea and Russia, in the east by Lithuania, Belarus and Ukraine, in the south by the Czech Republic and Slovakia and in the west by Germany. The country is 312,685 km- in size, with a population of 38.7 million (Turner 2000). The communist-dominated 'Democratic Bloc' was elected in 1947 and resigned in 1988 due to the 'Solidarity' movement led by Lech Walesa, after which free parliamentary elections were instituted in 1991. It is the expectation of the European Union that priorities listed in the revised Accession Partnership will be completed by Poland over the next two years (2002–2003) (European Union, 2001); however, the country is not likely to join before the year 2004 (European Union, 2002). The present Constitution was adopted in 1997.

Poland's economy is one of the fastest growing of the post-communist countries in Europe, with real GDP 17 percent higher in 1998 compared to 1989 (Turner 2000). Coal is a major facet of the Polish economy, with levels of production exceeding 110 million tones in 1997, and with projected reserves of some 120,000 million tones (Turner 2000). It also has the largest agriculture sector in central Europe in terms of labour, employing 27 percent of the working population, but contributing only 6 percent of the GDP (Turner 2000). As a result of decades of communist neglect and the application of 'dirty' technologies (e.g. coal), environmental protection in Poland is becoming a higher priority (Michałowski, et al. 1994). The consequences of significant industrial activity are many, including the mass dying of forests and the extreme level of pollution in the Baltic Sea, considered the most polluted in the world (Michałowski, et al. 1994). Environmental problems were not officially recognized until the early 1970s, and action has taken place only after the Solidarity movement began agitating in the early 1980s.

In 1997 Poland received about 87.8 million international tourists, 56 percent of which were from Germany. Many of these visitors have consistently shown an interest in ecotourism (Waśniewski 1998), a sector that has been introduced through companies like Eko-Tourist, which was developed in 1989 (Dąbrowski 2000). The interest in ecotourism has been especially important economically for local areas (the market estimated to be about 10 percent, as suggested by Dębski 1999), especially in rural areas where there is high population and low employment rates (Kamieniecka 1995; Kajszczak 1999; Wilkin 1999).

Ecotourism: supply and policy

The natural landscape of Poland consists of three relief groups: the lowlands, highlands and mountains. Physiographically, the country includes coastal plain, the lake region and central lowlands, the Małopolska uplands, the Sudeten and the Carpathians. There are also zones of forest-steppe vegetation and Eastern European subtaiga. The average elevation of the country is only 568 feet above sea level, and more than three-quarters of the land lies below 650 feet. Poland contains 2,250 species of seed plants, 630 mosses, 200 liverworts, 1,200 lichens and 1,500 fungi. The vertebrate fauna includes nearly 400 species, including more than 200 native birds (Wydawnictwo Naukowe PWN 2000).

There are 23 national parks in Poland totaling over 301,717 ha (Dębrowski, nd). Furthermore, there are a number of other protected area categories, including 1,183 nature reserves covering 128,001 ha (106 nature reserves on 4,687 ha of land with no human integration); 30,205 nature monuments; 106 landscape parks (totalling 2,136,268 ha); 7 Biosphere Reserves (LOP 1999–2000); 41 health and climatic resorts; and over 8,000 monumental gardens and parks surrounding castles, palaces and country houses (Pawlikowska-Piechotka 2000). In particular, the Group of Yura Landscape Parks (*Zespół Jurajskich Parków Krajobrazowych*) are rich in biodiversity, with 400 species of moss, over 1,200 mushroom species, 173 species of birds, 1,200 species of butterfy and 90 percent of Polish bats (Zwolińska 2000).

Ecotourism can be defined as

a form of tourism that fosters learning experiences and appreciation of the natural environment, or some component thereof, within its associated cultural context. It has the appearance, in the context of best practice, of being environmentally and socio-culturally sustainable, preferably in a way that enhances the natural and cultural base of the destination and promotes the viability of the operation (Weaver 2001: 346).

This global view of 'ecotourism' is not actively promoted by the travel agencies of Poland (Waśniewski 1998). Instead, agritourism and organized tours within parks and protected areas (which may be characterized as more of a conventional tourism experience) are more popular (Waśniewski 1998; Hall 2001). Rural areas in Poland comprise about 93 percent of the total area of the country, with a population of about 15 million (Wilkin 1998). Here, approximately 90 percent of tourism takes place. The Polish model of farming is based mainly on traditional development and differentiated farming – a unique remainder of European and world geological wealth – which may serve as an additional support mechanism or attraction for ecotourism development (Wilkin 1999).

Tatry National Park is an example of a park which has received an overwhelming degree of tourism pressure, generating about $US 120 million per year (Gąsienica-Byrcyn 1999). Significant interest has been shown in other areas, including the Biebrza river, one of the wildest in Poland, where 40,000 individuals kayaked in 1998, with twice that number predicted for 2001 (Korbel 2000). This has prompted members of the Popradzki Landscape Park in Beskid Sądecki, to commit to an ecotourism strategy based on the principles of 'deep ecology' (Styczyńska & Styczyński 1991). Their efforts resulted in the establishment of an educational trail and a number of attractive environmental trips and camps, supported and organized by experts. Thus, in light of the political, economic and environmental restructuring of Poland, the principles of ecotourism are starting to be considered as a means by which to address many of its economic and environmental woes (Kamieniecka 1995, 1998a, 1998b; Waśniewski 1998; Skupiewski 1999; Dębski 1999). Although ecotourism is a new term in the Polish literature, the tradition of environmental protection and contact with nature has deep roots in pre-communist Poland. For instance, organizations such as the Liga Ochrony Przyrody (LOP) [Environmental Protection League] which is the oldest pro-ecological organization in Poland established in 1928 (LOP 1998), the Polskie Towarzystwo Turystyczno Krajoznawcze (PTTK) [Polish Tourist Country-Lovers Association] established in 1950 through the merging of the Polish Tatra Mountains Society (established in 1872), and the Polish Landscape Society (established in 1907), have also been embedded in the country's commitment to environmental education and tourism (Dąbrowski nd).

Consistent with the budding interest in ecotourism is the Polish government's adoption of the spatial management policy of 1994, which incorporates principles of sustainable development as the basis of all planning efforts. Article 5 in the Constitution states that the 'Republic of Poland ... ensures protection of the environment, following the principle of sustainable development' [translation], a definition developed by the Institute for Sustainable Development (ISD), Warsaw (Kamieniecka & Wójcik 1999: 9). For tourism, laws for the protection of the environment are assessed, modernized, or replaced by new laws in concert with those of the European Union (Pudlis 1996; M. Wallstrom pers. comm. 2000, online at *http://www.ecp.wroc.pl/stanowisko_ngos_ang.html*). The implementation of these measures, however, is constrained by a number of factors, including: (i) lack of cooperation between different levels of government; (ii) non-existent planning and management plan; (iii) financial barriers; (iv) a low level of environmental awareness of Polish society and tourism operators; and (v) abuse of the term 'ecotourism' as a result of not understanding 'accepted' definitions of the term (Michałowski, *et al.* 1994; Waśniewski 1998; Kamieniecka 2000; Kopta 2000; Mateuszewska 2000; Pawlikowska-Piechotka 2000; Symonides 2000). As Poland endeavours to more fully develop its ecotourism potential, it must do so with an eye towards the education of the domestic market, as well as those working within the ecotourism sector. Consequently, it is important to understand the extent to which Polish nationals are sympathetic to a form of tourism based on nature and natural resources. While it appears as though there is a commitment from government to embark upon initiatives which are sustainably based, it remains to be seen how supportive government will be.

With this in mind, the present study is designed to replicate the work of Fennell and Smale (1992), through the application of the Canadian Tourism Attitude and Motivation Study (CTAMS) scale – a database of the general attitudes, motivations and benefits of travellers – to two groups of travellers in Poland: Polish ecotourists and mainstream Polish tourists. The purpose is thus to examine whether there are differences between these two groups in terms of their profile and the important attractions and benefits sought. The research will also examine how Polish ecotourists differ from Canadian 'hard core' ecotourists visiting Costa Rica, as profiled in the work of Fennell and Smale (1992). Hard core ecotourists are defined as a small portion of the overall ecotourist market which is strongly ecocentric, in search of meaningful interaction with the natural world, minimal services, with interests in conservation and sustainability (see Weaver 2001). Further to the central purpose of the paper, this study addresses two other areas which are deemed important for future research. The first is that Poland appears to be greatly under-represented in the tourism literature, at least from the English language perspective. This paper is an attempt to bridge the gap between scholarly work in Polish and the available research on the topic reported in English. Second, the paper addresses the need to focus on the development of tourism in a post-communist country and the various institutional constraints which are present from the legacy of this past regime. In doing so, it may help to develop a discourse on the potential for ecotourism development in Poland, as well as in many other countries in the region which have struggled through similar conditions, and who may yet benefit economically, socially and ecologically from appropriate tourism planning and management. Stated more succinctly, the paper examines who the Polish ecotourists are (as compared to mainstream Polish tourists), and the institutional context they find themselves in.

Methodology

Due to a limited understanding of the supply and demand aspects of ecotourism in Poland, it was appropriate to employ a judgmental sampling method based entirely on the professional judgement of the researcher in the identification of an ecotourism sample. In general, Polish ecotourists were identified on the basis of the type of experience sought in a Polish vacation (e.g. natural areas, environmental education, and so on), as well as their affiliation with various conservation organizations. The survey used in this study was designed after the one used by Fennell and Smale (1992), with only minor modifications to the income section and translation into the Polish language. The survey consisted of three sections. The first part covered questions related to the travel experience, the second included CTAMS questions on benefits and attractions, and the third contained questions on socio-demographics. A letter of information was presented when dealing with organized tour agencies and operators.

In total, 120 surveys were distributed among various groups of eco-tourists and tourists in the city of Częstochowa, Poland. Ninety-nine surveys were collected for a return rate of 82.5 percent. The self-administered survey was personally delivered to and collected from five groups of ecotourists ($n=64$) and two groups of mainstream tourists ($n=35$); numbers which are large enough to conduct statistical research (Johnson 1984), but which underscore the non-parametric nature of this study. Surveys were collected from ecotourists visiting Ojcowski National Park Museum, from elementary school teachers living in a community within the National Park and affiliated with LOP [Environmental Protection League] (see Curry 1992; Domka 2000), from ornithologists (Ogólnopolskie Towarzystwo Ochrony Ptaków-OTOP) [Polish Society for the Protection of Birds], and from members of the Polish Tourist Country-Lovers Association (PTTK). All ecotourist sub-groups were classified based on the traveller's interest in sustainability, natural areas and environmental education, as outlined in many contemporary ecotourism definitions, as well as their affiliation with various pro-ecological and conservation organizations. With regard to sub-groups within the sample of Polish mainstream tourists, surveys were collected from two travel agencies. According to the judgmental survey sampling, the researcher established the classification of each sub-group and each of the two categories through numerous informal interviews with locals, academics in this topic area and employees of the travel agencies. As such, the two groups were thought to be homogeneous within their respective categories

Results

Socio-demographic data

According to the findings of this study, Ecotourists in Poland differed only marginally from Polish mainstream tourists with regard to socio-demographics (Table 1). On average, ecotourists were slightly older ($\chi=35.92$ years) than the mainstream tourists ($\chi=33.66$ years); both groups were predominantly female, with over two-thirds of both groups as such; and both groups were well educated, although 51.6 percent of ecotourists attained an MA/MSc/MBA or equivalent, compared to only 34.3 percent of mainstream tourists. Few respondents had attained a PhD or MD, which is contrary to the results of past studies involving ecotourists (see below). Results of gross household income illustrate that the ecotourist sample appear to earn more money (note: incomes were converted from Polish currency, where 1 CDN=3 PL.) This is particularly evident in view of the last two income categories, where none of the mainstream tourists were represented, while 8 percent of the ecotourists were.

Table 1 Demographic characteristics of Polish ecotourists compared with conventional tourists

Characteristic	Ecotourists		Tourists	
	n	%	n	%
Age[a]				
18 to 27	15	23.4	13	37.1
28 to 37	22	34.4	5	14.3
38 to 47	19	29.7	14	40.0
48 to 57	7	10.9	2	5.7
58 to 67	1	1.6	1	2.9
Gender				
Male	21	32.8	10	28.6
Female	43	67.2	25	71.4
Education				
Some high school			2	5.7
High school	17	26.6	10	28.6
College diploma	6	9.4	8	22.9
Undergraduate degree	7	10.9	3	8.6
MA/MSc/MBA or equivalent	33	51.6	12	34.3
PhD/MD or equivalent	1	1.6		
Gross household income (CDN) [b]				
Below 3,333	16	25.8	9	34.6
3,334 to 5,000	22	35.5	5	19.2
5,001 to 6,666	4	6.5	3	11.5
6,667 to 8,333	5	8.1	4	15.4
8,334 to 10,000	8	12.9	3	11.5
10,001 to 11,666	2	3.2	2	7.7
11,667 to 13,333	3	4.8		
13,334 and above	2	3.2		

[a]Average age of Polish ecotourists was 35.92 years and of Polish tourists was 33.66 years.
[b]Gross household income groups were calculated from Polish to Canadian currency where 1 CDN=3 PL.

Contrary to the results of this study, Fennell and Smale (1992) reported that Canadian ecotourists visiting Costa Rica were relatively older, compared to ecotourist profiles in Costa Rica and other regions, at 54.0 years of age. These authors also found a slight predominance of males to females in their study, whereas 67.2 percent of the ecotourists in this study were female. In addition, while this study found that ecotourists in Poland were quite well educated (to Masters level), only 1 respondent held a Doctoral degree. A much higher percentage (17%) of respondents held a doctorate in the Canadian study, confirming the trend suggesting that ecotourists are generally better educated, and have higher incomes, than their mainstream counterparts (see Kellert 1985; Applegate and Clark 1987; Wilson 1987; Fennell & Smale 1992; Reingold 1993). This fact, however, may be a reflection of an international, specialist and high cost experience sample of tourists, and not a true reflection of such a comparison.

Ecotourists in Poland, on average, spent more money on all items of their trip than did Polish mainstream tourists (Table 2). Most money was spent on food (χ=144.44 CDN), followed by accommodation (χ=139.21 CDN), tour operator (χ=98.57 CDN) and transportation (χ=63.57 CDN).

Attractions

On the basis of independent sample t-tests, the results illustrate similar response patterns reported by both Polish groups in terms of the importance placed on attractions (Table 3). Only one attraction ('nightlife & entertainment') was more important to the mainstream tourists at a statistically significant level (p=0.036). None of the attractions was identified as more important to the ecotourists. Among the most important attractions for both ecotourists and tourists were: 'learning about nature', 'mountains', 'different climate', 'national parks & reserves', 'historic sites & parks' and 'wilderness/undisturbed areas'. The attractions identified as least significant for both groups were: 'gambling', 'indoor sports', 'first class hotels', 'amusement/theme parks', 'high quality restaurants' and 'big cities'.

The results of this study are inconsistent with the findings of Fennell and Smale (1992) in their research on Canadian ecotourists. In terms of attractions, these authors discovered that Canadian ecotourists represented a distinct segment within the tourism industry, by this group's tendency to place more importance on certain attractions considered fundamental to the ecotourism experience. Although ecotourists in Poland were not

Table 2 Trip expenditures of Polish ecotourists and conventional tourists

Expenditures (CDN)[a]	Ecotourists		Tourists	
	Mean	sd	Mean	sd
Accommodation	139.21	344.45	119.02	472.89
Food	144.44	260.68	121.38	457.92
Transportation	63.57[b]	106.52	42.42	108.55
Tour operator	98.57	241.79	37.56	2.92
All inclusive	653.62	5,385.52	346.32	995.77

[a]Expenditure Mean scores were calculated from Polish to Canadian currency, where 1 CDN=3 PL.
[b]Ecotourists spent more money on transportation than tourists (p=0.034).

Table 3 Relative importance of attractions to Polish ecotourists and conventional tourists[a]

Destination attractions	Ecotourists		Tourists	
	Mean[c]	sd	Mean	sd
Important attractions to ecotourists	Not found		Not found	
Important attractions to tourists[d]				
Nightlife and entertainment	2.04	1.04	2.57 [b]	1.07
Attractions with no significant difference				
Learning about nature	3.34	0.55	3.39	0.61
Mountains	3.26	0.86	3.25	0.89
Different climate	3.21	0.73	3.38	0.75
National Parks and Reserves	3.18	0.74	3.10	0.75
Historic sites and parks	3.18	0.57	2.97	0.66
Wilderness/undisturbed areas	3.17	0.87	3.13	0.68
Predictable weather	3.08	0.74	3.33	0.68
Seaside	3.07	0.84	3.39	0.84
Beaches for sunning and swimming	2.98	0.88	3.23	0.90
Budget accommodation	2.91	0.87	3.10	0.80
Inexpensive meals	2.87	0.73	3.13	0.72
Lakes and streams	2.84	0.81	3.14	0.85
Small villages and towns	2.63	0.96	2.75	0.75
Outdoor adventure activities	2.62	0.84	2.81	1.00
Cultural activities	2.58	0.84	2.48	0.78
Local festivals and events	2.53	0.80	2.38	0.86
Rural areas	2.38	0.94	2.33	0.96
Local crafts	2.25	0.91	1.96	0.86
Resort areas	2.25	0.91	2.12	1.03
Shopping	2.13	0.91	2.15	0.92
Big cities	1.91	0.87	1.68	0.72
High quality restaurants	1.81	0.97	1.50	0.76
Amusement/theme parks	1.79	0.88	1.73	0.72
First class hotels	1.67	0.90	1.38	0.80
Indoor sports	1.48	0.62	1.88	1.07
Gambling	1.21	0.71	1.04	0.20

[a]Differences between groups statistically significant at 0.05 level based on independent sample t-tests
[b]Attraction more important to tourists than to ecotourists ($p=0.036$)
[c]Scale: 1='very important'; 4='not at all important'
[d]Attractions are in descending rank order based on mean scores of ecotourists

found to be separate from the mainstream tourist group in the same way (as compared to the Canadian study), there appears to be a great deal of homogeneity with respect to the importance of attractions for both Polish samples, with ecotourism-based attractions foremost in importance. These include 'learning about nature', 'mountains', 'different climate', 'national parks & reserves' and 'wilderness'. At the other end of the scale, consistency was also found among attractions identified as least significant, both by the Polish tourists and ecotourists, and by the sample of Canadian ecotourists, including 'amusement/ theme parks', 'gambling' and 'indoor sports'.

Benefits sought

Similar to the previous section on attractions, a high level of homogeneity was observed between ecotourists in Poland and mainstream tourists when considering the types of benefits sought by these groups (Table 4). Only one benefit ('visiting friends & relatives') was more important to the mainstream tourists at a statistically significant level ($p=0.031$). No benefits were identified as more important to the ecotourists. Among the most important benefits for both ecotourists and tourists were: 'going new places', 'simpler lifestyle', 'getting a change from busy job', 'having fun/being entertained', 'seeing as much as possible' and 'thrills & excitement'. The benefits identified as least significant for both groups were: 'participating in sports', 'watching sports', 'visiting places my family came from', 'feeling at home away from home', 'taking advantage of reduced fares' and 're-living past good times'. Findings from this section are consistent with results from the previous section on attractions – ecotourists in Poland were not selective in terms of attaching more importance to different attractions than were mainstream tourists.

As in the previous section on attractions, the results on benefits are also inconsistent with the findings of Fennell and Smale (1992), who reported differences in the relative importance of benefits between ecotourists and mainstream tourists. Despite the apparent differences on the basis of statistical significance, some similarities between the present study and the Canadian study were observed. The benefit 'visiting friends and relatives' was identified as statistically more significant to the Polish tourists than to ecotourists – consistent with the Canadian general population.

Discussion: the institutional context

Findings of this study indicate that Polish ecotourists and mainstream tourists compose a very homogeneous travel sector, both in terms of their

Table 4 Relative importance of benefits to Polish ecotourists and conventional tourists[a]

Benefits sought	Ecotourists		Tourists	
	Mean[c]	sd	Mean	sd
Benefits important to ecotourists	Not found		Not found	
Benefits important to tourists[b]				
Visiting friends and relatives	1.96	0.89	2.41[b]	0.87
Benefits with no significant difference[d]				
Going new places	3.48	0.59	3.67	0.48
Simpler lifestyle	3.32	0.71	3.53	0.63
Getting a change from busy job	3.23	0.80	3.30	0.92
Having fun, being entertained	3.16	0.82	3.30	0.88
Seeing as much as possible	3.13	0.68	2.90	0.84
Thrills and excitement	3.05	0.79	3.29	0.76
Being physically active	2.95	0.78	3.10	0.80
Places I feel safe and secure	2.86	0.80	2.96	0.88
Getting away from demands	2.84	1.02	2.84	0.92
Being daring and adventuresome	2.66	0.85	2.93	0.94
Meeting people with similar interests	2.64	0.78	2.77	0.90
Rediscovering myself	2.58	0.96	2.74	0.86
New and different lifestyles	2.56	0.92	2.69	0.93
Doing nothing at all	2.49	0.99	2.77	0.94
Trying new foods	2.44	0.92	2.21	0.68
Re-living past good times	2.33	1.01	2.30	1.07
Taking advantage of reduced fares	2.31	1.04	2.65	1.32
Feeling at home away from home	2.06	0.93	2.19	1.04
Visiting places my family came from	2.06	0.95	2.12	1.07
Watching sports	1.73	0.75	1.74	0.90
Participating in sports	1.63	0.75	1.85	1.10

[a]Differences between groups statistically significant at 0.05 level based on independent sample t-tests
[b]Benefit more important to tourists than to ecotourists ($p=0.031$)
[c]Scale: 1='very important'; 4='not at all important'
[d]Benefits are in descending rank order based on mean scores of ecotourists

demographic characteristics, and the importance placed on attractions and benefits sought. This may be due to any one or a combination of the following. First it may be that, despite the varying educational levels of the respondents, there is an absence of environmental sensitivity that would otherwise partition tourists. This may be a consequence of the long years of environmental neglect by the Polish government under communism, as well as lack of social leadership in the direction of sustainability or environmental thought. It may also be a result of the relatively new market for ecotourists in Poland and their expectations of the resource in light of the environmental conditions of Poland over the last few decades. It is worth restating that a significant portion of ecotourists engaging in ecotourism activities in Poland are, in fact, international tourists. Had this study included these tourists, there may very well have been differences among ecotourists and non-ecotourists.

Furthermore, it may very well be that what has been identified as an ecotourism market in Poland, may be better conceptualized as a more broadly based tourism segment. This may include tourists who are interested not only in nature and natural history, but also in culture and adventure in various contexts. This may be explained conceptually through the ACE framework as developed by Fennell (1999) and the NEAT framework developed by Buckley (2000). In the former case, ACE includes various hybrids of adventure tourism, cultural tourism and ecotourism as, for example, developed by service providers, or as required by tourists (i.e. tourists not wanting a completely natural history-based experience). In the latter case, Buckley writes that NEAT is a hybrid of nature-based tourism, ecotourism and adventure tourism. Although the authors are not able to substantiate the link between ACE tourism or NEAT and the Polish tourists, some of the data suggest an enticing avenue for future research. In this study, the adventure component was supported by the importance of benefits like 'going to new places', 'thrills and excitement'; the culture component was supported by interest in attractions like 'historic sites and parks', as well as the multitude of available heritage resources offered by the country (Hall 2001); while the ecotourism component was supported by an interest in attractions such as 'mountains' and 'national parks and reserves'. Consequently, different forms of ecotourism may be developing in Poland as they are in other countries around the world.

These results lead us to conclude that researchers cannot generalize about the profile of ecotourists in a universal sense. Canadians, Americans, Africans and Eastern Europeans, for example, may all differ in terms of their interest in attractions and benefits, especially with regard to international travel where countries differ dramatically in terms of natural history and culture. In this sense, the homogeneity across groups may be consistent with the current social and ecological situation in Poland, and the slow 'greening' of the tourism industry and of the country as a whole. Unfortunately, the lack of empirical research on the Polish ecotourist, or even the East European ecotourist, makes it difficult, if not impossible, to substantiate the significance of these findings (Hall and Kinnaird 1994; Kamieniecka 1998a, 1998b). As such, it is left to compare the Polish ecotourist to ecotourists in other studies, as reported here, where Canadian ecotourists were found to be more hard-core or eco-centric on the basis of their responses to attractions and benefits.

Given its overall image, Poland, understandably, will have trouble competing for a share of the international market of ecotourists. It is perhaps more reasonable to think that ecotourism in Poland should be developed within and for the Eastern European market, with perhaps limited markets from outside the broader region (e.g. Germany, as suggested earlier). Notwithstanding, Poland is rich in culture and history, often connected with the natural environment and incorporated within the landscape, which may enable the country to build an ecotourism market based upon nature in combination with the vast cultural attraction base (e.g. ruins, old castles, surrounding botanical parks and gardens). The opportunity for adventure, in combination with nature, is possible, as supported by the interest in kayaking on some of the main river systems, and by the relatively young age of the market, as supported here.

Even at this initial stage of conceptualization, however, a strategy for ecotourism development in Poland is constrained by a number of problems. Lack of coordination between government levels/ministries and local communities, lack of government funding for national and local projects, lack of national and local empirical research studies within this area, reliance on Western frameworks of tourism development, and the organizational adjustments to standards of the EU in light of the country's integration. This is compounded by misconceptions and misunderstandings on how ecotourism ought to fit into the political, social, ecological and economic fabric of the country, as outlined below.

Defining the philosophical basis of ecotourism in Poland

While the concept of ecotourism is relatively new in Poland – as it is everywhere – the principles on which it is built are not, as can be seen in this quote from 1912: 'To maintain the original character of the Tatry Mountains is to capitalize on its value. Development has taken this direction' [translation] (Pawlikowski, as cited in Dąbrowski 2000: 6). Also, the Polish Country-Lovers Association (PTTK), which was established in 1950, focuses its efforts on preserving the natural environment and cultural heritage through activities, such as promoting and encouraging ecotourism; training staff of the tourist centres; organizing seminars, conferences and meetings; publishing books, magazines and documents; encouraging member participation in field work; and cooperating with domestic and international ecological organizations (Dąbrowski nd).

Defining the term, however, appears to be more problematic. Some authors interpret ecotourism as a form of nature-orientated tourism, the most important aspect of which is to derive satisfaction from learning and experiencing nature through various kinds of activities: intellectual, physical, or emotional (Dąbrowski 2000). In a similar fashion, a Polish encyclopedia defines ecotourism as a 'form of tourism, which actively promotes being close to nature, and establishing closer and fuller under-standing of human relationship with the natural environment, on the basis of significant and individual experience' [translation] (Encyklopedia Powszechna (PWN) 1995, as cited in Waśniewski 1998). In addition, the Małopolski Serwis Informacyjny [Polish Information Service] (1999) describes ecotourism as a narrow notion consisting of benefits from protec-tion of the natural environment and regional development, and as ethical travel in small groups to places of natural and cultural interest, where local people are fully aware of potential benefits and costs. These defin-itions appear to be much closer to the Western understanding of ecotourism, which view it as educational, sustainable, focused on natural history, and ethical (see Blamey 1997 and Acott, et al. 1998).

On the other hand, however, Kamieniecka (1998a) suggests that nature becomes an object of value to the client only when it is the most impor-tant motive for travel. In this latter case, ecotourism is seen as a wide-spread movement of pro-ecological thinking, behaviour and techno-organizational solutions, which allows for the long-term consump-tion of the resource base (Kamieniecka 2000). This definition is some-what worrisome because it opens the door for various interpretations of consumption which may not provide the basis for differentiating ecotourism (decidedly non-consumptive in its orientation) from other forms of natural resource-based tourism, such as fishing and hunting, which are much more consumptive. Indeed, others (see Styczyńska & Styczyński 1991) write that ecotourism is synonymous with mass recre-ation, and that it does not lead to limiting numbers of participants in its various forms. These differences serve to illustrate the tremendous vari-ability that exists across definitions in Poland, which is a problem that also exists elsewhere.

Discrepancies between definitions are potentially harmful, especially in regards to policy and public knowledge. With the potential of increased profits, tourist numbers often increase along with the infrastructure to support them. For example, the majority of agritourism farmers in Poland who were given funds and loans, have been found to build new modern houses rather than to improve or preserve the old (see Matejek: Dyskusja/ Discussion 1998). While new developments are often needed, regardless of the sustainable technologies that may have been used, there is the danger of environmental impact through inadequate planning, a loss of tradition and a loss of uniqueness.

Education about ecotourism has a critical role to play in the public's understanding of the concept. From this study, there appears to be a significant lack of it, both in terms of the professionalism of those who work in the tourism sector (researcher as participant on several ecotourism trips), but also with regard to the general public (Hall and Kinnaird 1994; Michałowski, *et al.* 1994; Kamieniecka 1995, 1998a, 1998b; Waśniewski 1998). One of the principal reasons for this is the lack of literature which policy makers and researchers may use to further conceptualize the idea (Hall and Kinnaird 1994). A shortage of information constrains the ecotourism industry, especially *in situ,* where it is needed to educate the public and encourage active participation by various stakeholders (Hall and Kinnaird 1994). Furthermore, the rather obscured understanding of ecotourism has also been shown to result in a lack of initiative and support from the local communities in developing this type of tourism in their area (see Mazul 2000; Symonides 2000; Wiatr 2000a; Wieczorek 2000; Wójcik 2000).

The importance of education, as a reference point for ecotourism development, has been demonstrated in a recent study by Smulska (1996). The study found a relatively low level of environmental knowledge among Polish society. Tourists in this study were found to be anthropocentric, expressing price and health as main motivations for the purchase of environmentally friendly products (Smulska 1996). The Polish government is beginning to address the problem through the establishment of a National Program of Environmental Education (Zarząd Główny Ligi Ochrony Przyrody 2000).

Ecotourism in Poland's National Parks

The formal Act allowing tourism within protected areas was developed in 1969, along with the first definition of National Parks (Mateuszewska 2000; Szczęsny 1982, cited in Baranowska-Janota 1995). Since the definition did not specify the scope of the parks' accessibility, tourism appears in a rich variety of forms, including recreation and sport, consumption of vegetation and driving (Baranowska-Janota 1995). Due to the high tourist interest in the Polish National Parks, which are visited yearly by some 10 million travellers, the Polish Management Board of National Parks (KZPN) is looking towards the implementation of ecotourism within all parks as a potential tool for the protection of the natural environment (Baranowska-Janota 1995). However, the attractiveness of ecotourism in Poland, as elsewhere, is derived from the need for the urban population to seek natural areas. Unfortunately, Polish cities continue to lose their available green spaces, with 14 m²/resident, and only 9 m²/resident in Warsaw (1994 figures), which is far below the recommendations of the EU, at 30 m²/resident (Pawlikowska-Piechotka 2000). The result is more pressure on existing natural areas (Baranowska-Janota 1995) and, although the Board (KZPN) has suggested that tourism is secondary to conservation, the recreational carrying capacity of many parks continues to be exceeded. In 1994, 8,482,000 tourists visited 20 of Poland's National Parks, 2,400,000 in Tatry National Park alone (Mateuszewska 2000).

Unlike the management of North American national parks, Poland shares its protected areas with people who live and work within them (as do the national parks of England and Wales, for example). These national parks are living, working landscapes, with a strong connection to the country's culture (Główny Urząd Statystyczny 1997). Consequently, the designation of a National Park does not affect land ownership and, further, the local population views it appropriate for these areas to have a range of socio-economic activities, subject to strict controls (Phillips 1985; Dąbrowski 2000; Gąsienica-Byrcyn 2000; Mazul 2000; Symonides 2000). Controls, however, are often ineffective (Gąsienica-Byrcyn 2000; Symonides 2000) and often viewed as further Draconian measures to restrict growth and prosperity (Curry 1992). Historically, local communities within or adjacent to parks have rejected ecotourism, associating it with increased controls and regulations which would threaten their livelihoods (Symonides 2000). More recently, however, successful cases have been documented (see Kowalkowski, et al. 1996; Kowalik 2000; LOP Europejskie Centrum Ekologiczne 2000; Mazul 2000; Wójcik 2000: 5, 8, 32; Wiatr 2000b). The following two examples are representative of the differing perspectives on tourism in Poland's parks system.

(1) Created forty five years ago, Tatry National Park's legal standards (Article 14, Bill 2, regarding environmental protection as the first priority) are far below those of other national parks. It is the only park in Poland which lacks a new version of decree by the Board of Ministers, possibly due to problems with private property within the National Park, inhabited mostly by the native mountain people (górale) (Gąsienica-Byrcyn 2000). The agreement established between the Minister of Environment, the local government of Tatry, and the Forest Partnership, completely ignored the Tatry wilderness and intended to implement demands of the local government-business lobby, which consequently began reshaping the park into a recreation and sports area (Symonides 2000). Experts on the park were omitted from negotiations, and the park's level of protection was subsequently lowered by the Ministry of Environment.

(2) In comparison, the conservation and environmental protection of Białowieski NP has many supporters. First of all, the Białowieża primeval forest and National Park has been placed by UNESCO on its list of 50 disappearing wonders of the world (Wieczorek 2000). It is the last of the old primeval forests (12,000 species of fauna and 5,000 species of flora) still exploited economically (Wieczorek 2000). The

Ministry of Environment plans to enlarge the National Park to an area of 60,000 ha in order to encompass all the Białowieża primeval forest, a decision supported by the Polish Academy of Science, UNESCO, WWF and Polish experts, such as Czesław Miłosz, recipient of the Nobel Prize (Wieczorek 2000). The contract signed in 1998 ensures tourism development, employment and government donations; however, the contract does not describe the direction or the type of tourism development (Wieczorek 2000). The park's extension will provide additional habitat for the 220 bird species nesting in Poland, a main cause (habitat) of declining bird populations in the country (OTOP 2000). Furthermore, the Coalition for the Protection of Białowieża sees the expansion of the National Park as a political manoeuver, with timber benefits being realized by the representative administration of State Forests (Symonides 2000). Instead, the Coalition would like the park to be developed with the best interests of the local residents and resource base in mind (see OTOP 2000: 5, 7–8, 32).

Conscious enjoyment of the wilderness demands a certain level of responsibility (Micułand). In view of the problems associated with low levels of environmental education and political corruption in Poland, industry codes of ethics would be valuable in protecting the natural environment, even if the codes were not supported by regulations (Kamieniecka nd; Przecławski 1997). Whereas hunters' codes of ethics are strengthened by national law in Poland (Zelek 2000), tourist codes of ethics are virtually non-existent, or follow codes developed elsewhere (Przecławski 1997). A recent European Green Card programme developed by the Environmental Protection League (LOP) European Ecological Centre in 1995 is designed to change this. It was the first professional discount card in Europe geared towards uniting people interested and active in the area of environmental protection, cultural heritage and a healthy lifestyle and leisure choices (LOP Europejskie Centrum Ekologiczne 2000). The card provides a list of various discounted travel choices (national parks, museums, vegetarian restaurants) in Poland and across Europe, and fulfills the function of travel information and a guide book. Anyone willing to follow codes of ethics for the protection of the natural environment and cultural heritage is able to join the programme for free. The Green Card is monitored by the LOP European Ecological Centre which publishes and distributes the cards and produces the list of appropriate locations, although Daniel Tarschys, the General Secretary of the European Board, personally supports and manages the programme beginning in August 1995. Another example, with a slightly different approach, is the establishment of legal regional groups called Guards for Preservation of Natural Environment (Straż Ochrony Przyrody), who intervene when codes of ethics are broken, and who provide information to various user groups (Mazul 2000).

Sustainable development

Considering the social and environmental conditions in Poland, some scholars feel that it would be more beneficial to shift from a focus on sustainability (e.g. Domański 1995 1996), to one which reduces unsustainability; and from one focused on equity, to one which attempts to reduce inequity (Asian NGO Coalition, IRED Asia and the People-Centered Development Forum 1994; Eichler 2000). From this perspective, Polish agritourism in rural areas (see Polish Federation of Country Tourism 'Hospitable Farms' 2000) could more easily evolve into an environmentally proactive and sustainably based form of tourism (Kamieniecka and Wójcik 1999). In other regions of Europe, as in Poland, agritourism represents an option for unstable agriculture-based economies (Dernoi 1983), which when transformed into a more sustainable form, could decrease inequity by provision of 'green' job positions and strengthening of the local economies (Kamieniecka 1995; Kowalik 2000).

The term 'sustainable development' was incorporated into policy in 1991 as the basis of national environmental politics and all planning efforts, as well as law, in 1997, regarding protection and shaping of the environment (Kamieniecka and Wójcik 1999). In addition, all decision-making structures which address sustainability are present in Poland, such as the *National Sustainable Development Coordination Body, National Sustainable Development Policy, National Agenda 21 Framework, Local Regional Agenda 21 Frameworks* (few), and *Environmental Impact Assessment Law* (WTTC 1999, cited in Hall 2001). Unfortunately, this has stimulated little in the way of pro-environmental transformation within Poland (Kamieniecka 1995). Furthermore, the new administrative divisions in the country were implemented for the purpose of conforming to EU environmental laws, allowing most decisions to rest with the lowest levels of administration (Tresenberg 2000). This has been constrained through a lack of legal regulations which have, in turn, resulted in dislocation between the various levels of government, and thus a move away from actions which would catalyse sustainability (Iwaniuk 2000; Małopolski Serwis Informacyjny 1999; Piontek 1997; M. Wallstrom pers. comm. 2000, online at *http://www.ecp.wroc.pl/stanowisko_ngos_ang.htm l*).

Recommendations and conclusion

Further studies on this topic, and region, may wish to refine the methods employed in this study through the application of a more randomized research design and, perhaps, through the distribution of surveys in major cities and among qualified operators. Efforts in creating national or even

regional research tools should be undertaken, both to support these findings and to encourage development of Polish research in this area. In
particular, the lack of Polish ecotourism data made it virtually impossible
to support or compare results of this study. Future research may also
attempt to provide a better understanding of the fundamental structure
of the ecotourism industry in Poland, including definitions/interpretations,
training and education (especially in the context of an industry that is
rurally based), codes of ethics and practice, community development, and
so on. In addition, a profile of operators would not only serve as a
marketing tool for the industry in general, but effectively categorize these
service providers according to their programme offerings. The proposed
environmental education programme should attempt to examine how
sustainability and ecotourism may help Polish society, economically,
socially and ecologically, as well as the many sustainably based industries
which may develop as a result of its incorporation. Also, as this study
touches only briefly on tourist–wildlife interactions, especially birds and
birdwatching, future studies may wish to examine the emerging area of
wildlife tourism (see Reynolds and Braithwaite 2001). Furthermore, future
studies may wish to examine the topic of ethnocentricity in the realm of
ecotourism, including the possible differences between ecotourists of
different cultural backgrounds and potential differences between the
domestic and the outbound ecotourists within a particular culture. As
such, Polish domestic ecotourists may be, in fact, very similar to the
Canadian domestic ecotourists, and not to the Canadian outbound
ecotourists, which is a focus not examined in this research.

This study found evidence to suggest that universal generalizations about
the ecotourist cannot be made. Ecotourism in Poland will thus evolve on
the basis of its unique social, political, economic and ecological conditions. This finding is cast in the light of the high homogeneity between
ecotourists in Poland and mainstream tourists with regard to their attraction preferences and benefits sought. Possible explanations for this might
be the relative immaturity of the sector, the long years of environmental
neglect by the Polish government under communism, as well as a lack of
social leadership in the area of environmental thought. While this was
not the main focus of the research, it could mean that those travelling to
Poland for ecotourism may demand better quality accommodation, food,
transportation, and so on. Given the financial difficulties of Polish society
and the minimal support from the government, the initial impetus may
need to come from private foreign operators, with the possibility for social
inequity and unsustainability if left unchecked (Turner 2000). The higher
quality demanded by visitors may stimulate a stronger commitment to the
management of parks and protected areas, as well as to the greater need
for policy to become practice. In this regard, it appears as though the
policy structure for ecotourism is in place (i.e. decision-making abilities

of communities). What is required, however, is effective leadership. The district that is able to capitalize on information (research), environmental education, lobbying and an understanding of domestic and international tourists (Gössling 1999) within the context of Polish policies and laws will be advantaged by ecotourism. Indeed, such a model is required for the benefit of a country which has endured through a legacy of environmental and social misfortune.

References

Acott, T. G., La Trobe, H. L. and Howard, S. H. 1998. An evaluation of deep ecotourism and shallow ecotourism. *Journal of Sustainable Tourism* 6(3): 238–53.

Applegate, J. E. and Clark, K. E. 1987. Satisfaction levels of birdwatchers: An observation on the consumptive–nonconsumptive continuum. *Leisure Sciences* 9: 129–34.

Asian NGO Coalition, IRED Asia and the People-Centered Development Forum. 1994. Economy, ecology and spirituality: Toward a theory and practice of sustainability (Part II). *Journal of the Society for International Development* 4: 67–72.

Baranowska-Janota, M. 1995. Ku ekoturystyce w Polskich Parkach Narodowych. [Towards ecotourism in Polish National Parks]. *Parki Narodowe i Rezerwaty Przyrody, Tom* 14(4): 119–28.

Blamey, R. K. 1997. Ecotourism: The search for an operational definition. *Journal of Sustainable Tourism* 5(2): 109–30.

Buckley, R. 2000. Neat trends: current issues in nature, eco- and adventure tourism. *International Journal of Tourism Research* 2: 1–8.

Curry, N. 1992. Controlling development in the National Parks of England and Wales. *Town Planning Review* 63(2): 107–21.

Dąbrowski, P. 2000. (July–August) Łatwiej powiedzieć niż zrobic! [Easier said than done!] *Ekoprofit* 7/8(45): 6–9.

Dąbrowski, P. no date. *Poland: The most valuable natural trails*. Warsaw: PTTK 'Kraj.'

Dębski, J. 1999. (July–August) Bez zagrożeń dla środowiska. [Without dangers to the natural environment]. *Ekoprofit*, 7/8(34): 14–15.

Dernoi, L. 1983. Farm tourism in Europe. *Tourism Management* 4: 155–66.

Domański, R. 1995. Structural changes in geographical systems fulfilling the conditions of sustainable development. *Geographia Polonica* 65: 79–89.

Domański, R. 1996. Towards a more operational form of the idea of sustainable development. *Geographia Polonica* 67: 121–39.

Domka, L. 2000. Spotkania edukacyjne z piosenkπ ekologiczną. [Educational meetings with environmental song]. *Eko i My* 7/8: 18–19, 28.

Eichler, M. 2000. In/equity and un/sustainability: Exploring intersections. *Environments: A Journal of Interdisciplinary Studies. Theme Issue: Linking Equity and Sustainability* 28(2): 1–9.

Europa World Yearbook. 1999. *The Europa world yearbook, 1999* (Vol. 2). UK: Europa Publications Limited.

Fennell, D. A. 1999. *Ecotourism: An introduction*. New York: Routledge.

Fennell, D. A. and Smale, B. J. A. 1992. Ecotourism and natural resource protection: Implications of an alternative form of tourism for host nations. *Tourism Recreation Research* 17: 21–32.

Gąsienica-Byrcyn, W. 2000. Tatrzański Park Narodowy. [Tatrzański National Park]. *Eko Styl* 1(31): 20–3.

Główny Urząd Statystyczny. 1997. *Ochrona Środowiska*, 1997: Informacje i opracowania statystyczne. [Protection of the natural environment, 1997: Information and statistical papers]. Warsaw, Poland: author.

Gössling, S. 1999. Ecotourism: A means to safeguard biodiversity and ecosystem functions? *Ecological Economics* 29: 303–20.

Hall, D. 2001. Sustainable tourism development and transportation in Central and Eastern Europe. *Journal of Sustainable Tourism* 8(6): 441–57.

Hall, D. and Kinnaird, V. 1994. Ecotourism in Eastern Europe. In *Ecotourism: A sustainable option?*, ed. E. Cater and G. Lowman, pp. 111–36. England: John Wiley & Sons.

Iwaniuk, H. 2000. Zgodność i działania dostosowawcze Polskiego prawa do wymogów Unii Europejskiej w zakresie ochrony przyrody. [Compatibility of Polish environmental protection law and adjustment thereof to EU requirements]. In *Ekorozwój w polityce regionalnej: Ekonomiczne aspekty ekorozwoju, Tom 1*, ed. H. Sasinowski, pp. 143–61. Białystok, Poland: Politechnika Białostocka.

Johnson, R. 1984. *Elementary statistics*. Boston: Duxbury Press.

Kajszczak, W. 1999. Atutem – nie tylko. [Argument – not only]. *Ekoprofit* 7/8(34): 16–19.

Kamieniecka, J. 1995. *(Eko)turystyka zielonym rynkiem pracy: Przyczynek do wdrazania zasad ekorozwoju w Polsce, Zeszyt 6*. [Ecotourism as green job market: Contribution to the implementation of eco-development principles in Poland, Volume 6]. Warsaw, Poland: Instytut na Rzecz Ekorozwoju (InE).

Kamieniecka, J. 1998a. *Ekopolityka w turystyce: Raport o zmianach mozliwych i potrzebnych, Zeszyt 2*. [Ecopolitics in tourism: Report of possible and needed changes, Volume 2]. Warsaw, Poland: InE.

Kamieniecka, J. (ed.). 1998b. *Polityka zrównoważonego rozwoju w turystyce*. [Politics of sustainable development in tourism]. Warsaw, Poland: Urzπd Kultury Fizycznej i Turystyki, InE.

Kamieniecka, J. 2000. Powrót do normalności. [Return to normality]. *Ekoprofit* 7/8(45): 15–16.

Kamieniecka, J. no date. *Ekorozwój i ekoturystyka*. [Sustainable development and ecotourism]. Jelenia Góra, Poland: Wojewódzki Ośrodek Doradztwa Rolniczego w Jeleniej Górze.

Kamieniecka, J. and Wójcik, B. 1999. *Potrzeba ekologizacji gospodarstw agroturystycznych*. [The need to ecologize the agritourism farms]. Jelenia Góra, Poland: Dolnośląski Wojewódzki Ośrodek Doradztwa Rolniczego z/s w Świdnicy, Oddział w Jeleniej Górze.

Kellert, S. R. 1985. Birdwaching in American society. *Leisure Sciences* 7(3): 343–60.

Kopta, T. 2000. (July) Ratujmy trolejbusy! [Save the trolleybuses]! *Aura: Ochrona Ś·rodowiska* 7: 13–15.

Korbel, J. 2000. Globalna ekoturystyka. [Global ecotourism]. *Dzikie Życie* [Online]. Available: http://www.most.org.pl/pnrwi/dz/Dz64/06.htm

Kowalik, T. 2000. Bank jako lekarz środowiska. [Bank for the protection of the environment]. *Eko i My* 7/8: 10–11.

Kowalkowski, A., Ciosek, W., Pałys, A., Sikora, A. and Tutka, K. 1996. Założenia i metody opracowania przewodnika ekoturystycznego po Górach Świętokrzyskich. [Principles and methods of the development of ecotourism guide-book for Świętokrzyskie Mountains]. In *Agroturyzm Świętokrzyski: Materiały sesji naukowej 21–22 września 1995*, ed. Wyższa Szkoła Pedagogiczna im. Jana Kochanowskiego w Kielcach, pp. 105–10. Kielce, Poland: KWANT.

Liga Ochrony Przyrody (LOP). 1999–2000. Poland: Author.

Liga Ochrony Przyrody (LOP). Europejskie Centrum Ekologiczne 2000. Europejska Zielona Karta. [European Green Card]. *Przyroda Polska* 7: 10.

Maletz, A. 1998. Liga Ochrony Przyrody w regionie Częstochowskim [Environment Protection League in the Częstochowa region]. Częstochowa, Poland: Liga Ochrony Przyrody.

Małopolski Serwis Informacyjny. 1999 (July–August). Ekoturystyka czy ekoterror. [Ecotourism or eco-terror]. *Eko Bałtyk* [Online serial], *64/65*. Available: http://www.region-malopolska.pl/kom-spol/turyst/ekotur.htm

Matejek, K. 1998. Dyskusja [Discussion] In *Polityka zrównowazonego rozwoju w turystyce*. [Politics of sustainable development in tourism], ed. J. Kamieniecka, p. 71. Warsaw, Poland: Urząd Kultury Fizycznej i Turystyki, InE.

Mateuszewska, D. 2000. (February) Turysta w Parku Narodowym – Intruz czy sojusznik? [Tourist in the National Park – Intruder or an ally]? *Parki Narodowe* 2: 28–9.

Mazul, M. 2000. Ludzie i park – Współpraca i rozwój. [People and the park – Cooperation and development]. *Parki Narodowe* 2: 9.

Michałowski, S., Jacyna, I. and Szulczewski, M. 1994. *Ekologiczne wyzwania Polski ... Zagrozenia a świadomość społeczeństwa*. [Environmental challenges in Poland ... Environmental threats and public awareness]. Warsaw, Poland: KOPIA.

Micuła, G. no date. *Przewodnik po Parkach Narodowych w Polsce*. [Guide-book for the National Parks in Poland]. Warsaw, Poland: PZU S.A. Sponsor Generalny Europejskiego Centrum Działań Ekologicznych Młodziezy w Warszawie.

OTOP – Ogólnopolskie Towarzystwo Ochrony Ptaków. 2000 (February). *Ptaki.* Poland, Gdańsk: author.

Pawlikowska-Piechotka, A. 2000. Symboliczny 'kosmiczny obraz świata'. Zabytkowe parki i ogrody na rynku nieruchomości (II). [Symbolic 'cosmic picture of the world'. Monumental parks and gardens on the market of real estate (II)]. *Ekoprofit* 7/8(45): 48–52.

Phillips, A. 1985. Socio-economic development in the 'National Parks' of England and Wales. *Parks* 10(1): 1–5.

Piontek, F. 1997. Ekorozwój a strategia zintegrowania restrukturyzacji na przykładzie Polski i województwa Katowickiego. [Eco-development and the strategy for integration of restructuring on the Polish example of Katowice voivodeship]. In *Ekorozwój i narzędzia jego realizacji*, ed. J. Sawicka-Demianowicz and A. Poskrobko, pp. 22–30. Białystok, Poland: Ekonomia i Środowisko.

Polish Federation of Country Tourism 'Hospitable Farms'. 2000. *Poland Agritourism Atlas*. Warsaw, Poland: Indeed Poland.

Przecławski, K. 1997. Etyka turysty. [Tourist ethics]. *Etyczne postawy turystyki*, pp. 39–50. Kraków, Poland: F. H.-U. 'Albis'.

Pudlis, E. 1996. (July) Fundament z prawa. [Foundation of the law]. *Środowisko i Życie* **69**: 33–4.

Reingold, L. 1993. Identifying the elusive ecotourist. In *Going Green*. Supplement to *Tour and Travel News* (October 25): 36–7.

Reynolds, P. C. and Braithwaite, D. 2001. Towards a conceptual framework for wildlife tourism. *Tourism Management* 22: 31–42.

Skupiewski, P. 1999. Supermarket czy . . . potrawa regionalna? [Supermarket or . . . a regional dish]? *Ekoprofit* 7/8(34); 13.

Smulska, G. 1996. (July) Świadomość zagrożeń i poczucie bezradności. [Awareness of dangers and the feeling of helplessness]. *Środowisko i Życie* 69: 35–6.

Styczyńska, H. and Styczyński, M. 1991. Ekoturystyka w Popradzkim Parku Krajobrazowym. [Ecotourism in Popradzki Landscape Park]. In *ZB* [Online serial], 12(30). Available: http://www.most.org.pl/zb/zb/30/ekoturys.htm

Symonides, E. 2000. Uchwała prezydium państwowej rady ochrony przyrody. [Decision of the state board presidium of environmental protection]. *Przyroda Polska* 7: 6.

Tresenberg, D. 2000. (May) Ochrona Środowiska problem moralny. [Environmental protection a moral problem]. *Zielona Liga* 47: 3, 19.

Turner, B. (ed.). 2000. *The Statesman's Yearbook 2001*. NY: Macmillan Press.

Waśniewski, P. 1998. *Ekoturystyka*. [Ecotourism]. Unpublished license paper, Wyższa Szkoła Humanistyczna, Pułtusk, Poland.

Weaver, D. B. 2001. *Ecotourism*. Milton, Australia: John Wiley and Sons.

Wiatr, A. 2000a. Strategia marketingowa dla doliny Biebrzy. [Marketing strategy for the Biebrza Valley]. *Parki Narodowe* 2: 18–19.

Wiatr, A. 2000b. Wielkie koszenie. [Large mowing]. *Parki Narodowe* 2: 26.

Wieczorek, O. 2000. Bitwa o puszczę. [Battle for primeval forest]. *Zielona Liga* 47: 4.

Wilkin, J. 1998. Wielofunkcyjny rozwój terenów wiejskich. [Multi-functional development of country areas]. In *Polityka zrównoważonego rozwoju w turystyce*. [Politics of sustainable development in tourism], ed. J. Kamieniecka, pp. 46–52. Warsaw, Poland: Urząd Kultury Fizycznej i Turystyki, InE.

Wilkin, J. 1999. Wieś przed nową szansą. [Rural areas before a new opportunity]. *Ekoprofit* 7/8(34): 12.

Wilson, M. 1987. *Nature oriented tourism in Ecuador: Assessment of industry structure and development needs*, No. 20. (FPEI). North Carolina State University, Raleigh, North Carolina.

Wójcik, B. 2000. Przyglądamy się jak problemy ochrony przyrody, a w tym ochrony ptaków, uwzględniane są w procesie przygotowań Polski do wstąpienia do Unii Europejskiej – Projekt realizowany wspólnie przez InE i OTOP. [Observation of how conservation issues, especially regarding birds, are integrated in the process of joining the EU by Poland – Project managed by the Institute for Sustainable Development (InE/ISD) and the Polish Bird Conservation Association (OTOP)]. *Ptaki – Biuletyn Ogólnopolskiego Towarzystwa Ochrony Ptaków (OTOP)*, 2: 23–5.

Wydawnictwo Naukowe PWN. 2000. *Mała Encyklopedia PWN. Wyadanie Trzecie*. [Small Encyclopedia PWN. Third Issue], pp. 621–5. Poland, Warsaw: author.

Zarząd, Główny Ligi Ochrony Przyrody. 2000 (July) Narodowy program edukacji ekologicznej oraz warunki jego wdrożenia. [National program of environmental education and its conditions of implementation]. Przyroda Polska 7:2.

Zelek, M. 2000. Łowiectwo – Pasja czy snobizm. [Hunting – Passion or snobism]. *Eko Styl* 1(31): 8–9.

Zwolińska, A. 2000. Czynne formy ochrony przyrody. [Active forms of environmental protection]. *Eko Styl* 1(31): 10–11, 14.

Relationships between International Tourism and Migration in Hungary: Tourism Flows and Foreign Property Ownership

SÁNDOR ILLÉS & GÁBOR MICHALKÓ

ABSTRACT *Tourism and migration are increasingly important elements of human mobility, but surprisingly little effort has been made to investigate the interrelationship between these in Hungary. Reviewing the literature on the tourism–migration nexus, the article identifies a number of relevant themes for applying to the Hungarian case, as well as a number of theoretical and empirical challenges. In this paper, two main themes are emphasized. First, the seasonality of tourism flows and, secondly, property acquisition by foreigners. These themes are examined from a macro perspective, using secondary, register-based data. Although the main emphasis has been placed on analysing the spatial patterns of the phenomena studied, the social characteristics are also considered. A number of conclusions are discussed about the relationships between tourist and migration flows, and foreign property ownership, set in the context of the European Union's freedom of movement provisions, and the implications for Hungary in terms of near future.*

Introduction

Tourism and migration are two of the principal elements of human mobility. The developmental phases, causes and consequences of migration are not independent of one another, and the more recent form of mobility, tourism, and *vice versa*. Changes in the volumes and directions of tourism and migration often complement and substitute each other (Bell and Ward 2000). While a substantial part of migration flows is motivated by aspirations of improving life conditions (broadly defined), tourism is driven by the motivation to acquire experiences. Both involve searches for advantageous locations, and sometimes these coincide (Illés 2000; Michalkó and Rátz 2003).

Although the connections between tourism and migration have been emphasized in the international literature (Williams and Hall 2000a, 2002; Truly 2002; Coles and Timothy 2004; Niedomysl 2005), these have not been explored systematically in Hungary and, indeed, in most of the transition economies of Central and Eastern Europe. This poses a serious challenge for those researchers trying to distinguish and identify the characteristic features, similarities, differences and overlaps of, and between, these two phenomena. Moreover, the processes of globalization have made both tourism and migration increasingly complex phenomena. Understanding the interconnections between them inevitably calls for an interdisciplinary approach (Böröcz 1996; Melegh *et al.* 2004).

There has, hitherto, been relatively little research on the interrelationships between these two phenomena in Hungary. Studies of international migration focus mainly on the spatial consequences of the places of residence of foreign migrants living in Hungary (Dövényi 1997), their impact on the everyday life of the host communities (Sik 1998; Michalkó 2002), and the peculiarities of their employment (Gagyi and Oláh 1998; Borbély and Lukács 2001; Illés 2004) demonstrate the way in which the international movements of migrants are shaped from the point of view of quasi-touristic practice. Hajdú and Lukács (2001) discussed tourism within the context of the social welfare system of the European Union (EU). The subject has also been examined from the perspective of tourism, mainly in work devoted to second homes (Dingsdale 1986; Csordás 1999) and the property purchases of foreigners in Hungary (Kasper 2001; Berényi *et al.* 2003). Nemes Nagy (1998) argued that the connections between tourism and migration, and the exploration of the points of interaction between these two major phenomena, can only take place when analysing the role of spatiality. Additionally, connections between tourism and migration have been examined in relation to Hungary's geographical position, historical heritage and resulting geopolitical relations, together with the natural resources waiting to be exploited by the tourism industry (Bora and Korompai 2001). There are, however, major gaps in our knowledge which demand further research into a number of specific topics.

The data for this paper were prepared at the Geographical Research Institute of the Hungarian Academy of Sciences. The original data files on tourism flows were provided by the Hungarian Central Statistical Office and are based on border and commercial accommodation statistics. The data on foreign property purchases originated from the legal register of the Local Governments Department of the Ministry of Interior. The original data files were selected, checked and harmonized by the authors.

The research adopted a holistic approach (Williams and Hall 2002: 3) that, in particular, has meant combining quantitative and qualitative methods. An initial analysis of the literature in this field was the main tool for identifying the key themes in relation to the tourism–migration nexus. Except for the general description of the context, shares and rates were utilized as statistical tools in the analysis. This avoids the distortions that are associated with relying on absolute numbers and facilitates an analysis of underlying processes. However, in some cases absolute data (shown in parentheses) will be utilized in order to clarify the meaning of the relative data. Cartographic presentations are also used to to explore further some of the relationships between migration and tourism.

The aims of the paper are five-fold. First, the international literature on the tourism-migration nexus is reviewed critically in order to identify key themes in the Hungarian context. Secondly, the seasonality of international tourism inflows is analysed in order to explore one of the contact zones between the two phenomena. Quantitative methods are used to identify the main macro-factors that influence the levels of international tourism and migration. Thirdly, the spatial pattern of foreign purchases is investigated in relation to the types of properties and the citizenship of the owners. Fourthly, some proposals are formulated for future research. Finally, the potential for further international comparisons is considered in order to extend the existing literature in this field, which has been highly ethnocentric, in being largely based on Australian, North American and north-western European experiences.

Literature Review

Researches on tourism and migration have tended to develop independently of one another in the second half of the twentieth century (Bell and Ward 2000). Some types of growth of tourism activity are considered increasingly to be a sub-type of migration in some areas of migration research. This is against a background of widespread increase in the numbers, formats and spatial distribution of tourism. The energy of tourism researchers was devoted to investigating the new flows, and the causes and consequences of the emerging phenomena (McKercher and Lew 2004). And exploration of the interrelationship between tourism and migration systematically started from the 1990s.

The continuum metaphor has become very popular in the literature which deals with the tourism–migration nexus. Longino and Marshall (1990: 233) found that vacationers anchored one end of the continuum of tourism–migration, while permanent migrants anchored the other. Warnes (1994), studying the displacement of northern Europeans to Spain, combined the analysis of mobility forms with an assessment of the tourist background and different types of housing ownership and use. This resulted in a number of forms, ranging from the one-week hotel holiday to permanent residence. O'Reilly (1995: 29) used the category of time spent in the destination, together with the way of life, to classify the international foreign community in Fuengirola, Spain. She identified five categories: expatriates, residents, seasonal visitors, returners and tourists. Later she distinguished migrant from tourist in terms of orientation to home, and identified four main groups: full residents, returning residents, seasonal visitors and peripatetic visitors (O'Reilly 2003: 305). These two kinds of typologies, produced by the same author researching a single area, reflect the fluidity of tourism–migration in reality.

Williams *et al.* (2000) created a provisional continuum where international retirement migration ranged from permanent legally registered residents, non-registered seasonal migrants, owners of second home staying for short period, to long-term tourists. Bell and Ward (2000) stated that tourism, as temporary movements, and permanent migration formed part of the same continuum of population mobility and proposed a unified classificatory framework, with time and space dimensions. Rodríguez (2001) stated that, in practice, there was a continuum of situations which were difficult to assess quantitatively, but did not generate new categories of international retirement migration. Krakover and Karplus (2002: 117) argued those potential immigrants represented a special case whereby their status on the tourist migrant continuum was not fixed but, rather, was changeable and conditional. Williams and Hall (2000a: 3) also placed tourism-led migration and migration-led tourism at two ends of the continuum of personal mobility. After a decade of research, it seems that a general consensus has emerged as to the existence of blurred or grey zones between permanent migration and tourism, invovling complex forms of mobility (Williams and Hall 2000b: 20).

The grey zones in the continuum contstitue different research areas that need further exploration. Williams and Hall (2000b) identified five important interdisciplinary themes relating to the symbiotic tourism–migration relationships: tourism and labour migration, tourism and return migration, tourism and entrepreneurial migration, tourism and retirement migration and second homes. These have been relatively neglected in mainstream tourism and migration studies except for second home development (Flognfeldt 2002; Müller 2002a; Haldrup 2004; Hall and Müller 2004; Müller and Hall 2004; Williams *et al.* 2004; Dijst *et al.* 2005).

There is a multitude of questions to be addressed concerning the relationships between migration and tourism, particularly relating to where the dividing line or zone can be drawn between the two phenomena (Bianchi 2000). This overlapping zone has tended to grow due to a process of convergence between work and leisure time activities (Clarke 2004), the increasingly changeable labour markets, and rapid ageing in the developed societies, combined with changing income streams, the development of transport and telecommunication facilities and globalization tendencies (Hall 2005).

Tourism exerts a strong influence on labour migration (Szivás and Riley 2002). In places where the local labour force is not yet inclined to be mobile, growing tourism may induce the external processes for workers (commuting, temporary migration). In those places where there are few people who could be, or wish to be, employed in the tourism industry or the wages on offer are not satisfactory to attract local workers, an external – and perhaps foreign – labour supply will be generated, sooner or later (Gössling and Schulz 2005). The flow of key personnel is particularly prevalent today to the developing countries, where much of the senior management in the hospitality industry originates from rich countries (King 1995).

In connection with production-orientated migration, Aitken and Hall (2000) pointed out those connections between these models of international migration and flows of technology and information. Beyond their corporeal presence, and varying amounts of money, immigrants bring intellectual capital with them, which manifests itself in the form of know-how, practical knowledge and marketing skills (Kaufmann *et al.* 2004).

Bianchi (2000) and Uriely (2001) approached the question from the angle of holiday workers (employees who work in tourism while they themselves are also tourists). This new type of worker is neither a tourist nor an employee in the classic sense. Their novelty is that the life style they have chosen is likely to constitute a temporary phase within their own life cycle. This new type of nomadism can be a metaphor for physical, intellectual and sexual freedom in which work goes hand in hand with a tourist's experiences. Above all, it has to be understood that the boundaries between tourism and work-orientated migration are not impenetrable. However, the connections between migration and tourism cannot be understood without appreciating the transformation of post-industrial societies. Our point of departure has to be the fact that connections between work and free time have become blurred in the post-industrial world. The social characteristics of holiday workers are no longer as clearly marked as they used to be – they include the new middle classes as well as the less educated, marginalized strata.

The geographical expansion of family and friendship ties (networks) has meant that international visits to friends and relatives (hereafter VFR) have become more commonplace (Lew and Wong 2002). The internationalization of working lives and other forms of migration have meant that families and friends have become increasingly geographically dispersed, but with VFR tourism becoming an important way to maintain contact with each other. The geographical redistribution of various ethnic minorities is also becoming an increasingly important motivating factor for VFR tourism (P. P. Tóth 1999; J. Tóth 2000). The presence of diasporas also plays an important part in tourism. This 'ethno-tourism' is a social factor, which refreshes and strengthens the relationships of a diaspora with the mother country (Duval 2004).

Several researchers working in the field of migration and tourism have noted that one of the more important forms of mobility is a unique form of commercial activity – that is, shopping (trading) tourism. Commercially motivated travel in border regions has increased drastically in the past decade (Timothy 1995, 2005; Michalkó and Timothy 2001). Trading tourism is probably a side effect of the transition period in post-state socialist societies. It is a short-lived phenomenon, which emerged temporarily and in changing forms on the boundaries between the one-time shortage economies and the functioning market economies, often constituting a strategy for survival and original capital accumulation on the part of the citizens of the post-socialist countries. These forms of trading or shopping-based mobility are constantly changing in response to institutional and economic changes. For example, Hungary's EU membership made it more difficult for people from surrounding non-EU countries to pay visits for reasons related to trading tourism (Hall 2000; Michalkó and Váradi 2004). It is not difficult to understand that this sort of border is slowly relocating to the south-east following EU enlargement.

The first part of the literature review yielded general insight into the tourism–migration nexus. The second part concentrates on connections between tourism and labour migration, the emerging VFR tourism and commercially motivated travel. These topics have considerable relevance for the two specific themes dealt with below: the seasonality of tourism flows and foreign property ownerships in Hungary.

Foreigners Resident in Hungary: Tourists and Migrants

Despite the fact that both international practice and Hungarian official statistical data collection only consider a person to be a tourist if they spend at least one night at the target location, it is not easy to delimit the concept of the tourist (Kovács and Probáld 1997). The most difficult point in clarifying the definitional questions regarding tourists and migrants is represented by foreigners who cross the border with tourist status, have no residence or work permit, and yet participate illegally within the economy (Szivás and Riley 2002). Their boundary crossing is legal, their stay as a tourist for the first three-month period did not break the rules, but their economic activity without a work permit, or owning a business, are illegal. A recent survey established that in 24.7 percent of Hungarian settlements at least one firm employed workers informally, including foreign illegal employees (Sik 2003).

The story of international tourism inflows to Hungary started earlier than large-scale international immigration in recent decades. The explanation is embedded in contemporary economic history. The medium-run effects of the first oil crises in 1973 caused a huge imbalance in the country's international financial position. One response to the ensuing fiscal crisis was the liberalization of access to, and encouragement of, international tourism to Hungary. International mass tourism flows started one and a half decades before the metamorphosis of the former regime (Rátz 2004; Szivás 2005) and the international tourism inflow was long independent of international immigration (Illés 2004). Since the political transition, there has been an average of 35 million foreign arrivals across the border each year, which is significant both when compared to the area or population of the country and in a European or even world-wide context (Baláz and Williams 2005). These annual absolute figures mean that transborder flows are approximately three and a half times the total population of Hungary (10.2 million inhabitants in the latest census, 2001) and about two hundred times higher than the annual volume of international migration inflow.

In investigating the connections zone between tourism and migration in Hungary, the primary sources of data are border crossing and accommodation statistics, as well as the databases on international migration. Initially, the number of foreigners arriving in Hungary, which is officially recorded at all border stations, is analysed (arrivals). The number of foreigners entering Hungary in 1996 was nearly 39.8 million and, in 2001, was around 30.7 million. The decrease in numbers was continuous until 1998 (28.8 million), but after that a slight increase was recorded. In the six years between 1996 and 2001, 75 percent of visitors arrived from the neighbouring countries (including Austria), followed by Germany (10.1%) and other European countries (12.9%), while the share of non-European arrivals was negligible. Concentrating on the surrounding countries, one finds that Austria is at the top of the list of arrivals (16.3%). This was followed by the citizens of Slovakia (13.5%), Romania (12.7%), Croatia (11.5%), Serbia-Montenegro (11.3%) and Ukraine (6.2%), while the lowest rate (2.9%) came from Slovenia. The citizens of the neighbouring countries are allowed, after a basic entrance procedure, to stay and move freely in Hungary for 90 days as tourists. All tourists need to contact the immigration office only if they wish to stay for longer than three months.

Before 1988, international migration to Hungary was very limited. The annual emigration fluctuated between 3–4,000 people after the 1956 revolution. Meanwhile, annual immigration was 1–2,000 in the same time period. The international migration balance was significantly negative and its long-run multiplier effect on the Hungarian population loss was even higher due to the young age structure of the net international migrants (Illés and Hablicsek 1997). A new epoch started after the fall of the Berlin Wall. The former sending country became a receiving and transit country. Between 1988 and 1992, 20–40,000 people immigrated and 5–15,000 emigrants moved away annually. From 1993 until 1997 the international migration flows decreased to an average of 15,000 immigrants and 3,000 emigrants annually. A relatively new period started in 1998 when, related to closer relationships during the accession procedure to the EU, Hungary became a popular destination among 'second-round country' citizens. Parallel with this process, the number of citizens of the EU living in Hungary as immigrants increased (Illés 2004). The continuation of old waves, together with the development of new ones, has resulted in an annual average of 20,000 immigrants and 2,000 emigrants, so that the migration balance has been increasing considerably from 1998 until recent years.

From 1996 until 2001 the majority of the 103,000 immigrants (who stayed more than one year in Hungary) arrived from Romania (39.6%), the Ukraine (11.5%), Serbia-Montenegro (8.2%), China (7.1%), Germany (4.1%), Slovakia (3.0%) and the USA (2.6%). The citizens of Russia accounted for 2.3 percent, followed by Vietnam with 1.8 percent, while neighbouring Croatia (1.0%) and Austria (0.8%) were relatively unimportant. There were also immigrants from France (1.1%), the UK (1.0%) and the Netherlands (0.6%). The largest increases are observed in the case of Romania and Ukraine; in the former, the yearly number of immigrants has tripled since 1996, in the latter case it has doubled in the same period. Chinese immigration has been decreasing continuously since 1996, and a similar process is observable in the case of the Vietnamese since 1998.

One can conclude that the pattern of time series for tourist and migration flows was very similar. New international tourism flows, caused by mainly political factors, started earlier compared to international migration inflows, but at the start of the political, economic and social transition, there were strong increases in both processes. The peaks were in the early 1990s, followed by a slight decrease. Both phenomena have revived since the end of the 1990s, with marked increases in volumes.

Returning to arrivals, and taking into account their use of commercial accommodation, only 8.8 percent of foreigners arriving in Hungary took advantage of commercial accommodation from 1996 to 2001. This extremely low proportion looks unfavourably even smaller if one concentrates only on visitors from the surrounding countries. Most striking is the fact that only 0.7 percent of all the Slovakian citizens entering Hungary make use of commercial accommodation and, even the highest rate among the neighbouring countries, which is for Austrians, barely exceeds 4 percent. Altogether it can be emphasized that only 2.0 percent of visitors from the surrounding countries use commercial accommodation. This means that although citizens of the neighbouring countries do arrive in Hungary in large numbers, this is not accompanied by a similar rate of touristic activity in the classic sense. If the countries that are market leaders in terms of using Hungarian commercial accommodation (countries which sent at least 100,000 tourist/overnight visitors to this country in 2001) are examined, the picture is reversed. The UK (58.2%), USA (46.0%), Netherlands (46.3%), France (41.6%) and Italy (37.9%) show the highest relative levels of demand for commercial accommodation compared to the total number of arrivals from countries. The situation is also quite favourable in the case of Germany (25.9%) and Poland (18.2%), which have intermediate positions. The market leader countries make up 33 percent of the total arrivals but they represent 63 percent of the total users of commercial accommodation. In the following sub-section, the seasonality of arrivals and of those using commercial accommodation facilities (tourists) are considered, but there is great opportunity to draw further links between tourism and migration.

The monthly distribution of arrivals and those using commercial accommodation is revealing. The seasonal nature of mass tourism in Hungary has always been influenced, to a considerable extent, by the holiday opportunities at Lake Balaton in the summer months, particularly in August, and by the holiday habits of the arrivals (Figure 1). In the case of EU-15 visitors (except for Austria) this has meant that, while in January only 5 percent of the total of arrivals was registered at the border stations, in August this proportion was 17 percent, with the share of tourists moving in synchrony with this monthly distribution, with only minor discrepancies. The EU diagram shows a profile of typical touristic behaviour. The peculiarity of Slovakian international tourism to Hungary is that the share of overnight visitors exceeded 25 percent in the summer peak month. The 8-percentage point discrepancy between arrivals and tourists in August was greatest amongst the countries studied. The touristic activity of the majority of the surrounding countries (with the exception of Slovakia) is atypical. The relative evenness of monthly distributions, in other words, narrows differences between the lowest and highest monthly arrivals and users of commercial accommodation, allowing one to conclude that these people are not participating in

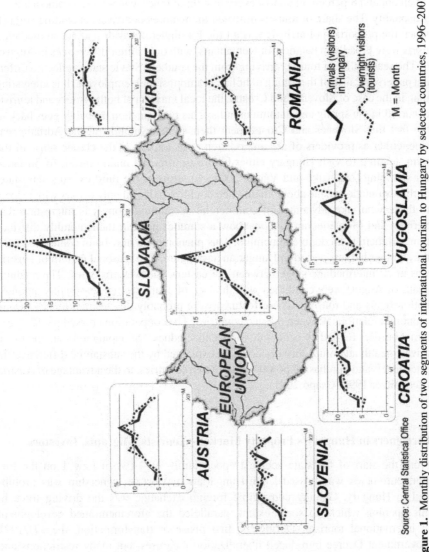

Figure 1. Monthly distribution of two segments of international tourism to Hungary by selected countries, 1996–2001

Source: Central Statistical Office

traditional forms of free-time activity (holiday-making, sightseeing tours) but contribute to the continuance of shopping tourism, VFR and fuelling illegal employment (Wallace *et al.* 1996). In the case of Ukrainians, the proportion of arrivals is between 7 percent and 8 percent in almost every month; in other words there is practically no seasonality. The share of tourists mirrored the features of arrivals excluding August, when the proportion of arrivals was a little bit higher. Arrivals and accommodation users were broadly in balance for Romanians, with only minor differences in August.

The seasonality of tourists arriving from the southern Slavic states reflects a different pattern because of the timing of holidays amongst their employers. It is interesting that, in the case of Slovenia and Croatia, the local maxima of both visitors and tourists occurred in the spring and autumn months. This phenomenon probably goes back to the fact that Slovenes and Croats spent their summer months at the Adriatic seaside, either as providers of accommodation or as tourists in the classic sense of the term, tending to visit Hungary either before or after the main season, for instance for shopping (Michalkó and Váradi 2004). In terms of the third ex-Yugoslav state, Serbia-Montenegro, the above-mentioned double maximum only occurs with respect to those who take advantage of commercial accommodation. It is interesting that Serbian and Montenegran visitors show a summer peak in their monthly distribution and there is no double maximum. This phenomenon may be in connection with the summer harvest period in Hungarian agriculture. The seasonal pattern of Austria was at an intermediate stage between the eastern and western types. The medium peaks of August were combined with the lack of characteristic seasonality amongst both arrivals and tourists. These features were probably due to traditionally strong economic relations between the two countries. The cooperation crossed the EU's external borders fuelled by economic interconnectedness. Shopping tourism and using private health and other services could be explained by the substantial differences in price levels and purchasing power between two countries, to the advantage of Austria (Rechnitzer 1999; Csapó 2001).

Foreigners in Hungary's Property Market – Tourists, Migrants, Investors

From the start of the state socialist epoch untill 1974 (when Law 1 on the foreign currencies was passed), non-Hungarian real estate ownership was prohibited in Hungary. Gaining convertible foreign exchange was the driving force in this opening which, to some extent, paralleled the aforementioned development of international tourism. During the first phase of transformation, the 171/1991 Government Decree introduced liberalization measures, but many restrictions and time-consuming bureaucratic measures remained in force. Foreign citizens did not like this fluid situation. A broad liberalization took place in 1996 and this measure induced growing foreign interest in the Hungarian real estate market (Berényi *et al.* 2003).

From 1998 onwards, during the accession negotiations to the EU, the acquisition of real estate by non-Hungarian citizens, considered as the flows of capital (direct foreign investment), were not completely free. During each of the earlier enlargements of the EU, similar sets of issues were discussed amongst the current member states and the potential entrants (Coles and Hall 2005). One of the key themes was the free movement of people. However, a strong interrelationship developed between the free movement of capital and free movement of people, as two principles. The EU-15 insisted on the right of individual member states to impose restrictions on international migration from the new member states, and a 2+3+2 years derogation period was introduced as a potential barrier to labour migration (Lukács 2002); initially, only the UK, Ireland and Sweden did not insist on imposing these restrictions. As a direct consequence of this, the responsible Hungarian body postponed the complete liberalization of the domestic property market. Five years after the accession (1 May 2009), the market conditions for real estate will be revised in view of progress in relation to the free movement of people.

According to current regulations (7/1996 Government Decree), property purchases by foreigners are subject to the approval of the home county (19 territorial units of Hungary in at NUTS 3 level) or capital city public authority administration. The aim of this section of the paper is to give a national-scale picture of the type of properties purchased by foreigners and the spatial distribution of their new owners, according to nationality. The quality of the data available is relatively poor, being partial and inconsistent, until 2001, which means that it is not possible to carry out a longitudinal national-level analysis. This is due to the fact that, until 2001, the public administration offices of counties and capital were not obliged to create a formally unified database; thus every office collected and summarized the data regarding property purchases by foreigners as they deemed most appropriate and taking into account their IT resources. This means that a coherent national database was available only for 2001 and 2002.

In 2001, 6,266 properties were purchased by foreigners in Hungary and, in 2002, this figure dropped to 4,973. The most sought-after areas were the capital, Budapest, and the main targets of foreign property purchases were towns and villages in Somogy, Zala, Győr-Moson-Sopron, Vas and Veszprém counties (in diminishing order), located in Transdanubia, the western part of the country (Figure 2). Compared to the estimates of the second half of the 1990s (Berényi et al. 2003), most counties show a decrease. One of the exceptions is Budapest. The increase in the capital may be due to a one-off and passing reaction to the earlier hostile attitude to foreign buyers on behalf of the local office, and reflects the changes that have taken place since 2002. It is remarkable that in the case of the counties which remain the least popular (Nógrád and Szabolcs-Szatmár-Bereg counties) a slight growth was experienced contrary to the national trend. Nógrád county is situated in the northern part of Hungary with a depressed industrial base (rustbelt county) and high population loss caused by natural decrease and out-migration. Szabolcs-Szatmár-Bereg borders

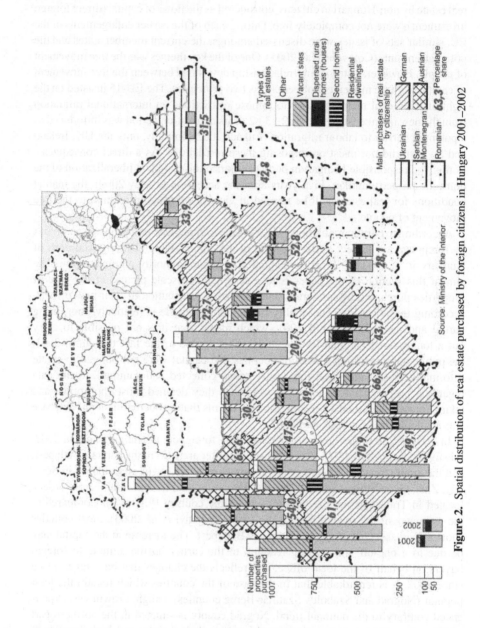

Figure 2. Spatial distribution of real estate purchased by foreign citizens in Hungary 2001–2002

Ukraine in the north-east part of Hungary, and has faced a number of economic crises combined with a high unemployment rate but a slight population loss caused by high fertility.

On the national level, the majority of the properties purchased in 2001–2002 were residential dwellings (flats and houses, 63%) and vacant sites (22%), while the rates of second homes (holiday and weekend houses, 5%) and of dispersed rural houses (cottages 3%) were negligible. The purchase of holiday and weekend houses exceeded the national average in Somogy and Veszprém counties (at the shore of Lake Balaton), Fejér county (on the shore of Lake Velencei), Bács-Kiskun and Pest counties (at the Great Hungarian Plane) and Baranya county near the Croatian border. The appearance of demand for dispersed rural houses (cottages) in Bács-Kiskun (35%), Csongrád (27%) and Pest (10%) counties goes back to the geographical settlement characteristics of the Great Hungarian Plane (Kovács 2002). Naturally, based on macro data, it is difficult to know precisely whether the purchase was fuelled by recreational, immigration or business motives (Flognfeldt 2002). Nevertheless, the foreign purchase could represent almost all forms of the mobility-motility (Kaufmann et al. 2004) spectrum. It is possible that the low rate of summer holiday homes and weekend houses can be retraced to the possibility that most of these were sold off in the previous years. Moreover, the purchases of vacant sites could have been motivated by the mixture of a weak supply of residential buildings, hot investment and future residential intentions. The spatial distribution of sites echoed the most popular areas of the second half of the 1990s: the border regions of Austria (Zala, Györ-Moson-Sopron and Vas counties), the counties of Lake Balaton (Somogy, Veszprém) and Pest county surrounding the capital. It may be anticipated that, after the saturation of the market segment of residential dwellings, the second phase of the foreign purchases, focused on vacant sites, has started since the millennium in the prosperous part of Hungary. The remaining countryside was underdeveloped in the first phase, when the supply of purchasable residential dwellings and dispersed, vacant rural houses was not exhausted.

The distribution according to the nationality of purchasers for the two years under examination shows that the majority of foreign-owned property (42%) belongs to Germans, while further significant participants are Austrians (20%), Romanians (8%) and Dutch people (7%). If the national groups, which dominate the various counties of Hungary, are examined, some interesting results arise. Germans represent the majority of foreign property owners in 12 counties and in Budapest. In Somogy county their rate among foreign citizens is 70.9 percent, which means the highest rate in contrast to Budapest, where Germans – although also the leading buyers – only accounted for 20.7 percent of foreign owners. Austrians dominate in Györ-Moson-Sopron and Vas counties in the common borderland. In the former they represent 63.6 percent, in the latter, 54.0 percent. Not surprisingly, Romanians are in a majority in two counties (Hajdú-Bihar, Békés) in the south-eastern part of Hungary. Ukrainians dominate in Szabolcs-Szatmár-Bereg county (31.5%) and citizens of Serbia-Montenegro in

Csongrád county (28.1%). These indicators allow one to conclude that Germans can be considered potential buyers in the whole of the country, and do not display particular territorial preferences (except for Tolna and Baranya counties, which contain a considerable ethnic German minority). One of the factors explaining the dominance of German purchasers, and their spatial distribution, is likely to be the presence of other German-origin buyers in Hungary. As an example of the role of ethnic networks, they recruited new investors from their circle of friends and relatives due to their positive experiences of property ownership in Hungary. A similar trend also seemed to be occurring in Sweden (Müller 2002b: 178), although this is derived from a substantially different set of circumstances. Other citizens, mainly those from the surrounding countries, prefer to buy in the counties near the border with their own country, which is probably motivated by access considerations, combined with different attractions. Moreover, the possibility of circulation between the countries would play an important role.

It is interesting that Romanian citizens dominate in Pest county, surrounding the capital, relatively far from the Hungarian–Romanian boundary. This can be explained in terms of commuting to Budapest, where they are employed dominantly. Another motivational factor is the low prices of real estate in rural areas. Additional explanatory factors include the network of mainly ethnic Hungarians, who immigrated earlier to this county (Gödri and Tóth 2005) and provided reliable information for the newcomers. Ethnic networks could play an important role in most of the neighbouring countries, where c. 3.5 million ethnic Hungarians live (Kocsis and Kocsis-Hódosi 1995). Naturally, if foreign purchasers find a desirable environment near the border, they are unlikely to add to their expenses by travelling to more distant areas within Hungary. These facts show the strong distance dependency which characterizes purchases by foreigners. There is one characteristic exception, namely Slovakia. Despite the long common boundary and the substantial ethnic Hungarian community, there is no Hungarian county where Slovakian citizens are the dominant buyers. (In the previous section, it was noted that the seasonality of Slovakian arrivals and tourists were very characteristic but the extent was limited.) The level of international immigration to Hungary is very low compared with Romania, Ukraine and Serbia-Montenegro. These facts could reflect the influence of mobility experiences upon foreign property purchases. The distance dependency is high (for similar findings, see Müller 2002b), but the purchasing power and ethnic network of buyers – together with the uneven economic, social spaces in the receiving country – could modify the quasi-linear relationship.

Conclusion and Discussion

Before the mid-1970s both international tourism and migration were limited in Hungary; tourist trips abroad were the main channel of emigration from the country. This was a one-way connection between two phenomena. The tourist status was transformed into a migrant status in the receiving country and there was little or no chance that the emigrants would return to Hungary as tourists. This phenomenon borrowed a unique element of the connection between tourism and migration and developed the potential reserve of international VFR tourism and return migration into Hungary. The international mass tourism inflows started one and a half decades before the metamorphosis of the former era, and the international migratory upheavals in Europe. During the change of political regime, as a consequence of liberalization measures affecting the inflow of foreigners and outflow of Hungarians, international mobility multiplied. Trade-related tourism emerged temporarily on the boundaries between shortage economies and market economies, in parallel with huge refugee and migration flows. Shopping tourism took place in informal markets, and the illegal employment of persons entering the country and staying as tourists were everyday phenomena. Some of the ethnic Hungarians living in neighbouring countries showed intentions of settling in Hungary. Their impressions, during VFR in the motherland (statistically registered as arrivals), triggered resettlement. Hungary also attracted international tourists and migrants from Europe and outside of Europe, especially former Hungarian emigrants who were potential buyers of domestic real estate. The time series trends of tourist and migration processes were very similar after 1988. Strong increases happened in both at the start of the transition. The peaks were in the early 1990s, followed by a small decrease. Both processes have revived since the end of the1990s and increases in volumes have been measured. Substitution was the core of the relationship between the two phenomena before 1988. After that the complementary character became stronger, with a slight multiplication effect. The different quality of relationship underlined the interconnectedness of two forms of mobility studied.

Both tourism and migration were also expansive processes in numbers, forms and terms in the last decades. It was increasingly difficult to distinguish one from another, applying traditional terminology when trying to explore the emerging new phenomena within the tourism migration continuum. Research on the seasonality of tourism, in addition to foreign property purchase, was conducted in the blurred zone between international tourism and migration to Hungary. The composition of the tourism and migration flows in terms of the country of origin, and the vast discrepancy between the number of tourists and the amount of money spent, reflected the role of ethnicity. In other words, a significant portion of tourists was not arriving to Hungary in order to spend money and take advantage of commercial accommodation but to earn money and to stay with friends and relatives. Another proof of the presence of ethnic factors is related to the difference among seasonal patterns of arrivals and overnight visitors in the case of Romania, Ukraine and Serbia-Montenegro, where ethnic Hungarians lived in large numbers. On the one hand, a discrepancy appeared in the relative evenness of arrivals, and on the other hand the atypical pattern of touristic activity (without a peak season) was linked to the citizens of the countries mentioned above.

Turning to the second set of research results, two-thirds of the properties purchased by foreigners were flats and houses, at the national level. One-fifth were vacant sites while the rates of second homes and dispersed rural house purchases was below 10 percent. The most popular areas were the capital, Budapest, and Somogy, Zala, Györ-Moson-Sopron, Vas and Veszprém counties in Transdanubia, the western part of the country. Nógrád and Szabolcs-Szatmár-Bereg counties, situated in north and eastern Hungary, were the least popular. Germans represented the majority of foreign property owners. The extent of German investors in Hungary was far less than it had been earlier in the countries of southern Europe (Friedrich and Kaiser 2001) but more than, for instance, in Sweden (Müller 2002a). This intermediate position reflected the fact that Hungary was not a peripheral destination within the German system of direct private investment abroad. They could be considered as potential buyers in the whole of the country without particular territorial preferences. Other citizens, mainly those from the surrounding countries, prefer to buy in the counties near the border. This fact, combined with the diminishing German share in the east, showed that the distance dependency was high, but financial, ethnic and spatial forces modified the quasi-linear relationship.

In this paper it has only been possible to present a partial picture of the relationships between migration and tourism. Williams and Hall (2000b), Hall and Williams (2002), Müller and Hall (2004) and Coles and Hall (2005) have all identified a number of important interdisciplinary themes, which this paper has only begun to address. Three overlapping sets of issues could be fruitful for further research in the Hungarian context. The first covers the interrelationship between tourism and labour migration at the frontier of legality and illegality. Tourism and return migration by different birth and emigration cohorts should be the second main focus of future investigation. The symbiotic relationship between tourism and retirement migration represents the third major research direction for the near future in the context of the rapidly ageing Hungarian population. Given its macro-level approach, the present study has tried to take account of officially registered events and processes. Another way to complete our knowledge of the tourism–migration interrelationship is the adoption of the methods and techniques of multi-level analysis. Population registers provide a unique opportunity for creating a methodologically sound sample framework for the surveys and indepth interviews.

Acknowledgement

Thanks are expressed to the editors and three anonymous referees for their helpful comments on earlier draft of this paper. Any remaining errors are entirely the responsibility of the authors.

References

Aitken, C. & Hall, M. C. (2000) Migrant and international skills and their relevance to the tourism industry: fact and fiction in the New Zealand context, *Tourism Geographies*, 2(1), pp. 66–86.

Baláz, V. & Williams, A. M. (2005) International tourism as a bricolage: an analysis of Central Europe on the brink of European Union membership, *International Journal of Tourism Research*, 7(2), pp. 79–93.

Bell, M. & Ward, G. (2000) Comparing temporary mobility with permanent migration, *Tourism Geographies*, 2(1), pp. 87–107.

Berényi, I., Illés, S. & Michalkó, G. (2003) A turizmus és a migráció kapcsolatrendszere [Systems of tourism and migration], *Tér és Társadalom*, 17(1), pp. 51–65.

Bianchi, R. V. (2000) Migrant tourist-workers: Exploring the 'contact zones' of post-industrial tourism, *Current Issues in Tourism*, 3(2), pp. 107–137.

Bora, Gy. & Korompai, A. (2001) *A Természeti Erőforrások Gazdaságtana és Földrajza [Economy and Geography of Natural Resources]* (Budapest: Aula Kiadó).

Borbély, A. & Lukács, É. (2001) Munkavállalás és vállalkozás az Európai Unióban [Work and employment in the European Union], in: É. Lukács & M. Király (Eds) *Migráció és Európai Unió [Migration and European Union]*, pp. 169–191 (Budapest: Szociális és Családügyi Minisztérium).

Böröcz, J. (1996) *Leisure Migration. A Sociological Study on Migration* (Oxford: Pergamon).

Clarke, N. (2004) Mobility, fixity, agency: Australia's Working Holiday Programme, *Population, Space and Place*, 10(3), pp. 411–420.

Coles, T. & Hall, D. (2005) Tourism and European Union enlargement. Plus ca change?, *International Journal of Tourism Research*, 7(2), pp. 51–61.

Coles, T. & Timothy, D. J. (2004) 'My field is the World.' Conceptualising diasporas, travel and tourism, in: T. Coles & D. J. Timothy (Eds) *Tourism, Diasporas and Space*, pp. 1–29 (London: Routledge).

Csapó, T. (2001) A falvak helyzete Vas megyében [The state of villages in Vas county], *Vasi Szemle*, 55(3), pp. 283–296.

Csordás, L. (1999) Second homes in Hungary, in: A. Duró (Ed.) *Spatial Research in Support of the European Integration. Proceedings of the 11th Polish–Hungarian Geographical Seminar*, pp. 145–160 (Pécs: HAS Centre of Regional Study).

Dijst, M., Lanzendorf, M., Barendregt, A. & Smit, L. (2005) Second homes in Germany and the Netherlands: ownership and travel impact explained, *Tijdschrift voor Economische en Sociale Geografie*, 96(2), pp. 139–152.

Dingsdale, A. (1986) Ideology and leisure under socialism: the geography of second homes in Hungary, *Leisure Studies*, 5(1), pp. 35–55.

Dövényi, Z. (1997) Adalékok a Magyarországon élő idegenek területi megoszlásához [Mosaic on spatial distribution of foreigners in Hungary], in: E. Sik & J. Tóth (Eds) *Migráció és Politika [Migration and Politics]*, pp. 97–105 (Budapest: MTA Politikai Tudományok Intézete).

Duval, D. T. (2004) When hosts become guests: return visits and diasporic identities in a Commonwealth Eastern Caribbean Community, *Current Issues in Tourism*, 6(4), pp. 267–308.

Flognfeldt, T. (2002) Second-home ownership. A sustainable semi-migration, in: C. M. Hall & A. M. Williams (Eds) *Tourism and Migration. New Relationships between Production and Consumption*, pp. 187–203 (Dordrecht: Kluwer).

Friedrich, K. & Kaiser, C. (2001) Rentnersiedlungen auf Mallorca? Möglichkeiten und Grenzen der Übertragbarkeit des nordamerikanischen Konzeptes auf den "Europäischen Sunbelt", *Europa Regional*, 9(4), pp. 204–211.

Gagyi, J. & Oláh, S. (1998) Vendégmunkások utazási formái Maros megyéből Magyarországra [Travel forms of migrant workers from Maros county, Romania, to Hungary], in: E. Sik & J. Tóth (Eds) *Idegenek Magyarországon [Foreigners in Hungary]*, pp. 49–56 (Budapest: MTA Politikai Tudományok Intézete).

Gödri, I. & Tóth, P. P. (2005) *Bevándorlás és Beilleszkedés [Immigration and Integration]* (Budapest: KSH Népességtudományi Kutatóintézet).

Gössling, S. & Schulz, U. (2005) Tourism-related migration in Zanzibar, Tanzania, *Tourism Geographies*, 7(1), pp. 43–62.

Hajdú, J. & Lukács, É. (2001) Népességmozgások és szociális védelem az Európai Unióban [Population movement and social protection in the European Union], in: É. Lukács & M. Király (Eds) *Migráció és Európai Unió* [*Migration and European Union*], pp. 271–306 (Budapest: Szociális és Családügyi Minisztérium).

Haldrup, M. (2004) Laid-back mobilities: second-home holidays in time and space, *Tourism Geographies*, 6(4), pp. 434–454.

Hall, C. M. (2005) *Tourism: Rethinking the Social Science of Mobility* (Harlow: Prentice-Hall).

Hall, C. M. & Müller, D. K. (2004) Introduction: second homes, curse or blessing? Revisted, in: C. M. Hall & D. K. Müller (Eds) *Tourism, Mobility and Second Homes. Between Elite Landscape and Common Ground*, pp. 15–32 (Clevedon: Channel View Publications).

Hall, C. M. & Williams A. M. (2002) Conclusion: tourism–migration relationships, in: C. M. Hall & A. M. Williams (Eds) *Tourism and Migration. New Relationships between Production and Consumption*, pp. 277–289 (Dordrecht: Kluwer).

Hall, D. (2000) Sustainable tourism development and transformation in Central and Eastern Europe, *Journal of Sustainable Tourism*, 8(6), pp. 441–457.

Illés, S. (2000) *Belföldi Vándormozgalom a XX. Század Utolsó Évtizedeiben* [*Internal Migration in Hungary in the Late Decades of Twentieth Century*] (Budapest: KSH Népességtudományi Kutatóintézet).

Illés, S. (2004). *Foreigners in Hungary: Migration from the European Union*. Working Papers on Population, Family and Welfare 5 (Budapest: HCSO Demographic Research Institute).

Illés, S. & Hablicsek, L. (1997) A külsö vándorlások tovagyürüzö hatásai [Multiplication effects of international migration], in: E. Sik & J. Tóth (Eds) *Migráció és Politika* [*Migration and Politics*], pp. 89–96 (Budapest: MTA PTI).

Kasper, M. (2001) Ausverkauf Ungarns? Eine Angebotsananalyse der Freizeitwohnsitze für den deutschsprachigen Raum, *Europa Regional*, 9(2), pp. 70–77.

Kaufmann, V., Bergman, M. & Joye, D. (2004) Motility: mobility as a capital, *International Journal of Urban and Regional Research*, 28(4), pp. 745–756.

King, R. (1995) Tourism, labour and international migration, in: A. Montanari & A. M. Williams (Eds) *European Tourism. Regions, Spaces and Restructuring*, pp. 177–190 (Chichester: Wiley).

Kocsis, K. & Kocsis-Hódosi, E. (1995) *Hungarian Minorities in the Carpathian Basin. A Study in Ethnic Geography* (Toronto-Buffalo: Matthias Corvinus Publishing).

Kovács, Cs. & Probáld, Á. (1997) Turizmus Magyarországon 1996. [Tourism in Hungary, 1996] *Turizmus Bulletin*, 1(1), pp. 22–25.

Kovács, Z. (2002) *Népesség- és Településföldrajz* [*Population and Settlement Geography*] (Budapest: ELTE Eötvös Kiadó).

Krakover, S. & Karplus, Y. (2002) Potential immigrants. The interface between tourism and immigration in Israel, in: M. C. Hall & A. M. Williams (Eds) *Tourism and Migration: New Relationships Between Production and Consumption*, pp. 103–118 (Dordrecht: Kluwer).

Lew, A. & Wong, A. (2002) Tourism and Chinese diaspora, in: M. C. Hall & A. M. Williams (Eds) *Tourism and Migration: New Relationships Between Production and Consumption*, pp. 205–220 (Dordrecht: Kluwer).

Longino, C. F. & Marshall, V. W. (1990) North American research in seasonal elderly migration, *Ageing and Society*, 10(2), pp. 229–236.

Lukács, É. (2002) Magyarország európai uniós csatlakozásával összefüggö kérdések [Questions on Hungarian accession to European Union], in: Gy. Berke, T. Gyulavári & Gy. Kiss (Eds) *Külföldiek Foglalkoztatása Magyarországon* [*Employment of Foreigners in Hungary*], pp.153–169 (Budapest: KJK-Kerszöv Kiadó).

McKercher, B. & Lew, A. A. (2004) Tourist flows and the spatial distribution of tourists, in: A.A. Lew, C. M. Hall & A. M. Williams (Eds) *A Companion to Tourism*, pp. 36–48 (Oxford: Blackwell).

Melegh, A., Kondratina, E., Salmenhaare, P., Hablicsek, L. & Hegyesi, A. (2004) *Globalisation, Ethnicity and Migration. The Comparison of Finland, Hungary and Russia.* Working Papers on Population, Family and Welfare 7 (Budapest: HCSO Demographic Research Institute).

Michalkó, G. (2002) The future of shopping tourism on the periphery of a Europe without borders, in: A. Montanari (Ed.) *Human Mobility in a Borderless World,* pp. 143–154 (Roma: Societá Geografica Italiana).

Michalkó, G. & Rátz, T. (2003) A sátorverésen túl. A turizmustudomány magyarországi állapotairól [Beyond the start. The state of art of tourism study in Hungary], *Magyar Tudomány,* 48(6), pp. 447–457.

Michalkó, G. & Timothy, D. J. (2001) Cross-border shopping in Hungary: causes and effects, *Visions in Leisure and Business,* 20(1), pp. 4–22.

Michalkó, G. & Váradi, Zs. (2004) Croatian shopping tourism in Hungary: Case study of Barcs, *Turizam,* 6(4), pp. 351–359.

Müller, D. K. (2002a) Reinventing the countryside: German second-home owners in southern Sweden, *Current Issues in Tourism,* 5(5), pp. 426–446.

Müller, D. K. (2002b) German second home development in Sweden in: C. M. Hall & A. M. Williams (Eds) *Tourism and Migration. New Relationships between Production and Consumption,* pp. 169–185 (Dordrecht: Kluwer).

Müller, D. K. & Hall, C. M. (2004) The future of second home tourism, in: C. M. Hall & D. K. Müller (Eds) *Tourism, Mobility and Second Homes. Between Elite Landscape and Common Ground,* pp. 273–278 (Clevedon: Channel View Publications).

Nemes Nagy, J. (1998) *A Tér a Társadalomkutatásban. Bevezetés a Regionális Tudományba [Space in Social Studies. Introduction to Regional Science],* (Budapest: Hilscher Rezsö Szociálpolitikai Egyesület).

Niedomysl, T. (2005) Tourism and interregional migration in Sweden. An explorative approach, *Population, Space and Place,* 11(2), pp. 187–204.

O'Reilly, K. (1995) A new trend in European migration: a contemporary British migration to Fuengirola, Costa del Sol, *Geographical Viewpoint,* 23(1), pp. 25–36.

O'Reilly, K. (2003) When is a tourist? The articulation of tourism and migration in Spain's Costa del Sol, *Tourist Studies,* 3(3), pp. 301–317.

Rátz, T. (2004) *European Tourism,* (Székesfehérvár: János Kodolányi University College).

Rechnitzer, J. (1999) Határ menti együttmüködések Európában és Magyarországon [Transborder cooperations in Europe and Hungary], in: J. Rechnitzer & M. Nárai (Eds) *Elválaszt és Összeköt – a Határ [Divide and Link – the Border],* pp. 9–72 (Pécs-Györ: MTA RKK).

Rodríguez, V. (2001) Tourism as a recruiting post for retirees, *Tourism Geographies,* 3(1), pp. 52–63.

Sik, E. (1998) Külföldiek Magyarországon (1995–1997) [Foreigners in Hungary, 1995–1997], in: E. Sik & J. Tóth (Eds) *Idegenek Magyarországon [Foreigners in Hungary],* pp. 9–14 (Budapest: MTA Politikai Tudományok Intézete).

Sik, E. (2003) Piacok és feketemunka [Market places and irregular work], *Önkormányzati Tájékoztató,* 13(5), pp. 19–26.

Szivás, E. (2005) European Union accession: passport to development for the Hungarian tourism industry? *International Journal of Tourism Research,* 7(2), pp. 95–107.

Szivás, E. & Riley, M. (2002) Labour mobility and tourism in the post 1989 transition in Hungary, in: C. M. Hall & A. M. Williams (Eds) *Tourism and Migration. New Relationships between Production and Consumption,* pp. 53–72 (Dordrecht: Kluwer).

Timothy, D. J. (1995) Political boundaries and tourism: borders as tourist attractions, *Tourism Management,* 16(7), pp. 525–532.

Timothy, D. J. (2005) *Shopping Tourism, Retailing and Leisure* (Clevedon: Channel View Publications).

Tóth, J. (2000) Az elmúlt évtized diaszpórapolitikája, in: E. Sik & J. Tóth (Eds) *Diskurzusok a Vándorlásról* [*Discourses on Migration*], pp. 218–251 (Budapest: MTA PTI Nemzetközi Migrációs és Menekültügyi Központ).

Tóth, P. P. (1999) *Szórványban* [*Living in Diasporas*] (Budapest: Püski Könyvkiadó).

Truly, D. (2002) International retirement migration and tourism along the Lake Chapala Riviera: developing a matrix of retirement migration behaviour, *Tourism Geographies*, 4(3), pp. 261–281.

Uriely, N. (2001) 'Travelling workers' and 'working tourists': variations across the interaction between work and tourism, *International Journal of Tourism Research*, 3(1), pp. 1–8.

Wallace, C., Chmouliar, O. & Sidorenko, E. (1996) The eastern frontier of western Europe: mobility in the buffer zone, *New Community*, 22(2), pp. 259–286.

Warnes, T. (1994) Permanent and seasonal international retirement migration: the prospects for Europe, *Nederlandse Geografische Studies*, 173(1), pp. 69–79.

Williams, A. M. & Hall, M. C. (2000a) Guest editorial: tourism and migration, *Tourism Geographies*, 2(1), pp. 2–4.

Williams, A. M. & Hall, M. C. (2000b) Tourism and migration: new relationships between production and consumption, *Tourism Geographies*, 2(1), pp. 5–27.

Williams, A. M. & Hall, M. C. (2002) Tourism, migration, circulation and mobility: the contingencies of time and place, in: C. M. Hall & A. M. Williams (Eds) *Tourism and Migration. New Relationships between Production and Consumption*, pp. 1–52 (Dordrecht: Kluwer).

Williams, A. M., King, R. & Warnes, T. (2004) British second homes in southern Europe: shifting nodes in the scapes and flows of migration and tourism, in: C. M. Hall & D. K. Müller (Eds) *Tourism, Mobility and Second Homes. Between Elite Landscape and Common Ground*, pp. 97–112 (Clevedon: Channel View Publications).

Williams, A. M., King, R., Warnes, T. & Patterson, G. (2000) Tourism and international retirement migration: new forms of an old relationship in southern Europe, *Tourism Geographies*, 2(1), pp. 28–49.

From 'Bricklaying' to *'Bricolage'*: Transition and Tourism Development in Central and Eastern Europe

DEREK HALL

ABSTRACT   *This paper aims briefly to review literature on tourism development in Central and Eastern Europe, to highlight major contemporary issues and to indicate future research needs and suggest a research agenda. It does this by addressing the EU enlargement context, conceptions and applications of 'transition', the 'mobility turn' and issues of identity within post-communist processes. It concludes with a proposed research agenda that emphasizes the need to interrogate a number of issues flowing from the policy neglect of tourism within the institutions of the EU.*

Introduction

This paper briefly reviews some of the literature on tourism development in Central and Eastern Europe (CEE), highlights major contemporary issues, indicates future research needs and suggests a research agenda. The nature of, and preparations for the European Union (EU) enlargements of 2004 and 2007, incorporating ten former communist states of CEE and two major Mediterranean island states, have important implications for the structural and spatial pattern of European tourism development. Indeed, from Gosar's (2005) notion of trans-border 'bricklaying' of tourism resources to Baláž and Williams' (2005) *'bricolage'* of international mobility, conceptions of CEE 'transition' and tourism's mutual relationship with it, have, of necessity, been set within the context of the inexorable progression of EU enlargement processes.

In this review, the notion of 'bricklaying' is understood to represent processes of gradual development through consolidation, integration and mutual confidence building, based upon systematically laid solid foundations. It is a term that has been employed in a wide range of contexts to indicate gradual, prudent but solid progress.

The more recent use of the term *'bricolage'* is meant to convey a notion of diverse, fragmented and perhaps confused – or at least not easily understood – patterns of activity. The two terms might even be thought of as representing, respectively, 'modern' and 'post-modern' states of reality.

The 2004/2007 accession states (Table 1) included both relatively long-established tourism destinations (such as Cyprus, Bulgaria and Malta) and (re-)emergent ones (such as Slovenia and the Baltic states). The World Tourism Organization (WTO 2004) predicted that EU enlargement would foster the conditions for a 'more complete and coherent' European tourism industry, albeit predicated on the implementation of a European Constitution that would afford appropriate prominence to the role of tourism (Anastasiadou 2006). As Europe has been losing its market share as the world's leading receiving region, development of unique and innovative products in the accession countries may be crucial for the future health of European tourism (Smith and Hall 2006b).

The accession states' tourism resources include:

- Mediterranean and Black Sea destinations primarily identified with coastal mass tourism, facing issues of sustainability and re-imaging (Bachvarov 1997, 1999; Light and Dumbrâveanu 1999; Bunja 2003; Konečnik 2004, 2006);
- Substantial wilderness areas, such as Baltic lake and forest environments, the Julian Alps of Slovenia, the Tatra mountains in Slovakia, Carpathians in Romania and Rhodope mountains in Bulgaria (Abrudan and Turnock 1998; Staddon and Turnock 2001; OECD 2003); and
- High quality urban and rural cultural heritage, notably in the region's capitals and in a wide range of smaller cities (e.g. Kraków, Brno), towns (e.g. Rila, Sighişoara) and villages (Jordan 2006; Puczkó and Rátz 2006).

Although in the latter case, appraisals of post-communist urban forms and processes have tended to marginalize the function of tourism and recreation, the roles and potential of, for example, built heritage (Ashworth and Tunbridge 1999; Urtane 2000) and retailing (Nagy 2001; Švab 2002), are substantial. Such concepts as cultural capital (Kearns and Philo 1993) and the production and reproduction of cultural heritage (Johler 2002) have been unevenly developed and applied, although the tourism potential of communist-era heritage has received some attention (e.g. Light 2000a, 2000b).

The European Commission (e.g. 2003, 2004b) has identified tourism frequently as a significant contributor to employment and income generation and to social benefits for local communities as well as providing a framework for the stewardship of distinctive cultures and environments. However, there is no dedicated EC commissioner: tourism represents just one of several diverse units within the Enterprise Directorate-General in Brussels (European Commission 2004a) and, in the 1990s, was beset with organizational concerns (e.g. White 1995). Partly as a result of this, the EU's

Table 1. Transition states in perspective

Country	Total population ($\times 10^6$)[a]	Area ($\times 10^3$ km^2)	Population density (per km^2)	% Urban population	GDP PPP ($\$ 10^9$)	GDP per capita PPP ($\$ 10^3$)	Unemployment rate (%)[a]	Life expectancy at birth — Female	Male	Infant mortality rate (per 10^3 live births)	Estimated Internet users (per 10^3 pop.)	Tourism receipts (as % of GDP [PPP])
2004 EU entrants												
Cyprus	0.8	9.3	82	70	17.8/4.5[b]	22.7/7.1[b]	5.5/5.6[b]	80.3	75.4	7.0	373	18.1
Czech Republic	10.2	78.9	130	75	221.4	21.6	8.4	79.7	72.9	3.9	500	2.1
Estonia	1.3	45.2	30	69	26.0	19.6	5.8	77.8	66.6	7.7	531	3.7
Hungary	10.0	93.0	110	65	172.7	17.3	7.4	77.1	68.5	8.4	305	2.7
Latvia	2.3	64.6	37	60	35.1	15.4	6.7	76.9	66.1	9.4	448	1.0
Lithuania	3.6	65.3	53	69	54.0	15.1	4.5	79.5	69.2	6.8	330	1.7
Malta	0.4	0.3	1239	91	8.1	20.3	7.8	81.3	76.8	3.9	318	9.6
Poland	38.5	312.7	124	63	542.6	14.1	14.9	79.2	71.0	7.2	275	1.2
Slovakia	5.4	49.0	110	58	96.4	17.7	10.2	78.9	70.8	7.3	463	1.3
Slovenia	2.0	20.3	98	49	46.1	22.9	9.6	80.3	72.6	4.4	550	4.0
2007 EU entrants												
Bulgaria	7.4	110.9	72	67	77.1	10.4	9.6	76.1	68.7	19.9	297	3.2
Romania	22.3	238.4	94	55	197.3	8.8	6.1	75.3	68.1	25.5	215	0.5
The neighbours												
Albania	3.6	28.8	119	43	20.2	5.6	14.3[a]	80.3	74.8	20.8	2	4.3
Belarus	10.3	207.6	48	70	80.7	7.8	1.6	75.0	63.5	13.0	330	0.3
Bosnia and Hercegovina	4.5	51.1	84	43	24.8	5.5	45.5[a]	81.9	74.4	9.8	178	2.3
Croatia	4.5	56.5	78	58	59.4	13.2	17.2	78.5	71.0	6.7	333	12.6
Georgia	4.7	69.7	72	57	17.8	3.8	12.6	79.9	72.8	18.0	374	1.3
Macedonia, FYR	2.1	25.7	79	59	16.9	9.2	35.0	76.6	71.5	9.8	191	0.5
Moldova	4.5	33.9	108	41	9.0	2.0	8.0	69.9	61.6	38.4	89	1.4
Montenegro	0.6	14.0		(52)[c]	3.4	3.8	27.7	74.5	70.0	(13.2)[c]	79	nd
Russia	142.9	17075.4	8	73	1723.0	12.1	6.6	74.1	60.5	15.1	165	0.3
Serbia	9.4	102.2	104	(52)[c]	44.8	4.4	31.6	76.0	71.0	(13.2)[c]	149	nd
Turkey	70.4	774.8	87	66	627.2	8.9	8.5	75.2	70.1	39.7	227	2.9
Ukraine	46.7	603.7	81	68	355.8	7.6	9.5	75.6	64.7	9.9	114	0.9

[a] Actual figure likely to be much lower due to a significant grey economy.
[b] Figures for South/North Cyprus.
[c] Figure for Serbia and Montenegro combined.
Source: CIA (2007), UNECE (2007), WTO (2006), author's additional calculations.

involvement in tourism has lacked co-ordination and policy coherence (Smith and Hall 2006a), with a lack of funding measures dedicated solely to tourism (Roberts and Hall 2001; European Commission 2004b; Coles and Hall 2005). Yet, the impress of EU policies on tourism has been widespread and far-reaching (WTO 1998), often because of the impact of other policy areas – environment, transport, agriculture and consumer affairs – on tourism rather than through any explicitly stated tourism policy or strategy (Anastasiadou 2006).

'Transition', Tourism and European Space

The concept of 'transition' has its roots in biology and population dynamics. It can be defined as 'a gradual, continuous process of societal change where the structural character of society (or a complex sub-system of society) transforms' (Martens and Rotmans 2005: 1136).

'Transition' thus entails movement between two specific points, the final point in the case of CEE being integration into the world economy and Western institutions, notably the EU (Agnew 2000). In the 're-territorialisation of Europe' (Dingsdale 1999: 149), EU territory is conceived as the economic, social, political and cultural core of the continent. Spatial and structural core–periphery relations – both within an enlarged EU and between it and its (new) eastern neighbours – are implicit in this conceptualization.

The core of this 'transition project'– transforming the former communist states of Central and Eastern Europe into 'Western democracies'– has been articulated in the terms defining fitness for purpose for EU accession and, most notably, in the 1993 'Copenhagen Criteria' (e.g. Vachudova 2005). These itemized political, economic and human rights requirements of applicant states were intended to indicate and enhance directly their capacity to become full EU members. Application for membership thus assumed compliance with EU rules for assistance and acceptance of EU protocols and terms of trade (Dimitrova and Dragneva 2001; Miošič-Lisjak 2006).

Although a holistic process, the 'transition project' in Europe has been driven by a specific political economy agenda that has often ignored or marginalized social, cultural, psychological and wider environmental dimensions (Marangos 2003; Hall 2004b, 2004c; Hall and Roberts 2004). As such, use of the term 'transitions' has become synonymous with prescriptive forms of post-communist restructuring processes. This is despite the fact that: (a) a variety of other types of 'transition' has long been conceptualised, such as the demographic; (b) societies can experience political and/or economic transformation from a non-state socialist condition, as in South Africa; and (c) some state socialist societies, such as China, can pursue economic transformation without apparent ideological change.

Tourism's role in relation to 'transition' has tended to be viewed within the same narrow and prescriptive parameters. However, while the English language literature on tourism development within post-communist processes has been substantial (e.g. see

Hall [1998] for an earlier review), the conceptual and theoretical strength informing much of this work has been limited.

Hanson (1998) pointed to an inability to accommodate conceptually the dynamics of formation and decline of 'the Stalinist socio-economic system'. None of the dominant frameworks of political economy could account sufficiently for the diversity of post-communist economic and social dynamism on its own. While modernization theory could accommodate processes taking place in Central Europe, world-systems theory illuminated forms of 'dependency' emerging in the Caucasus and Central Asia. Rational choice analysis assisted an understanding of the 'devolution' of state structures in countries where the *nomenklatura* – party, bureaucracy and managerial elites – were able to maintain control over most national wealth.

'Transformation', as an alternative framework concept to 'transition', while accommodating fundamental structural change, is less concerned with an end state, being open-ended and allowing for the substantial (converging and diverging) differences that exist between former communist countries. This negotiated approach to the unknown, with an emphasis on means rather than ends (Saltmarshe 2001), suggests more flexible, less dogmatic and certainly less prescriptively econocentric philosophical approaches to social change at a number of levels. These approaches can respect cultures, sovereignty and peoples' apprehensions, and can be imbued with ideals of equity and sustainability that may be difficult to accommodate within 'transition'.

Intriligator (1998) argued that both democratic and undemocratic, and collapsing and expanding economies could be accommodated in a simple conceptual model of 'post-communist systems'. He pointed to the apparent failure of 'shock therapy' economic policies for transition to a market economy in Russia, which adopted the 'Washington consensus package' of stabilization, liberalization and privatization (SLP). By contrast, the perceived success of China's economic policies for transition to a market economy is related to a rejection of SLP in favour of the institutions, competition and government (ICG) approach. Vietnam, whose political economy draws on SE Asian, Chinese and Leninist cultural elements, has also experienced 'non-democratic' 'transition' to a market economy with no change in political regime occurring. Fforde (2002) referred to this as a 'conservative' 'transition'. It complements conceptions of transformation, and does not assume an (interdependent) outcome of both economic and political change.

Path dependency (Stark 1992; Linz and Stepan 1996; Stark and Bruszt 1998) assumes that each country has had a distinctive and unique path of extrication from communism. In this conceptualization, particular variables play a crucial role in facilitating certain outcomes while constraining others (Meurs and Begg 1998). But Levi (1996) has argued that pathway analysis cannot assume outcomes are determined or predictable since continuing social and technological change influences choices and decisions. Examination of those sub-national trajectories impacting on specific cities, towns, villages and peripheral regions (e.g. Eikeland and Riabova 2002) may highlight local adaptations to dynamic economic, political and cultural conditions.

This is important as 'transition' processes may actually reinforce and rejuvenate long-standing core–periphery, urban–rural, class, ethnic, gender and regional inequalities perpetuated from situations under central planning (Staddon 1999, 2001). For example, the post-communist privatization of power has often been pervaded by vertical and horizontal networks of reciprocity –'survival networks' (Kewell 2002) – which have their roots in the communist period, and which may support or impede restructuring processes (Grabher and Stark 1997), such as the privatization of hotels and other tourism assets and infrastructure (e.g. Koulov 1996). Under such conditions, local empowerment may be difficult to achieve and such networks may expose structural cleavages in society including those of gender (e.g. Hall 2001).

Two groups of 'gatekeepers' of structural transformation in tourism have been identified (Phillips 1996): 'new' tourism managers who relied on old vertical structures and entrenched cultural expectations, and those entrepreneurs who, while apparently comfortable with new conditions, were likely to be 'reconstructed' communist *nomenklatura*. Fforde (2002) in Vietnam referred to the mechanisms involved as 'adaptive social relations'. Where the construction of the institutions of civil society has been slow, mafia-type organizations may have emerged to fill vacuums (e.g. Frisby 1998).

'Transition' and the Mobility Turn

Distinctions between tourism and other forms of temporary mobility, migration and cross-border activity have long been blurred (Hall 2000; Williams and Hall 2000; Coles *et al*. 2004). Use and meaning of the term 'tourist' has become increasingly ambiguous, particularly as successive enlargements of the EU stimulate employment migration, second-home development and other forms of transnational (temporary) mobility.

Drawing on Lefebvre's (1968) social construction of space and place, a mobilities perspective –'the mobility turn' – in social science research 'sees tourism as just one of several forms of intricately connected human mobility' (Church and Coles 2007: 279; see also Coles *et al*. 2005). This has led Urry (2000a, 2000b, 2003, 2004; Larsen *et al*. 2006; Urry and Sheller 2004) to recognize the ironies of heightened 'corporeal mobilities' alongside highly structured 'material immobilities', as represented by the proliferation of personal information technology use. Forms of tourism are thus drawn into concepts of 'meetingness' and 'networked sociality' within processes of transnationalism. These are developed through lenses focused on: (a) embodiment and corporeal mobility (Haldrup 2004); (b) transience – notions of the tourist body sensing landscapes as it passes through them (Larsen 2001); (c) grid theory, and its application to the temporary transnational mobilities of tourism and migration (Duval 2006); and in (d) concepts of 'halfway populations', such as cross-border petty traders, occupying 'thirdspace' in borderland areas (Sofield 2006).

Conceptualization of transnational mobilities of 'transition' in Europe has been a feature of the work of Williams and Baláž (2002a, 2002b, 2005; Baláž 2006; Baláž and Williams 2005; Williams *et al.* 2001). In their analyses focusing on tourism and cross-border petty trading, they have conceived the confusing and fragmented tapestry of different mobilities as '*bricolage*'. Regional cross-border mobility is a significant by-product of post-communist restructuring. It reflects forces both of integration– tourism, labour migration, shopping – and of disintegration, or at least dislocation – refugee flight and the need for informal petty trading and exchange (Sik and Wallace 1999; Thuen 1999; Aidis 2003; Egbert 2006). Indicating the intricate web of link-ages and networks on both sides of borders (Galia 2006), such mobility experiences have grown considerably, raising important issues for local and regional integration (Williams and Baláž 2000; Scott 2006).

Social costs of tourism may arise from the promotion of foreign investment op-portunities. Media publicity highlighting low property and land prices has led to an increased awareness among Western Europeans of potential second homes in se-lected locations and regions (Vágner and Fialová 2004). One consequence of this may be that, as elsewhere in Europe, local residents find themselves priced out of their own local housing markets, whether in desirable urban sectors, rural regions or coastal locations. Foreign direct investment in major infrastructure, accommodation and attraction projects may also leave new member states vulnerable to the power of transnational corporations and the vagaries of global market conditions (Behringer and Kiss 2004; Bachvarov 2006).

The introduction and growth in operations of low cost airlines (LCAs) to regional airports in the accession states has been significant for intra-European mobilities. The market for air transport users has been deepened and widened substantially by the LCAs' business model of stripped-down costs, relatively low fares and exploitation of personal information technology (Alderighi *et al.* 2004; Dobruszkes 2006). LCAs now carry more than twenty percent of European air passengers compared to five percent in 2000 (Roberts and Harrison 2006). Yet the role of LCAs in facilitating labour mobility within an enlarged EU ideologically (if not always in practice) promoting the free movement of labour is a relatively new element in spatial restructuring and remains a matter of some debate.

Williams and Hall (2002) recognized the economic and cultural mechanisms that influence search spaces, demand and investment, and adopted an idealized four-phase model of relationships emphasizing that not only can tourism lead to migration, but that migration may generate tourism flows, notably through the spatial exten-sion of friendship, ethnic and kinship networks. The scale, intensity and scope of such linkages will have increased significantly in recent decades, encouraged by EU enlargement.

Cultural disparities between source and host region may be important in determin-ing the welfare implications of (tourism) migrant workers (Hall and Brown 2006). Inferior–superior structural relationships may reinforce segregation from the local population in terms of their accommodation, working hours, and their ethnic and religious backgrounds. However, in the literature on tourism destinations – compared to wider migration studies, such as those on gender-related mobility (e.g. Iredale 2005) – relatively little research has been undertaken on issues such as the welfare of tourism migrants, the impacts of such movement on family life, particularly when employment is seasonal, the socio-economic consequences for the source areas, and the implications for subsequent service provision in both source and host regions.

The increasing diversity of both tourists and workers in the tourism industry and the growing competitiveness of destinations and businesses requires internationally transferable skills that can enhance employability (Aitken and Hall 2000). However, while there is widespread recognition of the need for such skills, there is often a reluctance to acknowledge its importance within individual businesses. Crucial to regional transformation and restructuring has been the need to establish and consolidate 'new mentalities' (e.g. Cottrell and Cutumisu 2006), even though an underlying continuity and resistance may persist through the pre-existing business/political ('survival') networks, noted earlier.

This may be reflected in inadequate levels of service, information and market research. For example, in Bulgaria (Anastassova and Purcell 1995; Bachvarov 1997, 1999, 2006), culturally entrenched 'residues of communist ideological practice'– whereby tourism quality is defined as that necessary to satisfy demand as perceived by the providers – have constrained the raising of service levels. As a model of good practice, the Lithuanian rural tourism information and development centre provides professional advice to current and potential rural tourism entrepreneurs, acting as an intermediary between tourists and rural tourism providers (Lordkipanidze *et al.* 2005). More remote regions may have suffered from problems of access to training, although comprehensive online provision should now be able to ameliorate this constraint.

Evidence varies concerning whether tourism employment reinforces existing social and structural differentiation or allows new socio-economic groups to emerge locally to reduce socio-economic inequalities. Verbole (2003) has shown in Slovenia that relatively homogeneous 'communities' who respond to tourism can become fragmented, with the emergence of local sub-groups assuming different stances in respect of development. This can result in both local winners and losers from tourism development processes. Enhanced opportunities can result from being located in an advantageous structural position: those owning land in key locations can reinforce their structural position or sell to developers for substantial financial gain. For those with more education or training, tourism may provide new opportunities in managerial positions and thereby open further fractures in local stratification systems (Cooper and Morpeth 1998). On the other hand, regions of strong employment traditions may see local men shunning 'demeaning' tourism-related work (Ateljevic and Čorak 2006).

Tourism can assist labour market adjustment, but may also remain one of the lowest paid sectors (although real earnings and benefits may be significantly greater than those officially recorded). In Hungary, although new entrants to tourism employment had transferred from a variety of occupations, Szivas and Riley (2002) detected a relatively low level of spatial mobility, suggesting that it may have been replaced by occupational mobility. Workers moved between employment sectors but tended to stay in the same geographical area, rather than seeking employment in a more prosperous region.

This raises questions of how tourism quality is affected by such employee diversity and what mechanisms are in place to assist the necessary adaptation and socialization processes to accompany or precede training and education. New entrants to the sector bring experience that may be different from their tourism employment requirements. However, in the short to medium term, the use of such labour may encourage the persistence of the poor service attitudes noted earlier (Szivas and Riley 2002).

Debates on the benefits of employment migration and of the role of remittances for labour-source countries are considerable (de Haas 2005). Circular migration and development are conjoined in a reciprocal relationship whereby migration is both a constituent part of the development process and is an independent factor influencing development in both source and receiving countries (CDR 2002). Although 'brain drains' of well-educated professionals from the accession countries, such as that of doctors from Poland (e.g. France 24 2006; Pidd and Harding 2006), have been well publicized, Bhagwati (2003) pointed to potential 'brain gains' for source countries in terms of the counterflow of remittances, trade relations, the gaining of new knowledge, skills, innovations, attitudes and information.

A recent World Bank report (Mansoor and Quillin 2007) emphasized the important role of remittances for a number of less advanced CEE countries in assisting economic growth. For Albania, Bosnia and Moldova they represented between 15 and 27 percent of GDP in 2003/4, and the latter figure for Moldova was exceeded globally only by Haiti and Tonga. For CEE as a whole, three-quarters of remittances by value arrive from migrants in the EU and about ten percent from those in Russia. Taylor (1999), however, argued that migration is no panacea for development, and that remittances are often viewed over-optimistically, their role and value crucially depending upon the selectivity of migration and on the geographical and temporal scale of analysis of their impact.

Indeed, for migrants' source areas, tourism employment migration can act to postpone long-term rural or regional development. Remittances may be used for consumption to (self-) build a larger house or buy a new car rather than being invested to help upgrade local infrastructures or improve structural employment opportunities. Return migrants – whose homecoming may be voluntary or forced (IOM 2004) – may be coming back to a home area that itself acts as a tourism (and, indeed, migration) destination.

Refining and Redefining Identity Through Tourism

Tourism's role may assist a strengthening, re-affirmation or redefinition of identity at a number of levels: national, ethnic, destination/place and gender/household. This 'hierarchy', may be characterized by differing conceptions of nation and of national collective identity, individual attitudes and value orientations. There is also constant change in the meaning and structure of 'identity' (Pickel 1997). Issues relating to destination image and branding development have become linked inextricably with identity formation. In this way, international tourism and marketing imagery represent vehicles through which identity can seek expression (Hall 2002; Light 2006).

The identity-building requirements of the global market place emphasize the importance of the interrelationships between imagery and the need to respond to new political and economic circumstances; between tourism branding and national/regional identity; and between cultural, political and economic re-imaging requirements. The competitive and nationalistic imperative to differentiate a country clearly from its neighbours and competitors has important cultural and economic implications for attracting tourism and inward investment. In addition, EU candidates have been required to emphasize a 'Europeanness' and disassociation from the ideologies and instability of the recent past.

Needing to respond to new and changing market demands and increasing market differentiation, CEE destinations have needed to reassure (former) markets that quality and value have been (re-)established, even if the destination in question has experienced conflict and has changed its political status (and perhaps even its name) in the process. For a country whose former markets were familiar with 'Yugoslavia' (and particularly the *Yugotours* brand), Croatia, through such promotions as 'A New Welcome – An Old Friend' has needed to portray itself as a 'new' country, yet a familiar and safe European destination integral to Mediterranean tourism.

Part of the escape strategy from the past has been to emphasize the diversity and uniqueness of cultural and natural resources (Meler and Ruzic 1999; Hall 2003, 2004d; Light 2006). Many rural areas are being re-imaged (Roberts and Hall 2001, 2004) in the promotion of traditional, 'idyllic' portrayals of timeless sustainability. This has encouraged a growth of eco- and nature tourism, gastronomy, heritage trails and activity holidays, although enthusiasm has often preceded appropriate infrastructure and training provision.

The promotion of urban 'cultural' destinations, has often employed imaging strategies emphasizing (again potentially paradoxically) 'European' heritage and progress, to appeal both to tourism and wider economic investment markets (e.g. Young and Kaczmarek 1999; Bachvarov and Wiluš 2005; Rátz et al. 2006). Employment of the (renewed) city of Dubrovnik as an icon of the Mediterranean culture and leisure experience has been particularly notable in Croatia's post-Yugoslav war recovery (Hall 2004a).

However, negative destination images can be generated easily to confound what may have been years of careful nurturing by national and regional authorities to develop high value niche roles in, for example, cultural tourism. Deeper market penetration of LCAs has raised potential image problems for some destinations. Major problems have arisen for the destination branding of countries and destinations seeking a positive new or rejuvenated image projection. For example, some tour-operators have specialized in 'stag' and 'hen' weekend packages to Latvia, with Riga targeted as a 'hot spot' (Naish 2004). As a result, state and city authorities have needed to act to reduce advertising of sex-related tourism products in order to prevent Riga becoming a European sex tourism capital (Druva-Druvaskalne, Ābols and Šļara 2006; see also Endzina and Luneva 2004).

Positively, such unsustainable situations may stimulate diversification and added value to tourism products. At least one report has suggested that what low-cost air travellers are saving in travel costs they are spending to upgrade the quality of their accommodation (EU Business 2005). The growth of LCAs may also be seen to have facilitated regular travel to second homes and easier international student exchange mobility (Richards 2006), both contributors to imagery and identity formation.

Conclusion: Future Research Needs and Agenda

This paper has selectively reviewed literature relating to tourism and the concept of 'transition', EU enlargement as the end of point of prescriptive transitional processes, and tourism as an element of the emerging mobilities within that context, together with image and identity issues related to renewal, restructuring and EU accession.

The tourism 'transition' literature is gradually drawing upon conceptual models and ideas emerging elsewhere in the social sciences, and stronger, theoretically informed critiques are gaining momentum (e.g. see Alejziak 2006; Saarinen and Kask 2006). None the less, much bricklaying remains to be undertaken within the academy, and the current *bricolage* of empirical and theoretical research approaches, while healthily broad, is nevertheless relatively inchoate. This fact is brought home when attempting to produce a representative review.

A research agenda for further conceptualization and strengthening of empirical methodology might include a number of interrelated themes (Smith and Hall 2006b). The way in which the interplay of processes of both continuity and change can be represented and interpreted is important for understanding the nature and impact of survival networks, persisting 'old mentalities', and how they can be incorporated into pathway analyses.

The policy significance of the relatively miserly position attributed to tourism within the institutions of the EU, despite its important economic and integrating role in Europe, requires further interrogation. At least five areas of significance flow from this. First, further work is required on the reality and representation of interrelationships between different mobilities – tourism, labour migration, cross-border petty trading and shopping, retirement, second-home residence and other seasonal attachments. In relation to these mobilities, the nature and role of transport and transport infrastructures, personal information technology and the role of internal and external borders in Central and Eastern Europe require more detailed scrutiny.

Secondly, within this context, the ongoing roles and impacts of low-cost airlines raise a number of issues. These arise from mutual ease of access between east and west

Europe, spatial shifts in the balance of mass and 'niche' activities and of conceptions of core and periphery, facilitation of labour movement, and the role of EU boundaries in relation to destinations in the former Soviet and Yugoslav federations. Such issues include relationships between EU environment and mobility policies, the fragmented nature of regional development processes, niche market development and concerns for destination imagery.

Indeed, thirdly, there is the wider issue, as yet little researched beyond anecdote, of the nature and roles of individual destination, regional and national imagery as an integral component of transformation and of the ever-evolving relationships between markets and destinations. Marketing, branding, their relationships with general and specific conceptions of the 'new Europe', and the impact of imagery for destination stakeholders, offer a range of opportunities for development, segmentation and added-value within the region.

Fourthly, there is a need for debate and strategy directed at developing conceptions of a tourist Europe in relation to future potential EU enlargement (and the challenges of reduced carbon-based fuel use). Further extension of the EU in the Mediterranean and Black Sea regions and the renewed emphasis this will bring to the continuing role of mass tourism requires careful consideration. Complementing this is the need to recognize further the region's unique attributes in supporting related opportunities in culture/heritage tourism, nature/eco-tourism, health/wellbeing tourism and adventure/sports tourism.

Fifthly, the interrelationships between tourism, education and culture (and implicitly issues of citizenship) deserve closer attention. In particular, the mobilities of student exchange, placement and gap-year activities, while significant, appear poorly documented and conceptualized.

References

Abrudan, I. & Turnock, D. (1998) A rural development strategy for the Apuseni Mountains, Romania, *GeoJournal*, 46(3), pp. 319–336.

Agnew, J. (2000) How many Europes?, in: D. Hall & D. Danta (Eds) *Europe Goes East: EU Enlargement, Diversity and Uncertainty*, pp. 45–54 (London: The Stationery Office).

Aidis, R. (2003) Officially despised yet tolerated: open-air markets and entrepreneurship in post-socialist countries, *Post-Communist Economies*, 15(3), pp. 461–473.

Aitken, C. & Hall, C.M. (2000) Migrant and foreign skills and their relevance to the tourism industry, *Tourism Geographies*, 2(1), pp. 66–86.

Alderighi, M., Cento, A., Nijkamp, P. & Rietveld, P. (2004) *The Entry of Low-Cost Airlines*, Discussion paper TI 2004-074/3 (Rotterdam: Tinbergen Institute).

Alejziak, W. (2006) Tourism research in Poland, *Tourism Recreation Research*, 31(2), pp. 91–93.

Anastasiadou, C. (2006) Tourism and the European Union, in: D. Hall, M. Smith & B. Marciszewska (Eds) *Tourism in the New Europe: the Challenges and Opportunities of EU Enlargement*, pp. 20–31 (Wallingford, UK: CABI Publishing).

Anastassova, L. & Purcell, K. (1995) Human resource management in the Bulgarian hotel industry: from command to empowerment?, *International Journal of Hospitality Management*, 14(2), pp. 171–185.

Ashworth, G.J. & Tunbridge, J.E. (1999) Old cities, new pasts: heritage planning in selected cities of Central Europe, *GeoJournal*, 49(1), pp. 105–116.

Ateljevic, I. & Čorak, S. (2006) Croatia in the new Europe: culture versus conformity, in: D. Hall, M. Smith & B. Marciszewska (Eds) *Tourism in the New Europe: the Challenges and Opportunities of EU Enlargement*, pp. 288–301 (Wallingford, UK: CABI Publishing).

Bachvarov, M. (1997) End of the model? Tourism in post-communist Bulgaria, *Tourism Management*, 18(1), pp. 43–50.

Bachvarov, M. (1999) Troubled sustainability: Bulgarian seaside resorts, *Tourism Geographies*, 1(2), pp. 192–203.

Bachvarov, M. (2006) Tourism in Bulgaria, in: D. Hall, M. Smith & B. Marciszewska (Eds) *Tourism in the New Europe: the Challenges and Opportunities of EU Enlargement*, pp. 241–255 (Wallingford, UK: CABI Publishing).

Bachvarov, M. & Wiluš, R. (2005) Cultural tourism – a new challenge in Central-eastern Europe. Paper presented at the ATLAS Annual Conference: *Tourism, Creativity and Development*, Barcelona, 2–4 November.

Baláž, V. (2006) Slovakia: EU accession and cross-border travel, in: D. Hall, M. Smith & B. Marciszewska (Eds) *Tourism in the New Europe: the Challenges and Opportunities of EU Enlargement*, pp. 92–103 (Wallingford, UK: CABI Publishing).

Baláž, V. & Williams, A.M. (2005) International tourism as bricolage: an analysis of Central Europe on the brink of European Union membership, *International Journal of Tourism Research*, 7(2), pp. 79–93.

Behringer, Z. & Kiss, K. (2004) The role of foreign direct investment in the development of tourism in post-communist Hungary, in: D. Hall (Ed.) *Tourism and Transition: Governance, Transformation and Development*, pp. 73–81 (Wallingford, UK: CABI Publishing).

Bhagwati, J. (2003) Borders beyond control, *Foreign Affairs*, 82(1), pp. 98–104.

Bunja, D. (2003) Modernizing the Croatian tourism industry, *International Journal of Contemporary Hospitality Management*, 15(2), pp. 126–128.

CDR (Centre for Development Research) (2002) *The Migration–Development Nexus* (Copenhagen: CDR).

Church, A. & Coles, T. (2007) Tourism and the many faces of power, in: A. Church and T. Coles (Eds) *Tourism, Power and Space*, pp. 269–283 (London: Routledge).

CIA (Central Intelligence Agency) (2007) *The World Factbook* (Washington DC: CIA). Available at www.cia.gov/cia/publications/factbook (accessed 19 January 2007).

Coles, T.E., Duval, D.T. & Hall, C.M. (2004) Tourism, mobility and global communities: new approaches to theorising tourism and tourist spaces, in: W. Theobald (Ed.) *Global Tourism*, 3rd edn (Oxford: Butterworth-Heinemann).

Coles, T. & Hall, D. (2005) Tourism and EU enlargement. Plus ça change?, *International Journal of Tourism Research*, 7(2), pp. 51–61.

Coles, T.E., Hall, C.M. & Duval, D.T. (2005) Mobilizing tourism: a post-disciplinary critique, *Tourism Recreation Research*, 30(2), pp. 31–41.

Cooper, C. & Morpeth, N. (1998) The impact of tourism on residential experience in Central-Eastern Europe: the development of a new legitimation crisis in the Czech Republic, *Urban Studies*, 35(2), pp. 2253–2275.

Cottrell, S. & Cutumisu, N. (2006) Sustainable tourism development strategy in WWF pan parks: case of a Swedish and Romanian national park, *Scandinavian Journal of Hospitality and Tourism*, 6(2), pp. 150–167.

de Haas, H. (2005) International migration, remittances and development: myths and facts, *Third World Quarterly*, 26(8), pp. 1269–1284.

Dimitrova, A. & Dragneva, R. (2001) Bulgaria's road to the European Union: progress, problems and perspectives, *Perspectives on European Politics and Society*, 2(1), pp. 79–104.

Dingsdale, A. (1999) New geographies of post-socialist Europe, *Geographical Journal*, 165(2), pp. 145–153.

Dobruszkes, F. (2006) An analysis of European low-cost airlines and their networks, *Journal of Transport Geography*, 14(4), pp. 249–264.

Druva-Druvaskalne, I., Ābols, I. & Šļara, A. (2006) Latvia tourism: decisive factors and tourism development, in: D. Hall, M. Smith & B. Marciszewska (Eds) *Tourism in the New Europe: the Challenges and Opportunities of EU Enlargement*, pp. 170–182 (Wallingford, UK: CABI Publishing).

Duval, D. (2006) Grid/group theory and its applicability to tourism and migration, *Tourism Geographies*, 8(1), pp. 1–14.

Egbert, H. (2006) Cross-border small-scale trading in South-Eastern Europe: do embeddedness and social capital explain enough?, *International Journal of Urban and Regional Research*, 30(2), pp. 346–361.

Eikeland, S. & Riabova, L. (2002) Transition in a cold climate: management regimes and rural marginalisation in Northwest Russia, *Sociologia Ruralis*, 42(3), pp. 250–266.

Endzina, I. & Luneva, L. (2004) Development of a national branding strategy: the case of Latvia, *Place Branding*, 1(1), pp. 94–105.

EU Business (2005) Luxury hotels cash in on tourism boom in new EU countries, *EU Business*, 21 June. Available at http://www.eubusiness.com/East_Europe/050622041934.nndypr28 (accessed 22 June 2005).

European Commission (2003) *Tourism and the European Union* (Brussels: European Commission).

European Commission (2004a) *Enterprise – Creating an Entrepreneurial Europe* (Brussels: European Commission).

European Commission (2004b) *EU Support for Tourism Enterprises and Tourist Destinations. An Internet Guide* (Brussels: European Commission).

Fforde, A. (2002) Resourcing conservative transition in Vietnam: rent switching and resource appropriation, *Post-Communist Economies*, 14(2), pp. 203–226.

France 24 (2006) Doctors, Poland needs you!, *France 24*, 1 December. Available at www.france24.com /france24Public/en/special-reports/Immigration-Europe/20061201-polish-doctors.html (accessed 15 January 2007).

Frisby, T. (1998) The rise of organised crime in Russia: its roots and social significance, *Europe-Asia Studies*, 50(1), pp. 27–49.

Galia, V. (2006) Kinship and transborder exchange at the Bulgarian–Serbian border in the second half of the twentieth century, *European Journal of Turkish Studies*, 4. Available at www.ejts.org/document607.html (accessed 4 January 2007).

Gosar, A. (2005) The cross-border bricklaying concept in the Alpen–Adria region, *Tourism Analysis*, 10(1), pp. 65–78.

Grabher, G. & Stark, D. (Eds) (1997) *Restructuring Networks in Post-Socialism: Legacies, Linkages and Localities* (Oxford: Oxford University Press).

Haldrup, M. (2004) Laid-back mobilities: second-home holidays in time and space, *Tourism Geographies*, 6(4), pp. 434–454.

Hall, D. (1998) Central and Eastern Europe, in: A.M. Williams & G. Shaw (Eds) *Tourism and Economic Development in Europe*, pp. 345–373 (Chichester, UK and New York: John Wiley & Sons).

Hall, D. (2000) Cross-border movement and the dynamics of 'transition' processes in South-eastern Europe, *GeoJournal*, 50(2–3), pp. 249–253.

Hall, D. (2001) From the 'Iron Curtain' to the 'Dollar Curtain': women and tourism in Eastern Europe, in: Y. Apostolopoulos, S. Sonmez & D.J. Timothy (Eds) *Women as Producers and Consumers of Tourism in Developing Regions*, pp. 191–207 (Westport: Praeger).

Hall, D. (2002) Brand development, tourism and national identity: the re-imaging of former Yugoslavia, *Journal of Brand Management*, 9(4–5), pp. 323–334.

Hall, D. (2003) Rejuvenation, diversification and imagery: sustainability conflicts for tourism policy in the eastern Adriatic, *Journal of Sustainable Tourism*, 11(2/3), pp. 280–294.

Hall, D. (2004a) Branding and national identity: the case of Central and Eastern Europe, in: N. Morgan, A. Pritchard & R. Pride (Eds) *Destination Branding: Creating the Unique Destination Proposition*, 2nd edn, pp. 111–127 (Amsterdam: Elsevier).

Hall, D. (2004b) Introduction, in: D. Hall (Ed.) *Tourism and Transition: Governance, Transformation and Development*, pp. 1–24 (Wallingford, UK: CABI Publishing).

Hall, D. (2004c) Key themes and frameworks, in: D. Hall (Ed.) *Tourism and Transition: Governance, Transformation and Development*, pp. 25–51 (Wallingford, UK: CABI Publishing).

Hall, D. (2004d) Rural tourism development in South-eastern Europe: transition and the search for sustainability, *International Journal of Tourism Research*, 6(2), pp. 165–176.

Hall, D. & Brown, F. (2006) *Tourism and Welfare: Ethics, Sustainability and Sustained Well-being* (Wallingford, UK: CABI Publishing).

Hall, D. & Roberts, L. (2004) Conclusions and future agenda, in: D. Hall (Ed.) *Tourism and Transition: Governance, Transformation and Development*, pp. 217–226 (Wallingford, UK: CABI Publishing).

Hanson, S.E. (1998) Development, dependency, and devolution: the anomalous political economy of communist and postcommunist societies, *Environment and Planning C: Government and Policy*, 16(2), pp. 225–246.

Intriligator, M.D. (1998) Democracy in reforming collapsed communist economies: blessing or curse?, *Contemporary Economic Policy*, 16(2), pp. 241–246.

IOM (International Organization for Migration) (2004) *Return Migration: Policies and Practices in Europe* (Geneva: IOM).

Iredale, R. (2005) Gender, immigration policies and accreditation: valuing skills of professional women migrants, *Geoforum*, 36(2), pp. 155–166.

Johler, R. (2002) Local Europe: the production of cultural heritage and the Europeanisation of places, *Ethnologia Europaea*, 32(2), pp. 7–18.

Jordan, P. (2006) Tourism and EU enlargement: a Central European perspective, in: D. Hall, M. Smith & B. Marciszewska (Eds) *Tourism in the New Europe: the Challenges and Opportunities of EU Enlargement*, pp. 65–80 (Wallingford, UK: CABI).

Kearns, G. & Philo, C. (Eds) (1993) *Selling Places: the City as Cultural Capital, Past and Present* (Oxford: Pergamon Press).

Kewell, B. (2002) Hidden drivers of organisational transformation in Poland: survival networks amongst state owned and privatised firms in the early 1990s, *Journal for East European Management Studies*, 7(4), pp. 373–392.

Konečnik, M. (2004) Evaluating Slovenia's image as a tourism destination: A self-analysis process towards building a destination brand, *Journal of Brand Management*, 11(4), pp. 307–316.

Konečnik, M. (2006) Slovenia: new challenges in enhancing the value of the destination brand, in: D. Hall, M. Smith & B. Marciszewska (Eds) *Tourism in the New Europe: the Challenges and Opportunities of EU Enlargement*, pp. 81–91 (Wallingford, UK: CABI).

Koulov, B. (1996) Market reforms and environmental protection in the Bulgarian tourism industry, in: D. Hall & D. Danta (Eds) *Reconstructing the Balkans*, pp. 187–196 (Chichester, UK and New York: John Wiley & Sons).

Larsen, J. (2001) Tourism mobilities and the travel glance: experiences of being on the move, *Scandinavian Journal of Hospitality and Tourism*, 1(2), pp. 80–98.

Larsen, J., Urry, J. & Axhausen, K. (2006) *Mobilities, Networks, Geographies* (Aldershot. UK: Ashgate).

Lefebvre, H. (1968) *Le Droit a la Ville* (Paris: Anthropos).

Levi, M. (1996) Social and unsocial capital: a review essay of Robert Putnam's 'Making Democracy Work', *Politics and Society*, 24(1), pp. 45–55.

Light, D. (2000a) An unwanted past: contemporary tourism and the heritage of communism in Romania, *International Journal of Heritage Studies*, 6(2), pp. 145–160.

Light, D. (2000b) Gazing on communism: heritage tourism and post-communist identities in Germany, Hungary and Romania, *Tourism Geographies*, 2(2), pp. 157–176.

Light, D. (2006) Romania: national identity, tourism promotion and European integration, in: D. Hall, M. Smith & B. Marciszewska (Eds) *Tourism in the New Europe: the Challenges and Opportunities of EU Enlargement*, pp. 256–269 (Wallingford, UK: CABI Publishing).

Light, D. & Dumbrâveanu, D. (1999) Romanian tourism in the post-communist period, *Annals of Tourism Research*, 26(4), pp. 898–927.

Linz, J. & Stepan, A. (1996) *Problems of Democratic Transition and Consolidation* (Baltimore: Johns Hopkins University Press).

Lordkipanidze, M., Brezet, H. & Backman, M. (2005) The entrepreneurship factor in sustainable tourism development, *Journal of Cleaner Production*, 13(8), pp. 787–798.

Mansoor, A. & Quillin, B. (2007) *Migration and Remittances: Eastern Europe and the Former Soviet Union* (Washington DC: The World Bank).

Marangos, J. (2003) Global transition strategies in Eastern Europe: moving to market relations, *Development*, 46(1), pp. 112–117.

Martens, P. & Rotmans, J. (2005) Transitions in a globalising world, *Futures*, 37, pp. 1133–1144.

Meler, M. & Ruzic, D. (1999) Marketing identity of the tourist product of the Republic of Croatia, *Tourism Management*, 20, 635–643.

Meurs, M. & Begg, R. (1998) Path dependence in Bulgarian agriculture, in: J. Pickles & A. Smith (Eds) *Theorising Transition*, pp. 243–261 (London: Routledge).

Miošič-Lisjak, N. (2006) Croatia and the European Union, *Policy Studies*, 27(2), pp. 101–114.

Nagy, E. (2001) Winners and losers in the transformation of city centre retailing in East Central Europe, *European Urban and Regional Research*, 8(4), pp. 340–348.

Naish, J. (2004) Baltics braced for new kids on the Bloc, *The Times Online*, 1 May. Available at http://www.timesonline.co.uk/article/0,160-1092380,00.html (accessed 2 May 2004).

OECD (Environmental Performance Reviews Poland) (2003) Nature and biodiversity, *Environment & Sustainable Development*, 8, pp. 126–151.

Phillips, R. (1996) Communism strikes back: cultural blockages on the road to reform in the post-Soviet tourism sector, in: M. Robinson, N. Evans & P. Callaghan (Eds) *Tourism and Culture: Image, Identity and Marketing*, pp. 147–164 (Sunderland, UK: Business Education Publishers).

Pickel, A. (1997) Creative chaos: concluding thoughts on interdisciplinary cooperation, in: K. Jarausch (Ed.) *After Unity: Reconfiguring German Identities*, pp. 196–207 (Oxford: Berghahn).

Pidd, H. & Harding, L. (2006) Why would you leave a place like Wroclaw?, *The Guardian*, 21 July.

Puczkó, L. & Rátz, T. (2006) Product development and diversification in Hungary, in: D. Hall, M. Smith & B. Marciszewska (Eds) *Tourism in the New Europe: the Challenges and Opportunities of EU Enlargement*, pp. 116–126 (Wallingford, UK: CABI Publishing).

Rátz, T., Puczkó, L. & Smith, M. (2006) Old city. new image: perceptions, positioning and promotion of Budapest. Paper presented at ATLAS annual conference, *The Transformation of Tourism Spaces*, University of Łódź, Poland, 20–22 September.

Richards, G. (2006) Tourism education in the new Europe, in: D. Hall, M. Smith & B. Marciszewska (Eds) *Tourism in the New Europe: the Challenges and Opportunities of EU Enlargement*, pp. 52–64 (Wallingford, UK: CABI Publishing).

Roberts, L. & Hall, D. (2001) *Rural Tourism and Recreation: Principles to Practice* (Wallingford, UK: CAB International).

Roberts, L. & Hall, D. (2004) Consuming the countryside: marketing for rural tourism, *Journal of Vacation Marketing*, 10(3), pp. 253–263.

Roberts, G. & Harrison, M. (2006) Budget airlines spread their wings to Africa, *The Independent*, 2 March, p. 3.

Saarinen, J. & Kask, T. (2006) Transforming tourism spaces in changing socio-political contexts: case of Pärnu (Estonia) as a tourist destination. Paper presented at ATLAS annual conference, *The Transformation of Tourism Spaces*, University of Łódü, Poland, 20–22 September.

Saltmarshe, D. (2001) *Identity in a Post-communist Balkan State: an Albanian Village Study* (Aldershot, UK: Ashgate).

Scott, J.W. (Ed.) (2006) *EU Enlargement, Region Building and Shifting Borders of Inclusion and Exclusion* (Aldershot UK: Ashgate).

Sik, E. & Wallace, C. (1999) The development of open-air markets in East-Central Europe, *International Journal of Urban and Regional Research*, 23(4), pp. 697–714.

Smith, M. & Hall, D. (2006a) Enlargement implications for European tourism, in: D. Hall, M. Smith & B. Marciszewska (Eds) *Tourism in the New Europe: the Challenges and Opportunities of EU Enlargement*, pp. 32–44 (Wallingford, UK: CABI Publishing).

Smith, M. & Hall, D. (2006b) Summary and conclusions, in: D. Hall, M. Smith & B. Marciszewska (Eds) *Tourism in the New Europe: the Challenges and Opportunities of EU Enlargement*, pp. 305–311 (Wallingford, UK: CABI Publishing).

Sofield, T. (2006) Border tourism and border communities: an overview, *Tourism Geographies*, 8(2), pp. 102–121.

Staddon, C. (1999) Localities, natural resources and transition in Eastern Europe, *Geographical Journal*, 165(2), pp. 200–208.

Staddon, C. (2001) Local forest-dependence in postcommunist Bulgaria: a case study, *GeoJournal*, 55(2–4), pp. 517–528.

Staddon, C. & Turnock, D. (2001) Think global act local? Negotiating sustainable development under postcommunist transformation, *GeoJournal*, 55(2–4), pp. 477–484.

Stark, D. (1992) Path dependence and privatisation strategies in East Central Europe, *European Politics and Societies*, 6(1), pp. 17–54.

Stark, D. & Bruszt, L. (1998) *Postsocialist Pathways* (Cambridge: Cambridge University Press).

Švab A. (2002) Consuming Western image of well-being: shopping tourism in socialist Slovenia, *Cultural Studies*, 16(1), pp. 63–79.

Szivas, E. & Riley, M. (2002) Labour mobility and tourism in the post 1989 transition in Hungary, in: C.M. Hall & A.M. Williams (Eds) *Tourism and Migration*, pp. 53–72 (Dordrecht: Kluwer).

Taylor, J.E. (1999) The new economics of labour migration and the role of remittances in the migration process, *International Migration*, 37(1), pp. 63–88.

Thuen, T. (1999) The significance of borders in the East European transition, *International Journal of Urban and Regional Research*, 23(4), pp. 738–750.

UNECE (United Nations Economic Commission for Europe) (2007) Trends in Europe and North America (Geneva: UNECE). Available at www.unece.org/stats/trend/trend_h.htm (accessed 16 January 2007).

Urry, J. (2000a) Mobile sociology, *British Journal of Sociology*, 51(1), pp. 185–203.

Urry, J. (2000b) *Sociology Beyond Societies: Mobilities for the Twenty-first Century* (London: Routledge).

Urry, J. (2003) Social networks, travel and talk, *British Journal of Sociology*, 54(2), pp. 155–175.

Urry, J. (2004) Small worlds and the new 'social physics', *Global Networks: A Journal of Transnational Affairs*, 4(2), pp. 109–130.

Urry, J. & Sheller, M. (Eds) (2004) *Tourism Mobilities: Places to Stay, Places in Play* (London: Routledge).

Urtane M. (2000) Visible archaeological remains in towns and parks, *International Journal of Heritage Studies*, 6(1), pp. 77–82.

Vachudova, M.A. (2005) The active leverage of the European Union, in: M.A. Vachudova, *Europe Undivided*, pp. 105–139 (Oxford: Oxford Scholarship Online Monographs).

Vágner, J. & Fialová, D. (Eds) (2004) *Regionální Differenciace Druhého Bydlení v Česku* (Prague: Karlova University, Department of Social Geography and Regional Development).

Verbole, A. (2003) Networking and partnership building for rural tourism development, in: D. Hall, L. Roberts & M. Mitchell (Eds) *New Directions in Rural Tourism*, pp.152–168 (Aldershot, UK and Burlington VT: Ashgate).

White, C. (1995) Audit damns EC tourism unit, *The European*, 10 February.

Williams, A.M. & Baláž, V. (2000) *Tourism in Transition* (London and New York: I.B. Tauris).

Williams, A.M. & Baláž, V. (2002a) The Czech and Slovak Republics: conceptual issues in the economic analysis of tourism in transition, *Tourism Management*, 23(1), pp. 37–45.

Williams, A.M. & Baláž, V. (2002b) International petty trading: changing practices in trans-Carpathian Ukraine, *International Journal of Urban and Regional Research*, 26(2), pp. 323–342.

Williams, A.M. & Baláž, V. (2005) Winning, then losing, the battle with globalization: Vietnamese petty traders in Slovakia, *International Journal of Urban and Regional Research*, 29(3), pp. 533–549.

Williams, A.M., Baláž, V. & Bodnárová, B. (2001) Order, regions and trans-border mobility: Slovakia in economic transition, *Regional Studies*, 35(9), pp. 831–846.

Williams, A. M. & Hall, C. M. (2000) Tourism and migration: new relationships between production and consumption, *Tourism Geographies*, 2(1), pp. 5–27.

Williams, A.M. & Hall, C.M. (2002) Tourism, migration, circulation and mobility: the contingencies of time and place, in: C.M. Hall & A.M. Williams (Eds) *Tourism and Migration*, pp. 1–52 (Dordrecht: Kluwer).

WTO (World Tourism Organization) (1998) *The Euro: Impact on Tourism* (Madrid: WTO).

WTO (World Tourism Organization) (2004) *WTO Welcomes EU Enlargement as a Stimulus for Tourism* (Madrid: WTO).

WTO (World Tourism Organization) (2006) *Tourism Market Trends, 2006 Edition* (Madrid: WTO).

Young, C. & Kaczmarek, S. (1999) Changing the perception of the post-socialist city: place promotion and imagery in £ódü, Poland, *Geographical Journal*, 165(2), pp. 183–191.

Estonian Tourism and the Accession Effect: the Impact of European Union Membership on the Contemporary Development Patterns of the Estonian Tourism Industry

JEFF JARVIS & PIRET KALLAS

ABSTRACT   *In this paper specific attention is placed on analysing the impact the EU accession of May 2004 had on the development trajectory of Estonia's tourism industry. Overall, it can be seen that the Estonian industry benefited significantly from the 'accession effect', with the industry roughly expanding by one third in two years. Three categories of positive impacts are defined. First, the accession, as well as NATO membership for the country, increased the perceived security associated with investment in the tourism industry, which in turn increased the supply of infrastructure, such as bed spaces as well tourism product. Secondly, the accession facilitated relaxed border controls and led to the opening of air access to the nation, which in turn led to the entry of low-cost airlines and stimulated a competitive response from the incumbent airline. Finally, the accession stimulated a significant increase in media attention, which resulted in an increase in the level of awareness amongst the general public and tour operators in the other EU states, which in turn stimulated demand. However it was also noted that the impact of the accession effect upon visitation patterns only lasted for a limited number of months.*

Introduction

Estonia, the most northern of the three Baltic States, is regarded increasingly as the most successful transition economy amongst the former Soviet republics of the USSR. Its transition has progressed to the extent that in recent years it has moved from being a borrower from the World Bank to becoming a donor partner (World Bank 2006).

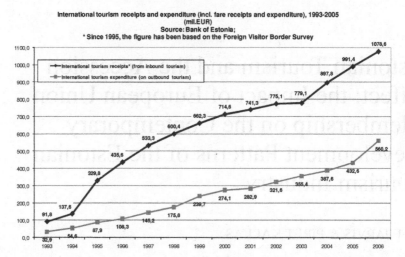

Figure 1. International tourism receipts and expenditure (€ million) in Estonia 1993–2006. *Since 1995, the figure has been based on the Foreign Visitor Border Survey. *Source*: Statistics Estonia (2007b)

In 2006, Estonia's economy was nominated (along with Latvia's) by the *Economist* magazine as one of Eastern Europe's 'Dyanamic Duo'. Significantly, between 2003 and 2006, the Estonian economy expanded by over 37 percent and, in 2006, the Bank of Estonia forecast economic growth to be 11.8 percent , making it the fastest growing Economy in Europe in 2006.

   One of the sectors fueling this economic growth is the tourism industry (*Economist* 2006), with industry earnings in 2006 exceeding €1 billion (Enterprise Estonia/Estonian Tourist Board 2006c). Between 2003 and 2005, overnight visitors increased by 30 percent, receipts from tourism by just under €200 million or 25 percent, the supply of bed spaces throughout the country by over 10,000 or 39 percent (Enterprise Estonia/Estonian Tourist Board 2006b) and the number of passengers on international scheduled routes at Tallinn airport grew by 89 percent (Tallinn Airport 2005a). Tallinn is also becoming increasingly attractive as a cruise destination within the Baltic Sea region. With 292,000 cruise passengers arriving in Tallinn in 2005, this made the city the third most popular cruise destination on the Baltic Sea after Copenhagen and St Petersburg. (Cruise Baltic 2006)

   Economically, it can be seen that Estonia has benefited greatly from the tourism industry, with just under €9 billion in receipts being generated between 1993 and 2006 (Enterprise Estonia/Estonian Tourist Board 2006c). The economic impact of the industry, as highlighted in Figure 1, has grown dramatically from €91.8 million in 1993 to €1.08 billion in 2006 (Enterprise Estonia/Estonian Tourist Board 2006) and is forecast to generate €1.3 billion by 2013 (Estonian Parliament 2006). In terms of total exports, the industry in 2003 accounted for 40 percent of all service exports and

13 percent of total exports, a rise from 32 percent and 9 percent in 1993 (Enterprise Estonia/Estonian Tourist Board 2006b).

Part of the success for the significant growth in Estonian tourism can be attributed to the fact that in 2002 the nation launched the 'Brand Estonia' campaign. Although the high cost of hiring foreign marketing specialists to design 'Brand Estonia' stimulated a wide domestic debate within the national press, it acted as a foundation stone on which to build a marketing strategy as the country moved towards EU accession. Branding is seen increasingly as crucial in the contemporary international marketing of tourism. Van Ham (2001) called the 'brand state' the outside world's ideas about a particular country that can have an impact on a country's economic and political attention, which he defined as a state's strategic equity.

Strategically, it can be seen that since 1995 the industry moved away from being over-reliant on same-day visitors (who predominantly came from Finland). However, a continuing strategic weakness is that, overall, the industry still exhibits an unhealthy reliance on the Finnish market, although this is gradually decreasing. The industry has also seen investment in and the development of product sectors such as the convention industry, 'off season' city breaks, high-yielding backpackers (Jarvis 1994; Clark & Jarvis 2005) and health spa tourism and infrastructure. The majority of this investment, however, is primarily flowing to Tallinn – the nation's capital city and international gateway – and not dispersing to rural areas.

The purpose of this paper is to examine the specific impact that the major event of the EU accession of May 2004 had on the development trajectory of the Estonian tourism industry.

The Methodology used for this study combined in depth qualitative interviews with key industry representatives with the re-analysis of existing statistics provided by the Estonian government. In addition other relevant secondary academic sources were analysed which focused on the historical patterns of tourism development in Estonia pre-accession.

The Evolution of the Tourism Industry in Estonia

The old town of Tallinn, the walled Hanseatic League city, is the major contemporary tourism attraction of Estonia. However, historically the development of tourism in Estonia was stimulated by the discovery that the sea mud from the small Baltic coast town of Haapsalu could be of therapeutic benefit. Subsequently, the first health resort built by the town doctor, Carl Abraham Hunnius, opened in 1825 and immediately became popular with the Russian aristocracy, intellectuals and artists, as well as the local Baltic Germans (Worthington, 2003). Within a few years, a number of 'spa resorts' had opened on the coastal areas of Estonia and the region had developed a thriving tourism industry. However, in a pattern that would become repetitive, the first geo-political shift to impact on the industry was World War I and, not unexpectedly, it had a major impact. The key Russian inbound market was cut off after the Communist revolution of 1917 and the majority of tourism infrastructure was either destroyed or lay in a state of decay after Estonia's battle for independence. This led to a forced market reorientation that saw the country promoted to her near neighbours, the Finns, Swedes and Latvians, many of whom were attracted to her coastal resorts (Unwin 1996). As had happened at the outbreak of World War I, just after recording a peak of 160,000 foreign visitors in 1936 (Kallas 2002), the industry suffered extensively during the Second World War as it was invaded by both Stalin and Hitler and eventually fell behind the Iron Curtain.

The Soviet Tourism Era in Estonia

The Soviet occupation of Estonia effectively saw the nation cut off from the rest of the world (Unwin 1996). For example, Worthington (2003) noted that the public in the coastal resort of Parnu were informed that the 'Rannahotel will no longer exist as a guest house but will be turned into a worker's rest home'. The tourism industry was problematic for the Soviet system under Stalin as it was regarded as 'non-productive', a fact that led to it being redefined as either a propaganda tool or as a means to 'recuperate the workforce' (Hall 1991). International tourism to Soviet Estonia increased substantially after the death of Stalin, as it was seen as a means of generating hard currency from the West and, to achieve this, the sea link to Finland was re-established in July 1965 (Jaakson, 1996). In its first year of operation some 10,000 foreigners came to Estonia on a quota system related to available bed spaces, organized through the Soviet travel agent *Intourist* and selected travel agents in Finland. This was supported by a marketing campaign and by brochures promoting 'Soviet Estonia' (Figure 2). As tourism in 'Soviet Estonia' was supply led, any new beds that came on line would lead substantially to increased arrivals. The opening of the 829 bed 'Hotel Viru' in 1972 increased supply and, by the end of the 1970s, it alone was accommodating between 40,000 and 50,000 visitors (Jaakson 1996). Estonia still remained a mainly closed country, with the majority of visitors permitted to go only to Tallinn; even the historic university town of Tartu was off limits due to the proximity of a military airport (Unwin 1996). The sailing regatta for the Moscow Olympics came to Tallinn in 1980 and this further stimulated Soviet hotel construction and, hence, visitor arrivals under the supply-driven industry. Under the freedoms gained during *Perestroika* in the late 1980s, restrictions on tourism were eased, which stimulated Estonians to fill the gaps left by *Intourist,* including the servicing of the ferry traffic by the provision of guided tours, excursions, folk entertainment and meals (Worthington 2001).

Tourism in Transition 1991–2003

With the ending of the Soviet occupation, tourism expanded rapidly in the first few years of transition, with the majority of international arrivals coming from Finland as Helsinki was only some 80 km from Tallinn by ferry. The number of Finnish visitors increased from an estimated 120,000 in 1985 (interview with Olaf Sööt, Director Intourist Estonia 1966–1991, November 2002) to 1.52 million in 1995, when they accounted for 72 percent of all foreign arrivals to Estonia. Unwin (1996)

Figure 2. Brochure promoting 'Soviet Estonia' produced in 1971. *Source:* Statistics Estonia (2007b).

argued that most of this increase can be attributed to same-day visitors who were attracted to Estonia by Tallinn's close proximity, the linguistic and historical cultural links and, significantly, by the economic incentive of cross-border trade. The level of cross-border trade expanded to the extent that in 1994 up to 40 percent of all retail purchases in the Estonian capital were attributed to Finns (Worthington 2001). Worthington (2001) also argued that the cross-border retail boom, in turn, acted as a stimulant in the overall transition process, and possibly even a catalyst as it stimulated foreign direct investment and technology and skills transfer.

In November 1995, Estonia submitted its application to accede to the European Union. From then to 2003 a steady market reorientation can be observed, highlighted in Figure 3. First, and most significantly, the lower yielding same-day visitor segment grew only by 8 percent between 1996 and 2003, while higher yielding overnight visitors increased by a substantial 120 percent to account for 43 percent of all international arrivals. Secondly, although Finnish visitors still dominated the market for total visitor arrivals, the reliance the Estonian tourism industry has on the market decreased, as, in 2003, visitors from Finland accounted for 53 percent of all arrivals compared with 72 percent in 1995 (Enterprise Estonia/Estonian Tourist Board 2004). Additionally, more Finns were encouraged to stay in overnight accommodation, with an increase of 230 percent from 1995 to 2003, accounting for 61 percent of the market. Finally, the later half of the transition phase saw increased market diversification via the growth in the number of overnight visitors from more distant EU markets, such as Germany and the UK. Additionally, the nearby Scandinavian markets of Sweden, Denmark and Norway also grew in total by 112 percent between 1996 and 2003 (Enterprise Estonia/Estonian Tourist Board 2004).

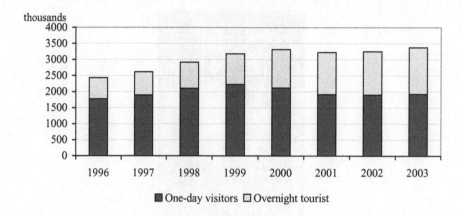

Figure 3. One-day visitors and overnight visitors to Estonia 1996–2003. *Source*: Enterprise Estonia/Estonian Tourist Board (2006b)

The 'Accession Effect' 2004–2006

Inbound tourism to Estonia grew dramatically in the EU membership year of 2004. Additional visitors staying in paid accommodation numbered 261,000, a significant percentage increase of 24 percent on 2003, while visitor nights increased by 21 percent (Tables 1 and 2) (Enterprise Estonia/Estonian Tourist Board 2005). This growth continued in 2005 and, in the two years post-2003, there were over 30 percent more visitors to Estonia and 31 percent more overnights spent in the country. However, this growth was not evenly spread, with the key market of Finland increasing only by 13 percent in visitors and by 12 percent in visitor nights. The accession growth was driven primarily by increases from the markets of the UK, Sweden, Germany and Norway, with Latvia and Russia also contributing (Table 1).

The fastest-growing major market for Estonia between 2003 and 2005 was the UK, which increased by 108 percent in terms of visitor numbers and 118 percent in terms of visitor nights (Table 1). The market is also relatively high yielding, as the British spent on average 26 percent more than the average visitor, at €258 per visit in 2005 compared to €173 by the Finns. Additionally, the UK market is highly independent, with 79 percent not booking any services via a travel agent, whilst 58 percent of Finns were on a package or group tour. Also 79 percent of UK travellers were first-time visitors, in contrast to only 4 percent Finns, a finding that highlights the fact that Estonia has been exposed to new visitors (Enterprise Estonia/Estonian Tourist Board 2006d).

Visitors from both the Swedish and German markets also grew substantially, by 62 percent and 60 percent, respectively, both to supply over 100,000 visitors per year, with German visitors also being high yielding, spending on average €276 per visit. These

Table 1. Arrivals (tourists) at accommodation establishments, 2003–2006

	Arrivals				Change			
	2003	2004	2005	2006	2006/03	2006/03	2006/05	2006/05
Foreign tourists	1 112 746	1 374 414	1 453 418	1 427 583	314 837	28%	−25 835	−1,8%
Finland	706 473	843 871	799 139	749 132	42 659	6%	−50 007	−6%
Sweden	66 751	89 042	108 234	105 939	39 188	59%	−2 295	−2%
Germany	68 151	85 643	109 346	90 073	21 922	32%	−19 273	−18%
Latvia	29 230	40 956	51 558	65 559	36 329	124%	14 001	27%
Russia	37 320	42 348	53 427	67 201	29 881	80%	13 774	26%
UK	30 151	38 903	62 926	61 393	31 242	104%	−1 533	−2%
Norway	29 842	35 798	41 273	48 863	19 021	64%	7 590	18%
Lithuania	14 320	20 555	24 703	29 889	15 569	109%	5 186	21%
Italy	13 127	25 642	26 712	26 753	13 626	104%	41	0%
USA	12 761	19 411	19 506	19 856	7 095	56%	350	2%
Poland	13 018	11 301	14 194	14 240	1 222	9%	46	0%
France	8 326	15 086	16 921	16 510	8 184	98%	−411	−2%
Spain	7 921	12 177	15 533	15 148	7 227	91%	−385	−2%
Denmark	14 894	13 915	15 407	16 206	1 312	9%	799	5%
Holland	7 826	10 490	12 714	13 688	5 862	75%	974	8%
Japan	6 901	7 362	8 066	8 093	1 192	17%	27	0%

Table 2. Visitor Overnights at accommodation establishments, 2003–2006

	Overnights				Change			
	2003	2004	2005	2006	2006/03	2006/03	2006/05	2006/05
Foreign tourists	2 267 873	2 746 806	2 982 459	3 020 367	752 494	33%	37 908	1,3%
Finland	1 411 623	1 664 799	1 581 685	1 501 481	89 858	6%	−80 204	−5%
Sweden	134 189	184 871	235 202	236 998	102 809	77%	1 796	1%
Germany	122 189	163 842	215 892	185 550	63 361	52%	−30 342	−14%
Latvia	42 682	59 532	74 880	101 300	58 618	137%	26 420	35%
Russia	81 321	101 546	138 508	176 862	95 541	117%	38 354	28%
UK	73 060	94 843	159 141	155 667	82 607	113%	−3 474	−2%
Norway	61 381	81 288	105 432	134 741	73 360	120%	29 309	28%
Lithuania	22 977	32 068	40 925	52 202	29 225	127%	11 277	28%
Italy	28 200	52 507	59 553	61 348	33 148	118%	1 795	3%
USA	30 254	44 492	44 349	49 460	19 206	63%	5 111	12%
Poland	77 320	22 681	26 459	31 802	−45 518	−59%	5 343	20%
France	15 350	28 962	33 990	35 817	20 467	133%	1 827	5%
Spain	13 631	21 878	28 634	29 362	15 731	115%	728	3%
Denmark	26 008	28 510	32 445	34 358	8 350	32%	1 913	6%
Holland	16 094	21 698	26 095	29 145	13 051	81%	3 050	12%
Japan	12 648	14 174	15 350	15 516	2 868	23%	166	1%

markets were also first-time visitors predominantly, with 41 percent of Swedes and 74 percent of Germans making their first trip to Estonia (Enterprise Estonia/Estonian Tourist Board 2006d). Interestingly all three fast-growing markets saw budget airlines establish links with London, Berlin and Stockholm, a factor that Hall (2006) identified as one of the major drivers of post-EU accession tourism development. As for the type of tourism that developed, the main growth has come from (1) city breaks to Tallinn, (2) tours combining Estonia with its neighbouring countries and (3) spa holidays, popular with tourists from Sweden and Finland (Enterprise Estonia/Estonian Tourist Board 2005).

Although the average length of stay in Tallinn has increased from an average of 1.58 nights in 2003 to 1.83 nights during the first ten months of 2006, 66 percent of tourists stayed for less than four nights in the country (Enterprise Estonia/Estonian Tourist Board 2006d). This highlights the fact that Estonia is predominantly a short-stay destination. Additionally, tourism is also highly concentrated, with 59 percent of all overnights in 2005 spent in Tallinn, with only 41 percent of nights in regional Estonia (Enterprise Estonia/Estonian Tourism Board 2006c). The statistics highlighted in Figure 4 also exhibit a bias towards Estonia attracting 'middle-aged tourists', with 50 percent of total arrivals being over 46 years old. However, the developing markets, such as the UK with 59 percent and Italy with 74 percent of visitors under 45 years old in 2005, run contrary to this trend; older tourists still dominate the markets of Finland and Sweden (Enterprise Estonia, Estonian Tourist Board 2006d). Thus, it can

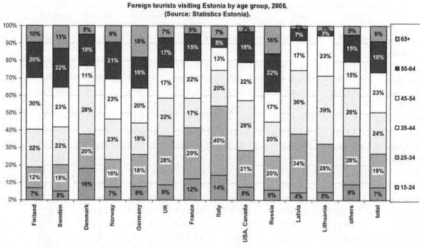

Figure 4. Foreign tourists visiting Estonia by age group 2005. *Source*: Foreign Visitor Survey (2005, in Enterprise Estonia/Estonian Tourist Board 2006d).

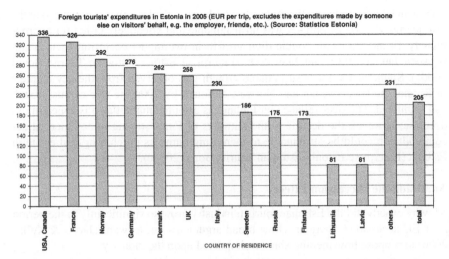

Figure 5. Foreign tourist expenditures in Estonia in 2005 (Euros per trip, excluding the expenditure made by someone else on the visitor's behalf). *Source*: Foreign Visitor Survey 2005, in Enterprise Estonia/Estonian Tourist Board 2006d), Statistics Estonia (2006).

be seen clearly that in the period after EU accession Estonia began to attract visitors from a more diverse range of source markets who were relatively high yielding, more independent and typically younger than the dominant Finnish market (Figures 4 and 5).

Interestingly, the overall figures for 2006 highlight the fact that the rate of increase in overall tourist arrivals have slowed from most major markets and decreased from the core market of Finland by six percent, or over 47,000 visitors, on the arrival numbers for the corresponding eleven months of 2005 (Table 1). Significantly, the UK market that had grown strongly between 2003 and 2005, declined by two percent in both terms of tourists and overnights, while Sweden was also down by two percent in arrivals but up one percent in overnights and German arrivals declined by 18 percent and 14 percent in terms of overnights (Tables 1 and 2). Growth, however, was seen in the markets of Norway, Latvia and Russia. In 2006, the Norwegian market was up by 18 percent in terms of visitors and 28 percent in terms of nights. This correlates closely with the arrival of the low-cost carrier 'Norwegian' on the Oslo–Tallinn route in May 2006, which, in 2007, was offering one-way fares for as low as €32 (www.norwegian.no). Overall foreign visitors declined by 1.8 percent, thus, it can be seen clearly that the substantial growth rates experienced in the two years post accession did not continue into 2006 as the 'accession effect' diminished.

From examining the statistical evidence, it is clear that the Estonian tourism industry experienced a positive growth phase immediately before and after joining the

European Union. However, the magnitude of the growth phase that commenced in the last quarter of 2003 essentially was unsustainable and effectively lasted for approximately 18 months, with double-digit growth in overnights occurring each month between January 2004 and May 2005 (Enterprise Estonia/Estonian Tourist Board 2006c). Significantly, more sustainable growth was observed from the key markets of Russia, the UK, Sweden and Norway, although by 2006 the rate of this growth had stabilized. The over-reliance on Finland as a source market also is appearing to decrease; however, the decline in the numbers of Finns staying in commercial accommodation could be attributable to increasing numbers purchasing real estate in Estonia (Enterprise Estonia/Estonian Tourist Board 2006c).

Analysing the 'Accession Effect'

So, why exactly did the Estonian tourism industry grow so significantly in the period after EU accession? There are three broad arguments put forward (Jarvis & Kallas 2006) to propose how membership has impacted upon the industry.

(a) EU Membership Fostered a Positive Business Climate and Stimulated Investment in Infrastructure (Increased Supply)

As Estonia moved towards membership of both NATO (March 2004) and the EU (May 2004), it provided a more stable business framework in which to attract both local and foreign direct investment to the country and the tourism industry. In fact, Estonia was ranked as the largest recipient of foreign direct investment per capita in Europe (*Economist* 2006). Membership of NATO was seen as significant as it removed the perceived security threat posed by Russia in the east. It also stimulated the government of Estonia to invest in the development of a branding strategy for the nation in 2002. The branding campaign entitled 'Welcome to Estonia', although debated widely within Estonia, provided the nation with a platform on which to capitalize on the imminent EU accession. Its major objectives focused on stimulating foreign direct investment in Estonia, increasing exports to European markets and to expand the tourist base beyond Sweden and Finland (Enterprise Estonia 2002). The linking of Estonia to the 'brand' of the EU conveyed some of the attributes associated with the union to 'Brand Estonia', most notably in regard to issues of perceived safety and security (K. Kont, managing director, Estonian Association of Travel Agents, interview November 2004). In branding theory, establishing a differentiation from other competitors is essential, as is developing a brand identity. Brand identity involves the development of a vision of how that brand should be perceived by its target market (Aaker and Joachimsthaler 2000; Grönroos 2000). The Estonian brand essence was described as 'positively transforming', which was based primarily on the successful transition the country had just experienced and the positive nature of the changes that were taking place (Enterprise Estonia, 2002). Additionally, the country was identified

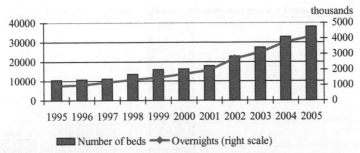

Figure 6. Supply of bed-spaces in Estonia and number of overnights of foreign and domestic visitors 1995–2005. *Source*: Statistics Estonia (2007).

as a 'Nordic country with a twist', and the Estonian people as radical and reforming, resourceful and environmentally minded, calm and peaceful (Gardner & Standaert 2003). Importantly, this differentiated the nation from the other Baltic States and Russia, and shifted the perception of Estonia towards the Nordic/Scandinavian region.

In expectation of a considerable increase in visitor flows (especially overnight visitors) after EU accession, the accommodation and spa sectors attracted substantial investments (D. Visnapuu, managing director, Estonian Hotel and Restaurant Association, interview November 2004). This investment flow resulted in a 33 percent increase in bed-places between January 2003 and July 2004. During the same period, the number of bed-places in Tallinn increased by 37 percent (Enterprise Estonia/Estonian Tourist Board 2005). Figure 6 shows the increase in the number of beds available in Estonia and the number of overnights. Basically it indicates that a significant capacity expansion occurred in 2002 and continued until 2005, which was, in turn, matched by substantial growth in overnights. This growth in supply is set to continue as bed-spaces in Tallinn are forecast to increase by 18 percent in 2007 (Enterprise Estonia/Estonian Tourist Board 2007). This, in turn, highlights the confidence that investors have in the future of Estonian tourism.

The substantial investment spike in accommodation that occurred as membership of the EU became closer is highlighted in Figure 7, with over €89 million having been invested between 2003 and 2005. This investment has continued, with more than 2000 additional bed-places in mainly four- and five-star hotels expected to become available in Tallinn during 2007, whereas, in Tartu, a new hotel with 400 beds is expected to increase the hotel capacity by 30 percent (Enterprise Estonia/Estonian Tourist Board 2007). Additionally, in order to develop the industry further, tourism infrastructure development and marketing funds were available for strategic projects under the EU's PHARE project prior to May 2004 (Enterprise Estonia Website 2007). This led to the refurbishment of old manor houses for tourism purposes, amongst other projects.

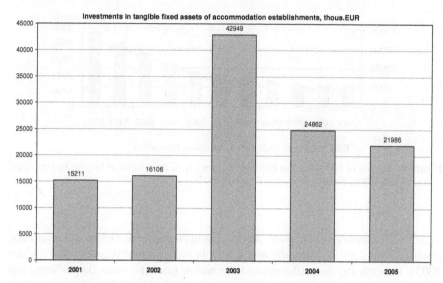

Figure 7. Investment (€ thousand) in accommodation establishments in Estonia 2001–2005. *Source*: Statistics Estonia (2007c).

(b) Regulatory Changes Associated with EU Membership Stimulated Increased Transport Access and Removal of Border Controls (Ease of Access Facilitated Increases in Demand)

The structural changes associated with moving toward EU membership facilitated streamlined border-crossing procedures and increased transport access to Estonia. The task of tourists arriving by road was made easier by simpler border-crossing formalities for EU nationals; this stimulated an increase in Finnish, Latvian, Lithuanian, Polish and German tourists travelling in Estonia by car, coach or caravan (Enterprise Estonia/Estonian Tourist Board 2005).

The 'open skies' policy of the EU and the competitive threats posed by low-cost carriers influenced the national carrier 'Estonian Air' to prepare for competition prior to accession to shore up its competitive position. This is a common strategy followed by other incumbent airlines in response to the threat posed by the arrival of low-cost carriers (Pender & Baum 2000). From late 2003 Estonian Air began to introduce substantially lower one-way airfares that were available for purchase over the internet (Enterprise Estonia/ Estonian Tourist Board 2005). Additionally, Estonian Air launched new routes to Amsterdam, Berlin, Oslo, Munich, Brussels and Dublin and increased frequency to Copenhagen, London and Hamburg.

Hall (2006) argued that the integration of the new entrants with the rest of Europe was aided by the arrival of low-cost airlines and this appears to be true for Estonia as well. Overall, EU membership saw the number of routes serviced from Tallinn grow substantially from 12 in 2002 to 22 by 2004 (Statistics Estonia 2007). The Italian carrier, Volare (May 2004) and Easyjet (November 2004) were the first to start flying between Tallinn and London, Berlin and Milan. They were followed into the market by the carriers Fly Nordic (March 2005), City Airline (March 2005) and Norwegian (May 2006), launching budget routes to Stockholm, Copenhagen, Oslo and Goteborg in Scandinavia. However, the potential pitfalls of a destination relying on budget airlines is highlighted by the fact that by January 2007 the only low-cost carriers still servicing Tallinn were Easyjet (Berlin and London) and Norwegian (Oslo). The rate of growth of air access also slowed, with Western European routes to Munich, Hamburg, Gothenburg and Manchester – opened in the 12 months after accession – all closing in 2005/6 (Tallinn Airport 2005b, 2006). Significantly, the arrival of the low-cost operator Easyjet on the London–Tallinn route stimulated a 185 percent increase in the number of British visitors in November and December 2004 (Enterprise Estonia/Estonian Tourist Board 2005) and, during the first four months of their flights to Tallinn, 10,000 additional British tourists stayed at accommodation establishments in Estonia (compared to the respective months the previous year) (Enterprise Estonia/ Estonian Tourist Board 2005). The arrival of Easyjet also helped push up the traffic numbers on the Tallinn–London route by over 100 percent between 2004 and 2005, to make it the most popular air route out of Estonia (Tallinn Airport 2005a). With Easyjet offering fares in 2007 as low as £14.99 one-way to Tallinn, it is understandable why the route has grown so quickly (Easyjet website 2007).

The boom in air passengers from 868,000 passengers on international scheduled routes in 2004 to over 1.2 million in 2005 (Tallinn Airport 2005a) correlates with the findings of Pender and Baum (2000) that low-cost carriers can stimulate new markets. However, there is some concern about the type of segments that can be attracted via budget airlines (Hall 2006). The *Economist* magazine commented on the number of British stag/hen weekends being attracted to Tallinn (*Economist* 2004) and BBC World's *Fastrack* TV series also raised the issue of the impact of stag parties on the image of Estonia (BBC World 2004). The arrival of the capacity associated with daily services of low-cost carriers has also stimulated a number of websites promoting such travel to Tallinn, for example 'pissup.com', a company that boasts of 'exporting' over 65,000 customers from the UK to Eastern European destinations in 2005 and 2006 (www.pissup.com). The emergence of the British stags, however, is not a unique problem for Tallinn as many cities across Eastern Europe are experiencing similar unwanted segment development, such as Bratislava, Krakow, Warsaw, Budapest, Vilnius and Prague (Kiralova, 2006). Hickman (2006) noted that although stags bring with them economic benefits, often they are short term and limited to a few businesses. In response to their arrival, a number of bars in Tallinn started to publicize that 'stag parties would not be served' in their establishments (BBC World 2004) (Figure 8). Coles and Hall (2005) warned of the potential long-term impact that such segments may have on the branding and positioning of destinations and this is supported by concerns

Figure 8. Sign posted at the door of an Estonian Bar in the old town to dissuade stag parties from visiting (November 2006).

about the contemporary tourism image of Riga in Latvia (Druva-Druvaskaline *et al.* 2006). In 2006, the *Marta resource centre for women* distributed brochures in bars and clubs in Riga to tourists warning of the issues surrounding human trafficking (Baltic Standbynews 2006a). The British Embassy in Tallinn was also sufficiently concerned about the damage that stag party visitors were doing to the image of the UK amongst the Estonians to host a special conference on the management of British groups in October 2006 for the benefit of the tourism industry (Baltic Standbynews 2006b). Although the number of stag party visitors out of the total arrivals to Estonia is small, the potential damage such segments can do to Estonia's brand image is highlighted in the following quote from the *Daily Telegraph* in 2004.

> Tallinn no longer takes pride in the title of 'favourite destination of British staggers'. Recently, such visitors have become an increasing source of trouble. The Brits, loitering on the streets in large groups, swilling beer and making lewd suggestions to girls, are known all over continental Europe (*Daily Telegraph* 7 August 2004).

(c) Imminent EU Membership Led to Increased Media Coverage of Estonia Both Within and Outside the EU (Stimulated Demand)

Within the context of international tourism marketing, media coverage is widely sought after. It is considered, first, to be low cost and, secondly, is regarded by consumers as far more believable than paid advertising (Cooper *et al.* 2005). An effective story in a targeted newspaper, magazine or television programme can be highly powerful, especially if it can convey the desired brand attributes and can communicate to a sought-after target segment. As the ten 2004 accession countries moved closer to the EU, this stimulated substantial media coverage (Coles & Hall 2005) and Estonia was no exception. In Estonia's case, the latent brand image within the other EU members may, in fact, have been non-existent or at least extremely limited, as the country had been occupied by the Soviet Union for over 50 years. In contrast to being a negative, this, however, could provide a unique opportunity for positioning the brand. This fact was identified in the background on the development of 'Brand Estonia' by the government in 2002.

> Our re-emergence on the European stage has given us a critical and rare opportunity to make a first impression on millions of European business people and potential tourists. For most of them the name Estonia will be unfamiliar, or, if they have any impressions at all they will more than likely than not be vague or even negative regarding Estonia's occupied past or perceived poor weather (Enterprise Estonia 2002: 46).

The EU accession delivered to Estonia a regular stream of reporters eager to 'discover' the country on behalf of their readers both within and outside of Europe. This pre-EU coverage was estimated to be worth millions of Euros in advertising; it built further on the increased exposure that Estonia secured in the European media during the hosting of the Eurovision Song Contest in 2002. In 2004 alone, newspapers and magazines, such as *Le Figaro, The Times, Newsweek, Wall Street Journal, Elle, Time, Economist, Le Monde, Marie France, Daily Telegraph* among others, all published articles promoting a positive image of Tallinn as a tourist destination (Estonian Foreign Ministry website 2005). In addition, television programmes as far away as Australia sent crews to Tallinn to explore the 'new' European country: 'It has cobbled streets and gingerbread facades, steeples, spires and a marvellous medieval wall . . . Get ready to step back in time ' (Channel 9 Australia 2005). The majority of these articles were positive in nature. The promotion of a positive image of a destination makes people more perceptive to favourable word of mouth and also helps them screen information, making it easier for the tourism board to communicate effectively (Grönroos 2000).

The following quotations provide some examples of the media coverage gained for Estonia: 'Tallinn, a magnet for the creative set, has developed a style that could be described as a mix of Scandinavian cool and urban hip' (*Wall Street Journal* 30 April 2004); 'Tallinn, architecturally one of Europe's most intriguing cities is a fusion of medieval cobbled streets and old town spires with a colourful café scene and eclectic nightlife' (*The Times* 24 January 2004); 'Word is starting to leak that Tallinn, Estonia's capital, is one of the coolest spots in Europe ... Tallinn's trump card is its seamless blending of medieval with modernity' (*San Francisco Chronicle* 24 May 2004).

This media coverage of Estonia has continued in the travel pages post-accession, with the *Sunday Times* (UK) listing Tallinn as one of the eight top winter weekend breaks (Newsom 2006) and the *Observer* (UK) describing the delights of a winter in the old town: 'Tallinn's Old Town is charming at any time of year, but its cosy candlelit cellar bars, opulent dining rooms and Art Deco patisseries are best appreciated when a chill wind is blowing in from the Baltic' (Ferguson 2006).

In addition to press coverage, a number of guidebooks designed for independent travellers now exist on both Estonia, and Tallinn in particular, with the Lonely Planet company releasing a 'Best of Tallinn' guide in 2006. However, despite the publicity generated in the press during the lead up to accession, research data highlights that the nation still remains almost invisible within the UK. When UK respondents were asked what comes to mind when thinking of Estonia as a holiday destination, 42 percent of the adult population did not know anything about the country and almost three-quarters were unlikely to consider going there in the next three years. However, for those who had been to Estonia previously, they were far more likely to return (Enterprise Estonia/Estonian Tourist Board 2006a).

Conclusions

From analysing the available data between 1993 and 1996 it is clear that the EU accession accelerated the development of the tourism industry in Estonia in the years following the event. Overall, it fostered the expansion of non-traditional source markets, such as the UK, Sweden, Norway and Germany amongst others, and attracted increasing numbers of first-time visitors. Three broad impacts can be associated with the 'accession effect'. First, it facilitated the increase in investment in the industry by – together with NATO membership – increasing the security associated with both local and foreign direct investment. This has led to an increase in the provision of accommodation and the supply of tourism products, as well as the increase in firms spending private funds on the promotion of Estonia. The improvement in the security perception also can be considered to have stimulated demand, as the view of Estonia as part of Europe directly countered the lawlessness perceived in the break up of the Soviet Union.

Secondly, the policy shifts associated with joining the EU, namely the easier border controls and the 'open skies' policy, has increased access to the country from the other EU member states and stimulated the national carrier to increase routes and reduce fares. Additionally, within months of Estonia joining the EU, the first low-cost carrier touched down at Tallinn airport, increasing access options and lowering access costs from the developing markets of Scandinavia, Italy, Germany and the UK.

Finally, the 'event' of Estonia joining Europe stimulated foreign media coverage of 'the new Europe' primarily within the EU, but also globally. This media coverage acted as free promotion of the country in key markets and it can be associated with stimulating the demand and acting as a platform for communicating the elements of the Brand Estonia strategy.

Once the customer demand was stimulated via the media, the budget carriers improved the ease of travel from new markets such as the UK, Sweden, Norway and Germany and the increase in the supply of infrastructure was available to host the visitors. Overall EU membership, increased supply of tourism infrastructure, facilitated increased access to the country and stimulated demand for visitors, primarily from other EU countries.

However, it can be seen that the 'accession effect' existed only for between eighteen months and two years, as the growth rates of 2004 and 2005 proved to be unsustainable in 2006. Within the context of tourism development, Estonia joining the EU had a similar impact to the hosting of a major special event. The legacy of the 'accession effect' has seen the Estonian tourism industry expand by around a third in two years, provided an increased range of affordable access options to the country, increased the industry infrastructure and raised awareness, albeit to a limited extent, of Estonia as a travel destination.

The research has highlighted a number of themes worthy of further research, which have wide-ranging implications for a number of destinations in the 'New Europe'. The first issue is attempting to measure the correlation between the growth of inbound tourism and the establishment of low-cost airline access. All of the fast-growing inbound markets to Estonia (the UK, Germany, Sweden and Norway) in the period post-accession benefited from budget airline access. Significantly, the only market out of those four to grow in 2006 was Norway, which saw the establishment of low-cost access in May 2006. The second research issue is associated with low-cost airline growth and concerns the management of the growth generated. The emergence of stag party tourism from the UK can be attributed to low-cost airlines and the current uncontrolled promotion of Tallinn via the internet could damage the perception of the destination amongst potential target customers. Additionally, this 'low-cost airline growth' appears to be highly concentrated in Tallinn and associated with a 'city break' product and, currently, only limited attempts have been made to encourage greater dispersion of visitors via self-drive products, such as 'The Great Baltic Touring Route' (www.gbtr.info). The third issue worth further research is associated with the management of 'Brand Estonia' and the ability of the national tourism office to control the brand when faced by larger budgets associated with low-cost airlines and internet-based companies promoting the destinations from outside the nation's borders. In effect, who has control of 'Brand Estonia'?

The 'accession effect' boosted tourism to Estonia; however, structural challenges still remain. The primary challenges for the tourism industry in Estonia are to build on the 'accession effect' as a platform to further develop the industry, increase length of stay and focus on attracting high yield international visitor segments, who will disperse outside of Tallinn to regional areas and spread the economic benefits through out the whole country. Finally, the marketing and management of 'Brand Estonia' requires further investment in both Europe and beyond.

References

Aaker, D. & Joachimsthaler, E. (2000) *Brand Leadership* (New York: The Free Press).

Baltic Standbynews (2006a) Tourists in Riga warned against sexual services. Available at http://www.standbynews.info/7182.0.html?&tx_standbynews_pi1[showUid]=21155& cHash=7078762f88 (accessed 15 January 2007).

Baltic Standbynews (2006b) Embassy and Enterprise Estonia hold stag party seminar. Available at http://www.standbynews.info/7182.0.html?&tx_standbynews_pi1[showUid]=21883& cHash=d21e9036b1 (accessed 15 January 2007).

Bank of Estonia (2006) Economic Forecast 2006–2008. Available at http://www.eestipank.info/pub/en/yldine/press/kommentaarid/Arhiiv/_157.html?objId=911003 (accessed 4 January 2007).

BBC World Television (2004) Fastrack TV Series, broadcast November.

Channel 9 Australia (2005) Getaway Program, 24 February. Available at http://getaway.ninemsn.com.au/article.aspx?id=17376 (accessed 10 January 2006).

Clark, G. & Jarvis, J. (2005) *Backpackers in Estonia: A Pilot Study* (Monash University: National Centre for Australian Studies, research paper).

Coles, T. & Hall, D. (2005) Tourism and European Union Enlargement. Plus ca change?, *International Journal of Tourism Research*, 7, pp. 51–61.

Cooper, C., Fletcher, J., Fyall, A., Gilbert, D. & Wanhill, S. (2005) *Tourism Principles and Practice*, 3rd edn (Harlow, UK: Pearson Education).

Cruise Baltic (2006) Basic Facts – a first eye opener to enjoy the Baltic region. Available at http://www.cruisebaltic.com/composite-20.htm (accessed 11 January 2007).

Druva-Druvaskalne, I., Abiols, I., & Slara, A. (2006) Latvia Tourism: Decisive Factors and Tourism Development, in: D. Hall, M. Smith & B. Marciszweska Tourism in the New Europe: The Challenges and Opportunities if EU Enlargement (CAB International: Wallingford).

Easyjet Website (2007) Fare quoted for 13 March. Available at http://www.easyjet.com/en/book/step2.asp (accessed 13 January 2007).

Economist (2004) A Baltic hot spot for boozy brits, *Economist*, 13 May.

Economist (2006) The Dynamic Duo, *Economist*, 16 December.

Enterprise Estonia (2002) *Brand Estonia Guide*. Available at http://www.eas.ee/?id=12 (accessed 7 January 2007 and 29 April 2005).

Enterprise Estonia (2007) Website. Available at http://www.eas.ee/?id=1198 (accessed 6 January 2007).

Enterprise Estonia/Estonian Tourist Board (2004) *Overview of Tourism in Estonia in 2005, as of June 2004* (Tallinn: Enterprise Estonia/Estonian Tourist Board).

Enterprise Estonia/ Estonian Tourist Board (2005) *Tourism in Estonia in 2004* (Tallinn: Enterprise Estonia/Estonian Tourist Board).

Enterprise Estonia/Estonian Tourist Board (2006a) Eesti maine puhkusesihtkohana: Suurbritannia elanikkonna küsitlus, aprill 2006 [The image of Estonia as a holiday destination in Great Britain: survey among the British population, April 2006] (Tallinn: Enterprise Estonia/Estonian Tourist Board).

Enterprise Estonia/Estonian Tourist Board (2006b) *Tourism in Estonia 1993–2005: Key Indicators* (Tallinn: Enterprise Estonia/Estonian Tourist Board).

Enterprise Estonia/ Estonian Tourist Board (2006c) *Tourism in Estonia in 2005* (Tallinn: Enterprise Estonia/Estonian Tourist Board).

Enterprise Estonia/Estonian Tourist Board (2006d) Foreign Tourists in Estonia: Selected results of the foreign visitor survey 2005 (Tallinn: Enterprise Estonia/Estonian Tourist Board)

Enterprise Estonia/Estonian Tourist Board (2007) *Tourism in Estonia in 2006* (as of 29 March 2007) (Tallinn: Enterprise Estonia/Estonian Tourist Board).

Estonian Foreign Ministry (2005) *Discovering Estonia*. Available at http://web-static.vm.ee/static/failid /098/avastades_eestimaad.pdf (accessed 6 January 2007).

Estonian Parliament (2006) Eesti riiklik turismiarengukava 2007–2013 [Estonian National Tourism Development Plan 2007–2013]. Available at https://www.riigiteataja.ee/ert/act.jsp?id=12755212) (accessed 17 January 2007).

Ferguson, E. (2006) Don't need the sunshine, *Observer*, 12 November.

Gardner, S. & Standaert, M. (2003). *Estonia and Belarus: Branding the Old Block*. Brand channel website, 3 March 2003. Available at www.brandchanel.com (accessed 7 January 2007).

Grönroos, C. (2000) *Service Management and Marketing – A Customer Relationship Management Approach*, 2nd edn (West Sussex: John Wiley & Sons Ltd).

Hall, D. (1991). *Tourism and Economic Development in Eastern Europe and the Soviet Union* (London: Belhaven Press).

Hall, D. (2006) Tourism and the transformation of European space, in: M. Smith & L. Onderwater (Eds) *The Transformation of Tourism Spaces: ATLAS Reflections 2006*, pp. 1–91 (Arnhem: ATLAS).

Hickman, L. (2006) Is it ok to go on a stag weekend?, *The Guardian*, 25 July.

In Your Pocket Guide to Tallinn (2005) Available at http://www.inyourpocket.com/estonia/tallinn/en /feature?id=55676) (accessed 29 April 2005).

Jaakson, R. (1996) Tourism and transition in Post Soviet Estonia, *Annals of Tourism Research*, 23(3), pp. 617–634.

Jarvis, J. (1994) *The Billion Dollar Backpackers* (Monash University: National Centre for Australian Studies).

Jarvis, J. & Kallas, P. (2006) Estonia – Switching Unions: Impacts of EU Membership on Tourism Development, in: D. Hall, M. Smith & B. Marciszewska (Eds) *Tourism in the New Europe: Challenges and Opportunities of EU Enlargement*, pp. 154–169 (Wallingford, UK: CABI International).

Kallas, P. (2002) Tourism and Holiday Business, *Estonian Encyclopedia* (Tallinn: Eesti Entsüklopeediakirjastus).

Kiralova, A. (2006) Tourism in the Czech Republic, in: D. Hall, M. Smith & B. Marciszewska (Eds) *Tourism in the New Europe: Challenges and Opportunities of EU Enlargement*, pp. 104–115 (Wallingford, UK: CABI International).

Newsom, S. (2006) Put on your snow shoes and dance, *The Sunday Times*, 12 November.

Pender, L. & Baum, T. (2000) Have the Frills Really left the European Airline Industry?, *International Journal of Tourism Research*, 2, pp. 423–436.

Statistics Estonia (2007a) Passenger traffic through airports. Available at http://pub.stat.ee/px-web.2001/I_Database/Economy/34Transport/02Air_transport/02Air_transport.asp (accessed 22 April 2007).

Statistics Estonia (2007b) Accommodation. Available at: http://pub.stat.ee/px-web.2001_Database/ Economy/32Tourism_and_accommodation/ 01Accommodation/01Accommodation.asp

Statistics Estonia (2007c) Financial data of accommodation, catering and tourist enterprises. Available at: http://pub.stat.ee/px-web.2001/L-Database/Economy/32Tourism_and_accommodation/ 06Economic_indicators_of_tourism_and_accommodation/06Economic_indicators_of_tourism_and_ accommodation.asp

Tallinn Airport (2005a) Tallinn Airport Traffic Report 2005. Available at http://www.tallinn-airport.ee (accessed 11 January 2007).

Tallinn Airport (2005b) Majandusaasta aruanne 2005 AS Tallinna Lennujaam [Annual Report 2005 of Tallinn Airport]. Available at http://www.tallinn-airport.ee/public/files/AS%20Tallinna% 20Lennujaama%202005%20aastaaruanne.pdf (accessed 22 April 2007).

Tallinn Airport (2006) Majandusaasta aruanne 2006. AS Tallinna Lennujaam [Annual Report 2006 of Tallinn Airport]. Available at http://www.tallinn-airport.ee/public/files/TLJ_aastaraamat_2006.pdf (accessed 22 April 2007).

Unwin, T. (1996) Tourist Development in Estonia: Images, Sustainability, and Integrated Rural Development, *Tourism Management*, 17(4), pp. 265–276.

Van Ham, P. (2001) The Rise of the Brand State: The Postmodern Politics of Image and Reputation, *Foreign Affairs*, 80(5), pp. 2–6.

World Bank (2006) Country Report on Estonia, September. Available at http://web.worldbank.org /WBSITE/EXTERNAL/COUNTRIES/ECAEXT/ESTONIAEXTN/0,contentMDK:20629083~menu PK:301081~pagePK:141137~piPK:141127~theSitePK:301074,00.html (accessed 11 January 2007).

Worthington, B. (2001) Riding the 'J' Curve – Tourism and Successful Transition in Estonia. *Post Communist Economies.*, 13(3), pp. 389–400.

Worthington, B. (2003) Change in an Estonian Resort: Contrasting Development Contexts, *Annals of Tourism Research*, 30(2), pp. 369–385.

Part II

Advancing post-communist change: Tourism as a transformative force

New Places in Old Spaces: Mapping Tourism and Regeneration in Budapest

TAMARA RÁTZ, MELANIE SMITH & GÁBOR MICHALKÓ

ABSTRACT   *The aim of this paper is to map some of the new developments that have been taking place in Budapest since 1989, in particular focusing on the role that tourism and cultural regeneration have played in transforming old spaces into new places. The redevelopment of former socialist cities is politically complex, as new power relationships need to be negotiated, heritage values must be reassessed, and widening economic and social disparities should be addressed. Tourism needs to be managed carefully if it is to contribute in a positive way to economic development, heritage conservation and promotion, and enhancement of the local quality of life.*
A number of examples are used to demonstrate the spatial transformations that are taking place in Budapest. In some cases, historic spaces have been accorded new and symbolic status (e.g. as World Heritage Sites); some attractions have been re-packaged as itineraries or trails (e.g. the Cultural Avenue project). Some socialist heritage has been removed to the outskirts of the city (e.g. Statue Park). Some previously derelict areas are being transformed and regenerated into national cultural or international business spaces. New shopping and leisure areas are also being created in accordance with Budapest's desire to be recognized as a dynamic and cosmopolitan city. Questions are then raised about the implications of these developments for the future planning of the city as a new tourism destination in a competitive market.

Introduction

This paper examines the process of spatial transformation and regeneration in Budapest since 1989, with emphasis on the initiatives and attractions that have been developed for tourism. Having cast off the shackles of the socialist past, many Central and Eastern European countries and cities were nevertheless keen to represent their communist heritage, a subject of tourist fascination (at least in the early 1990s). However, the need to be thought of as dynamic, modern and cosmopolitan is equally common to many post-socialist cities (Hall 2004), as is the desire to be thought of as quintessentially European, especially following accession to the EU (Smith & Hall 2006). Thus, CEE cities like Budapest find themselves in the position of trying to create new and unique experiences for visitors, whilst selecting which elements of the past to preserve and promote. This is further complicated by the need to enhance quality of life for local residents, many of whom are already disillusioned with post-socialist life and grappling with the economic and social polarization engendered by rapid transition.

The politics of post-socialism are complex and often extreme. This can have a major impact on the ways in which cities are transformed, especially in terms of how space is valued, how places are (re)created, and how new identities and images are constructed. This paper maps some of the ways in which old tourism spaces have been regenerated or re-packaged since 1989, especially in terms of symbolic accolades (e.g. World Heritage Site status, Cultural Avenue). It looks at how these are juxtaposed with the creation of new spaces and attractions, many of which could be viewed as more 'global' and less representative of Hungarian or even European culture. However, like many capital cities, Budapest is keen to be seen as an international city and, even prior to 1989, as a relatively Westernized one (Jancsik 1999). The fossilization of cities in transition for the purposes of tourism is therefore surely not to be advocated, yet in a competitive market, it is arguably the uniqueness of place that ultimately sells.

The rationale of the study is to explore the spatial development processes of tourism in a former socialist capital city in transition, and to examine some of the conflicting issues affecting tourism development that arise throughout the transition process, such as cultural and economic globalization, identity creation and heritage protection. The ideas summarized in the paper are based on secondary information concerning tourism development in Budapest, such as tourism development master plans and proposals (e.g. Almády 1900; Imre 1983; Juhász 1991; Horwath 1992; Lengyel 1993; Municipality of Budapest 1995; Szemrédi 1995; Horwath Consulting Magyarország Kft. *et al.* 2004; Meszter 2006), statistical data on Budapest tourism (e.g. Central Statistical Office 2006; TourMIS 2006), and the authors' previous empirical research experiences (e.g. Rátz & Puczkó 2003; Puczkó & Rátz 2006; Xellum Kft. & Szemrédi 2006; Puczkó *et al.* 2008).

Although many issues discussed below are common in most urban tourist destinations, the political and socio-economic transition process that Budapest is currently undergoing adds extra dimensions to tourism development patterns in the city. The continuously changing power relations create specific challenges for urban developers and tourism planners alike: illustrated, for example, by the high number of previous tourism development strategies listed above. While local and national authorities are generally in favour of supporting the city's tourism industry, the lack of consensus concerning the optimal direction and methods of development, and the shifting responsibility for tourism development from one body to another have so far prevented the actual implementation of any of these municipal strategies. Consequently, though district-level development projects as well as civil society-inspired organic development ideas have contributed significantly to the city's transformation, decision makers are faced continuously by the double challenge of adapting Budapest's tourism products to international trends as well as shaping the city in a way that appeals to international visitors and creates a sense of belonging among residents.

Space, Place and Identity in Destinations in Transition

The concept of the tourist-historic city, first developed by Ashworth and Tunbridge (1990) has subsequently been applied and adapted globally. They noted that the design attributes and physical form of cities will influence their heritage potential heavily. Heritage cannot be separated from other urban attributes, such as infrastructure or the organization of public space. These are all within the powers of local management authorities. Graham *et al.* (2000) noted that in the second phase of a heritage city's development, there is likely to be an old centre and a newer periphery. This phase seems to be especially typical of post-socialist cities that are anxious to modernize, whilst conserving their historic core and heritage values. However, this process is somewhat complicated by the existence of displaced heritage (e.g. former Communist buildings or icons), which create feelings of dissonance amongst local residents but are of great interest to tourists. The encroachment of modern developments (e.g. regenerated new business or shopping districts) on historic centres (e.g. World Heritage Sites) is not a problem unique to cities in transition, but the juxtaposition may appear to be more stark in the light of old socialist values, and facilities may not be affordable for local residents. Similar problems seem to have been prominent in Prague, Kraków and Budapest alike.

Graham *et al.* (2000) noted that the localization of heritage (i.e. its conservation at a local level) can lead ironically to a convergence of place identities. This can happen if conservation techniques are too standardized and contemporary developments are financed by globally active companies and replicate archetypes from other destinations. The tendency in transition cities to emulate developments that have been successful elsewhere (usually in Western cities) or to employ the services of 'expert' foreign companies is arguably higher than other locations.

Like other former socialist cities that were once planned centrally, one of the key issues for Budapest is therefore who is now responsible for the transformation of space. Under socialism, the public sector in the form of central government would have controlled spatial developments and practices, but increasingly the international private sector dominates. This has arguably led to greater disparities between rich and poor and emphasis on the global at the expense of the local. There are also several barriers to development and planning, which appear to hinder the flourishing of new heritage tourism attractions. Despite a number of historic and recent efforts to control the direction of tourism development in the city (e.g. Almády 1900; Imre 1983; Juhász 1991; Horwath 1992; Lengyel 1993; Municipality of Budapest 1995;

Szemrédi 1995; Horwath Consulting Magyarország Kft. *et al.* 2004; Meszter 2006), no serious attempts have been made to have any of the commissioned tourism development master plans actually implemented, which suggests something of a *laissez-faire* attitude and a lack of understanding of the nature of tourism. In addition, complex bureaucracy linked to the autonomy of the 24 districts has led to a lack of co-ordination and integration of tourism development. The Mayor of Budapest (responsible for the Municipality of Budapest, one of the central districts) has limited influence over the other 23 districts' planning procedures. His only real powers appear to be to protect the cityscape through limiting heights of buildings. In addition, state support is rarely available for attraction development, only for accommodation, and Budapest could not qualify for EU support since its GDP was higher than 70 percent of the EU average.

There are spatial limitations to development because of a general reluctance to expand beyond the city's core area (the central districts). At present, the relevant architectural legislation limits the opportunities for unusual buildings; therefore, unique architectural developments are rare. Since architectural and heritage boards are rather conservative, new functions are rarely welcome in old buildings. This means that the innovative conversions typical of many successful regeneration and tourism schemes are difficult to implement here. Developers usually are motivated by short-term profit, which is often supported by local governments. It is therefore not their priority to consider interesting, image-enhancing buildings. In addition, it is well nigh impossible to sell a property for hotel development or have a branded management company in many areas of the city (e.g. Buda, which would be attractive to visitors). Budapest also lacks the range of boutique hotels, which are typical of other cities, such as Prague. This is arguably because it is not yet attractive or chic enough for investors.

Arguably, brand identities can be created only where the unique selling propositions (USPs') are based on culturally distinctive features. Important decisions therefore need to be made about the transformation of old spaces (e.g. those of heritage value, which are unique to a place) versus the development of new spaces and attractions, many of which may be more globalized. Most Central and East European (CEE) cities have been criticized for their poor services and facilities, thus the temptation to encourage investment of global chain hotels, retail outlets and attractions can be overwhelming. Whilst quality upgrades are necessary, two major problems arise: one is the lack of affordability for domestic and local visitors; and the second is the lack of uniqueness for international tourists. The importance of place arguably still dominates, especially in transition destinations, which are in the process of boosting economic and social development through tourism whilst creating new and unique identities and images. Shaw and Williams (2004: 186), like many other theorists, emphasized the human component that differentiates space from place, noting how 'local populations and tourists inscribe (places) with values, while places contribute to identities'. Clearly, places are constructed actively by social processes, including tourism, and these processes change over time. The way in which cities and their spaces and places are valued and viewed by various user groups at any one time clearly has implications for their popularity, visitation levels, perceptions, image and identity. In terms of image, Budapest currently has a 'poor' rather than a 'rich' image in that visitors tend to know very little about it. Many international visitors questioned in perception studies by the Hungarian National Tourism Office (2002) variously had either no image of the city, perceived it to be grey, or imagined it would be similar to somewhere else (e.g. Prague, Vienna, Kraków) (Kiss & Sulyok, 2007). The city also seems to have an 'open image' as visitors tend to be pleasantly surprised by their visit, which then enhances their perception of the city (Puczkó *et al*. 2008). Therefore, the enhancement of the organic image of the city is needed, in particular.

The Budapest Tourism Development Strategy (Horwath Consulting Magyarország Kft. *et al*. 2004) suggested two strategic programmes for the capital's brand development: 'Live this city', and 'Your Budapest'. These slogans seem to appeal to Budapest's liveability and sense of place. According to the strategy, Budapest as a brand should be developed along the following five emotional values: 'Atmospheric Budapest' (diversity of architectural heritage); 'Entertaining Budapest' (vibrant cultural life); 'Pampering Budapest' (spa culture and gastronomy); 'Spectacular Budapest' (based on the impressive Danube panorama); and 'Dynamic Budapest' (fast-developing business centre). In terms of spatial transformation and development, this suggests the conservation of traditional heritage features coupled with the encouragement of global or cosmopolitan activities. Whether this leads ultimately to a uniqueness of place and product remains to be seen.

Budapest, Tourism and Transition

Budapest has always played a dominant role in the tourism of Hungary: approximately every third guest night is registered in the city, and about 70 percent of the country's international tourism revenue is generated in Budapest (TOB 2006). Budapest's share of all the international guest nights registered in Hungary exceeded 53 percent in 2005, and over 87 percent of the city's guest nights were spent by foreign tourists. These figures indicate the high spatial concentration of tourist demand in Hungary: Vienna, for example, accounted for only 8.9 percent of the total international guest nights spent in Austria (Budapest's other main regional competitor, Prague, however, proved to be rather similar to the Hungarian capital, with a share of 52.9 percent) (TourMIS 2006).

As the capital city of Hungary, Budapest is seen generally as the cultural gateway to the country. It is usually the first (and often the only) destination visited by the majority of international tourists. It is the only truly cosmopolitan metropolis in Hungary, in terms of population and area size, or the variety of cultural events. By combining political, economic, administrative, cultural and symbolic functions, it is clearly the centre of Hungary: every fifth citizen lives there (*c*. two million out of the country's total population of ten million), well above 50 percent of the GDP is produced in the city, almost all global companies have their local headquarters in Budapest, all national institutions have their seat in the capital, and only three internationally branded hotels operate outside the city (Puczkó *et al.* 2008).

Geographically, Budapest is located along the river Danube, which divides Hungary, at approximately equal distance from the western and the eastern borders of the country. Although Budapest as such is a relatively new administrative unit (it was created in 1873 by the unification of the independent towns of Buda, Pest and Óbuda), the hills of Buda and the plains of Pest have been inhabited since prehistoric times, and Buda has been the capital of Hungary since the fifteenth century. Budapest is the setting for the Hungarian nation's culture and history – it embodies the past, the present and the future of the country. It is the home of the country's major cultural institutions (e.g. the National Theatre, the Hungarian National Museum, the National Gallery) and principal heritage buildings (the House of Parliament, the former Royal Castle, the Chain Bridge or the Millennium Monument at Heroes' Square). Budapest's complex history of occupation means that its identity has been contested frequently, yet its majestic buildings are testimony to its distinctive Central European character and sense of place.

Due to its capital city status, and the limited conference capacities elsewhere in the country, Budapest plays a major role in business-related (MICE) tourism, since it provides the base for government operations, and it is the major economic centre of the country. In addition, Budapest is the hub of Hungary's star-shaped transport infrastructure, where most highways and railway lines meet, and Budapest Ferihegy Airport used to be the country's only international airport for decades.

Following the political changes of 1989–90, both the internal and the external image of Budapest have changed. During the socialist period, Budapest was seen both in Hungary and abroad as the 'most Western of the Eastern European capitals' (Jancsik 1999). This perceived position referred to an absolute superior quality in Eastern Europe where Budapest was indeed the most developed and Westernized city; however, in Western Europe, it only indicated a relative superiority compared to the other, less developed Eastern European cities (Puczkó *et al.* 2008). Today, Budapest is perceived by Hungarians as the only truly international Hungarian city (Gyáni 2005), while foreign visitors generally see it as a relatively attractive place in transition that has already lost most of its former socialist flavour, but has yet to develop in many aspects to reach Western European standards (Lengyel 2004; Meszter 2006).

In terms of its tourism and service development trends, Budapest is rather typical of many post-socialist destinations. Almost half a century within an ideological 'bloc' left the CEE countries with suppressed national and regional identities. Therefore, in the newly independent CEE countries of the 1990s, there was a clear desire to re-assert individuality and difference. On the other hand, a conflicting, but equally important priority was to achieve the same living standards as Western Europeans had, by consuming the same products and services, buying the same brands or enjoying the same kind of cultural experiences. The parallel objective of being acknowledged as unique and equally developed at the same time creates a challenge in many fields of socio-cultural and economic development: how to copy popular global trends in an individual way?

Tourism obviously has an important role to play as an emblem of the assertion of identity, especially as diversity and uniqueness are often the keys to a successful tourism industry and a distinctive brand image. Culture and heritage as the basis of tourism development may provide an answer to the development challenge, since each nation's heritage is exceptional *per se*; however, efficient and effective attraction and interpretation design are needed to develop heritage as a consumable product that is able to attract visitors. In addition, Budapest – as most Eastern European cities– suffers from the lack of a distinctive destination image, and potential international visitors are often unaware of the city's diversity and rich supply of attractions and services. Possible key elements of differentiation and positioning that might be used in international destination marketing include Hungary's socialist heritage on the one hand, and the UNESCO World Heritage status of the city's major tourist sights on the other; two seemingly very different factors that are both related to heritage and history.

Budapest, as with most Eastern European cities in transition, is often criticized for attempting to become dynamic, modern and cosmopolitan by promoting standardized facilities and attractions rather than cultural diversity. While it is, indeed, true that accommodating standardized retailing and entertainment facilities may decrease a city's international competitiveness in terms of unique image and identity, it may also increase local inhabitants' satisfaction with the socio-economic development of their city, and may even improve certain aspects of their perceived quality of life. In addition, the encouragement of international businesses may offer a better guarantee of quality for international visitors, especially in the field of MICE tourism. However, it is also true that the aspiration towards adequate service provision can undermine the cultural character and the uniqueness of a destination. In the case of Budapest, the World Heritage Site attractions at least reflect the distinctiveness of the city's architecture, and the river views are unmistakably unique to Budapest. Popular cultural events, such as exhibitions and festival programmes as well as museum collections, are based generally on international artists, which might be perceived as a both positive and negative trend: although foreign tourists are less likely to be motivated by such events and attractions, the local population's access to international cultural heritage and arts increases.

Spatial Transformation of Tourism in Budapest

The spatial structure of Budapest was defined in the late nineteenth century by the Council of Public Works, established in 1870. The Council formulated an imposing master plan, which laid down the main features of spatial development, setting the directions of expansion, defining the functions of the different areas, and dividing the city into land-use zones. As a consequence of this planning process, Budapest can be divided into seven major zones, with distinct socio-economic, functional and architectural characteristics. The current concentric structure is the outcome of the city's organic growth of the last 140 years, with the expansion of Budapest occurring concentrically from the city centre outwards (Kovács 2005).

The seven major zones of metropolitan Budapest include: the city centre (the City in Pest and the Castle District in Buda); the inner-urban residential quarter; the transition zone of mainly industrial and transport functions, as well as lower quality working class housing; the socialist housing estates built mainly in the 1960s and 1970s; the zone of the so-called 'garden towns' (i.e. the outer residential ring); the villa quarter in the Buda hills; and the agglomeration zone comprising suburban settlements around Budapest. The tourism industry of the city – attractions, services, facilities – has concentrated traditionally in the city centre and in the inner-urban residential quarter, although post-socialist development initiatives also aim to promote tourism in the transition zone and in the outer residential ring.

The city centre is the oldest part of Budapest. Although the area traditionally has been the political, economic and tourist centre of Budapest (in addition to its residential function), the rapid and intensive reinvestment at the urban core that characterized the post-socialist urban development resulted in the spectacular regeneration and expansion of this area (Kovács & Wiessner 2004). The power structures of the past produced heritage spaces of national and regional value, whereas the power structures of the present are creating economic spaces of international value. The reasons for this should be sought in the wider restructuring of the economy, which brought about high dynamism of tertiary activities, especially in the field of business services, commerce and tourism. Generally, this led to a growing demand for non-residential space in the city centre. The re-establishment of the real estate market, based upon land rent, made possible a rapid functional conversion in the centre of Budapest. Many new firms bought residential flats in the centre for office purposes, and gradually changed the function of the buildings (Kovács 1994).

Significant changes have also taken place within the transition zone – the industrial and commercial belt – during the last 20 years. Although the decline of the zone's industrial function had started already in the 1970s and 1980s, when several heavily polluting industrial plants were closed down, the expansion of derelict industrial spaces was intensified further by the collapse of the state socialist industry following 1989–90. However, the economic transition has also brought about new development in this zone, particularly at locations with good accessibility and transport connections. Geographically, these investments – mainly office buildings and retail outlets – concentrate mainly along the radial main roads (Váci road in the 13th district and Üllői road in the 9th district), but the development of the Innovation and Technology Park (InfoPark) adjacent to the Budapest University of Technology and Economics and the Eötvös Loránd University in the 11th district also represents the transition of the city's former industrial areas.

The visual milieu of Budapest – particularly that of the most visited central areas – is dominated by nineteenth century architecture. Many of the city's popular tourist attractions, such as the monumental Heroes' Square, the Parliament, the buildings of the Castle District (e.g. the Fishermen's Bastion, the Mathias Church and the Royal Palace housing the National Gallery, the Budapest History Museum and the National Széchényi Library), as well as the elegant residential buildings along the World Heritage-listed Andrássy Avenue, were constructed or reconstructed in the second half of the nineteenth century, celebrating the 1000-year history of the Hungarian state. However, due to its long and turbulent past, the capital has also preserved the architectural heritage of earlier periods, including the ruins of the ancient Roman city of Aquincum, the medieval houses of the Castle District, or the still popular Turkish baths. This architectural diversity is an inherent component of Hungarians' Budapest-consciousness (Bojár 2005) and it contributed significantly to the World Heritage listing of the central area. According to UNESCO's verdict, the site is one of the world's outstanding urban landscapes, displaying the continuity of history as an urban panorama and illustrating the great periods in the history of the Hungarian capital (Puczkó & Rátz 2006). Thus, the World Heritage Site is a good example of Lefebvre's (1974) multi-layering of space, where examples of different historical periods, power structures and social values are reflected.

During the past 15 years, the major tangible image components of the city – particularly the city centre, i.e. the most visited tourist area – have remained more or less the same, due to the lack of distinctive modern architectural developments. However, the atmosphere of Budapest has changed, mainly as a result of cultural and commercial globalization processes, and the city has witnessed the development of new urban centres. These may have a specific character and reinforce the sense of place, but it is more likely that a standardized 'fringe' emerges on the outskirts of more distinctive spaces. This is an example of how Budapest is still in the second phase of Ashworth and Tunbridge's (1990) Tourist-Historic City model, where the older centre and newer periphery are still largely separated.

Budapest is divided into 23 districts (marked by roman numerals on Figure 1), which are of differing economic, social and cultural character. Traditionally, tourism development is concentrated in the central area of the city (outlined and enlarged on Figure 1), which roughly includes districts 5–8 on the Pest side and the Castle Hill (district 1) on the Buda side. The centrality of this area is defined mainly by its current urban functions (particularly politics, business and culture), built heritage, accessibility and topography, while the difference between the centre and periphery is revealed rather well by the differences in architecture, atmosphere and services.

Figure 1 presents the spatial distribution of commercial accommodation capacity and guest nights in Budapest in 1997 and 2005. Grey shading indicates the growth of commercial accommodation capacity between 1997 and 2005, while data within the semi-circles present the number and domestic–international distribution of guest nights in the given years. Out of Budapest's 23 districts, only the 16th district offers

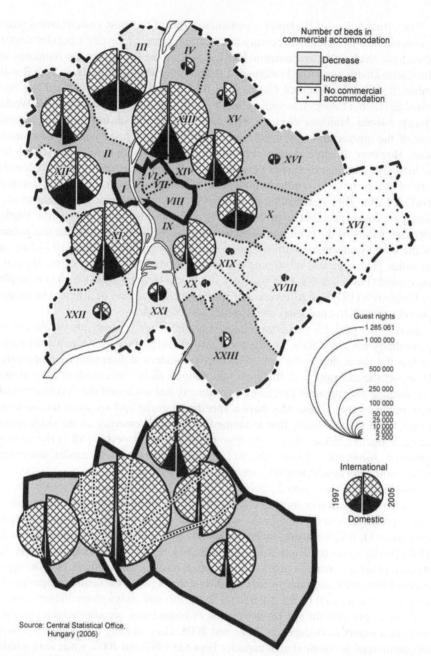

Figure 1. Spatial distribution of commercial accommodation capacity and guest nights in Budapest (1997, 2005)

no commercial accommodation, due to its distance from the city centre and the main transport hubs, and its relatively bad accessibility.

Between 1997 and 2005, the commercial accommodation capacity of Budapest increased by 12 percent, while the number of international guest nights grew by 48 percent (for all guest nights, the rate of increase was 46 percent). The figures indicate a significant improvement of occupancy rates and the transformation of the market, due, among others, to the dynamic increase of the budget airlines entering the Hungarian market. The traditional tourist centre of Budapest (the 1st and the 5th districts) experienced above-average growth in capacity and the success of Budapest's first comprehensive urban rehabilitation programme launched in the 9th district in the early 1990s is reflected clearly by the 300 percent increase in commercial accommodation capacity (Central Statistical Office 2006). However, it is an interesting question as to how far tourists are aware of the spatial implications of their accommodation choices, as they often select pre-visit according to price rather than geographical knowledge (with higher-priced, centrally located hotels being an exception).

The 5th district concentrates both Budapest's highest quality hotels – e.g. the Four Seasons Gresham Palace or the Corvinus Grand Hotel Kempinski – and the traditional tourist precinct of restaurant and shopping facilities, which has been popular among international tourists since the 1970s. In contrast, although also centrally situated, certain parts of the 7th and 8th districts are seen as the 'first real examples of ethnic-based urban ghettos in post-communist Eastern Europe' (Kovács 2005), due to the high concentration of poor, unemployed Roma people and the neglected, ill-maintained nineteenth-century residential buildings, which explains the relatively lower number of guest nights. However, hotel developers face the challenge of finding suitable buildings or available real estate within the whole central area, due to the complex and often unclear ownership structure of the old residential buildings, the district governments' rather slow and bureaucratic decision-making processes, as well as the conflicts of political and business interests.

In terms of guest nights, the most dynamic development was experienced in the 23rd district, but demand increased significantly in the 4th, 9th and 15th districts as well. Particularly interesting is the case of the formerly peripheral and relatively insignificant 9th district, where the expansion of bed capacity has been followed by an equally dynamic growth of mostly international tourist demand. The traditionally dominant 5th and 13th districts both preserved their relatively high market share between 1997 and 2005, but for different reasons: while the 5th district's success is based on its traditional significance in leisure tourism, tourist demand in the 13th district is mainly business-orientated, due to the development of a highly concentrated office zone along the metro line, and the consequent increase in business travel demand. Business travellers are often more interested in the standard of accommodation than in its location (i.e. proximity to cultural attractions is not a prerequisite). However, a gradual shift to the third and fourth phases of Ashworth and Tunbridge's (1990) model will mean that the commercial and heritage districts will eventually overlap.

In addition to the development of business life, accessibility and culture have also played a key role in the spatial redistribution of tourist demand in Budapest between 1997 and 2005. The rather spectacular increase in guest nights registered in the 4th, 15th and 23rd districts may be attributed partly to transit demand, due to the districts' location along the M3 and M5 motorways that connect Budapest to the north-eastern and the south-eastern parts of Hungary. The increase experienced in the 7th and 9th districts is related mainly to the cultural regeneration of the areas (the development of the semi-pedestrian Ráday street, the opening of the National Theatre and the Palace of Arts, as well as the World Heritage designation of Andrássy Avenue). This led to the opening of several new hotels in both districts and reflects the importance of culture in influencing tourist demand.

Guests nights within the central area of Budapest are almost exclusively generated by international tourist demand: the popularity of districts 1, 5 and 7 (roughly the World Heritage area) among foreign tourists significantly affects accommodation prices, which may explain why domestic demand accounted for less than 10 percent of all guest nights in these districts during the examined period.

In international tourism, the post-socialist period also means the re-discovery of Budapest after 50 years. During 1867–1945, it was the second-most important city within the Austro-Hungarian monarchy (after Vienna), but fifty years of socialism all but erased the former international centre from Europe's cultural and tourist map. The recent transformation of the city as a tourist destination may be attributed partly to conscious product development and the adaptation of global attraction management trends (e.g. in the case of the Museum of Fine Arts or the House of Terror) (Puczkó & Rátz 2006), and partly to political and economic factors (e.g. the EU accession and the growth of budget airlines serving Hungary have probably decreased the perceived distance between Budapest and the rest of Europe). Nevertheless, perception studies of budget airline travellers have also shown that many tourists have little or no clear image of Budapest as a destination, and instead select according to price and availability of routes (Mundruczó 2005; TOB 2006; Xellum Kft. & Szemrédi 2006).

Figure 2 presents the main tourist attractions of Budapest and their spatial distribution (selection criteria included visitor numbers and reputation, but recommendations by international travel forums, and the authors' own experiences were also taken into consideration). Traditional attractions (marked by circles) are the city's well-known, 'must-see' sights, which are based on a combination of landscape features – the Danube and the Buda hills – and historic built heritage. Even the youngest of these attractions was built or established in the nineteenth century, and they are all located centrally within or near the World Heritage area. The spatial distribution of these heritage attractions delineates the traditional tourist space in Budapest: practically all international leisure tourists move within this space, but it is also very popular among Hungarian visitors to the capital, due to their monuments and sights as well as their historic atmosphere.

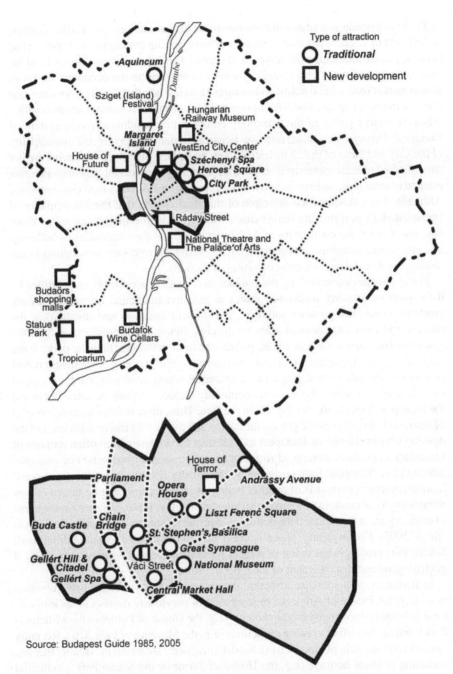

Figure 2. Traditional and new tourist attractions in Budapest

The less concentrated spatial distribution of the new attractions (marked by squares) is the result of a combination of conscious urban planning aiming to create new urban centres, private alternative initiatives, and financial and spatial constraints within the expensive and crowded city centre. However, in addition to the economic power of global market forces, local political structures also clearly influence the production and transformation of space. The development of new attractions is not without conflict, which is related partly to the extremely complex public administration system of Budapest. This system is based on a two-tier arrangement comprising the municipality of the City and those of the 23 districts. The City and the district governments are not subordinated to each other: the districts independently exercise the powers and rights granted to local governments within the framework of the Act on Local Governments. Although it is a fundamental principle of this dual system that the Municipality of Budapest shall perform the duties that concern the whole of the capital or more than one district, the complexity of decision making and the uncertainty of authority on certain occasions have definitely hindered heritage protection, destination brand management or the development of visitor attractions.

The challenges generated by the bureaucratic system are complicated further by the variety of property ownership found in the city: municipal as well as private property, in addition to state authority, government agencies and institutions, the church, and even international rules for foreign diplomatic representations. Public spaces in Budapest – such as roads, public transport networks, tunnels, parks – are controlled by the Budapest municipal government, while district governments control certain former state-owned properties acquired in whole or in part, but buildings of mixed ownership, where the resident community includes tenants, private owners and the local government, are also typical in the area. Thus, there is often a strong conflict of interests between creative private initiatives and the district municipalities, and the development of the city of Budapest as a creative urban destination often remains of secondary importance compared to financial and residential interests. For example, although the Budapest Tourism Strategy specifically lists the so-called 'ruin pubs' (converted inner courtyards of derelict buildings in the centre) among the city's key attractions, local municipalities make all attempts to close these initiatives in the name of urban regeneration, and sell the buildings in prime locations to real estate developers (Bojár 2005). Consequently, space is often sold to the highest (often international) bidder, thus eroding what is left of a local sense of place and heritage, especially if gentrification and displacement of local people follow.

In Budapest, post-socialist attraction development includes brand new constructions (e.g. the Palace of Arts), the regeneration of previously derelict areas into cultural or business-orientated establishments (e.g. the House of Future in the Millenáris Park), and the facelift of existing attractions (e.g. the Museum of Fine Arts). Recently opened and currently planned leisure tourist attractions are based on various themes, including political heritage (e.g. the House of Terror or the Statue Park), industrial heritage (e.g. the Millenáris Park or the Gas Factory), modern and contemporary culture (e.g. the Sziget Festival or the Palace of Arts), spa (e.g. the complete restoration and modernization of the Rác Spa), and shopping (e.g. the WestEnd City Center or the regeneration of the Váci street pedestrian area). In addition, the development of MICE facilities (e.g. the renovation of the Budapest Congress Center as the Budapest Congress & World Trade Centre in the 12th district, as well as the current redevelopment of the Hungexpo exhibition complex in the 10th district, and the construction of a new 5,000-capacity congress centre in the 9th district, next to the National Theatre and the Palace of Arts) may contribute to the positioning of Budapest as a leading MICE tourism destination in Eastern Central Europe. In addition to the construction of new attractions, 'virtual' spatial transformation processes are also taking place in Budapest: in some cases, historic spaces have been accorded new and symbolic status (e.g. as World Heritage Site), and some attractions have been re-packaged as itineraries or routes (e.g. the Cultural Avenue project). Whether some of the recent attractions and developments contribute to a new sense of place is a subject of debate.

A significant element of the city's transformation is the creation of new shopping and leisure areas in accordance with Budapest's desire to be recognized as a dynamic and cosmopolitan city. Before 1989–90, leisure shopping facilities, including special 'hard currency' shops – offering mainly souvenirs and otherwise unavailable Western consumer brands – and restaurants, were concentrated in the Castle District and in Váci street, probably the best known shopping street in Eastern Central Europe. In addition to these mainly tourism-orientated areas, the area within the Nagykörút (Grand Boulevard) (the inner parts of the 6th, 7th and 8th districts) was the traditional shopping centre of Budapest, offering functional consumer goods for a mainly local and domestic clientele. However, the development of new shopping malls outside this central area (e.g. the WestEnd City Centre and the Duna Pláza in Pest, and the Mammut Shopping Mall in Buda) and the construction of highly concentrated retail and commercial facilities along the motorways leading out of Budapest (e.g. the Budaörs shopping malls) have significantly transformed the spatial distribution of shopping demand within the city. The concentration of retail outlets and leisure services in the modern shopping malls, together with good accessibility and easier parking, has led to the decline of smaller, independent shops in the traditional shopping districts, and several once-popular department store buildings have been destroyed so that the properties can be converted into residential, business or leisure spaces.

Shopping spaces are essentially global in character, thus, however popular they are with local residents they arguably contribute little to a touristic sense of place. One exception is, perhaps, Váci street. This has preserved its position as a major shopping street in Budapest tourism (it is marked as a both traditional and new attraction on Figure 2), due to the regeneration and the pedestrianization of the whole length of the street, which now connects two traditional key attractions of the city. First, the Central Market Hall (a beautiful example of historicist architecture, as well as a socialist symbol of prosperity and abundance and a proof of the superiority of Hungarian agriculture, but also a common shopping outlet for many local residents both before and after 1989–90). Secondly, the Gerbeaud Café, which was seen as an icon of elegance, refinement and style in socialist Hungary, and considered a beautiful heritage building and an example of the typical Central European café today. Although Váci street has always been considered rather 'touristy' by Hungarian customers due to its location within the tourist district, the consequently inflated prices and the supply of mostly tourist-orientated products, today international high street retail stores (such as H&M or Zara) also attract local customers. However, despite its continuous success, Váci street seems to be losing its position as the number one Hungarian shopping street to Andrássy Avenue: following the opening of a Louis Vuitton store in 2006, further luxury brands are also likely to open stores here, while Váci street and the new shopping malls are preferred mainly by high street retailers.

The Significance of World Heritage Designation and the Development of the Cultural Avenue Project in the World Heritage Area of Budapest

The banks of the Danube and the Buda Castle Quarter in Budapest were inscribed on UNESCO's World Heritage list in 1987 as one of the world's outstanding urban landscapes that illustrates the great periods in the history of the Hungarian capital. The site, which displays the continuity of history as an urban panorama, includes the House of Parliament, the bridges spanning the Danube, the Gellért Hill, and the Buda Castle. In 2002, the site was extended to Andrássy Avenue and the Millennium Underground. The extension area is a representative example of late nineteenth century social development and urban planning, and it reflects the latest technical achievements of the day. The buffer zone of the extension area includes the old Jewish quarter of Pest.

Both the Buda Castle Quarter and Andrássy Avenue have traditionally been the most visited districts of the city, due to their monuments and sights as well as their historic atmosphere. Practically all the international tourists to Budapest visit the key attractions of the World Heritage Site, but they are also very popular among Hungarian visitors to the capital. However, the site's key success factor is its heritage value and its nationwide and international renown, and the concentration of visitors in the area is not related directly to its World Heritage status. Thus, the socially and politically welcomed World Heritage designation of the areas has not significantly altered visitation patterns or preferences within the city, although it may serve as a seal of approval for tourists' choice. However, the World Heritage status presents an additional challenge in heritage management and conservation: the title may heighten tourists' expectations and at the same time it increases the local community's associated responsibility (Rátz & Puczkó 2003).

Although the Budapest World Heritage Site is the most visited urban destination in Hungary, the development of tourism services has been rather unsystematic in the past, and only moderate changes have been experienced to date. Compared to the more established tourism product offered by the Buda Castle quarter, the development of

Andrássy Avenue has been more spontaneous and also more dynamic in the period following the 2002 World Heritage designation. This has resulted, unintentionally, in new urban spaces, such as the cluster of cafés and restaurants in Liszt Ferenc square or the theatreland (the so-called 'Pest Broadway Project') being created around Nagymező street.

Although the area's World Heritage status symbolically connects many different attractions and services located relatively far from each other, further marketing initiatives were considered necessary by local experts to draw visitors' attention to relatively less known sights and attractions within the traditionally popular central tourist space. The initial idea of the Cultural Avenue project was born in 2000, while physical implementation started in 2002, with the help and financial support of the Cultural Tourism Department of the Ministry of National Cultural Heritage (Puczkó & Rátz 2006).

The virtual Cultural Avenue re-packages the area's tourist resources by linking attractions that are similar and different at the same time, their common characteristics being their location along a virtual axis of Budapest and their individual willingness to be represented in the project. In addition, similarity also lies in certain – subjectively measured – cultural and historic aspects, while differences are manifested in the variety of stops along the trail – e.g. museums, churches, cafés, historical buildings, theatres and even a spa – that represent the history, culture and traditions of Budapest.

When selecting the stops of the Cultural Avenue, a wide and flexible understanding of culture, history and heritage was applied, from high culture (e.g. the Museum of Fine Arts) to common, popular or alternative culture (e.g. the Erzsébet Square Cultural Centre – also known as 'the Hole' – hosting bands and exhibitions). This approach concluded with 59 stops along the route, most of which form part of the World Heritage Site.

One of the key purposes of the route is to encourage visits to less popular or not too well-known areas, to divert traditional tourist flows and to provide an alternative itinerary. Almost all tourists visit the Castle District and Heroes' Square or the Great Synagogue, but only a very few are aware of the hidden treasures around these key attractions, e.g. the Museum of East Asia, the House of Photography or the former Jewish Ghetto. The intention of the Cultural Avenue project is to make tourists realize that the cultural and heritage assets of Budapest are too numerous and complex to discover in just one visit. As a result of the project, a clear sense of place emerges, however multi-layered and diverse.

Socialist Heritage-based Attraction Development in Budapest

Image is a major attraction in tourism, and a significant part of Hungary's international image is the combination of its recent socialist past combined with older heritage. Considering the domestic image of Budapest, however, the major elements are the well-known heritage sights (such as the Danube panorama or the Heroes' Square), the shopping facilities and the city's crowdedness and fast pace (Michalkó 1999). The differences in perception may be attributed to the fact that international visitors compare Budapest to other European (or global) cities, while domestic travellers use the less-developed, more provincial towns of the Hungarian countryside as the basis of their comparison. As stated by Castells (1978), space is always socially constructed, in this case by different groups with vastly different mental maps and perceptual understandings.

In the competitive global tourist market, the socialist heritage attractions of Eastern European cities may be seen as a valid differentiating factor, although, in recent years, this unique selling point has begun to wane as first-time 'curiosity' visitor numbers are decreasing. The country is also changing rapidly, and the visible, intangible signs of the socialist system are fast disappearing. In fact, returning foreign tourists also complain that Budapest is losing its 'exotic eastern' image and 'it's not like it used to be' (Szarvas 1998). Therefore, the creation of socialist heritage-based attractions was seen to be necessary for various reasons: in addition to preserving the memory of the period for Hungarian generations who are too young to remember, they also provide a unique opportunity for foreigners to get a glimpse of the country's past behind the Iron Curtain. It is actually ironic to realize the impact of 45 years of socialism on the 1000-year-old country's international and even internal image. Nevertheless, 'being a former Socialist country' is probably the most significant part of this image, so the destination must offer suitable visitor attractions (Rátz 2004).

Both the House of Terror and the Park of Socialist Statues (or, as it is better known, the Statue Park) are based – partly or fully – on the heritage of socialism, but the similarity ends here: the two attractions differ in their location, their style, the experience offered to visitors, or the initiation and implementation of the project idea.

The House of Terror is located in the city centre, in an elegant former apartment building on the World Heritage-listed Andrássy Avenue. The building itself has symbolic significance in Hungary: from 1940 it served as the headquarters of the Nazi-affiliated Arrow Cross party; following the Soviet liberation and occupancy of the country in 1945, it was taken over by the Communist Secret Police (ÁVH), and it was the ÁVH's interrogation centre until the 1956 uprising. The Statue Park is located on the periphery of Budapest and the area itself has no symbolic value whatsoever. Most probably the only selection criterion for the park's location was the availability and the price of real estate at the time of the Park's foundation. However, the peripheral location may also suggest the only marginal importance of such a collection of displaced and unwanted heritage icons.

The House of Terror, a state project initiated by the Prime Minister, opened with a bang on 24 February 2002, the eve of the memorial day of the victims of Communist terror. The Statue Park opened in 1993 as a private initiative, on a much smaller scale in financial terms. It was affected much less by national politics and, although it also caused controversy at the opening, the issues raised were mainly related to the question of whether any socialist relic should be preserved at all.

While promoted as such, the House of Terror is not a real museum in the general understanding of the term (Bloch 1997). Although it has a varied collection of items, such as clothes, weapons or personal objects from the 1940s and 1950s, the original objects on display would hardly be sufficient for a comprehensive exhibition on totalitarian terror, including wartime fascism and post-war communism in Hungary. In addition, the House of Terror is more committed to education and research than to collections management, so it should be defined rather as a heritage centre. However, the House of Terror is a good illustration of the new kind of museum whose function has gradually evolved from passive to interactive and from the authenticity of the object in the museum's collection to the authenticity of the visitor's experience. On the other hand, the Statue Park is a museum in the sense that it presents an open-air collection of public statues removed from the streets after the change of the political system in 1989–90. Compared to the innovative and high-tech House of Terror, the Statue Park represents a traditional-style attraction: although the spatial arrangement of the statues aims to convey a symbolic message, most visitors only experience a static collection of socialist-realist statues with no interpretation. The statues in the collection are not particularly beautiful or artistic. They are inherently symbolic objects whose ideological significance has never been stable (James 1999). Their attraction lies in their relative political value; they are reminders of an era, but do not entertain or excite. In the case of the House of Terror, the professional design of the interpretation also limits the visitor experience: the headphones, the intense use of music and film, combined with the careful control of lighting and the use of tight spaces, and a teleological progression in the narrative means there is much less room for alternative readings. Although most Hungarian visitors – at least over a certain age – have background information that may complicate the presented narrative, for the typical international tourist the experience they share represents the true history of communist Hungary (or Eastern Europe). In the Statue Park, the lack of interpretation provides an opportunity for visitors to develop their own understanding of the collection's significance and meaning. However, it also requires either a willingness to make a mental effort or a rather high level of previous background knowledge: the 'placelessness' of the icons requires a significant leap of the imagination to give them a context.

Conclusions

This paper has demonstrated that Budapest's situation as a tourism destination since 1989 has been based generally more on the (re)packaging and promotion of existing attractions than the development of new ones. This is partly due to the political complexity of post-socialist transformation, where the production and transformation of space is subject to new power relationships and negotiations. Like other cities in transition, Budapest is keen to modernize, but care must be taken that its shifts through the various phases of the Tourist-Historic City model do not lead to the erosion or overlaying of unique heritage with more standardized, commercial developments. A global and cosmopolitan image may seem attractive in the short term, but the long-term consequences are likely to be an erosion of distinctiveness and unique character of place. New developments and attractions should aim to reflect the post-socialist character of Hungary, whilst recognizing her multi-layered pre-socialist past (e.g. the Austro-Hungarian, Turkish or Roman heritage). For the first time in over 500 years of history, Hungary has the opportunity to define exactly what it means to be an independent nation, as well as an EU member and an international tourism destination, with the capital city Budapest as its flagship.

Creative initiatives, which serve to showcase the city's unique heritage as well as its contemporary cultures, are emerging slowly. In addition, lesser-known areas of the city are being transformed through regeneration, with the ultimate aim of providing not only higher quality residential and recreational areas for locals, but also unique and attractive quarters for tourism. With a less short-sighted political agenda and a more innovative, better co-ordinated, tourism strategy, such areas could serve to transform Budapest from a city of national and regional interest to one of international acclaim. The sacrifice of the city's Hungarian identity need not be an inevitable consequence of globalization. New spaces can attempt to reflect the multi-layered cultures of the city, providing a dynamic sense of continuity in the construction of post-socialist place.

References

Almády, G. (Ed.) (1900) *Budapest idegenforgalmának emelése érdekében tett intézkedések ismertetése* (Budapest: Pesti Nyomda).
Ashworth, G.J. & Tunbridge, J.E. (1990) The Tourist – Historic City (London: Routledge).
Bloch, S. (1997) Museums, *Insights*, 10, pp. D7–12.
Bojár, I.A. (2005) *Budapest, a kreatív város – a lehetségek kapujában. Egy XXI. századi európai főváros víziója* (Budapest: Demos Magyarország).
Castells, M. (1978) *City, Class and Power* (London: The MacMillan Press Ltd).
Central Statistical Office (2006) *Kereskedelmi szálláshelyek forgalma–statisztikai adatok* (Budapest: Central Statistical Office).
Graham, B., Ashworth, G.J. & Tunbridge, J.E. (2000) *A Geography of Heritage: Power, Culture and Economy* (London: Arnold).
Gyáni, G. (2005) Budapest túl jón és rosszon, *Beszélő – Politikai és kulturális folyóirat*. Available at http://beszelo.c3.hu/node/274/print (accessed 14 June 2006).
Hall, D. (2004) Branding and National Identity: the Case of Central and Eastern Europe, in: N. Morgan, A. Pritchard & R. Pride (Eds) *Destination Branding: Creating the Unique Destination Proposition*, pp. 111–127 (Oxford: Butterworth-Heinemann).
Horwath Consulting Magyarország Kft. et al. (2004) *Budapest főváros turisztikai stratégiája és 2010-ig szóló fejlesztési programja, a "Budapest, mint márka" marketingszempont érvényesítésével* (Budapest: Horwath Consulting Magyarország Kft.).
Horwath, W. (1992) *Budapest als Fremdenverkehrsstandort – Aktionsräume und Gästestrukturen* (München: Ludwig-Maximiliens-Universität).
Imre, J. (1983) *Budapest hosszútávú idegenforgalmi fejlesztésének koncepciója* (Budapest: KERSZI).

James, B. (1999) Fencing in the Past. Budapest's Statue Park Museum, *Media Culture Society*, 21(3), pp. 291–311.

Jancsik, A. (1999) Turisztikai bevételek és kiadások Magyarországon, valamint ezek várható alakulása az Európai Unióhoz való csatlakozás után, *Turizmus Bulletin*, 3(1), pp. 10–18.

Juhász, L. (1991) Budapest idegenforgalmának fejlesztési stratégiája 2000-ig. Stratégiai menedzsment a turizmusban, CSc Dissertation, Budapest University of Economic Sciences, Budapest.

Kiss, Y. & Sulyok, J. (2007) Magyarország turisztikai imazsa, *Turizmus Bulletin*, 11(1/2), pp. 2–11.

Kovács, Z. (1994) A City at the Crossroads: Social and Economic Transformation in Budapest, *Urban Studies*, 31(7), pp. 1081–1096.

Kovács, Z. (2005) Population and Housing Dynamics in Budapest Metropolitan Region After 1990. Paper presented at the European Network for Housing Research International Housing Conference, Reykjavík, 29 June–3 July.

Kovács, Z. & Wiessner, R. (2004) Budapest – Restructuring a European Metropolis, *Europa Regional*, 12(4), pp. 22–31.

Lefebvre, H. (1974) *The Production of Space* (Oxford: Blackwell).

Lengyel, M. (1993) Budapest turizmusának fejlesztési koncepciója I-II, *Kereskedelmi Szemle*, 34(2), pp. 29–37 and 34(3), pp. 29–38.

Lengyel, M. (2004) *A turizmus általános elmélete* (Budapest: Heller Farkas Gazdasági és Turisztikai Szolgáltatások Főiskolája – KIT Kereskedelmi és Idegenforgalmi Továbbképző Kft.).

Meszter, L. (2006) Budapest főváros turisztikai stratégiája és 2010-ig szóló fejlesztési programja–Felzárkózási stratégia, *Turizmus Bulletin*, 10(3), pp. 7–17.

Michalkó, G. (1999) *A városi turizmus elmélete és gyakorlata* (Budapest: MTA Földrajztudományi Kutatóintézet).

Mundruczó, Gy. (2005) A diszkont légi járatokkal Budapestre érkező külföldi turisták jellemzői, *Turizmus Bulletin*, 9(2), pp. 55–61.

Municipality of Budapest (1995) *Budapest turizmusának fejlesztési koncepciója. Előterjesztés a Fővárosi Önkormányzat Közgyűlésére 09-229/1995* (Budapest: Municipality of Budapest).

Puczkó, L. & Rátz, T. (2006) Managing an Urban World Heritage Site: the Development of the Cultural Avenue Project in Budapest, in: A. Leask & A. Fyall (Eds) *Managing World Heritage Sites*, pp. 215–225 (Oxford: Butterworth-Heinemann).

Puczkó, L., Rátz, T. & Smith, M. (2008) Old City, New Image: Perception, Positioning and Promotion of Budapest, *Journal of Travel & Tourism Marketing*, 10(4), pp. 429–451.

Rátz, T. (2004) *European Tourism* (Székesfehérvár: Kodolányi János University College).

Rátz, T. & Puczkó, L. (2003) A World Heritage Industry? Tourism at Hungarian World Heritage Sites, in: M. Gravari-Barbas & S. Guichard-Anguis (Eds) *Regards Croisés sur le Patrimoine dans le Monde à l'Aube du XXIᵉ Siècle*, pp.467–481 (Paris: Presses de l'Université de Paris-Sorbonne).

Shaw, G. & Williams, A.M. (2004) *Tourism and Tourism Spaces* (London: Sage).

Smith, M.K. & Hall, D. (2006) Enlargement Implications for European Tourism, in D. Hall, M.K. Smith & B. Marciszewska (Eds) *Tourism in the New Europe: The Challenges and Opportunities of EU Enlargement*, pp. 32–43. (Wallingford, UK: CABI).

Szarvas, Zs. (1998) "Valóság" és valóság: finn turisták Magyarország képe, in: Z. Fejős (Ed) *A turizmus mint kulturális rendszer*, pp. 145–149. (Budapest: Néprajzi Múzeum).

Szemrédi, J. (1995) Budapest turizmusának fejlesztési koncepciója (Budapest: unpublished manuscript).

Tourist Office of Budapest (TOB) (2006) *Visitor Profiles of Budget Airline Passengers. Promotion of Budapest by Budget Airlines* (Budapest: TOB, research report).

TourMIS (2006) City Tourism in Europe. Available at http://tourmis.wu-wien.ac.at (accessed 8 January 2007).

Xellum Kft. & Szemrédi, T.T. (2006): *A diszkont légitársaságok utasai körében végzett megkérdezés előzetes eredményei (2005. augusztus – 2006. július)* (Budapest: Xellum Kft. & Szemrédi, T.T., research report).

Transforming Tourism Spaces in Changing Socio-Political Contexts: The Case of Pärnu, Estonia, as a Tourist Destination

JARKKO SAARINEN & TIIT KASK

ABSTRACT   *The need to understand tourist destinations and their change has grown considerably in past decades, and this has become an especially relevant matter with respect to destinations located in the transition economies of Central and Eastern Europe, where international tourism and tourists are increasingly becoming characteristic features of the changing societies. This paper aims to analyse the historical transformation process of the town of Pärnu, Estonia. The local manifestations of wider socio-political contexts and changes are discussed and a narrative is provided of the transformation of Pärnu as a destination. This transformation has been characterized by changing periods of development and reorientation, which have created specific, complex socio-spatial constructions. Based on the changing contexts and their socio-spatial manifestations, the transformation and touristic identity of Pärnu is divided into four historically contingent periods, which are further discussed in relation to path-dependent and path-creative perspectives.*

Introduction

The recent discussion regarding tourist destinations and their changes has stressed the meaning and role of space, spatiality and contextuality in new ways (see Gordon and Goodall 2000; Franklin and Crang 2001; Ateljevic and Doorne 2002; Gale and Botterill 2005). As a spatial unit, a tourist destination refers to a varying range of scales and structures in tourism and, instead of being purely physical and location-based units, destinations are increasingly coming to be seen as socio-spatial constructions (Meethan 2001), 'spatial realities' which are transformed by social forces, systems and relations specific to certain contexts (Saarinen 2004). Nowadays these forces constructing and transforming destinations are increasingly proving to be non-local ones.

The issue of non-locally driven development and processes of globalization are not new perspectives in tourism and related studies. Tourism and its development has been non-locally orientated from the very beginning of its modern existence, but now the industry and destinations of tourism and their socio-spatial nature are being transformed much more rapidly and on a more distant basis than ever before (see Britton 1991; Terkenli 2002). As noted by Williams and Baláž (2002: 39), the most obvious manifestation of the stretching and deepening of social relations and institutions across space and time is the massive growth in international tourism. This is quite evident in the current situation of the transition economies of Central and Eastern Europe (CEE), where new tourism activities and tourists have become increasingly characteristic features of the rapidly changing societies, their production and consumption systems and their transforming landscapes (see Williams and Baláž 2000; Hall 2004). These processes that allude to the idea of globalization are not solely driven from 'out there', however, as local actors also contribute to them and their local outcomes (Teo 2002; Pearce 1997). In addition, these processes of non-locally driven transformations are not faced for the first time in the CEE context: the current changes and the 're-internationalization of tourism' (Baláž and Williams 2005: 79) represent only the latest outcomes of the process of transforming tourist destinations and societies.

This article analyses the transformation of a tourist destination, taking the town of Pärnu in Estonia as an example. The purpose is twofold: to emphasize the role of the societal and political context of tourism development and its local manifestations in the transformation process, and to analyse the nature of transformation in terms of the path-dependent and path-creative perspectives in tourism development. Although the paper is orientated theoretically, it aims to emphasize the empirical analysis of development by focusing on the historical transformation process of the study area.

Recently the transition economies of CEE have been increasingly in the focus of tourism development studies, not least because of the European Union enlargement processes (see Coles and Hall 2005; Hall *et al.* 2006). Since the 1990s the central issues in research have remained about the same: how tourism development is influenced by the transition from a system of central planning towards liberal market economy conditions and what role tourism plays in the process (Williams and Baláž 2002: 37; see Bachvarov 1997; Hall 1998). Naturally there has been other popular themes in research, such as post-communist or socialist identities, images and heritage in tourism (see Young and Kaczmarek 1999; Light 2000), but many of these issues have also been integrated into the challenges in (tourism) development (see Unwin 1996; Hall 2004). One of the outcomes in research has been the emphasis that in transition economies, such as those of Estonia, the development of tourism and destinations has not been a linear process or a single evolutionary cycle (see Jaakson 1996; Hall 2000; Hall *et al.* 2006). Rather, the transformation has been characterized by changing periods of development, with varying emphasis of path-dependent and path-creating perspectives (Williams and Baláž 2000). Based on the changing contexts and their socio-spatial manifestations, the transformation process undergone by Pärnu as a tourist destination is divided here into four historically contingent periods.

The main empirical data are based on historical archives in the possession of the City Museum of Pärnu, the Estonian State Archives and the Estonian Historical Archives, which have been discussed partly by Kask (2004) and in other studies focusing on development in Pärnu (Worthington 2003). In contrast to these previous studies of tourism development in Pärnu, the purpose here is both to contextualize and conceptualize the tourism transformation process and to discuss the transformations further in relation to path-dependent and path-creative perspectives. The main concern, therefore, will not be with exploring the detailed societal changes but with how those changes were manifest in tourism development processes on a local scale. The paper concludes with a discussion of the changing orientations and possible future transformations of the resort.

The town of Pärnu (population 43,788 in 2006) is a seaside tourist destination located on the Baltic Sea coast in south-west Estonia (Figure 1). In spite of its relatively peripheral location in Estonia, the town has a long history of tourism and, during the 1990s, after the dissolution of the Soviet Union and the regaining of independence by Estonia in 1991, Pärnu became the most attractive health and spa tourism destination in the country for international tourists. Nowadays it receives over 300,000 visitors a year and accounts for approximately 20 percent of the total overnight visits to the country (EAS 2005). According to Pärnu Tourist Information (2006), the town's commercial accommodation capacity is approximately 3,000 beds. In addition, there are increasing but unknown numbers of international and domestic second homes in Pärnu.

The Transformation of Tourist Destinations

As stated by Richard Butler (1980: 5) 'there can be little doubt that tourist areas are dynamic, that they evolve and change over time'. This changing nature of tourism in destinations has interested tourism researchers for almost as long as tourism studies have been conducted (see Jones 1933; Gilbert 1939, 1949). Scholars have been particularly attracted by peripheral destinations and seaside resorts.

Butler's (1980) original notion was based on the idea of the tourism area life cycle (TALC) (see Stansfield 1978), which conceptualizes a tourist destination as a place-bounded physical unit of analysis, the development of which is to be evaluated primarily based on local-scale impacts and processes. Although wider changes in, for example, fashion and competition are referred to, the main focus of analysis in the model is the evolving tourist numbers and their local impacts on the transforming character of the destination (Butler 2004, 2006). The model has been applied widely and, in a stable political context and relatively closed destination system, such as

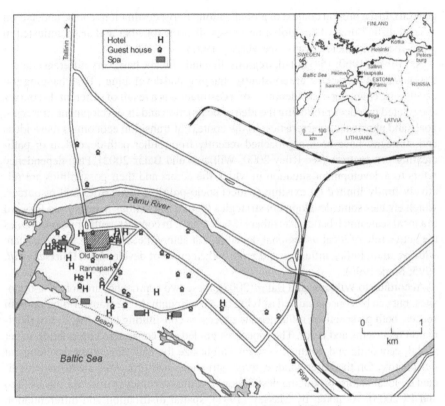

Figure 1. Location of the town of Pärnu in Estonia

an island resort, it often represents a fruitful approach (see Cooper 1989; Weaver 2006). In complex socio-spatial situations and contexts, however, the model does not necessarily 'take into account the tourism system in its entirety' (Gale & Botterill 2005: 159). Especially in an unstable transition situation, it may overlook exogenous economic and political forces (see Butler 1994; Williams and Shaw 1997).

Another basis for the idea of a tourist destination as a physical structure located in space but also as a culturally, politically and socially bounded and contextualized idea can be sought for within the geographical concepts of region and place based on spatial realities constructed by historically contingent practices (see Gilbert 1960; Pred 1984; Paasi 1991). Destinations can be seen as historically produced structures, which are experienced, represented and developed through different economic, political, social and cultural forces, and discursive practices (Saarinen 2004, see Cosgrove 1985). Through these forces and practices the destination is transformed as a part of a larger regional (spatial) system and as part of the awareness of the tourists (and the public in general). In the present context of globalization, tourist destinations can be understood as spatial structures where global processes all come together and are manifested in place-specific, concrete ways (see Massey 1991).

As Gilbert (1960: 158) noted, 'regions, like individuals, have very different characters' and these characters 'are constantly changing and developing'. This changing and developing character – the identity – of a destination is a result of different discourses and related practices producing the idea of destination and its development strategies, goals and physical characteristics. In the context of transition economies these ideas and strategies have been approached recently from either path-dependent or path-creating perspectives (see Riley 2000; Williams and Baláž 2002). Path-dependence refers to a development situation in which the actors and their possibilities are relatively firmly limited by existing (wider) socio-political boundaries and resources, which enables some development strategies (paths) and actions to be carried forward at a local scale much better than others (Stark 1994). In contrast, path-creation stresses the active role of local or regional development actors; i.e. (local) social forces can, within certain limits, influence and modify the course of development (Nielsen *et al.* 1995; Stark 1996).

According to Williams and Baláž (2002), these two approaches are not polar opposites, but can be conceptualized as lying on a continuum. In the transforming tourism spaces, both perspectives influence the processes constituting what the idea of destination represents and is for. The processes guided and constructed by existing wider social, economic and political systems emphasize the path-dependent development perspective. On the other hand, external structures and processes are always mediated by local actors, producing destination-specific outcomes in different places (Teo and Li 2003). As noted by Massey (1991), spatial distribution and differentiation in certain places is a result of wider social processes, but it also affects how those social processes work and are implemented in places. Thus, in practice and theory the line between the path-dependency and path-creative perspectives in development is not clear-cut but often a hybrid one. Therefore, the analysis should also address the plurality of development perspectives (Stark 1996: 996).

This is not to say that the analysis of path-dependency and path-creative perspectives in development is only a matter of position, from which the evaluation is constructed. There are social and cultural but also political and physical structures that emphasize one perspective more than the other in certain contexts, but path-dependency and path-creative perspectives do not hold 'an exclusive agency' in development. In addition, the hegemonic development path is often processed and selected through a failure of another, which makes the analysis of integrated (hybrid) development rather complex in practice (see Grabher and Stark 1998). Although the development perspectives usually are evaluated based on the bounded categories of time and space, it does not mean the processes outside the unit of analysis (e.g. interwar period or a certain region) would be excluded. By applying Raymond Williams' (1977) idea of a hegemonic culture, the identity of a tourist destination contains features from the present context and processes but also traces and continuation from the past and signs of future transformation processes of the destination.

The Transformation of Pärnu as a Tourist Destination

Creating the Idea and Structures of Bathing: the First Period (1830s–1915)

In the mid- and late nineteenth century, the urban space of the town of Pärnu faced major changes at the perceptional and structural levels, initiated by the change in its status. After the period of Swedish rule (1617–1710), Pärnu became a Russian fortress town, a status and meaning that it then lost in 1835 (Pärnu Museum 2002). This opened wider opportunities for economic activity and also for extending the urban space, which had been strictly limited earlier by the town walls and related strategic military and security functions. In addition, locally the change made it possible to search for alternative pathways and to diversify the entrepreneurial environment of Pärnu in the following decades (see Kask 2004).

Based on the contemporary examples of Livonian and Estonian resorts by the Baltic Sea (such as the Haapsalu mud bath, established in 1825), Pärnu tried to develop similar therapeutic bathing practices. Mud cures and related treatments were very popular with the Russian nobility in the imperial capital of St Petersburg (Schlossmann 1939; Worthington 2003) and tourism in the Baltic was based largely on the Russian market and associated with seaside activities, such as bathing (Pärnu Museum 2002).

An application for a bathing establishment on the sea front outside the fortified area of the town was submitted to the local magistrate in 1837. In the autumn of the same year, a contract was signed for the construction of an establishment with six bathrooms and four rooms for accommodating summer visitors as well as bathing huts and piers on the beach. The bathing facilities received their first visitors in 1838, the year regarded as marking the beginning of the tourist resort of Pärnu (Kask 2007). The initial venture was successful only for a short period of time, however, and activities had diminished by the 1850s and 1860s.

From a path-dependent perspective, this can be interpreted as a failure in the 'fitness test' for the diversification of development opportunities (see Grabher and Stark 1998; Williams and Baláž 2002). During the trade boom in the port of Pärnu in the 1860s–1870s, the development discourses started to address other options rather than tourism, and the numbers of bathers decreased. As a result of this setback, Pärnu returned to the position of a recreational place of local importance (Pärnu Museum 2002: 98).

Tourism and recreation activities in Pärnu typically developed spontaneously and in a relatively small scale in the early period, based on local private investments. This spontaneous development led to a relatively dispersed structure of services. However, for a long time, no supporting spatial structures were in place that could have connected and integrated the town area with the beach and seaside facilities that had evolved. Thus, the relationship between the old structures (e.g. the old town and fortress) and the new spatial practices of tourism and recreation were weak or even non-existent for practical purposes (Kask 2004). Even so, in spite of its local character and economically modest outcomes, the first part of the period (1830s–1880s) played a significant role in that it promoted both an expansion of the urban space towards the sea and the initial development of the idea of a resort and related activities.

The second – and touristically more successful – part of the first period was governed by several internal and external processes, which stimulated growth in the late nineteenth century. First, based on plans laid down by the magistrate of Pärnu, the town established a park area, *Rannapark* (Beach Park), between the old town and the original seaside mud baths. This park was constructed in 1882 (Worthington 2003) and, in view of the earlier economic problems in tourism development (e.g. a lack of capital), the mud bath facilities were taken over by the town council in 1889 (Pärnu Museum 2002). After the green zone was established, connecting the town with the beach and its evolving 'Bathing Street', the resort area and the historical town centre were perceived increasingly as integrated spatial structures. At the same time, business efforts were made to develop high-class seaside services and increase the visibility of the resort by advertising it. Pärnu was included in the list of Russian imperial health resorts in 1890 and this official recognition encouraged the town council to publish advertisements in the larger newspapers in Moscow and St Petersburg, for example (Kask 2007).

Secondly, early tourist transport was based largely on mail coaches and, later, on sea connections. Regular boat traffic began between Pärnu and Riga in Latvia in the 1870s, but overland transport was more problematic. There was no proper river crossing between Pärnu and Tallinn (Reval at that time), but the situation was partly resolved when a railway line was opened in 1896 (Worthington 2003), although a more modest (indirect) access route by a combination of train and steamboat or mail coach had already existed since the 1860s.

The town council's goal in this new development phase was to create a large, well-maintained health resort, based on co-operation between the public and private sectors (Kask 2004) in order to ensure the necessary capital for development. The local town council was also active in wider tourism management connections, which manifests path-creating perspectives in its development practices. The town by-laws stated, for example, that the owner of a new building plot had to construct at least one villa for the use of summer visitors within two years (Worthington 2003). Although tourism activities and business increased, the flows of visitors were still relatively small at the turn of the century. Thus, where there were 100 summer visitors (i.e. staying in Pärnu for the whole summer season) in 1890, the number of visitors had multiplied to 800 by 1898 and to 2,500 by 1908 (Figure 2).

Although Pärnu become known as a health and holidaymaking resort, especially among Russian visitors, during the first decade of the twentieth century, the evolving political and power changes in Tsarist Russia resulted in a decrease in summer visitors in the 1910s; so that there were 1,700 summer guests in 1911 but the number had

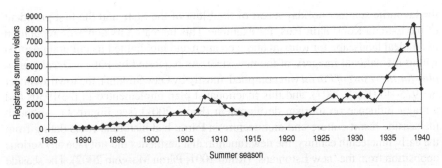

Figure 2. Numbers of summer visitors during the latter part of the first development period and in the second period, 1889–1940. *Source*: City Museum of Pärnu, Estonian State Archives and Estonian Historical Archives.

fallen to 1,100 by 1914. Finally, the outbreak of World War I put an end to the first development period.

Developing and Internationalizing the Beach: the Second Period (1919–40)

After World War I and the Russian revolution, the town of Pärnu had to resume tourism activities and the development of the resort area under new political and economic conditions. Estonia became independent in 1918, and tourism development was slow in the 1920s, after its War of Independence (1918–20), as the local domestic demand was too small to sustain the previously developed structures and the town's tourism infrastructure had been damaged during the political struggles.

The construction of the new nation-state began to influence the image of Pärnu in the late 1920s and 1930s. The place increasingly came to be known as an ideal landscape for recreation and health activities for Estonians, which encouraged people to visit it. The town council also took an active organizational role in the development of the resort. The green zone was restored and new mud bath facilities were opened in 1927; these were extended in 1930 and 1936, for example. By the mid-1930s, the whole tourism infrastructure and supporting urban structures had been re-developed (Pärnu Museum 2002). This was in accordance with the town council's strategy, which strongly emphasized the role of tourism in regional development, regarding it as the most promising pathway to local development and as a source of local income in the short term (Worthington 2003). This strategy was supported indirectly by the state government, which aimed to develop internal links within the country. The railway line was improved and a new bridge across the Pärnu River was built, which, together with road improvements, created more direct and faster links between Tallinn and Pärnu.

The improvements in the basic infrastructure and active path-creating processes were influenced by the evolving national identity. By the 1930s, Pärnu had become

the favourite summer holiday resort of the Elder of the State and the first president
of the Estonia Konstantin Päts, for example. This increased its domestic reputation
as an ideal landscape for tourism and recreation and highlighted its cultural position
within the national imagery of the new state. As requested by Päts, a *Development
plan for the resort of Pärnu* was compiled, mostly by Olev Siinmaa, the town architect
in 1925–40 (Kask 2007), and this functionalist plan implemented in the 1930s had
a major influence on tourism development (Kalm 2001) (see Figure 1). Although
the seaside resort culture and architecture in Pärnu had historical roots dating from
the early nineteenth century, the new functionalist aesthetics did not face any serious
opposition from the 'new Estonians' (Kalm 2001; Pärnu Museum 2002). The seaside
resort culture was still a relatively novel thing for Estonians and it did not have major
traditions or connotations for them, which may have conflicted with the emerging new
style of architecture. The main principles of functionalism – an abundance of light,
air and sun and a healthy lifestyle – were easy to integrate with the beach culture,
its symbolic meanings and activities at the time. Especially after the completion of
the grandiose *Rannahotell* (Beach Hotel) in 1937 and the functionalist *Beach Café*
(with 1,200 seats) in 1939, Pärnu became a very fashionable resort both nationally
and internationally (Kalm 2001; Kask 2007), as is evident from the flows of visitors
in the late 1930s (Figure 2).

While the internal transportation system in Estonia was being upgraded, connections with Finland and the Scandinavian countries, especially Sweden, were also
developed, which opened new international perspectives for the tourism sector. Steam-
boats were operating regularly between Helsinki and Tallinn and between Stockholm
and Tallinn, while the railway connection from Latvia, Lithuania, Poland and Germany had been re-established. Estonia was also one of the cheapest destinations in
the region, and Pärnu attracted increasing numbers of international visitors. The proportion of foreign tourists rose from 30–40 percent to 60 percent of the total in the
years 1929–39 (Kask 2004) and, by the end of the decade, Pärnu had become 'the
premier resort for foreign tourists' in Estonia (Worthington 2003: 374). The international markets were dominated by the Swedes (who had historical connections with
the town dating back to the seventeenth and early eighteenth centuries) and the Finns,
but there were also visitors from Germany, Poland, Great Britain and the other Baltic
states. Again, it was the outbreak of war that brought tourism in Pärnu to an end for
several years.

Organized Recreation in the Soviet System: the Third Period (1944–90)

Under the rule of the Soviet Union after World War II the resort structure of Pärnu was
adapted to serve as a Soviet mass health tourism destination. Tourism in the Soviet
Union was governed by the same logic as any other industrial activity in that country:
it was organized, centrally planned and based on the idea of functional specialization.
Certain places were planned and developed to serve the recreational needs of the

workers (see Vuoristo 1981). For a long time individual tourism and private tourists were unknown concepts in the Soviet recreational system.

The Soviet era represented an intensive concentration of recreational practices and structures. As noted above, Pärnu had been included in the official list of Russian imperial health resorts before World War I, and after World War II it was once more included on the All-Union list of health resort towns. This reflects a certain continuity and hybridity in development paths, but the new and very influential dimension was that the All-Union sanatoriums (i.e. health establishments at resorts) were open all year round and not only in the summer season as had been the practice earlier in Pärnu. The infrastructure was re-developed and expanded, and the existing establishments were nationalized. The Functionalist *Rannahotel*, for example, was re-directed to serve as a workers' rest home. From the 1950s onwards, Pärnu started to gain an image as a health treatment resort and a Soviet summer resort of union-wide importance. The number of people undergoing health treatments grew rapidly: the number of people in treatments from 6,300 in 1948 to 14,000 in 1962, by which time Pärnu had developed into the largest health resort in the Estonian SSR.

Most of the tourism and recreation development, logistics and marketing decisions were taken in Moscow, and the local level was left to do the 'subcontracting'. This central co-ordination did not lead to a holistic or integrated form of planning and development, however. On the contrary, the different trade unions, industrial organizations and ministries built and managed their own recreational facilities, such as sanatoriums – a policy which restructured the Pärnu resort area but also expanded it, causing additional environmental impacts (see Kask 2004; Pärnu Museum 2002).

Pärnu maintained its status as a well-known and recognized tourist destination in the Soviet system, but mainly only for domestic (Soviet) visitors (see Unwin 1996). In this respect Pärnu (and Estonia in general) returned to the provincial role which it had during the first period of development. According to the Soviet classificatory system, it was placed in the categories of mud and climate resorts and, as such, it became recognized increasingly both as a health resort and as a holiday destination. The long tradition of visits by holidaymakers from St Petersburg and Moscow, who stayed for long periods in Pärnu at the turn of the twentieth century, was continued from the 1950s by the Soviet elite and intellectuals from Moscow and Leningrad. However, the emphasis on organized and controlled sanatorium and health-related holidays for Soviet workers was one of the most dominant forms of domestic tourism in Pärnu, as it was over the whole of the Soviet Union (see Jaakson 1996). Thus, the volume of tourism increased rapidly, being fostered by the extensive Soviet market, and the population of Pärnu would more than double during the summer season (Pärnu Museum 2002).

Demand exceeded supply during the 1950s, as the market was vast but the town's accommodation capacity was still rather limited. There were three rehabilitation centres in 1956, with a total of 830 beds, and Pärnu was able to take 14,000 visitors per year. Thus, the town's tourism system was dictated largely by the accommodation capacity. A new rehabilitation centre for agricultural workers, *Tervis* (Health), with an additional 125 beds, was opened in 1971 and, by the late 1980s, Pärnu had four rehabilitation centres with approximately 1,780 beds. In addition, there were 'numerous' smaller guesthouses and bed-and-breakfast places belonging to various authorities, including the military forces, which had been established to cope with the increasing demand from the 1960s onwards (Kask 2004). Although the emphasis was above all on the quantity rather than the quality of the services provided, Pärnu was still regarded as a 'prestige resort' by comparison with many other 'recreation destinations' in the Soviet Union (see Jaakson 1996).

The extensive growth of tourism in the late 1960s stressed a need for planning. There were already some evident environmental issues based on the uncoordinated development of the resort by different trade unions and state actors, but the growing industrial sector was also causing impacts. A *General Plan for Pärnu* was produced in 1973, made possible by the first tourism budget announced in the Estonian SSR in the same year, which channelled funds into the improvement of facilities and into planning (Worthington 2003). The plan outlined a 'public health zone' to protect the beach in the light of competition between the resort area and the growing industrial area. According to the plan, only service industries were allowed in the green zone and the major parts of the coastal areas were designated for recreational purposes (Pärnu Museum 2002; Kask 2004). The estimated number of visitors to Pärnu grew to 300,000 a year in the 1980s. No exact figures exist for the numbers of visitors during the Soviet period, but statistics on visits to the sanatoriums are available (Figure 3).

The data on sanatoriums suggest that flows of visitors grew in two sub-periods during the Soviet era (Figure 3). By the late 1950s their numbers had increased to the limit of the accommodation capacity at the time, after which a new period of growth started in the late 1960s, when additional small- and large-scale sources of tourist capacity were developed and continued until the late 1980s. Although there was some individual tourism activity involved towards the end of the period, Pärnu

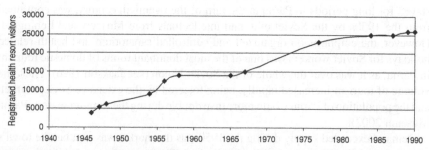

Figure 3. Numbers of visitors to sanatoriums in Pärnu during the third period of development, 1946–90. *Source*: City Museum of Pärnu, Estonian State Archives and Estonian Historical Archives.

during the Soviet era was mainly a destination for organized health tourism controlled by non-local authorities, which created a relatively strict path-dependent development situation at the end of the period.

Globalizing the Beach: the Fourth Period (1991– Present)

Following the collapse of the Soviet Union, Estonia regained its independence in 1991. This meant that the system of sanatoriums and other recreational facilities administered by the trade unions broke down and the number of customers receiving treatments diminished rapidly. The situation was a very challenging and risky one for tourism development plans and measures: the Soviet markets were gone, no Western markets (yet) existed and the domestic demand was still unknown. In addition, there were no substantial sources of private capital for the investments in development and renovation that were needed. In this unclear situation, the town council took the initiative in tourism development in order to re-build the supporting infrastructure and upgrade the tourism facilities in Pärnu (Kask 2004).

Although the existing health treatment establishments started to provide accommodation for 'new' visitors, the quality of their facilities and services was still related to the level of organized Soviet recreation, which was not attractive at an international level. On the other hand, the democratization of society gave people the right to travel freely within the country, enabling domestic visitors to come to Pärnu. A key issue from the public sector and path-creating perspectives was how the town council could regain its active position in practice as the owner of the main sea-front facilities, as had been the case during the successful inter-war period. Some of the smaller units serving tourism were returned to their previous (pre-Soviet) owners, but there were many unresolved ownership disputes. After complicated negotiations with various interest groups, the (hybrid) 'municipalization' of the main resort establishments was completed in 1994.

The municipally owned Pärnu Tourism Development Centre (PTDC) was founded in 1992 to organize tourism management and development measures, and the focus of marketing was turned towards the Finnish and Scandinavian markets (Raagmaa et al. 2000). The town also aimed to make the most of its location beside the planned Via Baltica (see Jaakson 1996), which was largely based on Finnish interests in creating a gateway from Finland to Central Europe (Worthington 2003). The expectations of growing international tourism initiated an early spurt in path-creating development when the Viking Hotel and Health Centre was opened in 1993, for example (later expanded in 2003). As a symbol of a new era of collaboration with Western tourism markets, the first post-war foreign cruise ship, the *Kristina Brahe* from Kotka and Helsinki, Finland, made two trips to Pärnu and the island of Hiiumaa in summer 1994. In addition, the town's collaboration with the 'Keep the Estonian Sea Tidy' association helped the Pärnu Yacht Club to gain the right to fly the European Blue

Flag in its harbour in the same year. This was the first Blue Flag to be awarded in the whole of Eastern Europe (Kask 2007).

The key concepts of Pärnu as a tourism destination in the early 1990s included terms such as tradition, heritage and continuity – all referring mainly to the pre-Soviet periods, especially to the powerful image surviving from the inter-war period. From a strategic perspective, new developments took place in the arranging of events and in international marketing (Kask 2004). When the PTDC re-identified Pärnu's tourism development priorities from the mid-1990s onwards, these were summed up under the themes of seasonality, zoning and regionality. In order to expand the current season, focusing strongly on summer, and to attract regular domestic visitors in particular, an annual calendar of events was created in 1995. Pärnu initiated its present Summer Capital campaign in 1996, and this has proved to be a successful marketing device, with a multitude of events targeted mainly at the domestic market. By zoning, the PTDC aimed to include an environmental management aspect in the development measures. This was done in order to maintain and increase the attractiveness of the town, and especially of the beach. While much attention was paid to monitoring the maintenance of the beach areas and the cleanliness of the water, there were also land-use pressures driven by the new wave of capitalism and neo-liberal development goals (see Jaakson 1996), which were reflected in relatively uncontrolled and poorly regulated building projects (see Kask 2007). The regionality aspects of the strategy were aimed at placing Pärnu as tourist destination within the wider regional tourism system. The main challenge was the domination of the international and domestic tourism markets and of investments in Estonia by the capital city, Tallinn (see Unwin 1996), which is still evident in regional tourism development discourses and practices in Estonia (see Jarvis and Kallas 2006).

Interestingly, the number of domestic summer visitors is influenced largely by the weather conditions, in that the relatively rainy summers of 1998 and 2000 are clearly reflected in the estimated numbers of summer visitors (Figure 4). This is not surprising, of course, in view of the role of the beach and sun–sea–sand activities as the main motives behind tourism in this case. The peak in visitor numbers in 2001 was connected with the celebrations for the 750th anniversary of the town, which encouraged major international marketing efforts in the fields of event, cultural and heritage tourism in order to be less weather-dependent and seasonal (Kask 2004).

However, the successful start made in event creation at the turn of the century has partly resulted in a passive, taken-for-granted situation in domestic tourism development and marketing. In addition to this, the estimated numbers of domestic tourists have probably decreased due to the growth in the Estonian economy, which has led increasing numbers of Estonians to travel abroad (see EAS 2005). In contrast, international tourism in Pärnu has grown (Figure 4), so that this category accounted for 50 percent of the total number of 300,000 tourists during the summer season in 2003. The majority of these tourists were from Finland (over 60%) followed by Sweden, Germany, Latvia and also Russia (Worthington 2003; Kask 2004). The overwhelming

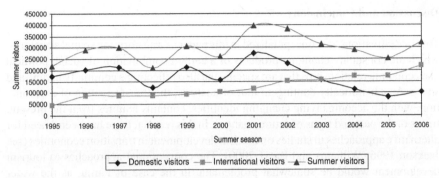

Figure 4. Domestic and international summer visitors to Pärnu in 1995–2006. *Source*: Kask (2004, 2007). There are no reliable yearly data, and the estimated numbers of summer visitors are based mainly on the Pärnu City Council Planning Department's Development and Tourism Service records.

majority of Finns is due to the relative proximity of that country, good accessibility and a favourable exchange rate for the Euro with the Estonian Kroon (see Jaakson 1996). Pärnu has also proved increasingly attractive to foreign investors, especially from Finland and Sweden. For example, the nearby new Beach and Golf Resort is developed and managed by Finnish and Estonian firms.

Pärnu has been active in international collaboration in both the public and private sectors in recent years. For example, it has been a full member of ESPA (European Spas Association) since 1999 and joined the European Federation of Conference Towns in 2001 (Kask 2007). These connections demonstrate the international aspects of Pärnu as a seaside health resort and tourist destination and they have encouraged both domestic and, increasingly, international investors to finance health- and welfare-related projects. One of the largest spas in the Baltic countries, *Tervise Paradiis* (Health Paradise), opened in 2004, for example, and international investors have been active, especially in the Tallinn region but also outside, since Estonia joined the EU in 2004.

The attractiveness of present-day Pärnu as a tourist destination is still based mainly on the same image of an *ideal landscape* for tourism and recreation, which was initiated in the first period of its development and deepened during the second period. As in the 1930s, Pärnu has turned into a popular destination for increasing numbers of tourists from neighbouring Western countries. Thus, there are strong elements of continuity in its development, although, in contrast to the second period, the current development is increasingly being shaped by non-local forces, through investments. Although Estonia is not yet in the Euro currency system, EU membership has created much-needed stability and creditability for foreign investors (see Coles and Hall 2005; Jarvis and Kallas 2006), which has fuelled and deepened the globalization of Estonian tourism and of Pärnu as a tourist destination.

Discussion and Conclusions

Tourist destinations are conceptualized in this paper as transforming spatial structures, which are constantly changing products of a certain combination of social, political and economic relationships that are specific but also reflecting a continuity in time and space. As a historically contingent unit of analysis, the transformation of a destination, with the accompanying changing identities, contains features from the present, traces of the past and signs of future changes. In this respect, there has been a need for alternative approaches in studies on tourism development in transition economies (see Jaakson 1996; Williams and Baláž 2000). The conventional approaches to tourism development would be somewhat problematic in the case of Pärnu, as the wider changes in the political and economic landscape of tourism development, which have been typical of destinations located in transition economies, cannot be considered fully by means of TALC, for example. The four phases identified here in the transformation of Pärnu as a tourist destination, do not cohere with a single evolution process or theoretically with any set of consecutive, 'constantly' rising cycles (see Baum 1998; Butler 2004, 2006). This is because the triggers for stagnation and (very sudden) decline really have not been related to carrying capacities or other similarly determined factors but to rapid changes in the wider socio-political context. In this respect, the major contribution of the paper and path-dependent and path-creative approaches is the incorporation of the contextual change in the process of destination development.

A similar role for contextual changes was identified in British seaside resorts and their decline (see Williams and Shaw 1997; Gale 2005). As Agarwal (2002) stated, the decline of British seaside resorts has been the outcome of an interaction between internal and external factors shaping their competitiveness under changing market conditions. In the case of Pärnu, the development has been influenced and steered strongly by international- and national-scale shifts in social, cultural and economic structures. Pärnu's transformation process can be contextualized based on alternating periods, socio-political contexts and orientations (opportunities and limitations), which do refer to market conditions but more importantly entail wider changes in societal structures (Figure 5). However, there has also been continuity in development with changing levels of hybridity in path-dependent and path-creative perspectives.

During the first period, which included two sub-phases, tourism development in Pärnu and in Estonia as a whole proceeded under Russian rule. The actions and decisions taken after losing the status of a fortified town and, especially, during the latter sub-phase of the period, demonstrate an active local path-creating approach to the transformation process through diversification of the entrepreneurial environment in the town. This development was constrained by its lack of connections with the West. The initial basis created by the idea and structures of bathing was, nevertheless, utilized and further developed during the First Republic of Estonia, which provided for the first significant growth in tourism activities and internationalization of the

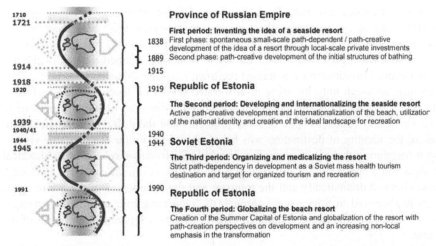

Figure 5. The changing periods, socio-political contexts and path-dependent/path-creative perspectives of the development of Pärnu as a tourist destination (see Kask 2004). The solid line and arrow implies the changing obstacles/limitations and orientations in tourism development and markets.

resort. On the other hand, this second period was constrained by the absence of links to the East, although this created opportunities and resources for alternative pathways, the new development being based increasingly on Western visitors, especially from Sweden.

In relation to the path-dependency and path-creation analysis, the first two periods could also be interpreted as one period in which the inter-war time would represent just the expansion of the first period's development perspectives. Indeed, many of the processes and practices initiated in the first period were deepened during the second one but there were also substantial structural changes, such as regained independence, the closure of Russian markets, Western-based internationalization and much higher level of development actions, which all created very different kinds of outcomes in the transformation process. Even though the development perspective remained about the same, the changed nature of transformation paved the way for Pärnu to develop from a provincial-level resort towards an international-scale tourist destination.

In contrast to the connections between the first and second periods, the Soviet period and its organized tourism were dramatically different to these earlier (path-dependent) path-creating perspectives. From the local perspective, the orientation of development changed towards a strict path-dependent process, which provided only minimal opportunities for alternative pathways at the local and regional levels. As noted, most of development decisions were made centrally in Moscow and the earlier development processes reverted to reactive or passive ones at the local level instead of proactive and innovative ones. Naturally, the Soviet period also created new opportunities and paths by introducing different modes of consumption and reorganizing and restructuring the services, etc. However, these new processes did not allow alternative paths in (local) development. Even so, Pärnu, as a part of the Estonian SSR, represented one of the most Western-orientated regions of the Soviet Union. This situation maintained the town's attractiveness and touristic infrastructure, although only by using an integrated model of development (see Pearce 1979), which led to problems in environmental issues and planning processes in the 1970s and 1980s. In spite of these problems and the different ideological situation, the identity of destination was based on rather similar elements for visitors as it had during the inter-war period: a healthy environment, relaxation, a historical milieu and a beach culture and related activities. However, the symbolic landscape was changed dramatically and the touristic and therapeutic use of the Pärnu resort was medicalized in Soviet times through the increasing role and number of organized health treatments in accordance with the ideological practices and goals of the state.

In contrast to the Soviet era, the present period of the Second Republic of Estonia is based more on path-creating perspectives of tourism development. Although there was considerable path-dependence and partial continuity in tourism activities in the transition economies, in general, during the early 1990s (see Stark 1996; Baláž and Williams 2005: 88), regained independence has resulted in a clear change in the transformation of Pärnu, while EU membership has increased the pace of development, with increasing investments and the effects of globalization in Estonia. These processes of globalization and their local outcomes may change and challenge the basis of the tourism attraction system in Pärnu from an ideal landscape, originating from the time of the second period of development, towards a commodified and international 'spa and golf estate landscape'.

Thus, the evolution of large-scale international tourism can produce spaces that are more representative of the ideas and values of non-local actors and global industry, or else a combination of paths may be possible. In transition economies, globalization has already resulted in development processes that can be interpreted as both path-creative and path-dependent (see Baláž and Williams 2005). Indeed, globalization and internationalization are currently creating new and wider possibilities for development in the transition economies, but also a potentially unequal distribution of tourism services and opportunities (see Coles and Hall 2005). In this respect, the era of deepening globalization, with the current market-driven economics, may lead to a similar kind of situation in Estonia as prevailed during the Soviet period, when development processes were controlled and influenced mainly by outside needs and interests. The initial signs of such processes are already evident, for in addition to the large-scale tourism development projects there are increasing, uncontrolled numbers of Western (mainly Finnish)-owned second homes in the town centre that are altering the nature of its social activities during the low season and potentially turning it into an elite landscape (see Hall and Muller 2004).

Local actors have nevertheless responded to the current nature of changes in the new development plan for Pärnu, which aims to co-ordinate development up to the year 2015 (Kask 2004). The underlying issue in this plan is the idea of Pärnu as a tourist destination and how the resort should be developed in the future. The initial development project has set the objective of maintaining the traditional idea of a bathing resort and the historical parts of town as the most attractive aspects of the future destination. Thus, in the era of globalization and multinational development projects, tourist destinations and their surrounding social structures are not only recipients of path-dependent (global/non-local) forces but are, or can be, actively involved in their own transformation. This kind of globalization from below may help Pärnu to maintain its distinctive character and identity dating from the first and second periods of the transformation.

The regaining of independence in Estonia and the more recent enlargement of the EU have provided new path-creative processes within local-scale development. However, at the same time, EU regional policy tools are urgently needed in order to reduce not only the historical inequalities in the peripheries of the transition economies but also the newly evolving structures of regional inequality created by increasing globalization in tourism and regional development. In this respect, the idea of the Via Baltica, connecting Tallinn to Warsaw (via Pärnu), is now recognized as a priority routing project by the EU (Worthington and Sedakat 2005: 130). In addition to the success of regional policy projects, such as this, one of the main issues in the future development of tourism in Pärnu will relate to the re-opening of development thinking and actions towards the Eastern markets. The Russian segment exists at present, but, given the strong emphasis on Western markets, its role has been minimal and is based mainly on individual travellers and interests. In the future, however, once the current freshness, the novelty factor and the advantage of lower pricing levels relative to Western markets have faded, tourism development in Pärnu will most probably need to search again for potential growth in the East.

References

Agarwal, S. (2002) Restructuring seaside tourism: the resort lifecycle, *Annals of Tourism Research*, 29(1), pp. 25–55.

Ateljevic, I. & Doorne, S. (2002) Representing New Zealand: tourism imagery and ideology, *Annals of Tourism Research*, 29(3), pp. 648–667.

Bachvarov, M. (1997) End of the model? Tourism in post-communist Bulgaria, *Tourism Management*, 18(1), pp. 43–50.

Baláž. V. & Williams, A. (2005) International tourism as bricolage: an analysis of central Europe on the brink of European Union membership, *International Journal of Tourism Research*, 7(2), pp. 79–93.

Baum, T. (1998) Taking the exit route: extending the tourism area life cycle model, *Current Issues in Tourism*, 1(2), pp. 167–175.

Britton, S. G. (1991) Tourism, capital, and place: towards a critical geography of tourism, *Environment and Planning D: Society and Space*, 9, pp. 451–78.

Butler, R. (1980) The concept of a tourist area cycle of evolution: implications for management of resources, *Canadian Geographer*, 24(1), pp. 5–12.

Butler, R. (1994) Introduction, in: R. Butler & D. Pearce (Eds) *Change in Tourism: People, Places, Processes*, pp. 1–11 (London: Routledge).

Butler, R. (2004) The tourism area life cycle in the Twenty-First Century, in: A. Lew, C.M. Hall & A. Williams (Eds) *A Companion to Tourism*, pp. 159–169 (Oxford: Blackwell).

Butler, R. (2006) The Conceptual Context and Evolution of the TALC, in: R. Butler (Ed.) *The Tourism Area Life Cycle Vol. 2: Concepts and Issues*, pp. 1–6 (Clevedon: Channelview).

Coles, T. & Hall, D. (2005) Tourism and EU enlargement. Plus ça change? *International Journal of Tourism Research*, 7(2), pp. 51–61.

Cooper, C. (1989) Tourist Product Cycle, in: S. Witt & L. Moutinho (Eds) *Tourism Marketing and Management Handbook*, pp. 577–581 (London: Prentice Hall).

Cosgrove, D. (1985) *Social Formation and Symbolic Landscape* (London: Croom Helm).

EAS (2005) *Eesti ja maailma turism (2004)* [Estonia and World's tourism 2004]. Available at http://public.visitestonia.com/files/statistica/Tourism_in Estonia2004.pdf (accessed 21 January 2007).

Franklin, A. & Crang, M. (2001) The trouble with tourism and travel theory, *Tourist Studies*, 1(1), pp. 5–22.

Gale, T. (2005) Modernism, post-modernism and the decline of British seaside resorts as long holiday destinations: a case study of Rhyl, North Wales, *Tourism Geographies*, 7(1), pp. 86–112.

Gale, T. & Botterill, D. (2005) A realist agenda for tourist studies, or why destination areas really rise and fall in popularity, *Tourist Studies*, 5(2), pp. 151–174.

Gilbert, E. W. (1939) The growth of island and seaside health resorts in England, *Scottish Geographical Magazine*, 55(1), pp. 16–35.

Gilbert, E. W. (1949) The growth of Brighton, *The Geographical Journal*, 114(1–3), pp. 30–52.

Gilbert, E. W. (1960) The Idea of the Region, *Geography*, 45, pp. 157–175.

Gordon, I. & Goodall, B. (2000) Localities and tourism, *Tourism Geographies*, 2(3), pp. 290–311.

Grabher, G. & Stark, D. (1998) Organising diversity: evolutionary theory, network analysis and post-Socialism, in: J. Pickles & A. Smith (Eds) *Theorising Transition*, pp. 54–75 (London: Routledge).

Hall, C. M. & Muller, D. K. (Eds) (2004) *Tourism, Mobility and Second Homes: Between Elite Landscape and Common Ground* (Clevedon: Channelview).

Hall, D. (2000) Tourism as sustainable development? The Albanian experience of 'transition', *International Journal of Tourism Research*, 2(1), pp. 31–46.

Hall, D. (2003) Rejuvenation, diversification and imagery: sustainability conflicts for tourism policy in the eastern Adriatic, *Journal of Sustainable Tourism*, 11(2/3), pp. 280–294.

Hall, D. (2004) Introduction, in: D. Hall (Ed.) *Tourism and Transition: Governance, Transformation and Development*, pp. 1–24 (Wallingford: CABI).

Hall, D., Smith, M. & Marciszweska, B. (Eds) (2006) *Tourism in the New Europe: the Challenges and Opportunities of EU Enlargement* (Wallingford: CABI).

Jaakson, R. (1996) Tourism in transition in Post-Soviet Estonia, *Annals of Tourism Research*, 23(3), pp. 617–634.

Jarvis, J. & Kallas, P. (2006) Estonia – switching Unions: Impacts on EU membership on tourism development, in: D. Hall, M. Smith & B. Marciszweska (Eds) *Tourism in the New Europe: the Challenges and Opportunities of EU Enlargement*, pp. 154–169 (Wallingford: CABI).

Jones, S. B. (1933) Mining and tourists towns in the Canadian Rockies, *Economic Geography*, 9(4), pp. 368–378.

Kalm, M. (2001) *Eesti 20. sajandi arhitektuur* [Estonian 20th century architecture] (Tallinn: Prisma Prindi Kirjastus).

Kask, T. (2004) Resort of Pärnu – the heritage, which generates today's success story and new tends of the Summer Capital of Estonia. Paper presented at the IGU Conference 'Recent Trends in Tourism: The Baltic and the World', University of Greifswald, 20–24 June.

Kask, T. (2007) *Pärnu: From Fortress Town to Health Resort Town* (Pärnu: Pärnu Town Government).

Light, D. (2000) Gazing on communism: heritage tourism and post-communist identities in Germany, Hungary and Romania, *Tourism Geographies,* 2(2), pp. 157–176.

Massey, D. 1991. The political place of locality studies, *Environment and Planning A,* 23, pp. 267–281.

Meethan, K. (2001) *Tourism in Global Society: Place, Culture, Consumption* (Basingstoke: Palgrave).

Nielsen, K., Jessop, B. & Hausner, J. (1995) Institutional change in post-socialism, in J. Hausner, B. Jessop & K. Nielsen (Eds) *Strategic Choice and Path Dependency in Post Socialism: Institutional Dynamics in the Transformation Process,* pp. 3–44 (Aldershot: Edward Elgar).

Paasi, A. (1991) Deconstructing regions: notes on the scales of spatial life, *Environment and Planning A,* 23, pp. 239–256.

Pearce, D. G. (1979) Towards a geography of tourism, *Annals of Tourism Research,* 6(3), pp. 245–272.

Pearce, D. G. (1997) Tourism and the autonomous communities in Spain, *Annals of Tourism Research,* 21(1), pp. 156–177.

Pred, A. (1984) Place as a historically contingent process: structuration and the time-geography of becoming places, *Annals of Association of American Geographers,* 74, pp. 279–297.

Pärnu Museum (2002) *Brief History of Pärnu* (Pärnu: Museum of Pärnu).

Pärnu Tourist Information (2006) *Pärnu, Estonia* (Pärnu: Tourist Information Centre of Pärnu).

Raagmaa, G., Kask, T. & Rein, A. (2000) Tourism in city marketing and regional development. The success story of Pärnu, Estonia, in: *Proceedings of ERSA's XII Summer Institute – Tourism sustainability and Territorial Organisation* (Faro: University of Algarve).

Riley, R. (2000) Embeddedness and tourism industry in polish Southern Uplands, *European Urban and Regional Studies,* 7(3), pp. 195–210.

Saarinen, J. (2004) 'Destinations in change': The transformation process of tourist destinations, *Tourist Studies,* 4(2), pp. 161–179.

Schlossmann, K. (1939) *Estonian Curative Sea Muds and Seaside Health Resorts* (London: Boreas).

Stansfield, C. A. (1978) Atlantic City and the resort cycle: background to the legalisation of gambling, *Annals of Tourism Research,* 5(2), pp. 238–251.

Stark, D. (1994) Path dependency and privatisation strategies in East-Central Europe, in: E. Milov (Ed.) *Changing Political Economies – Privatisation in Post-Communist and Reforming Communist States,* pp. 115–146 (New York: Lynne Reinner Publishers).

Stark, D. (1996) Recombinant property in East European capitalism, *American Journal of Sociology,* 101(4), pp. 933–1027.

Teo, P. (2002) Striking a balance for sustainable tourism: Implications of the discourse on globalisation, *Journal of Sustainable Tourism,* 10(6), pp. 459–474.

Teo, P. & Li, H. M. (2003) Global and local interactions in tourism, *Annals of Tourism Research,* 30, pp. 287–306.

Terkenli, T. (2002) Landscapes of tourism: towards a global cultural economy of space? *Tourism Geographies,* 4(3), pp. 227–254.

Unwin, T. (1996) Tourist development in Estonia, *Tourism Management,* 17(4), pp. 265–276.

Vuoristo, K.-V. (1981) Tourism in Eastern Europe: development and regional patterns, *Fennia,* 159(1), pp. 236–247.

Weaver, D. B. (2006) The 'plantation' variant of the TALC in the Small-island Caribbean, in: R. Butler (Ed.) *The Tourism Area Life Cycle vol. 1,* pp. 185–197 (Clevedon: Channel view).

Williams, A. M. & Baláž, V. (2000) *Tourism in Transition* (London and New York: I.B. Tauris).

Williams, A. M. & Baláž, V. (2002) The Czech and Slovak Republics: conceptual issues in the economic analysis of tourism in transition, *Tourism Management,* 23(1), pp. 37–45.

Williams, A. M. & Shaw, G. (1997) Riding the big dipper: the rise and decline of the British seaside resort in the twentieth century, in: G. Shaw & A. Williams (Eds) *Rise and Fall of British Coastal Resorts: Cultural and Economic Perspectives*, pp. 1–18 (London: Mansell).

Williams, R. (1977) *Marxism and Literature* (London: Oxford University Press).

Worthington, B. (2003) Change in an Estonian resort: Contrasting Development Contexts, *Annals of Tourism Research*, 30(2), pp. 369–385.

Worthington, B. & Sedakat, P. (2005) Kaliningrad – the last piece of the Baltic jigsaw? *International Journal of Tourism Research*, 7(2), pp. 123–134.

Young, C. & Kaczmarek, S. (1999) Changing the perception of the post-socialist city: place promotion and imagery in £ódü, Poland, *Geographical Journal*, 165(2), pp. 183–191.

Culinary Tourism Packages and Regional Brands in Czechia

JANA SPILKOVÁ & DANA FIALOVÁ

ABSTRACT *The paper discusses the 'Regional Brand' initiative as the regional quality certification with potential to build links with viable rural tourism products. This branding system is explained in the context of a multi-functional paradigm in the development of viable rural economies. A questionnaire survey of certified producers conducted for the first part of the research within this paper revealed mainly a strong awareness of the regional branding system, however, with underused further potential. In the second phase of the research, a qualitative study was conducted in the model region of Vysočina, Czechia, and the results of semi-structured interviews with entrepreneurs in culinary tourism about their involvement in the creation of tourist packages and their cooperation with regional brands were analyzed. The conclusion stresses the need for a significantly more effective interconnecting body at the regional level with the capability of creating fertile links between rural tourism and regional products.*

Introduction

During the 1990s, a number of fundamental societal and economic changes were introduced in Czechia. These changes also affected the diverse rural areas of the country, creating gaps between the leading urban regions and the lagging-behind peripheral areas. In spite of this factor, rural tourism and alternative agriculture could become the most promising activities in the most recent phase of rural development; however, a clear strategy supporting the creation of 'fertile links' is essential (Lacher & Nepal 2010). The once strongly centralized Common Agricultural Policy (CAP) of the European Union has shifted toward a model of multi-functional agriculture and a more pluralistic approach to rural development. The same shift also applies to the post-communist countries, which are quickly catching up with their western neighbors in adopting the latest trends (Hall 2008). However, the post-communist countries have witnessed a distinctively different development of their rural communities and their agricultural functions.

This paper discusses the 'Regional Brand' initiative of the Czech Association of Regional Brands and its potential to build links, which encourage the creation of viable rural tourism products and additionally harness and direct local entrepreneurs to take advantage of this potential to create attractive and feasible rural tourism products. The literature review introduces the role of tourism in rural development and the background of the branding system in Czechia in the next part of the paper in the context of the call for a multi-functional paradigm in the development of viable rural economies in the Czech countryside. As a part of the research for this paper, a questionnaire survey of certified producers in Czechia was carried out. The methodology of this survey is presented in the fourth part of the paper together with the main findings and discussion of the results. The fifth part of the paper consists of the results of a case study conducted in the Vysočina region, Czechia, and includes the results of semi-structured interviews with entrepreneurs in culinary tourism about their involvement in the creation of tourism packages and additionally, their cooperation with regional brands and certified products. The paper concludes with a summary of findings from the two segments of research: both the quantitative and qualitative ones. The concluding remarks point out the need for a significantly more effective interconnecting body or agent at the regional level with the capability of creating fertile links between rural tourism and regional products in a specific entrepreneurial environment.

Aims and Objectives

First, this paper aims to grasp the perception of regional brands and the branding scheme as relatively recent concept and quality measure newly introduced to the Czech market among the certified producers. Second, the paper focuses on the organization of the tourism system and its particular agents to create products with value added and foster the rural development. Here, the connection between food, culinary tradition, hospitality, and tourism comes to the surface as logical opportunity for less favored rural areas without any other strong attractions.

The objectives of the paper are:

1. to identify the certified producers' experience with the branding system and their involvement to utilize their articles to create a complex tourism products—tourism packages within the area of rural tourism;
2. to reveal the principles of tourism enterprising in a specific post-communist context on the example of culinary tourism in a rural region of Vysočina, Czechia, and possible links between the particular agents in the system—mainly the certified producers and traditional restaurant managers;

3. to sketch out some strategies to foster the mutual cooperation in the creation of rural tourism packages based on culinary tradition in areas with low experience of networking, trust, and self-generated activity distorted by 40 years of entrepreneurial practices under the communist regime.

Culinary Tourism and Its Role in Rural Development

The development of rural tourism in its various forms currently represents a potential means of an alternative development strategy and economic activity in peripheral areas (Kneafsey 2000; Wilson *et al.* 2001; Ribeiro & Marques 2002; Michael 2003; Clark & Chabrel 2007), which could especially be the case in the post-communist countries (Gannon 1994; Hall 1998). In the context of the new push toward a multi-functional and pluralistic approach to rural development (Gray 2000; Lowe *et al.* 2002; DuPuis & Goodman 2005; Feagan 2007), a key strategy of the CAP second pillar (rural development) has also been strong support for the non-productive functions of agriculture and forestry in the European countryside. In peripheral areas, however, it is always important to balance the short-run benefits of newly introduced economic activities with the possible costs of long-term environmental and socio-cultural degradation (Hospers 2003).

Many scholars have already discussed the commodification of the countryside and its products (Urry 1995) for the benefit of the interested consumers together with the local economies and communities. The former approach the rural as a place of a nostalgic, true and simple life, seeking health, authenticity, and quality (Smith & Phillips 2001), and the local economies and communities benefit from these new trends in consumption and tourism demand since they can be used strategically for progressive ends (Mc Carthy 2006). However, the tourism development cannot be effective in every region or locality. Specific market segments will generate niche markets for some areas, but 'the cost of supplying these markets could be prohibitive' (Wanhill 1997: 49). Geography, as a complex science, is capable to put together all the pieces of knowledge related to the research of peripheral areas, rural development strategies, environmental barriers, socio-cultural aspects, tourism management, etc. Ioannides (1995) stressed the importance of bridging the gap between the research in tourism and economic geography and highlights the geography's role in explaining the organization of agents involved in the tourism system. In a similar vain, Ioannides and Petersen (2003) make an appeal to more attention to tourism entrepreneurship within the current geography, especially the role that innovation plays in small and medium tourism enterprises. That is why the survey in this paper focuses on small producers of branded goods and consequently also on the management of small restaurants and accommodation facilities in a rural area and their potential cooperation to create innovative tourism products with value added.

The strengths of many rural areas usually lie in their undisturbed landscape and attractiveness of natural environments. Wanhill (1997: 50) states that this remoteness often correlated with lack of tourist infrastructure may cause that the visitors purchase essential supplies before setting on their way and limit their spending in the area. Therefore, the offer in rural areas has to include all the facilities and supplies required by the host, e.g., in the form of a tourism package. A complete tourism package is on the top of the list of factors for success in rural tourism (Wilson *et al.* 2001: 134), and it becomes obvious that rural communities who wish to attract visitors, entice them to stay longer, spend more money, and encourage return visits have to develop a package of attractions and businesses necessary to capture the attention of today's increasingly demanding clientele (González & Bello 2002). Briedenhann and Wickens (2004) argue that the clustering of activities and attractions, and the establishment of rural tourism products (such as packages, routes, etc.), stimulates co-operation between local areas and partnerships between particular local agents. Community participation and public sector support may create opportunities for the development of small-scale tourism projects in less developed areas.

The traditional regional foods and aliments became a part of today's shoppingscape and are rapidly gaining devotees among high-income consumers and becoming more frequently sought after (Parrot *et al.* 2002; Watts *et al.* 2005). Logically, it is the food that could form the focus of the potential rural tourism packages in remote areas without any stronger attractors. EU has also recognized the potential of food as important factor of regional development and introduced two pieces of legislation protecting regional and traditional food. First of them defines the so-called products with a Protected Designation of Origin (PDO) or Protected Geographical Indication (PGI), and the second creates a system of Certificates of Special Character (CSC). These products have a strong association with the regional development, since a great majority of PDO and PGI products come from the Less Favoured Areas. Thus, they provide a chance for the regionally distinctive products, which could represent an alternative development strategy for rural regions, less competitive within the global-ized, commodity-driven market (Parrot *et al.* 2002). These products should stimulate endogenous economic development in areas that lack any other kind of distinctive attractiveness or specific potential (Watts *et al.* 2005), such is the case of the Vysočina region presented in our case study.

Regional Branding and Its Implications for Rural Tourism in Czechia

The strategic goals of The National Strategic Rural Development Plan of the Czech Republic for the period 2007–2013 (Ministry of Agriculture of the Czech Republic) include the utilization of the cultural specifics of rural regions for tourism, the im-provement of public awareness as regards tourism potential as well as support for the non-productive functions of agriculture and forestry. The choice of tourism as a key alternative occupation in Czech rural areas has thus emerged as the logical outcome of recent development in policies given the potential of the unique cultural landscape, historic monuments, events and traditions stored in the Czech countryside.

In this context, during the spring of 2010, the Czech Ministry of Agriculture launched a new campaign which aimed at fostering consumer interest in regional food from specific regions of the country. As a part of this campaign, a brand 'Regional aliment' has been created. Producers can attain the 'Regional aliment' branding for individual products when meeting particular criteria. One of the most important criteria is that the product must be made from regionally traditional raw materials while the proportion of national raw materials must form at least 70% of the product, and the main raw material must be 100% originating from the specific region. Czech government, through its agency for tourism promotion—Czech Tourism, together with the Association of hotels and restaurants of Czech Republic also popularize the Czech regional gastronomy. The project 'Czech specials' serves to promote Czech cuisine to the foreign consumers via a variety of actions both within the country and abroad. EU funds also support the 'Culinary academy' focusing on meals from all around Czechia, where successful graduates receive an internationally recognized certificate. Together with the World Association of Chefs Societies, there is an effort to re-establish master exams—Master Chef Certification and WACS Global Master Chef Certification for the Chefs concentrating on Czech traditional meals of high quality.

Similarly, regional or quality/authenticity branding is a commonly recognized tool for the promotion of rural regions and their typical products. In the present-day quest for sustainability, branding may additionally become a way to support the sustainable social, cultural, and environmental development of rural regions with a rich natural or cultural heritage (Parrot *et al.* 2002). In the economic sense, branding enables the creation of links between small entrepreneurs or small or medium-sized enterprises from the region by offering a common marketing denominator and identification with the region itself. The diversification of economic activities in rural areas assists local inhabitants to retain their jobs and to specialize, and thus to prevent an outflow of people from rural areas. Furthermore, regional brands are a convenient tool for the development of rural tourism. The concept of regional brands in tourism contains not only the functional dimension (the product itself) but also its representative value. Moreover, sustainable tourism is fostered by regional brands as a result of enabling tourists to learn about social and economic life in a particular region. Branded products combined with the opportunity to meet the producers and visit their workshops or farms strengthen the attractiveness of a region for tourists (ARZ 2011).

The tradition of regional branding in Czechia started some five years ago with the first three regional brands (Krkonoše, Beskydy, and Šumava—traditional mountain regions of Czechia) which recently established the Association of Regional Brands (ARB) in the Czech Republic. Other regions followed and at the present time there are already 15 (April 2012) regional brands (Figure 1). The fourth region to join the system was the region of Moravský kras (Moravian Karst) as one of the most important karsts areas of Central Europe with more than 1000 caverns and gorges and an underground river. Next regions to follow thanks to the cooperation with an

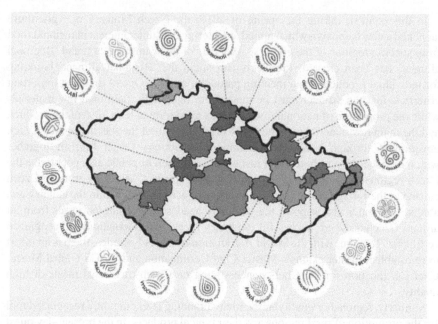

Figure 1. Regional brands of Czechia. *Source*: Association of Regional Brands 2012.

association for home made products were another Czech mountains—Orlické hory and their foothill region Podorlicko. During 2007 the region of Moravské Kravařsko joined and also the first cross-border region of Górolsko Swoboda on the boundary of Czechia, Poland, and Slovakia. In the same year, this time owing to the initiative of agricultural agencies and organic farmers, the regional brand in the region of Vysočina was created. In 2008, other two regions entered the Association: one foothill region of Podkrkonoší (in continuation of the regional brand in the Krkonoše mountains) and a traditional riverside region Polabí (river basin of the Elbe river). One year later the region of Haná, historically most fertile area of the Czechia with a strong tradition of agricultural production, followed, and one year later also the regions of Českosaské Švýcarsko (on the boundary of Czechia and Germany), Jeseníky (another mountain region in the Eastern part of the country), and Prácheňsko (historical region in Southern Bohemia with handcrafted goods tradition). In 2011, other regions followed: Broumovsko (a region known thanks to its rock towers), Kraj blanických rytířů (The 'Blaník knights' region in the Central Bohemia), Železné hory (a small mountain range in Eastern Czechia), and Moravská Brána (Moravian Gate).

Nevertheless, more regional brands are emerging as well as other brands not included in the Association, however, still working on a similar basis and using comparable principles. It appears that the Association fulfills the aims to raise awareness about regional branding and to promote the sale of certified products and services.

In the following part of the paper we rely on a survey among producers of certified goods and their involvement in the creation and operation of rural tourism packages based on quality and authentic local and traditional goods.

Regional Branding and Rural Tourism Packages: A Postal Survey of Certified Goods' Producers

At the beginning of 2011, there were 325 branded products and 22 service providers. Not surprisingly, the regional brands differ by the number of brand-granted products and conditions of their work, the amount of financial resources that can be used for promotion and their fund-raising abilities. As the first part of the research for this paper, we conducted a questionnaire survey targeting producers of certified goods—food, drinks or artisan products. The survey aimed to reveal how these producers perceive the process of certification, how they evaluate the benefit of certification for their enterprises, how they market their products, and what problems they face when making and selling certified products. The questionnaire covered a range of questions on the producers' experience of certification and regional brands, and it also dealt with the possibility of creating tourism packages in combination with other products or services within the region.

The questionnaires were sent via e-mail to all the listed producers with certificates of regional brands in Czechia. The total sample thus represented the entire set of all 282 producers (some of them have more than one certified product, in this case they were approached only once) existing as at 1 July 2011. From the total of 282 questionnaires sent, 13 were undeliverable, 269 respondents were approached (95.4%), and 91 questionnaires represented the usable response. In spite of all these obstacles, the response rate of 33.8% can be considered as representative.

Results and Discussion

The data obtained from the questionnaire survey were coded and transformed into the database, which was consecutively processed by the basic descriptive statistical tools and content analysis. The results of these analyses are presented in the following sections. One half of the respondents (51%) were producers of regional artisan goods, 37% produced certified food products, 7% were regional drinks producers, and 3% of respondents offered certified services. The distribution of the respondents according to the year when they obtained certification was quite balanced with 20% in 2005, 2% in 2006, 9% in 2007, 20% in 2008, 16% in 2009, 21% in 2010, and 12% in 2011; therefore the survey contained both the experienced producers and the newly-entered entrepreneurs.

First we analyze some interesting relations between the questionnaire categories with the cross-tabulations using the Pearson Chi-Square measures and Cramer's V for the coded nominal variables. There is a significant relation between the type of certified product and the importance attached to the branding process (Cramer's V, Pearson Chi-Square $p < 0.001$). The producers of artisan products clearly attach the greatest importance to branding schemes, followed by the producers of food. The importance of branding schemes is higher among the producers who joined the branding process recently (Cramer's V, Pearson Chi-Square $p < 0.001$). There is also an obvious relation between the type of certified product and the benefits from the certification, when mainly the producers of artisan products benefited from being certified (Cramer's V, Pearson Chi-Square $p < 0.001$). There is also a strong association between the type of product and the perception of success of the company, when the producers of regional drinks and providers of services evaluate themselves as mostly successful, followed by the producers of food and producers of artisan goods (Cramer's V, Pearson Chi-Square $p < 0.001$). When it comes to the involvement in the tourism packages, there are also some significant associations, e.g., the producers of food (45.8%) do not currently want to cooperate in the form of package, however, some 42% are interested and would like to be part of a tourism package. The percentage of those who would like to contribute to a package is highest among the producers of artisan goods (70.5%). Last but not least, we analyzed also the correlation between the type of certified product and the type of the desired tourism package to join (Cramer's V, Pearson Chi-Square $p < 0.00$): the producers of food mostly want to be part of packages in agro tourism or tourism related to fests and cultural events; the producers of drinks see their opportunities in the cultural events, incentive and congress tourism, and educational tourism, and the producers of artisan goods were clearly interested in the packages related to art, cultural heritage and monuments, and regional events tourism.

Second, we present the most interesting results of the survey with the figures depicting frequencies of particular responses. The vast majority of respondents (74%) thought that the attractiveness of their region was based mainly on the quality and beauty of the natural landscape and countryside, another 42% stated that it was the architectural heritage and historical monuments that made their region attractive; the same percentage of respondents (39%), however, also mentioned the local traditions and customs and local products as the main attractions of their regions. These results clearly coincide with the results of previous surveys (Fialová & Vágner 2006) and demonstrate that it is the natural heritage and typical landscapes that are the most valued assets offered by Czech rural regions. Furthermore, the preservation of natural environments and cultural attributes are among the most cited features of the new rural paradigm.

When it comes to the regional brands, 84% of the respondents agreed that certification in the form of regional brands and similar concepts was important for regional producers and service providers, 14% thought that the benefit of certification was only partial, and just one respondent answered negatively to the question on the importance of regional certification and branding. This provides clear evidence of the

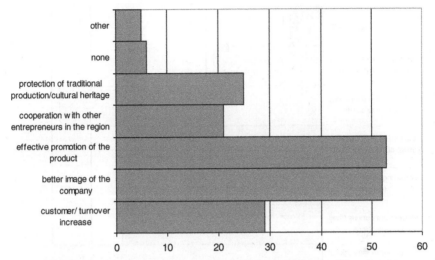

Figure 2. The main benefits of regional brands and certification. *Source*: authors.

success of the regional branding concept, which is also mirrored in the stable demand for certification and the first-rate reputation of this scheme throughout Europe.

The question on the benefits of certification (Figure 2) revealed that producers benefit from regional branding mainly in the areas connected with the image of the company or product and more effective promotion/marketing (64%, resp. 63% of respondents). Thirty-five percent of respondents also reported that being certified increased the number of their customers and/or their turnover. The protection of traditional production processes and cultural heritage was an important benefit of regional branding for another 30% of respondents.

When it comes to the reasons for the perceived success of regional products among customers, the most often stated reasons according to the producers were: first, the customers and tourists liked regional products, regional flavors, and traditional materials (55%); second, customers were willing to pay more for the higher quality they got (52%); third, 39% of respondents also believed that an important reason was the customers' curiosity and interest in trying new things; lastly, another 38% stated that it was the desire to know more about purchased products (Figure 3). These findings are comparable with similar surveys of regional products (Vieira & Figueiredo 2010) declaring the increasing hedonism of consumers, but also idealization of the 'rural as a more pure, authentic, and wholesome space' (Figueiredo 2003: 1649).

On the contrary, the respondents, who admitted to the economic hardship of their companies and low competitiveness of their products, perceived the main factors affecting their failure to be the unwillingness of customers to pay for quality regional

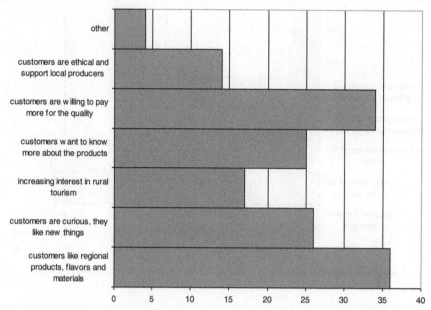

Figure 3. The main reasons for the success of regional products. *Source*: authors.

products and customer preference for unified products from industrial production (both 61%). Other important reasons cited by this group of producers included that the customers had no bonds with the area, so they did not feel the urge to buy regional products and they also lacked information about the concept of regional branding or the purpose of certification (44%). Other serious problems mentioned by the respondents and seen from the perspective of the company were the small scale of their production, lack of quality materials, as well as the fact that they often work as individuals and thus the income is not sufficient for the family, etc. (Figure 4).

The questionnaire next addressed issues more connected to the possibility of creating relationships between regional production and tourism activities in rural regions. When asked about the extent of interest in a potential regional association or group in which they would be able to participate, just over half of the respondents (52%) wanted to take part in an association focused on tourism for cultural heritage and monuments, one third (33%) were interested in associations related to eco-tourism, and 28% would choose to join in activities connected to culinary tourism. Given the fact that adrenaline tourism was mentioned by only 4% of the respondents, it was evident that the producers of regional products in the rural sector emphasized the peaceful and relaxing element of rural tourism, the quality of products and hospitality, culinary tourism sometimes associated with a certain hedonism, as a counter product

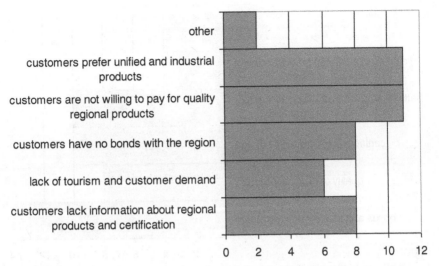

Figure 4. The main reasons for the rejection of regional products. *Source*: authors.

to adrenaline adventures, and the everyday stressful environment of the predominant type of tourism found in the capital city, Prague, or in popular skiing areas.

The question on the rural tourism packages, however, revealed very interesting results. Twenty-four percent of surveyed producers already took part in some type of tourism packages, 27% were not interested in such enterprises, however, almost one half of the respondents (48%) had not ever supplied products or services as part of a tourism package, although they indicated they would like to do so. There is thus great potential for the creation of fruitful liaisons between the regional products and tourism activities in rural regions. In this context, half of the respondents had some ideas on the formation of new rural tourism packages with their products and/or services included.

Those respondents who had already cooperated in the formation of rural tourism packages declared their biggest advantage was developing stronger bonds and relations with the region itself (62%). They also highlighted the importance of certification for improving the image of both the products and the whole packages (48%) as well as better presentation of the products which perform more successfully in the form of packages than they would alone (48%), (Figure 5).

The respondents who did not plan to become a part of a tourism package with their products explained their negative response was mainly due to lack of information about such possibilities or lack of potential packages in their region (49%) while others often stated that their production was too small or too seasonal to take part in a tourism package (48%), (Figure 6). As indicated by the answers of the respondents, this question revealed a serious lack of information and propagation of tourism

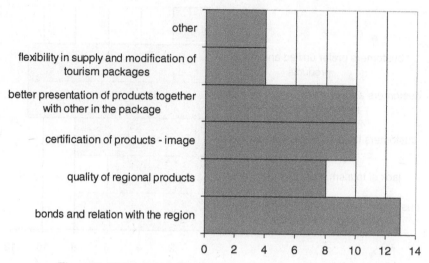

Figure 5. The main benefits of tourism packages. *Source*: authors.

packages that could help both the producers of regional products and the region itself in attracting tourists. It can therefore be assumed that there are substantial opportunities for improvement in this area.

Interestingly, those respondents who did not cooperate in tourism package creation but indicated they would either like to participate in an existing package or start their

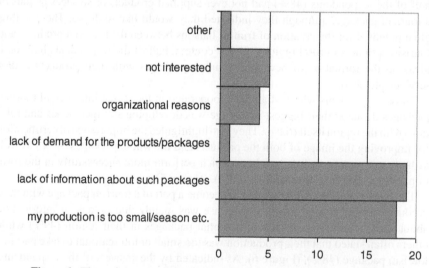

Figure 6. The main reasons for rejection of tourism packages. *Source*: authors.

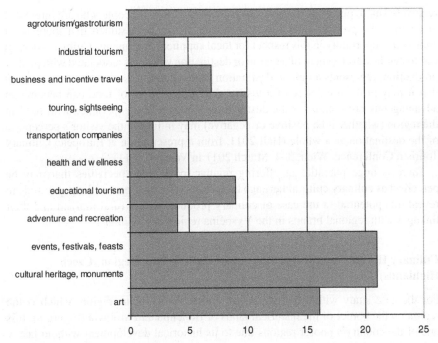

Figure 7. The areas of potential interest in tourism package creation. *Source*: authors.

own one, expressed their interest in a variety of tourism packages (Figure 7). Given the character of most regional products, the highest interest was evident for tourism packages related to special events, popular festivals and feasts, and cultural heritage (both 42%). Another important area of interest was agro-tourism, alongside culinary (here 'gastro') tourism and eco-tourism (36%).

The last presented results introduce us to the issues of event tourism and its possibilities (Getz 2008), but mainly to the natural appeal of the connection of rural tourism and hospitality with traditional and local food (Parrot *et al.* 2002). The producers and entrepreneurs themselves perceive the packages related to local resources, traditional food and cuisine as clearly linked and promising. Moreover, scholars have not left behind this area of blending between tourism and gastronomy. Food has an obvious relationship to tourism since every tourist has to eat, and food is an integral part of any tourist product. Gastronomy may be related to other tourism products and culinary tourism may bring an important economic benefit to the rural areas (Hall & Sharples 2003).

Nevertheless, the association between the food market and tourism is problematic in some aspects. While every tourist has to eat, it is obvious that not all tourists necessarily have to be culinary tourists. The segment of true culinary devotees is relatively small, however, there is also a growing group of people who are interested in testing new products and food. Therefore, it can be assumed that there is an enormous opportunity in this respect for local suppliers of aliments. Culinary tourism can foster the development of a region or destination when it is associated with quality production, represents a unique destination product, and it is attractive to the extent that it may prolong the stay of a visitor. A regional brand of food can become an advantageous promotion for the destination. However, the experience with food in the region (whether it be positive or negative) may influence the visitor's perception of the destination as a whole (Hall 2011, from a presentation at European Culinary Tourism Conference, Wien, 3–4. March 2011 in Vaníček 2011).

There is huge potential in offering regular local food specialties that may be perceived as culinary cultural heritage by tourists. The next part of the paper aims to reveal this potential in the case of culinary products within rural tourism and their linkages with regional brands in the Vysočina region of Czechia.

Culinary Heritage and Rural Tourism in the Vysočina Region (Czech Highlands)

For the case study within this paper, we chose the Vysočina region, which is the region on the border of the historical lands of Bohemia and Moravia (Figure 8). It is one of the country's poorer regions due to its historical development without heavy industrialization, and for this reason, the region now boasts an unspoiled environment and favorable conditions for recreation, relaxation, and holidays in the countryside. On the other hand, the region now ranks among the fastest developing in the country and is attracting new investments and people. The unspoiled landscape, rural character of the environment, tradition, and hospitality together with improved transport and tourist infrastructure, makes it a suitable region for a case study of potential links between rural tourism, especially culinary tourism, and regional products with (or without) certification.

Culinary traditions of Vysočina regions are based on the seasonal dishes and the use of fresh home made products (above all legumes, plums, mushrooms, and potatoes), thus the values that are acknowledged within the current return to local food consumption (Holloway & Kneafsey 2000; Goodman 2003). The basic meal was represented by bread, made from rye or, in the mountain areas, from oat. Peas consisted a regular part of the menu, in the form of puree with hulled grain or plums. Other legumes such lentils and beans were also widely consumed. Soups were served extensively and the same is true for different types of purees—from millet grains, hulled grains, semolina. Hulled grains were sometimes baked with plums. Sauces were also typical for the Vysočina's cuisine (with milk the white sauce was created, with blood and plums, the black one), mainly horseradish sauce, mushroom sauce, dill sauce or several types of fruit sauces. After the Napoleon wars, the potatoes were introduced in the Vysočina's culinary tradition and they were consumed baked,

Figure 8. The location of Vysočina region within the country. *Source*: ArcČR 500, 2012.

boiled or prepared as sweet or salty. Today's famous potato pancakes proceed from Vysočina (http://vysocina.fkaleidoskop.cz/).

There is an initiative called 'Heritage trails' sponsored by the European Union and Gastronomia Bohemica company aimed at the promotion and evaluation of the best regional restaurants offering traditional dishes and specialties. This initiative runs a web page www.stezky-dedictvi.cz where visitors may browse Czechia by regions and choose a recommended restaurant serving regional specialties. Leaflets and other promotional materials are also offered. Promoted and recommended restaurants are selected by a team of gastronomy and tourism specialists according to a given set of criteria.

There are 22 recommended restaurants and/or hotels in the Vysočina region. Although interviews were planned with all the 22 restaurant managers or owners, due to the time constraints on the part of some, it was only possible to conduct 19 semi-structured interviews, each lasting between 20 and 45 minutes. Survey question development was informed by the relevant literature and diverse knowledge about the situation and context. The questions in the interviews were structured around three main topics: knowledge and consciousness about the regional branding process and certification of regional products; the availability and offer of tourism packages and the potential links between culinary tourism packages and regional certified products. A range of topics included both open-ended and categorical questions. For open-ended questions, the answers were categorized, and comments and observations were recorded. Anecdotal notes from some respondents were truly valuable for understanding their perspectives of rural tourism and enterprising ventures in gastronomy.

The results showed that a majority of the interviewed managers were acquainted with certified products and had heard something about regional certification, its functions and operation. Some of them had seen certified products in tourist information centres, etc. However, the majority of interviewed people showed a lack of further information about the products, could not recall any of the products, and had no clear idea of where they could get the certified products or what type of products were being certified. Responses such as: 'Perhaps I have come across these products, but I think that they are not really promoted' (resp. 14) were very typical for the interviewed sample. This is a clear sign that the promotion of regional products had been inadequate and thus the effect and influence on the quality or potential of rural tourism cannot be considered truly successful in its current form.

In three cases, the selected businesses already cooperated with branded products and involved them within their production or their enterprise. 'Yes, we have this lady from Jihlava region, she makes this leather jewellery . . . very nice . . . we will organise a small exhibition of her products here in the pension and we are going to sell them as well' (resp. 1).

Eight of the 19 interviewed businesses did offer some kind of tourism package; most of these packages involved relaxation and wellness facilities or a romantic element while those packages related to horse riding were also among the more frequent plus there were some other specific packages available, focused on golf, bowling or other sports activities according to the individual demand of the visitors. Nevertheless, the packages on offer did not include any type of certified regional products. The process of certification runs alongside the process of creating tourism packages although these two have almost nothing in common. In a couple of cases, the interviewed businesses used local materials such as certified milk, meat or honey when cooking local specialities. This signifies cooperation with regional brands, however, at a very basic level only.

The most interesting part of the interviews was concerned with the potential building of fertile links between the regional products and rural tourism, mainly in its gastronomic form. The responses varied from pure and pragmatic rejection of cooperation with regional brands, 'We are just a restaurant' (resp. 9) or 'We are strictly a business hotel, we don't sell these things' (resp. 5) to interest in buying local products, but attaching no importance to brands: 'We use local materials to cook, but we don't care about the brand . . . anyway, I don't trust all these brands and labels . . . ' (resp. 6) to acknowledgement of some potential ' . . . yes, it would be possible, but only on a small scale—some jewellery, or crafts that we could sell . . . ' (resp. 2).

Very often, the interviewee mentioned the issues of price when the regional products and material were sold at higher prices than the materials available from wholesale stores. 'We cook with local ingredients as often as possible, it is only about the price... I, I would like it, but local products are often expensive, not everybody can afford it...' (resp. 7). 'We can talk about it, but the price is the deciding factor' (resp. 19).

In the majority of cases (9), however, the respondents expressed a clear interest in cooperation and admitted that it would provide a considerable fresh impetus to their enterprise. 'Well, we are just in the process of changing the menu... errr.. we wanted to include more local and fresh food like the goat cheese which is now quite popular again... so that would be a good impulse' (resp. 3), 'Yes, we have people coming here and asking for some packages and that stuff... we would love to try something new, but we don't know about it' (resp. 21) or 'We used to sell ceramics from local craftsmen, but then it somehow disappeared, ... I don't even remember why... but we would like to sell something new again' (resp. 20). In contrast, respondent 10 states, 'We certainly would be interested, now we are creating new packages. Our hotel is a conference hotel so we could use it for the propagation of local products on a greater scale... we are aware that brands attract...' (resp. 17).

Nevertheless, even these positive attitudes were clearly marred by the fact that the entrepreneurs interviewed had not been approached by local producers with any promising and mutually beneficial offers. 'Nobody has come and offered anything, but it is not a problem to use it, if it is favourable—what about a weekend with Czech cuisine?... That could work' (resp. 4) or 'We try to use local materials and products but we don't care about branded products, we don't ask them if they have the brand certificate or not. We would be interested, but so far, nobody has come and offered us anything... I would be delighted' (resp. 13).

Therefore, it is apparent that the price of the products and the lack of information and coordinated cooperation or linking were among the most serious reasons for the low penetration of regional products into the rural culinary tourism and complex tourism packages in the Vysočina region. One of the most interesting outcomes of the survey was the fact that in five cases, it was the researcher who brought the attention of respondents to the existence of promoted certified local products and notified them about the website or organizations where they could obtain information. It is thus obvious that the organizations of regional tourism and those responsible for the promotion of brands had not been operating in the most effective manner. In the complicated context of intensive competition within the relatively recently created market system, there are several actors and schemes that run alongside each other but are totally independent: the regional branding system; quality branding system; the competition for best regional aliments with its own certification system; support of tourism in the regions; support of multifunctional development of rural areas; rural tourism initiatives of individual entrepreneurs, etc. In this highly diversified environment of actors without any prior links, it is extremely important to introduce an element or agent that will effectively disseminate information and successfully package and market the particular elements of the regional production and rural tourism chain.

The promotion of regional products should be raised to a level whereby they are easily accessible to individual enterprises engaged in rural tourism that do not have the required resources to look for information of this kind nor to find the necessary contacts by themselves. These promotional and marketing activities have to be tailored to the particular needs of consumer demand and the scale of business thus in the case of a smaller pension, some smaller artisan goods or traditional products could be offered for sale as souvenirs at reception. On the other hand, a larger conference hotel could offer gift packages consisting of local products and goods, and additionally the hotel's restaurants and bars could provide and recommend to guests a range of local specialities made with or accompanied by some local products such as locally baked bread or locally brewed beer, traditional sweets or regional liquors.

Conclusions

The main conclusion to be drawn from the research, collected data and survey is that a relatively strong awareness of the regional branding system and its importance was displayed by the respondents. However, the main obstacles are still a lack of knowledge about products among consumers and a lack of information or wasted potential among producers in regard to more complex tourism products. As regards the second objective of the paper, it is recommended that there must be a precise and clearly-led strategy to support the creation of complex tourism products. Therefore, the existing funding schemes and programs should not only support individual producers and products, but in the first place, they should also foster cooperation and the establishment of joint activities leading to the creation of more complex tourism products.

The paper contributes to the current literature on the role of tourism in regional development and creation of viable links within the rural enterprising within a specific context of a post-communist entrepreneurial environment by examining the case of culinary tourism packages and regional branding system. There is a wide spectrum of opportunities for cooperation and creation of fertile links between the local branded products and rural and culinary tourism (as evidenced by foreign experience and also the results of the survey). The potential of culinary traditions in the rural tourism in Czech peripheral areas is highly promising. Nevertheless, Geciene (2004), in this respect, warns about merely transplanting Western models to post-socialist societies, where there may be many specific cultural patterns and different contexts.

There are conclusions important beyond the importance of this case study: within the specific entrepreneurial environment in transition economies, where the level of confidence, mutual trust, and the will to cooperate tends to be low (Spilková 2008), one cannot anticipate that these links will be created bottom-up (Spilková 2008; Golden

2011). Small entrepreneurs and producers do not have sufficient experience and knowledge about the certification schemes or the linkages within the tourism system, mutual mistrust and wariness prevail, entrepreneurs see each other as competitors—all these aspects present barrier to the development of complex tourism products with value added within this economic and socio-cultural background distorted by 40 years under communist regime. The need for a strong linking and reliable agent is thus even more pronounced. The challenge has to be met by people and organizations responsible for the development of regional tourism and the promotion of regional brands.

Acknowledgements

This work was supported by the Czech Science Foundation's project no. 404/12/0470 'Geography of alternative food networks and sustainable consumption' and project no. 403/09/1491 'The significance of tourist function of settlements and municipalities in the process of formation of regional identity and identity of regions in CR.'

References

Asociace regionálních značek. (2011) *Regional Branding Throughout Europe* (Praha: ARZ).

Briedenhann, J. & Wickens, E. (2004) Tourism routes as a tool for the economic development of ruralareas—Vibrant hope or impossible dream? *Tourism Management*, 25(1), pp. 71–79.

Clark, G. & Chabrel, M. (2007) Measuring integrated rural tourism, *Tourism Geographies*, 9(4), pp. 371–386.

DuPuis, E. M. & Goodman, D. (2005) Should we go "home" to eat? Toward a reflective politics of localism, *Journal of Rural Studies*, 21(3), pp. 359–371.

Feagan, R. (2007) The place of food: mapping out the "local" in local food systems, *Progress in Human Geography*, 31(1), pp. 23–42.

Fialová, D. & Vágner, J. (2006) New trends in second housing in Czechia, *Acta Geographica Universitatis Comenianae*, 48(3), pp. 263–271.

Figueiredo, E. (2003) Entre o vivido e o desejado. O papel do ambiente na nova dicotomia rural/urbano, in: J. Portela & J. C. Caldas (Eds) *Portugal Chao*, pp. 149–166 (Oeiras: Celta Editora)

Gannon, A. (1994) Rural tourism as a factor in rural community economic development for economies in transition, *Journal of Sustainable Tourism*, 2(1–2), pp. 51–60.

Geciene, I. (2004) Democracy and the middle class: Western theoretical models in a post- Communist context, in: C. Harrington, S. Ayman & T. Zurabishvili (Eds) *After Communism: Critical Perspectives on Society and Sociology*, pp. 235–255 (Bern: Peter Lang)

Getz, D. (2008) Event tourism: Definition, evolution, and research, *Tourism Management*, 29(3), pp. 403–428.

Golden, J. D. (2011) Place marketing in an environmentally sensitive area: Case study of the Barycz Valley, in: Asociace regionálních značek (Ed) *Regional Branding Throughout Europe*, pp. 106–114 (Praha: ARZ)

González, A. M. & Bello, L. (2002) The construct "lifestyle" in market segmentation: The behaviour of tourist consumers, *European Journal of Marketing*, 36(1/2), pp. 51–85.

Goodman, D. (2003) The quality turn and alternative food practices: Reflections and agenda. *Journal of Rural Studies*, 19(1), pp. 1–7.

Gray, J. (2000) The common agricultural policy and the re-invention of the rural in the European Community, *Sociologia Ruralis*, 40(1), pp. 30–52.

Hall, C. M. (2011) *Keynote speech at the European Culinary Tourism Conference* (Vienna).

Hall, D. R. (1998) Tourism development and sustainability issues in Central and South-Eastern Europe, *Tourism Management*, 19(5), pp. 423–431.

Hall, D. R. (2008) From "bricklaying" to "Bricolage": Transition and tourism development in Central and Eastern Europe, *Tourism Geographies*, 10(4), pp. 410–428.

Hall, C. M. & Sharples, L. (2003) *Food Tourism Around the World: Development, Management, and Markets* (Burlington, MA: Butterworth-Heinemann).

Holloway, L. & Kneafsey, M. (2000) Reading the space of the farmers' market: A preliminary investigation from the UK, *Sociologia Ruralis* 40(3), pp. 285–299.

Hospers, G. J. (2003) Localization in Europe's periphery: Tourism development in Sardinia, *European Planning Studies*, 11(6), pp. 629–645.

Ioannides, D. (1995) Strengthening the ties between tourism and economic geography: A theoretical agenda, *The Professional Geographer*, 47(1), pp. 49–60.

Ioannides, D. & Petersen, T. (2003) Tourism "non-entrepreneurship" in peripheral destinations: A case study of small and medium tourism enterprises on Bornholm, Denmark, *Tourism Geographies*, 5(4), pp. 408–435.

Kneafsey, M. (2000) Tourism, place identities and social relations in the European rural periphery, *European Urban and Regional Studies*, 7(1), pp. 35–50.

Lacher, R. G. & Nepal, S. K. (2010) From leakages to linkages: Local-level strategies for capturing tourism revenue in Northern Thailand, *Tourism Geographies*, 12(1), pp. 77–99.

Lowe, P., Buller, H. & Ward, N. (2002) Setting the next agenda? British and French approaches to the second pillar of the Common Agricultural Policy, *Journal of Rural Studies*, 18(1), pp. 1–17.

Mc Carthy, J. (2006) Rural geography: Alternative rural economies– The search for alterity in forests, fisheries, food and fair-trade, *Progress in Human Geography*, 30(6), pp. 803–811.

Michael, E. J. (2003) Tourism micro-clusters, *Tourism Economics*, 9(2), pp. 133–145.

Parrot, N., Wilson, N. & Murdoch, J. (2002) Spatializing quality: Regional protection and the alternative geography of food, *European Urban and Regional Studies*, 9(3), pp. 24–61.

Ribeiro, M. & Marques, C. (2002) Rural tourism and the development of less favoured areas—Between rhetoric and practice, *International Journal of Tourism Research*, 4(3), pp. 211–220.

Smith, D. P. & Phillips, D. (2001) Socio-cultural representations of greentrified Pennine rurality, *Journal of Rural Studies*, 17(4), pp. 457–469.

Spilková, J. (2008) Foreign investors and their perceptions of socio-institutional and etrepreneurial environment in the Czech Republic: A pilot study, *Journal of Geography and Regional Planning*, 1(1), pp. 4–11.

Urry, J. (1995) *Consuming Places* (London: Routledge).

Vaníček, J. (2011) Přeshraniční spolupráce vysokých škol cestovního ruchu, *Studia Turistica*, 2(1), pp. 84–88.

Vieira, C. & Figueiredo, E. (2010) Fruitful liaisons? Relationships between regional food productions and tourism activities in Serra da Estrela, Portugal. Paper presented at the 9th European IFSA Symposium, Vienna, July 4–7, 2010. Available at http://sa.boku.ac.at/cms/fileadmin/Proceeding2010/2010_WS4.1_Vieira.pdf (accessed 21 December 2012).

Wanhill, S. (1997) Peripheral area tourism: A European perspective, *Progress in Tourism and Hospitality Research*, 3(1), pp. 47–70.

Watts, D. C. H., Illbery, B. & Maye, D. (2005) Making reconnections in agro-food geography: Alternative systems of food provision, *Progress in Human Geography*, 29(1), pp. 22–40.

Wilson, S., Fesenmaier, D., Fesenmaier, J. & Van Es, J. C. (2001) Factors for success in rural tourism development, *Journal of Travel Research*, 40(2), pp. 132–138.

International hotel groups and regional development in Central and Eastern Europe

Piotr Niewiadomski

The influence of expanding hotel companies on economic development in host countries is one of the most under-researched aspects of the globalisation of the hotel industry. Aiming to contribute to this agenda this paper focuses on the expansion of international hotel groups into Central and Eastern Europe (CEE) after 1989 and enquires into their influence on economic upgrading in CEE following the fall of communism. The paper is grounded in the global production network (GPN) perspective and selected assumptions of evolutionary economic geography (EEG), a combination of which is argued here to be an effective theoretical platform from which the targeted set of processes can be addressed. The paper proposes a framework for analysing the influence of the hotel industry on regional development in host economies. Four areas of influence are distinguished: direct investment and infrastructure upgrading; employment creation; knowledge transfer; and forging local linkages. The first three of them are then analysed in more detail on the basis of Poland, Estonia and Bulgaria. It is demonstrated that the influence of hotel groups on regional development hinges upon the business model preferred by the group for a given hotel and, depending on various place-specific factors, it may have different manifestations in different markets. The paper also shows that it is often other actors from hotel groups' GPNs, rather than hotel groups themselves, that play a key role in creating and enhancing the value which the region captures and in influencing the path of development which the region follows.

Introduction

The impact of the international tourism production system on economic upgrading in host countries is a growing research agenda (see e.g. Goodwin, 2008; Hall & Page, 2006, 2009; Shaw & Agarwal, 2012; Wall & Mathieson, 2006; Williams, 2009). Despite that, it still seems to be a relatively long way until this complex set of processes is sufficiently explored and comprehensively theorised. By means of focusing on the varied ways in which international hotel groups foster regional development in host markets – one of the most under-researched aspects of the globalisation of the hotel industry – this paper aims to contribute to this important agenda both in empirical and theoretical terms. Given that the hotel industry is much more global than other service industries in terms of the number of countries covered by each large firm (Contractor & Kundu, 2000), which in turn implies a variety of complex interactions between international hotel companies (and their partners) and the different contexts into which they expand, the shortage of research on the developmental impacts of hotel firms is particularly appealing. Meanwhile, the hotel sector requires much more attention if the uneven geographies of the tourism production system are to be fully accounted for.

This paper focuses on the expansion of international hotel groups into Central and Eastern Europe (CEE) after 1989 and analyses the role which the hotel industry plays in fostering economic upgrading in CEE following the collapse of communism. Four areas of impact are distinguished: direct investment and infrastructure upgrading; employment creation; knowledge transfer; and forging local linkages. Due to the shortage of space, only the first three are discussed in more detail. Simultaneously, given that regional development has been a central objective for the formerly communist states in their transition to market, the paper also investigates in what way the impact of the hotel sector on economic upgrading in CEE is integral to post-communist transformations. The following two questions are answered:

(1) What is the influence of international hotel groups on regional development in CEE after 1989?
(2) To what extent do international hotel groups foster post-communist transformations in CEE?

Although the paper aims to generalise about the whole CEE, examples are mainly drawn from Poland − one of the biggest markets in CEE − and to a lesser extent also from Estonia and Bulgaria.

The paper is grounded in the global production network (GPN) perspective (Coe, Dicken, & Hess, 2008a; Henderson, Dicken, Hess, Coe, & Yeung, 2002; Hess & Yeung, 2006), which because of its attention to post-entry behaviour of expanding firms (unlike e.g. eclectic paradigm and other approaches used to explain the globalisation of services before − see Faulconbridge, Hall, & Beaverstock, 2008) is argued here to be a promising theoretical platform from which the impact of the hotel industry on economic development can be effectively addressed. In order to better account for the specific post-communist nature of the CEE region, the analysis is also informed by some of the theoretical advancements associated with the 'evolutionary turn' in economic geography (Boschma & Frenken, 2006; Boschma & Martin, 2007, 2010; Coe, 2010; MacKinnon, Cumbers, Pike, Birch, & McMaster, 2009; Martin & Sunley, 2006).

The paper draws from extensive research carried out in Poland, Estonia and Bulgaria in 2009. The research process focused on all 23 hotel groups from the world's top 50 (Gale 2008) that were active in CEE when the research commenced and consisted of 90 interviews in total. Twenty-four of them were conducted over the phone with HQ-level development executives from 21 out of the 23 analysed hotel groups. The following 56 interviews took place in the three focal countries (30 in Poland, 13 in Estonia and 13 in Bulgaria) and were mostly carried out face to face. They targeted general managers of international hotels, hotel developers and owners, local hoteliers, hotel experts from international consultant firms based in CEE, representatives of local authorities and representatives of trade unions. Ten popular business and tourist destinations across the three countries were addressed during this stage. The remaining 10 interviews were carried out over the phone and targeted hotel industry representatives in other CEE countries and hotel industry consultants based outside CEE. The interviews revolved around four main themes, each of which can be equated to one of the four areas of hotel industry impact listed above. This paper addresses three of them. The results are presented theme by theme in synthesised and generalised form. The discussion is supported by selected quotations.

It is demonstrated that the influence of expanding hotel groups (and their GPNs) on regional development depends on the business model selected by the group for a given hotel (i.e. the structure of the hotel GPN in a given location) on the one hand and various place-specific features of the host market on the other. Enhanced attention to these groups of factors is thus key to understanding the post-entry implications of the worldwide expansion of hotel groups. It is also argued that the role of hotel groups is not necessarily central to the whole process. Instead, it is often other actors from their GPNs that play a critical role in creating and enhancing the value which the region captures and in influencing the path of post-communist development which the region follows.

The paper consists of two main sections. The first one outlines the applicability of the GPN approach to research on services and economic development and proposes a framework for analysing the influence of hotel groups on regional development in host countries. The section also shows in what way the assumptions of evolutionary economic geography (EEG) can complement the GPN framework in accounting for the processes of regional development. The second main section provides an empirical example. Focusing on the expansion of hotel groups into CEE after 1989, the section analyses the impact of the international hotel industry on economic development in CEE following the fall of communism.

Global production networks (GPNs) and regional development

Developed in the early 2000s, GPN is 'a heuristic framework for understanding the developing geographies of the global economy' (Coe & Hess, 2011, p. 130). As a broad-based approach that is 'capable of grasping the global, regional and local economic and social dimensions of the processes involved in many (...) forms of economic globalisation' (Henderson et al., 2002, p. 445), the GPN framework 'emphasises the complex intra-, inter- and extra-firm networks that constitute all production systems, and explores how these are structured both organisationally and geographically' (Coe & Hess, 2011, p. 130). In general, the architecture of the GPN framework rests upon three conceptual categories – power, embeddedness and value (see Coe, 2009; Henderson et al., 2002; Hess & Yeung, 2006 for a detailed discussion). Of critical importance to this paper is the category of value which allows the GPN framework to consider how value can be created and enhanced and to what extent it can be captured by various locations and actors. Thus, one of the central concerns of GPN analysis is 'to reveal the dynamic developmental impacts that result both from the firms and the territories that they interconnect' (Coe & Hess, 2011, p. 130). More specifically, the framework's perspective on regional development revolves around the concept of 'strategic coupling of global production networks and regional assets, an interface mediated by a range of institutional activities across different geographical and organizational scales' (Coe, Hess, Yeung, Dicken, & Henderson, 2004, p. 469). Attention is paid both to endogenous growth factors within the region (such as local human, technological and institutional resources that are a necessary precondition for development to take place) and to the strategic needs of the translocal actors that coordinate GPNs. If the region's assets complement a transnational firm's strategic needs a coupling process takes place. However, to bring regional development, the process of coupling requires the presence of institutional structures that would promote local assets and attract translocal actors (Coe, 2009; Coe & Hess, 2011; Coe et al., 2004; MacKinnon, 2012; Yeung, 2009).

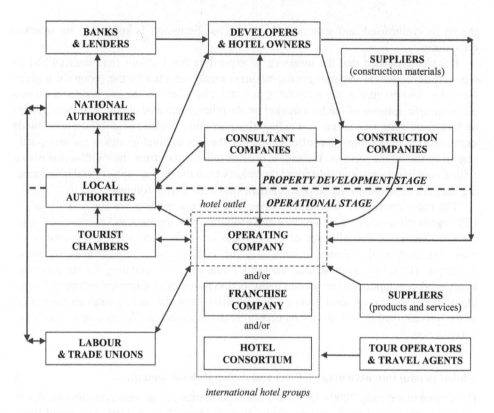

Figure 1.   A stylised example of an international hotel group's global production network.
Source: Niewiadomski (2013, p. 6; Figure 1).

The applicability to research on services is another key feature of the GPN framework. The research by Coe, Johns, and Ward (2008b) who enquired into the power relations between different stakeholders in the temporary staffing industry in Poland and the Czech Republic and by Coe and Wrigley (2007) who focused on host economy impacts of expanding retail corporations can serve here as good evidence. As this paper demonstrates, the GPN framework is also particularly useful in research on the hotel industry. Thus, to set the scene, Figure 1 demonstrates in what way the international hotel industry can be theorised as a form of GPN, whereas in order to delineate different types of hotel GPNs Table 1 provides a summary of five main business models of hotel groups, each of which implies a different relation between the hotel owner and the hotel group and thus a different structure of the hotel GPN. Building upon the concept of strategic coupling and the work of Dicken (2007) who identified major dimensions of GPN impacts on host economies, Figure 2 proposes a framework for analysing the impact of the international hotel industry on regional development in host countries.

However, while the applicability of the GPN framework to research on regional development cannot be questioned, the approach is not entirely free from shortcomings. Most importantly, the GPN framework does not fully account for the historical evolution of GPNs and regional assets over time – a limitation which according to MacKinnon (2012) can be easily overcome by combining the GPN framework with EEG. Indeed, drawing from evolutionary economics, EEG is concerned with the spatialities of economic novelty, how the spatial structures of macro-economy are shaped by the behaviour

Table 1.   Five main business models of international hotel groups.

Business model	Features
Operator owning	The hotel is both owned and operated by a given hotel group (i.e. hotel industry FDI) A high-commitment model and the slowest mode of expansion
Managing	The owner employs a hotel group to operate the business A medium-commitment model
Leasing	A hotel group rents the property in order to operate the business independently A high-commitment model
Franchising	The hotel owner/operator employs a hotel group to flag the hotel for a fee A low commitment model and the quickest mode of expansion
Hotel consortia	The hotel joins an affiliation of independent hotels to jointly conduct marketing activities The range of services offered by consortia is similar to that of franchisors

Source: Own elaboration on the basis of Cunill (2006), Go and Pine (1995), León-Darder, Villar-Garcia, and Pla-Barber (2011) and Niewiadomski (2014).

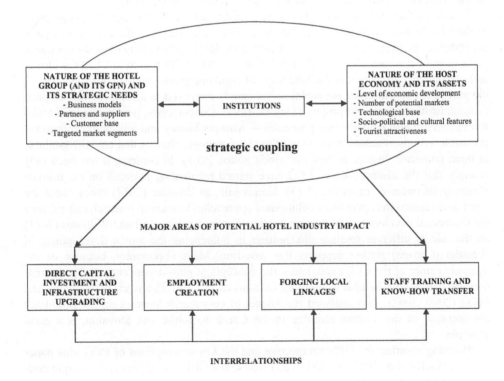

Figure 2.   Strategic coupling in the hotel industry and hotel industry host economy impacts.
Source: Own elaboration on the basis of Coe (2009, p. 560; Figure 2) and Dicken (2007, p. 461; Figure 16.4).

of economic agents and how the processes of path-creation and path-dependence interact to shape geographies of economic development (Boschma & Martin, 2007, 2010). In other words, shedding light on the economy as a dynamical and self-transformational system, EEG explores how the economic landscape is transformed over time (Boschma & Martin, 2007).

The central concepts of EEG are path-dependence, path-creation and lock-in. The idea of *path-dependence* assumes that the economic landscape does not tend towards a unique equilibrium but it rather evolves in ways shaped by its history and past trajectories of growth (Boschma & Martin, 2010). Thus, future outcomes depend on past events (Martin & Sunley, 2006). The idea of *path-creation*, in turn, suggests that actors may reproduce, transform and deviate from existing socio-economic structures, practices and development paths, or to put it more simply, that new paths of development are also possible (Martin & Sunley, 2006). Finally, the concept of *lock-in* refers to 'how regions can become "locked-in" to existing trajectories of development as the weight of inherited investments, practices and skills inhibits their capacity to adapt to wider processes of economic change' (MacKinnon, 2012, p. 233). Thus, while the concept of strategic coupling can account for the local assets which the region relies on and the role which different local actors play in stimulating further growth, the key notions of EEG draw attention to the historical context in which this growth takes place and the path of development which the region follows. In this respect, the assumptions of EEG are particularly useful in accounting for the nature of the places which various GPNs interconnect and on which they impact — something that over years has been one of the most under-theorised elements of the GPN framework (Coe et al., 2008a; Hess & Yeung, 2006).

Due to the fact that the traces of the communist past continue to shape the geographies of the CEE region (Smith & Timar, 2010), it is not surprising that the concepts of path-dependence and path-creation play a key role in explaining the variety of post-communist paths of growth across CEE (Smith, 1997; Sokol, 2001). With regard to CEE, the idea of path-dependence implies that the landscape of capitalist production is constituted out of the past relations which are not replaced but simply reworked in a complex way as post-communist transformations progress (Smith, 1997). Concurrently, post-communist transformations are also path-shaping processes — whereas history and legacies constrain the economic actions of actors, they do not foreclose strategic choices that are still available to them (Hausner, Jessop, & Neilsen, 1995; Sokol, 2001). In contrast, it has been only recently that the assumptions of EEG have started permeating research on the tourism economy (Brouder & Eriksson, 2013). Meanwhile, as Brouder (2014) notes, there are legitimate reasons to expect that evolutionary approaches to tourism research can enhance the theoretical development of tourism studies. The research by Gill and Williams (2011) on the role of different tourism stakeholders in influencing the tourist development of Whistler (Canada) further supports this assertion. Most importantly, because of the dynamic nature of the CEE capitalisms, the concepts of path-dependence and path-creation are particularly helpful in research on tourism in CEE. The work of Williams and Balaž (2000, 2002), who analysed the impact of communist legacies on the post-1989 development of the tourism industry in the Czech Republic and Slovakia, is a good example.

Bringing together the GPN perspective and the key assumptions of EEG, this paper follows MacKinnon (2012, pp. 231–232) who argues that 'the process of strategic coupling can be viewed in evolutionary terms, suggesting that regional institutions' capacities to bargain with TNCs will reflect the legacy of previous strategies and forms of investment'. Concurrently, '[n]ew forms of strategic coupling based on the meshing of regional assets and local firms in GPNs can be seen as a key mechanism of path creation' (MacKinnon, 2012, p. 234). Thus, links to external networks can provide access to extra-regional sources of innovation, investment and expertise (Coe et al., 2004; MacKinnon, 2012) – something that Martin and Sunley (2006) refer to as transplantation of new technologies, organisational forms and institutional arrangements from elsewhere, and which they consider a key mechanism of 'de-locking'. As Brouder (2014) and Brouder and Eriksson (2013) note, the nature of knowledge transfer through tourism networks and the ability of this transfer to overcome path-dependence and lock-in are an important gap in research on the tourism production system. Thus, apart from analysing the impact of hotel groups on economic upgrading in CEE per se, this paper explores the role which hotel GPNs play in 'de-locking' the regional economies of CEE from the legacies of communism.

The hotel industry and economic upgrading in Central and Eastern Europe

When in 1989 communism in CEE collapsed, the countries of the former communist bloc almost unanimously decided to embark on the path of transition from socialism to capitalism. Looking to be inserted into 'at least the margins of the wider global economy' (Hudson, 2000, p. 411) and hoping for a smooth closure of the wealth gap between the East and the West, the CEE states opted to implement liberal democracy and various forms of market economy (Sokol, 2001). A critical role in the transition was accorded to foreign direct investment (FDI) and, more generally, the expected influx of foreign firms, both perceived as crucial components of internationalisation and demonopolisation (Bradshaw & Swain, 2004; Pavlinek, 2004). It was argued that large inflows of foreign firms would generate widespread industrial restructuring, foster technology and knowledge transfers, implement modern production and management strategies and create jobs, thus bringing economic upgrading at all spatial scales (Pavlinek, 2004). The following section analyses the role of the hotel industry in this set of processes. The section enquires into the extent to which the processes of strategic coupling between hotel GPNs and regional assets and actors in CEE foster economic growth in CEE and help the CEE regions to overcome the post-communist path-dependence.

Direct investment and infrastructure upgrading

Given that each new hotel project implies a large injection of capital in real estate, the most basic role that the hotel sector plays in fostering regional growth in CEE is associated with direct investment (Brown, 1998; Franck, 1990; Go & Pine, 1995). However, whether the hotel industry is a source of external capital depends on where investors come from. Even if hotels are operated or franchised by international hotel groups, the invested capital may be local and the influence of hotel GPNs on economic upgrading may be in this respect fairly limited. Notwithstanding that, as Table 2 shows, despite the recession experienced by some countries in 2008–2009, the volume of FDI stocks in the accommodation sector has in many CEE states significantly increased in the last decade. The role of the international hotel industry as an important source of foreign investment in CEE cannot be therefore questioned. However, three potential negative aspects of this impact also should be recognised. First, the cost associated with obtaining FDI may be higher to host countries than that of local investments (e.g. as a result of tax holidays offered to foreign investors). Second, FDI in the hotel sector may contribute to the host country's dependency on foreign capital, thus affecting the country's autonomy in

Table 2. Hotel and restaurant (2002−2006) and accommodation and food service activities (2008−2010) FDI stocks in selected CEE countries (in millions of euro).

Country	2002	2004	2006	2008	2010
Bulgaria	63	97	243	558	677
Czech Republic	419	397	445	479	626
Lithuania	57	56	58	89	61
Poland	275	427	512	−	850
Slovenia	−	17	22	39	30

Source: Own elaboration on the basis of data retrieved in September 2014 from *http://epp.eurostat.ec.europa.eu.*

implementing economic policies (Dicken, 2007) − something that Coe and Hess (2011) refer to as the 'dark side' of strategic coupling. Third, the outflow of profits may in time outweigh the amount of capital invested initially, thus leading to considerable financial leakages (Brown, 1998; Dicken, 2007).

Therefore, the most important kind of value that the host country captures is the development of high-quality hotel infrastructure − something that many regions of CEE still often lack. This semi-permanent character of hotel base is perfectly reflected by the concept of 'spatial fixity' of tourism supply, i.e. the inability of many forms of tourism supply to relocate to different places (Urry, 1990; Hall & Page, 2009). As a general manager from an international hotel in Sofia observed:

> For the city it's a long-term investment. (...) And it is not something with which you can do whatever you want. If for any reason you have cheaper labour next door you move the factory. (...) But the hotel won't move because our business is local. We invest in the beginning, then we maintain it, develop it, which means we carry on with a certain plan to invest. (...) We can't move. We might build another hotel somewhere else, that's true, but this one will stay. (September 2009)

Moreover, the contribution of the international hotel industry to the development of the hotel infrastructure also has an important qualitative dimension. Because international hotel groups tend to be leaders in setting modern construction standards (Mitka-Karandziej, 1993), newly-built international hotels are often the most technologically-advanced developments in CEE. In addition, international hotels offer plenty of accompanying facilities such as leisure clubs or conference rooms, the shortage of which is still evident across CEE. A notable example is Warsaw where the biggest conference facilities are currently offered by the Hilton hotel.

Importantly, the value that the international hotel industry brings to CEE has a clear reflection in the physical landscape of cities and towns. In contrast to the obsolete post-communist hotel base, international hotels often stand out in the landscape and become hallmarks of whole districts − even in bigger cities where they are not the only new developments, the InterContinental Hotel in Warsaw and Swissôtel in Tallinn being good examples. For the same reasons, the international hotel industry contributes to the urban development of CEE cities and the regeneration of urban cores (Chang, Milne, Fallon, & Pohlmann, 1996; Watson, 1991). Multiple revitalisation projects that have been undertaken by CEE cities since the post-1989 closure of inefficient state-owned plants and the subsequent abandonment of whole industrial areas are the best evidence here. The Manufaktura shopping and entertainment centre in Lodz that has been developed in the place of an old industrial district and that also includes an international hotel is a prominent example.

The role of local authorities and other institutions in CEE such as convention bureaux and tourist chambers, all of which deliberately attract hotel GPNs through promoting regional assets and exposing the region to external influences, should not be unacknowledged. The ways in which local authorities stimulate the development of the hotel sector are therefore place-specific, i.e. they depend on the path of post-communist growth followed by the region and the specific features of a given institutional environment such as the political and personal attitudes of local decision-makers and the level of bureaucracy. For instance in Estonia, where local authorities claim to have a liberal approach and try not to get involved in the growth of any private sector, the responsibilities of local authorities are usually limited to elaborating general development plans, investing in public infrastructure and conducting city marketing (Interview with a senior official from the City Enterprise Department, Municipality of Tallinn, June 2009). Due to the high level of centralisation, the level of involvement of local administrations is also considerably low in Bulgaria. In contrast, Polish municipalities often foster the development of the hotel industry more pro-actively. Not only do they suggest what kind of investments they expect on various plots, but they also elaborate investment offers for potential investors and cooperate with consultant firms to carry out market research and look for hotel investors and operators. However, given that the extent of such endeavours largely reflects political ambitions of local authorities, it should not be surprising that wide regional variations in this respect can be observed across Poland. While on the one hand there are active and progressive cities such as Wroclaw and Gdansk, on the other there are numerous destinations that are still far less outward-looking and that especially pertains to non-metropolitan areas.

At the same time it is necessary to acknowledge that the development of hotel infrastructure can only bring expected results if it is synchronised in space and time with the development of other infrastructure – the infrastructure determining the city's accessibility (e.g. railways, airports), the business infrastructure (e.g. convention centres) and the entertainment infrastructure (e.g. stadiums, concert halls), which all generate demand for hotel services but which in CEE are still often 'in the making' (especially in secondary destinations). While on the one hand the shortage of the other infrastructure impedes the development of hotels, on the other the development of hotels stimulates the development of the other infrastructure and fosters regional growth through enhancing the attractiveness of the city and positioning the city as a tourist/business destination. This results in a higher number of cultural, business and sport events and in an increased number of foreign investments, all of which serve as important sources of technological, organisational and institutional innovations and useful mechanisms of de-locking. Thus, hotel GPNs have the potential not only to create and enhance the value that the region captures but also to help the region multiply that value by means of expanding into the market and improving its economic image. This path-shaping potential of the hotel sector was well addressed by a development executive from an international hotel group active in CEE:

> I think it goes both ways. (...) In the early 1990s (...) internationally-branded hotels were considered to be necessary business infrastructure. And I think that was why EBRD was funding hotel projects along with office buildings. Having modern hotels (...) was necessary for Western companies to come in and do business easily. (...) So once you have these (...) modern hotels, then obviously it helps the growth of international business in the destination. And then, in turn, it stimulates economic development. And when the economy develops, it may create hotel development opportunities. So it goes both ways. (November 2008)

However, although the potential of the international hotel industry to attract new busi-nesses cannot be questioned, it is necessary to recognise that in the majority of cases the hotel industry develops in a reactive way, i.e. it follows economic development. It is for this reason why the most significant hotel sector growth in CEE can be observed in capital cities (Warsaw, Tallinn and Sofia being good examples) and other relatively well-estab-lished business destinations such as Krakow, Wroclaw or Gdansk, whereas secondary and tertiary destinations across CEE continue to suffer from a largely undeveloped (inter-national) hotel base (e.g. Lublin in Poland, Bourgas in Bulgaria or Tartu in Estonia).

Finally, the way in which international hotel groups foster infrastructure upgrading in host destinations also depends on the group's business model. While injecting foreign capital and developing the hotel infrastructure is down to hotel developers, it is hotel operators and franchisors that dictate hotel developers what standards to pursue and that play a key role in importing novelty into CEE. It is also operators and franchisors who provide a brand and enhance the market's visibility. Thus, although the role of developers in fostering economic upgrading in financial terms outweighs that of operators and fran-chisors, the role of hotel operators and franchisors in implementing innovations and help-ing the CEE economies with overcoming the post-communist path-dependence is more significant than that of developers. What further supports this assertion is that, due to the high degree of scepticism which foreign developers still often express towards CEE, hotel groups that expand into CEE mainly rely on local developers who usually do not have access to the newest technological solutions to the same extent as their foreign counter-parts. Thus, it is through importing innovations that hotel GPNs initiate mechanisms of path-creation. This observation is expanded upon in the sub-section on knowledge trans-fer and staff training.

Employment creation

The role of the international tourism production system in generating employment has long been recognised and documented (Brown, 1998; Cukier, 2002; Ioannides & Timo-thy, 2010; Liu & Wall, 2006; Williams, 2009). However, because of the massive unem-ployment that hit CEE further to the collapse of communism (Dunford & Smith, 2004) and the great hopes that have been pinned in this respect on foreign firms (Pavlinek, 2004), the role of the international hotel sector in generating employment in CEE and how it differs between different countries and various types of destinations deserves par-ticular attention.

The impact of hotel groups on job creation in CEE can be analysed according to two criteria – the number of jobs and the quality of jobs in terms of skills, wages and labour relations. With regard to the first criterion, apart from numerous casual jobs, the most important jobs that the hotel industry generates are permanent jobs at each new hotel. Depending on the size of the hotel (i.e. the number of rooms) and the range of accompa-nying facilities (e.g. restaurants, spas, etc.) the number of newly-created jobs may differ widely. While in Western Europe the ratio of employees per room oscillates in the range 0.3–0.5 (and is only higher in luxury hotels), owing to the low cost of labour the ratio in international hotels in CEE ranges from 0.5 to 1.0 or more (interviews with representatives of international hotel groups active in CEE, November 2008–April 2009). Although from the employment perspective the higher ratio in CEE is a positive phenomenon, it can be expected that if the economic development in CEE progresses, the labour cost will increase and the employment ratios in CEE will have to be reduced. Despite that, as Table 3 shows, the level of direct employment in the hotel sector in the three focal countries has

Table 3. Employment in the hotel sector in Poland, Estonia and Bulgaria in 2004–2012.

	2004	2006	2008	2010	2012
Poland*					
Hotels and restaurants (2004–2006)					
Accommodation and catering (2010–2012)	250,000	289,000	–	303,000	316,000
Estonia**					
Accommodation	3100	7200	7700	7000	6200
Bulgaria***					
Hotels and restaurants (2004–2006)					
Accommodation and food service activities (2008–2012)	79,489	91,212	108,878	110,834	113,397

Source: *www.stat.gov.pl, **www.stat.ee, ***www.nsi.bg (data retrieved in September 2014).

significantly grown in the last decade and apart from Estonia, where the financial crisis of 2008–2009 affected the hotel sector significantly, it is still constantly growing.

Moreover, the international hotel sector also initiates jobs indirectly, for instance through generating additional demand for local products and services (Brown, 1998). This pertains to construction firms hired at the stage of property development, suppliers of food and beverage products and providers of services which hotels tend to outsource (e.g. cleaning, laundry, security). In other words, the volume of jobs created indirectly hinges upon the extent of local linkages forged by the developer and the operator. However, whether the employment created by the international hotel industry translates into a net gain of jobs for the local community also depends on potential adverse effects of the international hotel sector's expansion. As Dicken (2007) observed, the expansion of transnational corporations (TNCs) into a host economy may lead to a displacement of jobs elsewhere in the sector and a squeezing out of local firms. This is especially the case in secondary destinations across CEE where it is relatively easy for an international hotel (especially if it is the first international hotel in the destination) to quickly dominate the market and put some of the local competitors out of business. The Bulgarian resort destinations where international hotels are said to have a significant advantage over their local counterparts in terms of the quality of services are a good example here.

While building new hotels may impact on employment levels in CEE positively, the expansion of international hotel groups through acquiring state-owned chains or signing management or franchise agreements with existing hotels and re-branding (converting) them may sometimes have a negative influence. Given that new arrangements are usually sought when the business is not financially sustainable, reducing jobs is inevitably one of the ways in which profit-orientated operators look to achieve cost-efficiency. Because in communism many hotels were over-staffed, cutting employment is from the perspective of foreign hotel groups an economically justified necessity in the CEE context. As a development executive from an international hotel group active in CEE explained:

> If the owner and the operator are not looking at achieving efficiency (. . .) what would be the point for those parties in doing new arrangements? (. . .) Cutting jobs [is] not a goal in itself, but (. . .) those things inevitably happen when [necessary]. Obviously, we don't want to terminate people's employment, but if a particular hotel has far more people on its payroll than necessary and then some people may be friends and relatives, whoever, then what would you do? What would any rational business do? (November 2008)

Accor's acquisition of the Polish chain Orbis in the late 1990s serves here as a good example. As a formerly state-owned enterprise, Orbis was largely over-staffed and further to its privatisation, a reduction in staff was a critical change to be made. The gradual centralisation which Accor introduced to the whole network of Orbis hotels and which resulted in the transfer of the administrative functions from the individual hotels to the central office affected the level of employment even more. In 10 years, the total number of jobs at Orbis dropped from over 5000 to approximately 2000. Although this decrease in employment was massive and it serves now as a striking example of negative impact, the question remains what would have happened to Orbis if it had not been acquired by a foreign group. While it might be expected that in situations like this other paths of restructuring are possible and collective lay-offs may be often avoided, it should be simultaneously acknowledged that in some cases conversions and acquisitions save businesses from bankruptcy and although some jobs have to be lost others are eventually saved.

While the role of the (international) hotel industry in generating jobs in Poland and Estonia is largely subject to the processes and mechanisms described hitherto, mainly due to seasonality, the impact of the (international) hotel industry on job creation in Bulgaria has a very specific dimension. In contrast to business hotels in Sofia that are open the whole year, leisure hotels on the coast are only open from April to September and the majority of jobs which they offer are only seasonal. Apart from managers, employees (sometimes up to 90% of staff) are made redundant when the season is over, which forces them to either register as unemployed or find temporary jobs elsewhere, e.g. in ski resorts in the mountains where they can work in the winter. Therefore, the temporary employment generated by the hotel industry in the Bulgarian resorts is not as appealing an opportunity for local communities as it normally is in bigger cities. Thus, rather than looking for differences solely between countries in CEE, it is also useful to distinguish between resorts and business destinations.

While owing to the gradual increase in the number of hotels across CEE the overall impact of the international hotel sector on employment levels in CEE can be expected to be rather positive (although, as mentioned above, it is hardly possible to measure the actual net gain of jobs), the same cannot be said about the quality of jobs that the industry generates. With the exception of managerial positions, jobs offered at hotels are usually low-paid, labour-intensive and servile in nature (Baum, 1993, 2007; Ioannides & Debbage, 1998a; Zampoukos & Ioannides, 2011). Even if international hotels offer higher wages than their local competitors, they are still too low to markedly improve local people's well-being. Moreover, given that high-order decision-making functions are concentrated in hotel groups' HQs outside CEE, the development of the international hotel sector in CEE fosters 'a geographical bias in the pattern of types of employment at the global scale' (Dicken, 2007, p. 469). By the same token, with the exception of Poland where trade unions are traditionally strong, labour in the hotel industry in CEE is very weakly organised, which often results in stricter internal requirements and lower levels of job stability (see Baum, 2007).

Most importantly, similarly to injecting capital and upgrading infrastructure, different types of hotel GPNs impact on employment levels in CEE in different ways. While the quality of jobs is normally determined by the operator, it is the hotel investor whose entrepreneurial initiative creates new jobs and who therefore plays a more important role than the operator in creating employment in absolute terms. In contrast, given that both the scope of local linkages forged by the hotel and the position of the hotel in the local market depend on the strategic decisions made by the operator, the impact of the operator on the number of jobs generated or displaced elsewhere in the host economy is more significant than that of the hotel developer. In turn, the impact of franchisors and hotel consortia, which are usually not involved in daily operations, is almost non-existent. While the mechanisms of job-creation described in this sub-section demonstrate how the hotel industry impacts on economic development in CEE, the ways in which these mechanisms contribute to the processes of de-locking CEE from the post-communist path-dependence are dealt with in the next sub-section.

Knowledge transfer and staff training

Technology and knowledge transfer has long been recognised as one of the most important categories of long-term impact that foreign firms may have on the host economy (Darr, Argote, & Epple, 1995; Dicken, 2007; Glass & Saggi, 2002). As some commentators pointed out, international hotel groups are no exception in this respect (Jacob & Groizard, 2007; Pine, 1992). For this reason, as valuable sources of newest standards, innovations and know-how, hotel groups play an important role also in the CEE context.

First of all, as mentioned in the first sub-section, international hotel groups tend to promote the newest technological solutions. This influence starts as early as the stage of property development when operators and franchisors advise developers on what facilities to include and how to develop and arrange them in order to create a sustainable hotel product. While 30 years ago it would probably mean no more than air-conditioning, nowadays it implies well-equipped conference rooms, sophisticated spas and various facilities offered in guest rooms such as wireless internet, play stations or pay TV. Moreover, it also pertains to different kinds of software that are used by hotels of the same brand to store and exchange operating knowledge and to organise work in the same way. However, it should be recognised that although such innovations may be largely appreciated by local business owners and operators, some technologies such as cost-rationalising software may have undesired effects on hotel workers. For instance, by means of rationalising costs and increasing labour control they may heighten the pressure on staff and thus seriously affect the quality of jobs, not to mention that for the very same reasons they may also have a negative impact on employment levels.

In contrast to the modern technology that can be often acquired independently of franchise or management packages (although many local hotels in CEE still cannot afford it), professional knowledge – something that has to be learnt on the spot and that has a partly tacit character – is far more difficult to acquire without adequate guidance. In this respect the term 'knowledge' pertains to innovative management and marketing techniques, rules underlying the organisation of work (e.g. fire or health and safety regulations) and customer service standards which have long traditions in the West but which are still often under-developed in CEE (see Karhunen, 2008 for the example of Saint Petersburg). Importantly for the CEE regions that look for new sources of novelty in order to de-lock themselves from the post-communist path-dependence, the transfer of knowledge which hotel groups initiate also spills out beyond hotel GPNs. For instance, expatriate managers often serve as international tourism experts and help local administrations with elaborating city promotion strategies and planning destination management activities. Their expertise also often proves helpful in establishing new tourism-related legislation. Finally, customer service standards and corporate culture are acquired not only by hotel employees but also indirectly by their families and friends who subsequently export them to other sectors in the host economy (Fosfuri, Motta, & Ronde, 2001).

Despite that, one of the crucial types of knowledge transfer that the CEE regions can capture is associated with the professional training provided by hotel groups to local staff. As a development executive from an international hotel group active in CEE pointed out:

> If a local person works for an international company they have the opportunity to liaise with the organisation (...) which gives them a very powerful incentive. [Our hotel group] is a machine. We have [a few thousand] hotels around the world so we have certain standard operating procedures and ways of doing things and when you are trained and taught in those procedures and those ways you become a better business person and do things the way they're done by an international company. These are then transferable to whatever you may do in your life, whether you stay with the hotel business or you do something else on your own. (January 2009)

While on the one hand the professional training is firm-specific (i.e. it focuses on chain-specific procedures), it also inevitably includes general hotel knowledge. Every hotel group has a separate training system in which both kinds of knowledge are taught. Importantly, in order to secure a high level of consistency in terms of brand standards, every member of staff (regardless of the position) is offered the same level of exposure to training. Connected to this, many hotel groups also have special departments, often referred to as 'universities' (e.g. Accor Academie), whose objective is to provide high-level courses for talented employees.

Because of the shortage of professional hotel schools and the low level of development of service culture in CEE – obvious traces of the communist past which hotel groups have to deal with when expanding into CEE (Healey, 1994; Johnson & Vanetti, 2004) – this category of influence is particularly valuable in CEE. Its de-locking character was well captured by a hotel industry consultant from an international consultant firm active in Poland:

> We must have somewhere to draw good examples from and fortunately there are already a few sources of those [in Poland]. It's just like the Marriott in Warsaw that opened in 1989. All the people who worked there and were trained there are now scattered across the country and work now as general managers at other hotels in Warsaw and elsewhere. It's because they got this know-how from an international operator. (May 2009)

The advantage of international hotels over local hotels in terms of skills and knowledge of staff is also evident in the Bulgarian resorts. Not only can international hotels provide better customer service (as mentioned before) but also, as it was the case during the financial crisis of 2008–2009 when many local hotels went bankrupt, they are able to keep higher occupancy rates, perform better and thus more easily survive periods of economic downturn.

Despite that, just like with technology, the transfer of Western know-how should not be considered all-positive. Indeed, there is risk that local habits and ways of doing business are not always accounted for by international hotel groups which tend to rely on strictly pre-defined procedures. Assuming that even the most effective standards cannot be applied to the same degree all over the world, too high a level of standardisation may often restrict individual initiatives of local workers. In contrast to Poland and Bulgaria where local employees are often considered by foreign managers to be ambitious, open to innovations and willing to learn, problems like this can be observed in Estonia where standardisation is deemed to clash with the culture and mentality of Estonian staff (interview with a senior official from the City Enterprise Department, Municipality of Tallinn, June 2009). Therefore, although some generalisations about the whole CEE can be easily made, more detailed research would be necessary to comprehensively explore the need for and the effectiveness of knowledge transfer in the hotel industry at different spatial scales and in different cultural and social contexts across CEE.

Finally, it is also worth acknowledging that the technology and knowledge which the hotel sector imports to CEE are more easily diffused in the host economy than those imported by the industries where technological achievements are strictly guarded for commercial purposes. Due to the fact that such knowledge may be difficult to obtain without the international hotel industry's involvement, the value that the CEE economies capture is in the context of post-communist transformations an important engine of economic development and a powerful (although often unappreciated) mechanism of de-locking. Moreover, given that knowledge transfer is to a larger extent initiated by hotel operators, franchisors and hotel consortia, rather than by hotel developers, and that they share this knowledge with hotel developers which in CEE are still predominantly local firms, the hotel sector is a good example of how external forces (in this case hotel GPNs) can influence the path of development which a given economy follows.

Conclusions

In order to address one of the most under-researched aspects of the globalisation of the hotel sector – the impact of the hotel industry on economic development – and to contribute to the general understanding of the tourism production system's developmental impacts, this paper focused on the role of international hotel groups in stimulating regional development in CEE and analysed how the processes of strategic coupling between hotel GPNs and local firms and assets foster post-communist transformations in CEE. Four different areas of impact have been distinguished: direct investment and infrastructure upgrading; employment creation; knowledge transfer; and forging local linkages. The first three have been analysed in detail.

The paper has argued that the ways in which the value is created, enhanced and captured for the benefit of CEE regions hinge upon the structure of the hotel GPN in a given location (i.e. the business model selected by the hotel group for a given hotel and the relations between the hotel group and the hotel owner) and various place-specific institutional characteristics of the host country/region. It has been shown that the role of hotel groups is not always crucial as it is often other actors from their GPNs (notably hotel developers) that play a key role in fostering economic upgrading. However, although the most obvious categories of influence such as injecting capital and creating new jobs are down to developers, the important role of operators, franchisors and hotel consortia also has to be acknowledged. Indeed, by means of training hotel cadres and importing the newest technological solutions hotel operators and franchisors have the potential to foster economic development in CEE in no less important way. Despite that, some negative areas of influence can also be identified – repatriating profits and fostering the displacement effect are perhaps the most notable examples.

Most importantly, because of the knowledge transfer which hotel operators and franchisors initiate in CEE, the international hotel industry can be an important source of novelty to the CEE region, thus helping the national and regional economies of CEE to break away from the legacies of communism and develop in a more path-shaping way. Therefore, not only does the influx of international hotel groups into CEE help the CEE countries to connect with the wider networks of the global economy, but it also functions as a mechanism of de-locking the CEE economies from the post-communist path-dependence.

Finally, the paper also has important theoretical and methodological implications. In theoretical terms, it has been demonstrated that the assumptions of EEG can compensate for some of the shortcomings of the GPN approach and, if combined with the concept of strategic coupling (as suggested by MacKinnon, 2012), they can help the GPN framework to more effectively address the processes of regional development. Thus, while the concepts of path-dependence and lock-in account for the historical factors that affect a given territory's trajectory of growth, the concept of path-creation is particularly helpful in accounting for the effects which various GPNs can have on a given place when they couple up with local actors and assets. Because of the path-dependent nature of post-communist transformations in CEE and the important role of external processes in how the countries of CEE develop, the CEE region proves to be a good territorial case with regard to which a combination of GPN and EEG can be operationalised. By the same token, the international hotel sector serves as a good sectoral case through which the impact of external processes on regional development can be investigated in detail. In methodological terms, in turn, the paper has shown that while it is relatively easy to identify various mechanisms of regional development which the hotel industry initiates, it is difficult (if possible at all) to measure their scale and evaluate the net value which the host economy captures. Although the paper has aimed to focus on the issue of regional development empirically – something that is very rarely looked at 'on the ground' – more research is required if the processes of regional development in general and the influence of the tourism production system on economic upgrading in host economies in particular are to be comprehensively accounted for.

Acknowledgements

This paper is based on the author's PhD thesis which was completed in 2011 at The University of Manchester, UK. The author is grateful to his supervisors – Dr Martin Hess (The University of Manchester) and Professor Neil Coe (currently in the National University of Singapore) for supervising the PhD project. The paper was presented at the Annual Meeting of the Association of American Geographers in Los Angeles in April 2013 at the session entitled 'Evolutionary perspectives on the multinational corporation (MNC)-institutional nexus'. The session was organised by Dr Andrew Wood (University of Kentucky) and Dr Crispian Fuller (University of Aston) and sponsored by Economic Geography Specialty Group.

References

Baum, T. (1993). Human resource issues in tourism: An introduction. In T. Baum (Ed.), *Human resource issues in international tourism* (pp. 3–21). Oxford: Butterworth-Heinemann.
Baum, T. (2007). Human resources in tourism: Still waiting for change. *Progress in Tourism Management, 28*(6), 1383–1399.
Boschma, R., & Frenken, K. (2006). Why is economic geography not an evolutionary science? Towards an evolutionary economic geography. *Journal of Economic Geography, 6*, 273–302.
Boschma, R., & Martin, R. (2007). Editorial: Constructing an evolutionary economic geography. *Journal of Economic Geography, 7*, 537–548.
Boschma, R., & Martin, M. (2010). The aims and scope of evolutionary economic geography. In R. Boschma & R. Martin (Eds.), *The handbook of evolutionary economic geography* (pp. 3–39). Cheltenham: Edward Elgar.
Bradshaw, M., & Swain, A. (2004). Foreign investment and regional development. In M. Bradshaw & A. Stenning (Eds.), *East Central Europe and the Former Soviet Union* (pp. 59–86). Harlow: Pearson.
Brouder, P. (2014). Evolutionary economic geography: A new path for tourism research? *Tourism Geographies, 16*(1), 2–7.
Brouder, P., & Eriksson, R. (2013). Tourism evolution: Latent synergies of evolutionary economic geography and tourism studies. *Annals of Tourism Research, 43*, 370–389.
Brown, F. (1998). *Tourism reassessed: Blight or blessing?* Oxford: Butterworth-Heinemann.

Chang, T., Milne, S., Fallon, D., & Pohlmann, C. (1996). Urban heritage tourism: The global-local nexus. *Annals of Tourism Research, 23*, 284–305.

Coe, N. (2009). Global production networks. In R. Kitchin & N. Thrift (Eds.), *The international Encyclopedia of human geography* (pp. 556–562). Oxford: Elsevier.

Coe, N. (2010). Geographies of production I: An evolutionary revolution? *Progress in Human Geography, 35*(1), 81–91.

Coe, N., Dicken, P., & Hess, M. (2008a). Global production networks: Realizing the potential. *Journal of Economic Geography, 8*, 271–295.

Coe, N., & Hess, M. (2011). Local and regional development: A global production networks approach. In A. Pike, A. Rodriguez-Pose, & J. Tomaney (Eds.), *Handbook of local and regional development* (pp. 128–138). London: Routledge.

Coe, N., Hess, M., Yeung, H., Dicken, P., & Henderson, J. (2004). 'Globalizing' regional development: A global production networks perspective. *Transactions of the Institute of British Geographers, New Series, 29*, 468–484.

Coe, N., Johns, J., & Ward, K. (2008b). Flexibility in action: The temporary staffing industry in the Czech Republic and Poland. *Environment and Planning A, 40*, 1391–1415.

Coe, N., & Wrigley, M. (2007). Host economy impacts of transnational retail: The research agenda. *Journal of Economic Geography, 7*, 341–371.

Contractor, F., & Kundu, S. (2000). Globalization of hotel services: An examination of ownership and alliance patterns in a maturing service sector. In Y. Aharoni & L. Nachum (Eds.), *Globalization of services* (pp. 296–319). London: Routledge.

Cukier, J. (2002). Tourism employment issues in developing countries: Examples from Indonesia. In R. Sharpley & D. Telfer (Eds.), *Tourism and development: Concepts and issues* (pp. 165–201). Clevedon: Channel View Publications.

Cunill, O. (2006). *The growth strategies of hotel chains: Best business practices by leading companies*. New York: The Haworth Hospitality Press.

Darr, E., Argote, L., & Epple, D. (1995). The acquisition, transfer and depreciation of knowledge in service organizations: Productivity in franchises. *Management Science, 41*, 1750–1762.

Dicken, P. (2007). *Global shift: Mapping the changing contours of the world economy* (5th ed.). London: Sage.

Dunford, M., & Smith, A. (2004). Economic restructuring and employment change. In M. Bradshaw & A. Stenning (Eds.), *East Central Europe and the former soviet union* (pp. 33–58). Harlow: Pearson.

Faulconbridge, J., Hall, S., & Beaverstock, J. (2008). New insights into the internationalization of producer services: Organizational strategies and spatial economies for global headhunting firms. *Environment and Planning A, 40*, 210–234.

Fosfuri, A., Motta, M., & Ronde, T. (2001). Foreign direct investment and spillovers through workers' mobility. *Journal of International Economics, 53*, 205–222.

Franck, C. (1990). Tourism investment in Central and Eastern Europe. *Tourism Management, 11*, 333–338.

Gale, D. (2008). Hotels' 325. *Hotels, 7*, 38–52.

Gill, A., & Williams, P. (2011). Rethinking resort growth: Understanding evolving governance strategies in Whistler, B.C.. *Journal of Sustainable Tourism, 19*(4–5), 629–648.

Glass, A., & Saggi, K. (2002). Multinational firms and technology transfer. *Scandinavian Journal of Economics, 104*, 495–513.

Go, F., & Pine, R. (1995). *Globalization strategy in the hotel industry*. New York, NY: Routledge.

Goodwin, H. (2008). Tourism, local economic development and poverty reduction. *Applied Research in Economic Development, 5*, 55–64.

Hall, C., & Page, S. (2006). *The geography and tourism & recreation: Environment, place and space* (3rd ed.). Abingdon: Routledge.

Hall, C., & Page, S. (2009). Progress in tourism management: From the geography of tourism to geographies of tourism – a review. *Tourism Management, 30*(1), 3–16.

Hausner, J., Jessop, B., & Neilsen, K. (Eds.). (1995). *Strategic choice and path-dependency in postsocialism*. Aldershot: Edward Elgar.

Healey, N. (1994). The transition economies of Central and Eastern Europe: A political, economic, social and technological analysis. *The Columbia Journal of World Business, 29*, 61–70.

Henderson, J., Dicken, P., Hess, M., Coe, N., & Yeung, H. (2002). Global production networks and the analysis of economic development. *Review of International Political Economy, 9*, 436–464.

Hess, M., & Yeung, H. (2006). Guest editorial. *Environment and Planning A, 38*, 1193–1204.

Hudson, R. (2000). One Europe or many? Reflections on becoming European. *Transactions of the Institute of British Geographers, 25*, 409–426.

Ioannides, D., & Debbage, K. (1998a). Introduction: Exploring the economic geography and tourism nexus. In D. Ioannides & K. Debbage (Eds.), *The economic geography of the tourist industry: A supply-side analysis*. London, NY: Routledge.

Ioannides, D., & Timothy, D. (2010). *Tourism in the USA: A spatial and social synthesis*. London: Routledge.

Jacob, M., & Groizard, J. (2007). Technology transfer and multinationals: The case of Balearic hotel chains' investments in two developing economies. *Tourism Management, 28*, 976–992.

Johnson, C., & Vanetti, M. (2004). Market developments in the hotel sector in Eastern Central Europe. *Advances in Hospitality and Leisure, 1*, 153–175.

Karhunen, P. (2008). Managing international business operations in a changing institutional context: The case of the St. Petersburg hotel industry. *Journal of International Management, 14*, 28–45.

León-Darder, F., Villar-Garcia, C., & Pla-Barber, J. (2011). Entry mode choice in the internationalization of the hotel industry: A holistic approach. *The Service Industries Journal, 31*, 107–122.

Liu, A., & Wall, G. (2006). Planning tourism employment: A developing country perspective. *Tourism Management, 27*, 159–170.

MacKinnon, D. (2012). Beyond strategic coupling: Reassessing the firm-region nexus in global production networks. *Journal of Economic Geography, 12*, 227–245.

MacKinnon, D., Cumbers, A., Pike, A., Birch, K., & McMaster, R. (2009). Evolution in economic geography: Institutions, political economy, and adaptation. *Economic Geography, 85*(5), 129–150.

Martin, R., & Sunley, P. (2006). Path dependence and regional economic evolution. *Journal of Economic Geography, 6*, 395–437.

Mitka-Karandziej, U. (1993). Hotelarstwo [The hotel industry]. unpublished manuscript.

Niewiadomski, P. (2013). The globalisation of the hotel industry and the variety of emerging capitalisms in Central and Eastern Europe. *European Urban and Regional Studies*, published online on 18 September 2013, 1–22. doi:10.1177/0969776413502658

Niewiadomski, P. (2014). Towards an economic-geographical approach to the globalisation of the hotel industry. *Tourism Geographies, 16*(1), 48–67.

Pavlinek, P. (2004). Regional development implications of foreign direct investment in Central Europe. *European Urban and Regional Studies, 11*, 47–70.

Pine, R. (1992). Technology transfer in the hotel industry. *International Journal of Hospitality Management, 11*, 3–22.

Shaw, G., & Agarwal, S. (2012). Changing geographies of coastal resorts: Development processes and tourism spaces. In J. Wilson (Ed.), *The Routledge handbook of tourism geographies* (pp. 240–248). London: Routledge.

Smith, A. (1997). Breaking the old and constructing the new? Geographies of uneven development in Central and Eastern Europe. In R. Lee & J. Wills (Eds.), *Geographies of economies*. London: Edward Arnold.

Smith, A., & Timar, J. (2010). Uneven transformations: Space, economy and society 20 years after the collapse of state socialism. *European Urban and Regional Studies, 17*, 115–125.

Sokol, M. (2001). Central and Eastern Europe a decade after the fall of state-socialism: Regional dimensions of transition processes. *Regional Studies, 35*, 645–655.

Urry, J. (1990). *The tourist gaze: Leisure and travel in contemporary societies*. London: Sage.

Wall, G., & Mathieson, A. (2006). *Tourism: Change, impacts and opportunities*. Harlow: Prentice Hall.

Watson, S. (1991). Gilding the smokestacks: The new symbolic representations of deindustrialized regions. *Environment and Planning D: Society and Space, 9*, 59–70.

Williams, S. (2009). *Tourism geography: A new synthesis* (2nd ed.). London: Routledge.

Williams, A., & Balaz, V. (2000). Privatisation and the development of tourism in the Czech Republic and Slovakia: Property rights, firm performance and recombinant property. *Environment and Planning A, 32*, 715–734.

Williams, A., & Balaž, V. (2002). The Czech and Slovak Republics: Conceptual issues in the economic analysis of tourism in transition. *Tourism Management, 23*, 37–45.

Wrigley, N., Coe, N., & Currah, A. (2005). Globalizing retail: Conceptualizing the distribution-based transnational corporation (TNC). *Progress in Human Geography, 29*, 437–457.

Yeung, H. (2009). Regional development and the competitive dynamics of global production networks: An East Asian perspective. *Regional Studies, 43*, 325–351.

Zampoukos, K., & Ioannides, D. (2011). The tourism labour conundrum: Agenda for new research in the geography of hospitality workers. *Hospitality & Society, 1*(1), 25–45.

Non-planning and tourism consumption in Budapest's inner city

Melanie Kay Smith, Tamás Egedy, Adrienne Csizmady, András Jancsik, Gergély Olt and Gábor Michalkó

ABSTRACT

The relationship between urban planning and tourism consumption is presented through one of the most attractive and popular districts of Budapest (District VII). Budapest is the capital city of Hungary and has a population of 1.7 million inhabitants making it one of the largest metropolitan regions in Central Eastern Europe. Budapest is typical of many other post-socialist cities in that its urban development process has followed a somewhat different trajectory from many Western European cities until recently, for example the relatively slow rate of gentrification in the post-socialist years. The paper will focus in particular on one central district of the city (VII) which currently contains a high concentration of hospitality and entertainment facilities (especially 'ruin pubs') and attracts a large numbers of tourists. The planning and development history of the district will be explained, including many controversies and conflicts which have arisen over the years. In addition to analysing the significance of the areas' heritage and the intensive growth of the creative industries, the paper will also provide a case study about the Budapest-specific 'ruin bar' phenomenon, as well as data on the global issue of Airbnb, which is becoming an extremely topical and controversial issue in many other cities in the world today. 'Ruin bars' and Airbnb represent local and global examples of tourism consumption which have flourished despite or even because of an unstructured, often unregulated urban planning system. Through this examination, two main questions are addressed: to what extent has planning (or a lack of it) influenced urban development and the new trends of international tourism in Budapest? and what role has tourism played in the transformation of a central district within the inner city?

A brief overview of urban development in post-socialist cities

In many US and Western European cities, capitalist development tended to manifest itself in geographically uneven ways leading to the transformation of the inner city, but at the expense of local residents. This included gentrification and displacement as urban manifestations of geographically uneven development (Atkinson & Bridge, 2005; Nagy & Timár, 2012). Gentrification was defined as the change from working class to middle class residential composition in the inner city (Atkinson & Bridge, 2005).

Post-socialist city development tended to differ in some ways from that of its Western European counterparts. In some cities under post-socialist transformation there was a lesser degree of market-led gentrification and displacement than in others or new investment headed towards the suburbs (Brade, Herfert, & Wiest, 2009; Wiest, 2012). In many cases, the privatization of public housing functioned in such a way that sitting tenants were able to purchase their apartments at a very low price (Kovács, Wiessner, & Zischner, 2013; Sykora, 2005). As a result, a high degree of home ownership was evident in cities like Budapest compared to Western cities. However, the community of new owners did not have the financial resources to renovate the dilapidated houses in most cases (Sykora, 2005).

The gentrification of post-socialist cities intensified after the turn of the millennium. In the post-socialist countries, the process of gentrification depends primarily on the inflow of foreign capital, the extent of state subsidies, the regulations adopted, the development of the real estate market and the preferences of the population on the housing market. These processes have resulted in the spatial fragmentation of inner city areas and society (Marcińczak & Sagan, 2011 so in Central and Eastern European cities polarization has become the dominant process rather than the social upgrading caused by gentrification (Berki, 2014; Benedek & Moldovan, 2015). In upgrading areas, high status residents and elderly or disadvantaged low social status groups live next to each other. The introduction of functional mix alongside the residential function in such neighbourhoods has led to the development of tourism, gastronomy (restaurants and pubs) and offices (i.e. commercial gentrification). Districts with purely residential functions have been slowly transformed into working, entertainment and investment areas, including hospitality and tourism enterprises (Ashworth & Tunbridge, 2000; Eldridge, 2010; Judd & Fainstein, 1999;

Roberts, 2009; Roberts, Turner, Greenfield, & Osborn, 2006). There have been a number of new urban developments in cities like Warsaw, Prague, Bratislava and also Budapest. This includes office buildings, shopping centres, industrial and technological parks and (luxurious) residential complexes (Grubbauer & Kusiak, 2012; Keresztély & Scott, 2012). State or local authority-led rehabilitation played an important role in these processes.

Urban development and planning in Budapest

The gentrification of the inner city areas of Budapest was not very intense until relatively recently (Czirfusz et al., 2015; Kovács et al. 2013), despite predictions that the transition from socialist planning to a liberal market would create exponential gentrification (Smith, 1996) However, reinvestment and price increases were less significant than expected, and in the 1990s, the inner city districts actually started to decline instead (Kovács, 1998). Földi (2006) described how the legacy of more than 40 years of neglect by the socialist regimes led to a physically and socially dilapidated inner city. Higher-status residents tended to move away from the inner city to the suburbs or to higher status residential areas of Budapest on the Buda side (Csanádi & Csizmady, 2002; Csanádi, Csizmady, Kocsis, Kőszeghy, & Tomay, 2010). This also happened in many other cities in the region (Sykora, 2005).

On the other hand, displacement still occurred in the inner city areas, but not primarily because of market-led gentrification. The engines of socio-spatial changes were the local authorities and the state, and gentrification was most spectacular in designated rehabilitation areas of the city (Jelinek, 2010). Local authorities were unable and unwilling to preserve social housing stock, which lead to the displacement and exclusion of the lowest status residents and the Roma (Ladányi, 2008; Nagy & Timár, 2012). The relatively slow adoption of the social dimension of urban renewal (Keresztély & Scott, 2012) and the competition for investment were a consequence of the lack of adequate funding for local authorities (Vigvári, 2008). The dismantling of the social housing system and aesthetic refurbishments of public spaces were part of an attempt to make the inner city of Budapest more desirable for middle class residents, and eventually (as could be seen later) for the tourism and hospitality sectors (Boros, Fabula, Horváth, & Kovács, 2016).

In terms of urban planning, Budapest has not been lauded as an exemplary model. Indeed, many harsh criticisms have emerged over the past few years. One of the main challenges to urban planning is the fact that the city is divided into 23 districts, all of which have their own political, economic, social and cultural structure, but with very little focus on governance or collaboration with other districts. District mayors are often also MPs or prominent cadres of political parties which can significantly affect power relations between districts and the City Council. When it comes to implementing social or housing policies, or launching regeneration programmes and plans, these districts enjoy a high level of autonomy (Kovács et al., 2013). According to the Statute of Local Government, tourism development and management is typically the responsibility of Budapest City Council, so the districts have a limited vested interest in tourism (Michalkó, 2001). On the other hand, some individual districts have developed their own tourism strategies (e.g. District I and V), but few tourists would be aware of (or even interested in) where one district ends and another begins within a city. This approach is arguably detrimental to tourism infrastructure which often spans 2-3 districts, as well as slowing down attractions development because of conflicts between district authorities. Although the Budapest City Council should technically oversee district activities, in reality, the allocation of responsibilities and resources between the Municipality and the district governments is subject to constant political tensions and disputes, often resulting in complete inactivity for many years. This has affected major tourism areas of the city, for example, the Castle area or the City Park, where several municipality authorities could not agree on how to develop the areas further for tourism (Smith, Puczkó, & Rátz, 2009). Bontje, Musterd, Kovács, and Murie (2011) list this highly decentralized and bureaucratic system as being one of the most negative aspects of city development especially as it fails to solve the widespread deprivation and exclusion of lower skilled social groups in the inner city.

Even worse than the lack of coordination is the absence of legal and planning frameworks in the first half of the 1990s (Egedy, 2010) and frequent disregard for them thereafter, resulting in numerous scandals and corruption (Kauko, 2012). Barta, Beluszky, Czirfusz, Győri, and Kukely (2006) criticized some of the approaches that took place between 1990 and 2005, which are described as uncoordinated, irrational and unconsidered. He states that these often led to inefficient and incomprehensive conservation of architecture and heritage, created dubious 'science and technology parks', and cultural projects which tended to result in losses and missed opportunities. When the current government Fidesz was last in power from 1998 to 2002, 'flagship' architectural and cultural projects such as the House of Terror, Millennium Park and the National Theatre were constructed to establish a specific political vision and disrupt the existing urban flow (Palonen, 2013). Some of these have become tourism attractions too, for example, The House of Terror, but few international tourists are aware of the political intentions behind the construction and interpretation of such attractions (Smith & Puczkó, 2010). Kauko (2012) was especially critical of the period 2002–2010 in Hungary which he suggested resulted in economically and socially regressive developments. He states that 'during the period 2002–2010 in particular, Hungary has been nothing short of a disaster in terms of urban policy and planning issues' (Kauko, 2012, p.10). Unfortunately, there is little to suggest that urban planning has improved in recent years either. Since the election in 2010 when Fidesz won an unprecedented two thirds parliamentary majority and launched its radical re-shaping of the country, there have been numerous protests against the government's increasing centralization of power and abolition or takeover of formerly independent institutions (Akçalıa & Korkut, 2015). Palonen (2013) suggests that similarly to 1998–2002, the government is busy re-writing the national past, changing plans made by the previous government, and creating political divisions. Unfortunately, however, urban renewal policies which benefit deprived areas have not been forthcoming, and a low level of funding has been available for developments of this kind (Keresztély & Scott, 2012).

Tourism in Budapest

Although Budapest does not have a leading position among European capitals based on the number of guest nights, its position in Central and Eastern Europe is strong. Within the region its turnover lags behind Prague and Vienna, but it is far ahead of the capital cities of its neighbouring countries (CSO, 2016).

In Budapest, there is no longer a city agency which is responsible for tourism, as the Tourism Office of Budapest ceased to exist several years ago (the 'logic' being that tourists will come to Budapest anyway and that resources should be devoted to promoting the rest of Hungary which is relatively under-visited). Smith et al. (2009) research had concluded that tourism planning and management is extremely fragmented in Budapest, and turnover of staff working in tourism has been increasingly rapid in recent years since 2010, and it is not altogether clear today which stakeholders are responsible for which developments in the city. The state-owned Hungarian Tourism Agency is mainly focused on marketing and communications rather than planning or development.

Although Budapest had traditionally focused on heritage tourism in its product development and marketing, the global popularity of creative tourism and creative cities has also had an impact on Budapest since the late 2000s (Smith & Puczkó, 2012). Tourists are increasingly drawn to those cities which are deemed to be creative or to have creative districts or neighbourhoods (Marques & Richards, 2014). It will be seen later in this paper that the Districts in Budapest which have the highest concentration of Airbnb accommodation are those that would be considered to be the most creative. However, it is also well-documented that as creative districts become more popular with locals and tourists alike, gentrification often ensues, sometimes leading to displacement of the original inhabitants and erosion of the characteristics that made the area attractive in the first place (Zukin, 1987, 1995). The concomitant development of tourism can also risk turning such areas into enclaves and losing their appeal for creative people (Pappalepore, Maitland, & Smith, 2014).

The following analysis of District VII will show how the historical and contemporary processes of urban planning (or a lack thereof) have contributed to the development of a tourist area which often fails to consider the situation of local residents. Two phenomena are highlighted in particular: one is local and specific to Budapest, and that is the 'ruin bars', of which District VII has the highest concentration; the second is a global issue, which has started to impact negatively on numerous cities according to many of the authors in Colomb and Novy (2017), and that is the growth of Airbnb (also highly concentrated in District VII). 'Ruin bars' made Budapest much more desirable for tourism and it seems that this increased the demand for Airbnb too. However, the exact explanation behind the dynamics of the Airbnb phenomenon needs more research, some of which is provided in the latter part of this paper.

Case study of District VII

Although the focus of this section is on one central, inner city district in Budapest, it is important to discuss the wider area, especially District VI which borders District VII (Figure 1) and shares many of its characteristics (one of its central streets Király Utca is the District boundary). Indeed, the relationship between District boundaries, planning and tourism in Budapest is a complex and opaque one. Although the physical environment and the social status of inner city districts can be quite similar, district authorities often apply very different policies (see Kovacs, Wiessner, & Zischner, 2015). On the other hand, tourists are largely ignorant of where one District ends and another begins and move fluidly and unconsciously between them.

Districts VI and VII are historic inner city districts with mostly nineteenth century densely built housing stock, and until recently, this area was mainly a residential district with about 15,000 inhabitants per 0.5 sqKm. Under socialism, it had been one of the most neglected parts of the city and many of its buildings had become ruined or even

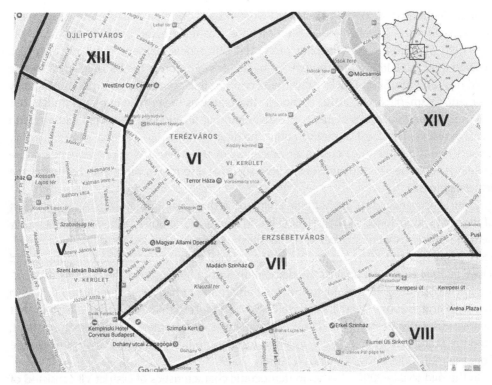

Figure 1. Location of District VII in Budapest. Source: Authors' own.

collapsed. This was followed by a 'laissez faire' urban policy which mainly benefitted private investors, local government officials and friends of the political élite. 'Ruin bars' appeared in so-called rehabilitation areas in both of these Districts. Most of them can be found in District VII, however three bigger 'ruin bars' can be found in adjacent District VI (although one of them closed in spring 2017 to give way to a hotel construction).

The two districts are rather similar in many aspects: extremely dense urban residential and commercial neighbourhoods with dilapidated housing stock built at the end of the nineteenth century. However, District VI was always a somewhat higher status area, especially because of the prestigious World Heritage Site area, Andrássy Avenue, the national Opera house and other theatres in the inner part of the District that is also called the Budapest Broadway. The autonomous districts after 1989 had different urban policies: the privatization process was more complete in District VI and foreign investors started to buy apartments in the area earlier. Corruption during the privatization process was present in both districts, however the heritage buildings along Andrássy Avenue were better protected and speculative investors were not allowed to demolish them as happened in District VII in many instances. The different heritage and related policies meant different conditions for functional changes and for the hospitality and tourism industry. As a consequence, fewer venues opened in District VI and the local authority could be more restrictive in their regulation of the night time economy. This meant that luxury shops and office investments along Andrássy Avenue became alternatives to 'party' tourism. District VI also attracts more cultural tourists because of its heritage attractions and architecture. In

District VII many of the heritage buildings were in bad condition, therefore, a 100-year-old plan based on the so-called Madách-Promenade was resurrected in 1990 (Román, 1998). The 1990 Madách-Promenade plan promoted office developments and the plan also allowed the local authority to prevent flat-by-flat privatization of the housing stock. Whole buildings and housing blocks thus remained in the ownership of the municipality (Csanádi, Csizmady, & Olt, 2012). Although the plan was never fully implemented, it was still used in the mid-2000s to justify the demolition of dilapidated heritage buildings with social housing. The local authority could maintain a higher proportion of municipality owned housing after the housing privatization of the 1990s. As a consequence, more buildings could be vacated and sold to investors that also meant more 'ruin bars' after the real estate crisis.

Controversy arose over the heritage buildings in these neighbourhoods. Although most of the area was included in the UNESCO World Heritage Site buffer zone from 2004, many heritage buildings were still being demolished or were scheduled for demolition. Architects, historians and other supporters of the cultural heritage established a group called 'Óvás' in 2004 to protest against the demolition and to help protect the heritage. According to Óvás, by 2007 40% of the former built environment had been demolished or was in danger (Perczel, 2007). Overall, Keresztély (2007) suggested that the historic Jewish district clearly and sadly demonstrated the consequences of incoherent urban management. Property scandals and corruption involving local authorities and politicians were also rife from the mid-2000s onwards (Sipos & Zolnay, 2009).

In the mid to late-2000s, the socio-democratic characteristics of District VII consisted of a high rate of elderly widows; lowering social status compared with the early twentieth century; decreasing Jewish and an increasing Roma population; and no marked segregation of different residents (Földi, 2006). The profile of the area changed further with the arrival of young people, students, artists, and independent ex-patriates who bought or rented flats for a relatively low price (Csanádi et al., 2012; Keresztély, 2007). Since the early 2000s a growing number of students rented apartments in low quality inner city buildings. Thus, the first signs of 'studentification' appeared relatively early in the neighbourhood (Fabula, Boros, Kovács, Horváth, & Pál, 2017). Csanádi et al. (2012) showed that the proportion of apartments shared by non-family members increased from below 1% in 2005 to more than 7% in 2010. After the rapid growth of tourism in the 2010s tourism accommodation mainly priced out students from this area. According to our interviews with property managers, even foreign students who could afford the higher prices turned away from the party district because they also complained about the noise. The mix of social housing and newly built condos has created considerable polarization. For example, on the opposite side of the same street we recorded an interview with a young professional in the IT sector who paid 1000 EUROs per month for his flat in a recently built condominium (in a country where the average salary is less than half of this sum) and a middle aged lady who struggled hard to pay 100 EURO per month for her low quality social housing.

In terms of tourism, District VII plays a very important role in the city. Although there are no traditional tourist attractions located in the district, one tenth of the restaurants in Budapest and one fifth of private accommodation are located here, and District VII has the highest occupancy rate in commercial accommodation in Budapest (CSO, 2016). Table 1 compares District VII to two of the other most popular tourism districts in Budapest (V and I).

Table 1. Importance of District VII compared to Districts I and V in Budapest tourism.

	Number of catering units	Guest nights by foreigners (1000)		Number of hosts in private accommodation	Occupancy rate in commercial accommodation (%)
		Private accommodation	Commercial accommodation		
Budapest	11,082	1106	8195	4047	50.6
District VII	1018	203	1359	868	60.1
District I	278	48	542	157	54.2
District V	866	208	2022	801	57.4

Source: CSO (2016).

Academic literature sometimes tends to refer to the practice of accommodating tourists in private apartments as an innovative business solution (Dervojeda et al., 2013). However, it is not a new trend in Budapest, as the utilization of the housing stock for tourism purposes dates back to the 1960s (Michalkó, 2001). As the annually rising demand could not be satisfied by the modest hotel capacity at that time, and the government did not possess the resources needed for investments, it seemed to be an obvious solution to use the housing stock in the tourism supply of Budapest. Since the mid-2000s, grand bourgeois homes have been turned into hostels. This trend continued after 2010 and it became possible for smaller apartments to be used for these purposes with the arrival of Airbnb around 2010. The current legislation defines the detailed conditions of operating a residential property as a tourist accommodation, and also regulates their administrative and tax obligations. Apartment rentals in Budapest are not restrained geographically or in terms of the number of guest arrivals, and the tax rules are particularly beneficial for hosts who operate only one apartment.

Many religious monuments and institutions can be found in this neighbourhood, for example, one of the largest synagogues in the world. The ghetto of Budapest was also located here between 1944 and 1945, and many tourists, often with Hungarian origins visit as part of remembrance and commemoration. The revival of the ghetto area was helped by Jewish families returning from Israel and U.S.A. after the change of regime (1990). These second or third generation Jews started to establish various enterprises which contributed to regeneration. However, as a typical example of the lack of planning and irresponsible political leadership during the rehabilitation of a building, the only remaining segment of the ghetto wall was demolished by the construction work. It was restored only with the help of the Óvás civil group. Thanks to their work tourists can still visit it.

The growing popularity of the area for tourists has partly also been due to the growth of the creative industries. In the late 2000s, there were a growing number of venues with artistic projects and art galleries as well as new cafés and restaurants (Csanádi et al., 2012; Keresztély & Scott, 2012). This area became the 'creative hub' of the city with a plethora of restaurants, bars, design shops, galleries, and festivals. In addition, the district hosts art exhibitions, workshops, and contains small theatres. In the heart of the area there is a renovated courtyard called Gozsdu Udvar which has a Sunday arts and crafts market as well as numerous restaurants, bars and cafés. The courtyard built in 1901 is a 200 m long promenade with seven buildings and six courtyards. After a long time of neglect, the run-down buildings were renewed between 2005 and 2008 (Photo 1).

Photo 1. Commercial gentrification with restaurants in the Gozsdu courtyard in District VII. Source: Authors' own.

The area's creative, aesthetic and atmospheric appeal has become attractive not only for tourists, but for artists and entrepreneurs as well (Tóth, Keszei, & Dúll, 2014). The historical buildings from the turn of the centuries (nineteenth and twentieth) combined with the creative environment of the present contribute to creating a unique tourist milieu (Michalkó & Rátz, 2006). However, one of the more recent developments since 2010 (when a new government was elected) was that artists in municipality-owned premises were forced to leave for political as well as economic reasons. The more profitable uses of bars and clubs priced out the creative mission especially after 2013. Artistic venues were squeezed out to the adjacent District VIII (not yet a flourishing tourism area), and most of them operate now in privately owned rather than publicly owned spaces.

The growth of the hospitality industry can also be partly explained by the 'ruin bar' phenomenon. The 2008 crisis stopped the real estate investment in the area and the in-between use of the empty buildings - the so-called 'ruin bars' (Csanádi et al., 2012; Lugosi, Bell, & Lugosi, 2010) – became a determinant factor of the development. Lugosi et al (2010) describe 'ruin bars' or pubs as temporary (often seasonal) or semi-permanent (open for several consecutive years but with an uncertain future) hospitality venues which have been established in abandoned residential or office buildings, many of which are dilapidated (Photo 2).

At first, only local residents (mainly creative and bohemian individuals) tended to frequent the 'ruin bars', but since the early 2010s (which also coincided with the development of Airbnb, as discussed in detail later) tourists have become the main consumers. Because of low cost airlines and low prices compared to Western cities, Budapest has become competitive as a weekend party capital. Since 2013, the former Jewish District brand has almost completely changed to the image of a 'party district' where hundreds of tourists go out every night causing a great deal of noise and some distress for local residents. Many of them are enjoying 'stag and hen party' tourism as Budapest is becoming a

Photo 2. The 'ruin bar' Kőleves (Stonesoup) in Kazinczy street in District VII. Source: Authors' own.

more and more popular destination for this form of entertainment (Iwanicki, Dłużewska, & Smith, 2016). Problems with 'party' or 'alcohol' tourism have similarly been noted in Lisbon (Colomb & Novy, 2017), Berlin (Novy, 2017) and Prague (Pixová & Sládek, 2017).

The following sections present empirical research on two of the aforementioned phenomena in Budapest, which are closely connected to tourism consumption. These are the 'ruin bar' phenomenon and Airbnb. These phenomena are closely connected as the highest concentration of Airbnb accommodation is located in the area which has the most ruin bars in the city.

Methodology for the empirical research

It is acknowledged that several methods could have been used to illustrate the ways in which a lack of coherent planning and clear regulation has influenced urban development and tourism in Budapest. Airbnb is one of the most topical and controversial subjects in global tourism today, which is why it was selected for this study. The data from District VII is contrasted with other popular tourism districts to demonstrate the relative geographical concentration of accommodation. The 'ruin pub' phenomenon was selected because it is one of the current Unique Selling Propositions for Budapest's tourists and is thought to be one of the main causes for the increase in tourism and the growth of Airbnb in District VII (and to a lesser extent, VI). Research was, therefore, undertaken to analyse the development of 'ruin bars' in Budapest and their role in hospitality and tourism using qualitative data, and to examine the scope and concentration of Airbnb using big data.

'Ruin bar' research

Ethnographic research on the regeneration and gentrification of District VII was undertaken from 2006 and the conflict between the residential and hospitality/ tourism function emerged. From 2009, in-depth interviews were undertaken during which local residents were asked more specifically about their perception of the hospitality industry and tourism. Fifteen interviews were recorded with local residents which focused on their conflicts with the 'ruin bars' and the local authority between 2010 and 2014. In addition, non-participant observation took place during several (heated) civil forums about the night noise in the area. Five of these meetings were organised by different actors such as the local authority, active citizens or bar owners between 2011 and 2014. Some monthly meetings of bar owners were also attended. During this period, eight interviews were recorded with 'ruin bar' owners who talked about their enterprise and their conflicts with residents and the authorities. Attempts to approach local politicians were largely unsuccessful and their responses to questions were vague. Their interests are often conflictual, i.e. they need local entrepreneurs for income tax but have to appease residents to gain the popular vote. The role of the press played an important role in the conflict, therefore, 43 newspaper articles were analysed. In the early 2010s, many of the articles supported the freedom of entrepreneurship and the Hungarian success story of the 'ruin bars'. Later, the picture became more mixed as mass tourism and cheap alcohol became the main features of the area, and journalists became more critical about the party district.

Airbnb research

Airbnb like several other companies in the so-called 'sharing economy', operates a peer-to-peer market through its platform (Einav, Farronato, & Levin, 2015). The majority of the transactions in the sharing economy are internet-based, thus the buying processes (from the initial information search to the feedback events) generate a large amount of data, making the sharing economy one of the significant sources of publicly available 'big data' (Mayer-Schonberger & Cukier, 2013). It must be noted, however, that research methods based on 'big data' retrieved from the internet have some important limitations: firstly, the technical difficulties can make the data incomplete or imprecise, lowering the trustworthiness of the results; secondly, the interpretation of the results is not always straightforward, questioning the objectivity of the research (Boyd & Crawford, 2012).

In order to investigate the operational characteristics of Budapest's private accommodation market, data from the Internet was collected monthly between October 2014 and September 2016. The data collection was carried out with web-scraping technology, which means using a software that opens up the given pages of a website one after the other, and saves the information found on them in a database (Olmedilla, Martínez-Torres, & Toral, 2016). The homepage of Airbnb was the focus of the investigation from where all accessible data was collected apart from the users' written reviews. This involved listing data concerning properties and hosts as well. The main data groups included data on supply, demand and operation, as well as users' scores. Based on the observed data, several derivative data types were developed: the number of guest nights was estimated on the basis of occupation and capacity data, and the volume of revenues was modelled by adding the prices. Since the number of beds per listing varies between 1 and 16, the uncertainty of the estimation of guest nights is significant. In order to achieve a better approximation, a segmentation-based modelling was carried out using the data scraped from the Booking.com website, which contains information about the segment of the reviewers (solo travellers, couples, families, groups of friends, business travellers). The majority of Airbnb properties may be suitable for more than one segment. In these cases, the number of guests was determined on the basis of the segment proportions observed on Booking.com and the various characteristics of the listing itself (e.g. number of beds, rooms, bathrooms, range of services, etc.).

As the database contains the geographical coordinates of properties, it is possible to plot their locations on a map. However, it should be noted that due to privacy protection reasons, Airbnb generally shows the position of properties somewhere within 100–200 m of their actual location; therefore, the maps used in this paper might also be slightly imprecise.

Findings

'Ruin bars': conflicts over residential and tourism functions

The inner part of District VII and also a part of the adjacent District VI has become a world-famous party district according to Trip Advisor. The process of this functional change from a low status, dilapidated inner city area to a touristic attraction was completely unplanned and quite unexpected. As mentioned above, the original regeneration plans proposed a higher status residential area, however the corruption inherent in the privatization process slowed down this particular development. After the buildings were vacated, they remained in the hands of the local authority and stood empty for several years. Hospitality entrepreneurs operating in the area negotiated with the local authority to use the buildings temporarily for 'ruin bars' or 'gardens'. The venues operated only in the summer months and paid low rent to the municipality. The bars were so-called because they were operating in dilapidated or partly ruined buildings, and investment in these short- term venues remained minimal until the planned residential real estate investments actually took place (Lugosi et al., 2010).

After a few years of this uncertain operation, in 2005, the local authority decided to restrict the number and type of venues and gave out fewer licences and only for venues that had a cultural function as well. The licensing was in the hands of the local authority and they could deny the permission for operation without further explanation. The motivation for this restriction was clear: the success of the venues frequented mostly by the local bohemians of Budapest started to disturb local residents and the elections in 2006 were approaching. Most of the buildings remained empty that year and privatization progressed.

Because of the corrupt privatization process mentioned earlier, the area mainly attracted speculative investors and the buildings stayed empty for years even after privatization. The plan was simply to gain more on the increasing real estate prices. Some artists could make a deal with one of the owners and paid low rent for an empty building which was in poor condition to use it temporarily as a workshop, warehouse or even illegal housing. The most successful 'ruin bar', Szimpla Garden, also started to operate in a privately owned building in 2004 (Photo 3).

Meanwhile, other artists could occupy publically owned buildings and retail spaces with one year contracts or even illegally. Everybody expected a rapid change, and imagined a short term operation, but as mentioned earlier, they were evicted only after 2010. The great change in the scene came after the 2008 crisis. The then privately owned

Photo 3. Szimpla Garden in District VII, the first 'ruin bar' in Budapest. Source: Authors' own.

buildings were utilized by their new owners as ruin bars, but this time with much longer (usually 5+5) year contracts and consequently with much bigger investments. Ruin bars started to operate in a 'pop-up' fashion in the early 2000s but after 2009 they rather operated as proper enterprises, which was made possible by the change of regulation as well. They contributed to the 'creative' atmosphere and increased the number of hospitality venues, as well as new accommodation such as small hotels and youth hostels.

The constant growth of the tourism industry and low cost airlines was an important factor in the commercial success of these bars. 'Ruin bars' are still not part of the official tourism marketing of the city; however, low cost airlines and other private tourism entrepreneurs heavily advertise the night life of Budapest. The number and capacity of venues has been growing constantly since 2009, and by 2013, there were more than 300 bars and pubs in the area and large capacity dance clubs appeared as well. Instead of the previous minimal investments of the early 2000s, some new venues opened after a few million EURO investments in the building and these places wanted to attract higher status consumers and better off foreigners. These new venues operate in vacated buildings but many of them are definitely not 'ruin bars', although they advertise themselves under this umbrella. The artistic flavour of these places often completely disappeared and there are only a few smaller clubs that have an offer beyond drinks and mainstream electronic music. Some bars also serve as restaurants and there are hostels or other forms of accommodation within the building as well.

Hungarian legislation tends to favour entrepreneurs and new investments instead of the right of residents for peace and quiet at night as declared by the ombudsman for civil rights in 2008. This results in situations where local residents feel helpless against night noise and neglected by authorities and politicians. In the Hungarian situation, the regulation of commercial activities changed according to the EU legislation in 2009 and the local authorities only had the right to restrict opening hours within their territory between 10 pm and 6 am if the service activity caused a 'dangerous amount' of noise. In District VI, the regulation introduced compulsory closing time after 10 pm with only a few exceptions when residents living close to the venue gave permission for late night operation. This regulation caused many heated debates in the press because the ruin bars were one of the few Hungarian 'success stories'. After 2012, the regulation changed the closing time to midnight and a local committee decided about exceptions rather than local residents.

In District VII, the local government did not react as quickly and the restriction of opening hours was introduced only in 2010, and even then, its implementation was controversial. In late 2012, the national level regulation changed which made it possible for the police to restrict opening hours or close down venues if they were 'dangerous' or causing 'too much trouble'. More than 20 pubs received some kind of fine or restriction in December 2012 in District VII. As the 'ruin bars' were even bigger success stories by then, the scandal was also greater than ever and even the initiator of the modification of the law explained that he did not intend to close down 'ruin bars'. By early 2013, there was no restriction of opening hours at all, and investment in hospitality venues grew exponentially.

Both regulations and planning measures were insufficient to control the functional change of the area and mitigate the negative social consequences of the changes. Residents feel displaced from their living environment and renters are priced out and excluded from the inner city where most of the low skilled service jobs often related to tourism can be found. The changing nature of tourism played an important role in the gentrification of the inner city. This transformation was never intended and was only a consequence of the post-socialist privatization process and pervasive corruption. Because of the success of the 'ruin bar' scene, Budapest and especially District VII became real tourist hot spots, even if official marketing does not focus on this. The transformation changed the spatial structure of tourism in Budapest away from the more conventional or classic cultural tourism and World Heritage Site attractions. It also impacted on the accommodation sector and consequently inner city housing and gentrification.

Main stakeholders and conflicts in the party quarter

Conflicts between local government and residents in Budapest emerged after the change of regime in the 1990s because local governments refused to privatize apartments, residents could not purchase them, and the quality of housing and building stock deteriorated as a result (Pap & Boros, 2015). In the second half of the 1990s (when development increased exponentially), conflicts increased as non-governmental organisations (NGOs) and private investors became new stakeholders in the area. Investors' interest in a quick return on investment by destroying old buildings and constructing new ones often clashed with heritage protection lobbies. Local governments tended to support the former rather than the latter. The heritage protection agency is viewed by local government as inflexible and a barrier to regeneration. Profitable renovation becomes almost impossible (Pap & Boros, 2015). New constructions, therefore, transformed the housing stock in some places, for example, in the Gozsdu courtyard at the heart of District VII, where large old flats were replaced by expensive small ones which were less suitable for local residents.

Since the turn of the Millennium (the mature/consolidation phase of development), conflicts between local residents and tourists, as well as young people looking for entertainment, have emerged in the area. The conflicts during this period can be predominantly linked to the expansion of 'ruin bar' culture and its impact on night noise. The local population has repeatedly turned to the local government in protest (legal disputes, lawsuits against bars, letters to their local authority representative or the mayor, collecting signatures to put pressure on their local politicians, and Facebook groups) and the local authority has already introduced more silence regulations in order to remedy the problem, but the situation has not yet been fully resolved. The local authority decided to divide the district into two very differently regulated parts: in the most central part of District VII where the 'ruin bars' and most other bars can be found there is no restriction of opening hours, while outside the Great-Boulevard shops and bars have to close by midnight. (The regulation of commercial activities in accordance with the EU directives gives priority to entrepreneurial freedom, and the local authority can only restrict the opening hours.) The local authority politicians often complain that their hands are tied by the national level legislation and under this regulation they cannot restrict the function or the type of venues opened in the area. The local authority also decided to introduce a local tax for bars that are open after midnight in the central part of the district. However, the close negotiations with the entrepreneurs resulted in this amount being very low.

According to some NGOs, the local government plays a 'double game' in this case, because the revenue from the consumption of tourists is as important to them as the satisfaction of local residents. Thus, since 2013, the central part of District VII has become a party district and other parts of the district are regulated. In the near future, there will be an increase in the number of conflicts between investors, as the flourishing of the area is a good opportunity for profit making. Recently, big entrepreneurs and developers appeared in the area and a transformation and concentration process in the ownership structure of the 'ruin bar' market began. Although 'ruin bars' were expected to be temporary and the whole party area emerged as an unintended 'by-product' of unplanned urban processes, it has proved to be much more than a 'pop-up' phenomenon after 15 years of ongoing developments.

The development of Airbnb in Budapest

The use of apartments for tourism accommodation became a promising business opportunity which resulted in a demand side boom after 7 years of real estate crisis and nominal decrease of property prices after 2008. It is important to note that gentrification was not induced automatically by former disinvestment or by the demand of affluent residents or students, but rather the growth of tourism that was fuelled partly by the emergence of 'ruin bars'. This functional change in the apartment sector has a double displacement effect: first, rents and property prices increase because apartments become the competition for hotel rooms, and second, the noise generated by bars and guests of Airbnb apartments decreases the use value of these apartments and residents often have no other option than to leave (Cócola Gant, 2016).

In order to understand the geographical distribution of the Airbnb accommodation in Budapest, it is important to look firstly at the concentrations of tourist attractions within the city. The vast majority of tourists visit only the inner districts (Rátz, Smith, & Michalkó, 2008). This smaller area includes the Castle District and Gellért Hill (District I), the inner city, the Lipótváros and the embankment of the Danube (District V) as well as other inner districts on the Pest side (Districts V–VIII). It should be noted that District V is popular because of its elegant architecture and concentration of more classic cultural tourism and heritage attractions. Although District VII also offers some cultural attractions (e.g. architecture, museums and synagogues), the World Heritage Site attractions are located along Andrássy Avenue (District VI) stretching between Heroes' Square and the City Park (District XIV) at one end and the Castle District (District I) at the other end. Other popular places are Margaret Island (District XIII), as well as some parts on the Buda side (riverbank of the Danube in District II and surroundings of the Gellért Spa in District XI). Evaluating the geographical location of Airbnb accommodation, we can conclude that they spread over a much smaller area than the catchment area of the main tourist sites mentioned above. Seventy-seven per cent of all Airbnb properties are concentrated in the inner districts of Pest (Districts V-VIII). In Districts VI and VII the number of active Airbnb listings was slightly more than 1700 per district in September 2016. During the research period, the number of Airbnb properties constantly increased in District VII (but not in V and VI), which may be connected to the attractiveness of the party atmosphere and 'ruin pubs'.

The geographical distribution of apartments within the area is uneven and the majority of listings are located in the more central parts of the districts. Thus, the high density of Airbnb apartments is located in the so-called 'party area' where most of the 'ruin bars' are located. During the research period, the number of apartments registered on the Airbnb

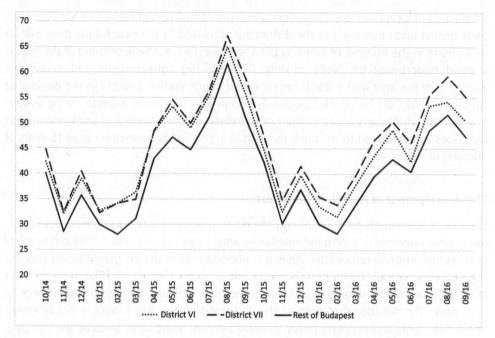

Figure 2. Monthly occupancy of Airbnb properties in Budapest. Source: Authors' own.

platform increased significantly in the case study area. Between October 2014 and September 2016, the number of listings in Districts VI and VII increased by 230% and 280%, respectively. However, the data also shows that many hosts did not manage to run a successful operation, as more than a thousand properties per district were withdrawn from the platform during the same period.

The monthly occupancy was higher in the case study district than in other districts of Budapest for the entire research period. The advantage of District VII has grown steadily: in autumn 2016, the occupancy indicator here surpassed the respective figure of District VI by 10%, and of other districts of Budapest by 15%.

Analysis of the daily occupancy figures highlights the characteristics of the demand side of the Airbnb market (Figure 2). It can be observed that occupancy at the weekends is about 10–20 percentage points higher than on weekdays. This trend changes only during the Sziget Festival in August. Other periods with outstanding occupancy are Easter weekends, 1 May and during the Formula 1 race in July. The most popular period is New Year's Eve, when Airbnb properties are almost fully booked (see Figure 3).

Airbnb apartment prices in Budapest are close to the four-star hotel prices (see Table 2; the apartment prices were calculated for two guests). However, annual price volatility of private accommodation is much lower than that of hotels. It is worth noting that the average price level differs, for example, prices in District VI are 10%–15% higher than in District VII. Figure 3 shows the daily capacity of Airbnb properties in Budapest and Figure 4 shows a map of Airbnb listings.

A comparison of prices at district level is made difficult by the variation in apartment sizes (their capacity varies between 2 and 16 persons per apartment), and by the different pricing policies used by the owners (e.g. listing rate dynamics according to the number of

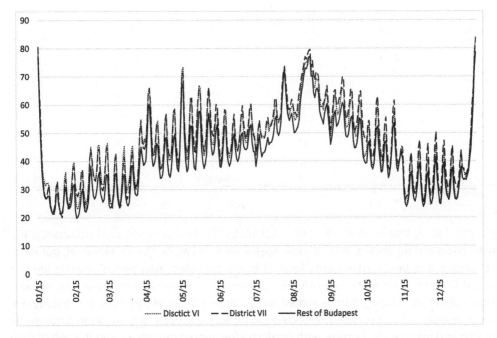

Figure 3. Daily capacity of Airbnb properties in Budapest. Source: Authors' own.

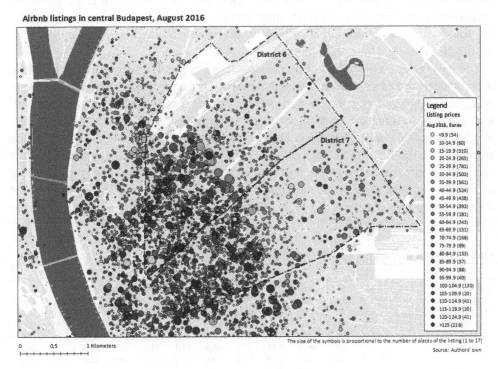

Figure 4. Airbnb listings in Central Budapest. Source: Authors' own.

Table 2. Airbnb listings in Budapest, September 2016.

District	Listings	Listings %	District	Listings	Listings %
I	324	4.0	XIII	481	5.9
II	238	2.9	XIV	144	1.8
III	75	0.9	XV	19	0.2
IV	25	0.3	XVI	20	0.2
V	1668	20.6	XVII	6	0.1
VI	1705	21.0	XVIII	10	0.1
VII	1714	21.1	XIX	20	0.2
VIII	863	10.6	XX	17	0.2
IX	399	4.9	XXI	10	0.1
X	10	0.1	XXII	15	0.2
XI	200	2.5	XXIII	5	0.1
XII	147	1.8	Budapest	8115	100.0

Source: Authors' own.

guests). Taking into account the prices calculated for two person-based occupancy, the differences are significant, and no clear spatial pattern can be drawn. However, our data-set shows that larger apartments located in the so-called 'ruin bar' quarter inside the Grand Boulevard are quite expensive for couples. This suggests that these accommodation facilities are supposed to be rented out by larger parties of travellers. In the party district, the guests of Airbnb apartments tend to be young groups who are often participants of stag and hen parties. Families with small children would probably avoid this area if they were well-informed enough about the nature of the District.

A much more homogenous picture of price levels appears if we analyse the prices per person at full apartment occupancy: the average price paid by guests in this case is around 15–20 EURO per night. Higher per capita rates (over 35 EURO) characterise the properties located closer to the city centre accommodating two–four persons. Actually, the 'ruin bar' quarter offers several affordable apartments also in this size category, making the area attractive for couples or families as well.

The data collected from the Airbnb website does not provide exact information about the characteristics of visitors, thus we cannot rely on it concerning segmentation. However, such information can be obtained with the help of data gathered from another platform which is Booking.com, as the guests' assessments are categorised by segments. The number of apartments registered in Booking.com is about 2000 in Budapest, of which around 450 are in Districts VI and VII. Table 3 shows the monthly average prices in 2015 and Table 4 shows that families and groups of friends generally make up a much larger proportion in private accommodation compared to the hotels. Furthermore, the ratio of couples and groups of friends in private accommodations and hotels, as well as the ratio

Table 3. Monthly average prices in 2015, EURO/night.

	1	2	3	4	5	6	7	8	9	10	11	12
All hotels	64,8	57,1	56,1	64,7	73,6	71,8	72,9	65,9	76,8	77,4	61,3	63,3
Three-star hotels	32,4	27,5	28,7	33,9	37,9	36,6	38,3	37,2	40,8	39,3	30,2	31,6
Four-star hotels	54,2	45,3	45,2	54,1	63,0	60,3	58,4	54,3	63,9	63,0	49,0	50,8
Five-star hotels	113,7	106,4	110,9	124,9	148,6	142,4	139,5	124,2	142,5	146,3	105,0	126,3
B&Bs	26,5	26,5	30,5	31,7	33,1	29,4	36,8	36,5	34,5	35,6	29,6	30,8
Airbnb (listing)	48,1	48,6	49,3	50,1	50,6	50,8	51,1	51,0	50,8	50,0	50,2	49,3
Airbnb District VI (listing)	52,5	52,7	52,8	52,9	52,9	52,9	52,7	51,9	52,2	51,4	51,2	50,1
Airbnb District VII (listing)	44,3	44,7	45,5	46,5	47,2	47,3	48,2	48,2	47,6	46,2	47,1	45,7

Source: Authors' own; Hotel and motel data – KSH (Central Statistical Office); Airbnb data –own research.

Table 4. Ratio of different guest segments in Districts VI and VII based on Booking.com data.

Accommodation type	Business	Solo	Couples	Families	Friends	Count
Hotels, District VI	10,41	16,10	46,44	11,46	15,59	22
Hotels, District VII	9,90	14,42	47,78	11,75	16,15	24
Apartments, District VI	6,23	10,25	34,17	23,54	25,81	454
Apartments, District VII	5,41	10,43	37,38	20,39	26,39	449
Hostels, District VI	3,94	39,96	21,74	4,17	30,19	32
Hostels, District VII	3,95	45,00	17,92	3,25	29,89	30

Source: Authors' own.

of single travellers in hostels are obviously higher in District VII. Our results presume that this area of the city appears to be a zone more suitable for parties and entertainment compared to other districts.

For now, it is still questionable whether and to what extent expanding the supply of Airbnb services causes one frequently mentioned undesirable consequence, which is the limitation of private housing facilities. Many properties in the affected districts are still neglected and a vast number of flats have been empty for the past few years. It has now become obvious, that in the districts of inner-Pest like VI and VII the process of perceptible gentrification has begun, with the Airbnb properties being its beneficiaries and to some extent, catalysts at the same time. The media and public opinion often tend to ascribe the negative effects of the above mentioned changes to Airbnb; however, there have not yet been any anti-tourism demonstrations, as there have been in some other popular destinations (Bock, 2015; Colomb & Novy, 2017).

Conclusions

It can be seen that not only has there been little planning for tourism due to the fragmentation of the city in terms of district management, but there has been very little coherent urban planning altogether in the post-socialist years. Tourism in Budapest has nevertheless increased and flourished largely due to the post-EU accession influx of budget airline tourists, coupled with the growing reputation of the city as a location for cheap entertainment (namely alcohol) and parties. In line with many other European cities, there has been a parallel development of a creative quarter (Districts VI and VII), which affords locals and visitors 'bohemian' entertainment, mainly in the form of 'ruin bars', coupled with the rapid growth of Airbnb apartments and hostels. Most of this process has taken place within less than 10 years. It is difficult to say whether one might be the consequence of the other, but it is clear that the two phenomena are closely connected. The Airbnb data shows that there is a strong concentration of accommodation in District VII, especially in the areas where 'ruin bars' are located.

The nature of the accommodation seems to cater more for groups of friends, supporting the idea that this area is more suitable for parties in recent years than for other groups or forms of tourism. The needs of local residents have been largely disregarded both in terms of the rapidly increasing property prices and consequent displacement, and the unreasonable noise levels and behaviour of tourists. There is little evidence to suggest that coherent urban planning has been used to attract tourism consumption to these districts of the city nor to contain or regulate it. Both the 'ruin bar' and Airbnb phenomena appear to have flourished independently of any kind of identifiable planning objectives.

Local government(s) in District VII (and VI) eventually seemed to have recognized the potential of this 'party area'. However, despite the government's attempts at centralization at all administrative levels, there is still no clear vision for the further development of the area. Planning still seems to be characterised by random and unpredictable decision-making. A Daily News Hungary report (2015) suggests that tourism is growing year on year in Budapest (5.2% growth from 2013 to 2014) but that tourists spend significantly less than in Prague. The low spending is attributed to the popularity of 'low-budget party tourism' based on the 'age of ruin pubs' and a 'flourishing' Airbnb market. It is suggested that local residents need to tolerate it or to pack up and move out. The area is still in an early phase of development, but the big question remains as to how local residents who live in the party area could benefit from future developments. Will the quarter become integrated better into the overall urban fabric or became an exclave within the district? Another uncertain question relates to the question of Airbnb. Partly in response to the protests of the hotel sector, the national government may pass restrictions against Airbnb similar to what happened in the case of Über (which has now been discontinued in Budapest). The sharing economy is still not fully understood or supported by governments around the world, therefore, the future of Budapest will also depend partly on how this relationship between the sharing economy and national governments develop. Evidence suggests that resistance to Airbnb and the 'sharing economy' among local residents in cities is also mounting (Colomb & Novy, 2017). The struggle over the night noise intensified in Budapest in 2017 when a group of residents started petitions, organised demonstrations and attracted the attention of the Hungarian media in the summer months. Pub and bar owners and their workers also demonstrated against the idea of an earlier closing time and highlighted the economic importance of tourism, which according to them, has increased because of the party district. At the time of writing, the decision of the local authority in District VII was still unclear, however adjacent districts introduced earlier closing times for terraces and open air venues and restricted the sale of alcohol in late night shops. It was decided that in order to represent the different stakeholders, a so-called 'night mayor' should be elected.

Despite the fact that Budapest shared a history that was more typical of former socialist cities, its future looks set to emulate that of many Western European or even global cities. It may become yet another tourist city featuring 'protest and resistance' like so many of those outlined in Colomb and Novy's (2017) recent book. The resistance to and rejection of the Olympic Bid in Budapest in 2017 was just one example. It is perhaps most similar to Prague, where the local residents are unhappier about the laissez-faire and corrupt approach of the municipal government than they are about tourism per se (Pixová & Sládek, 2017). Budapest is similarly grappling with the forces of property-led gentrification and a rapid growth in budget airline-fuelled party tourism based on the cheap availability of alcohol (albeit in the creative and bohemian milieu of the 'ruin bars'), reinforced by abundantly available and unregulated Airbnb options. The decentralised, fragmented and ad hoc approach to urban (tourism) planning arguably does not bode well for residents, even if it supports the current growth of tourism. Care must also be taken that these developments do not erode the very features that made them attractive to tourists in the first place.

Disclosure statement

No potential conflict of interest was reported by the authors.

References

Akçalıa, E., & Korkut, U. (2015). Urban transformation in Istanbul and Budapest: Neoliberal governmentality in the EU's semi-periphery and its limits. *Political Geography, 46*, 76–88.

Ashworth, G. J., & Tunbridge, J. E. (2000). *The tourist-historic city: Retrospect and prospect of managing the heritage city*. London: Routledge.

Atkinson, R., & Bridge, G. (2005). Introduction. In R. Atkinson & G. Bridge (Eds.), *Gentrification in a global context: The new urban colonialism* (pp. 1–17). London: Routledge.

Barta, G., Beluszky, P., Czirfusz, M., Győri, R., & Kukely, G. (2006). *Rehabilitating the Brownfield zones of Budapest centre for regional studies of Hungarian Academy of Sciences* (Discussion Paper No. 51). Budapest: Centre for Regional Studies of the Hungarian Academy of Sciences.

Benedek, J., & Moldovan, A. (2015). Economic convergence and polarisation: Towards a multi-dimensional approach. *Hungarian Geographical Bulletin, 64*(3), 187–203.

Berki, M. (2014). Return to the road of capitalism: Recapitulating the post-socialist urban transition. *Hungarian Geographical Bulletin, 63*(3), 319–334.

Bock, K. (2015). The changing nature of city tourism and its possible implications for the future of cities. *European Journal of Futures Research, 3*(1), 1–8.

Bontje, M., Musterd, S., Kovács, Z., & Murie, A. (2011). Pathways toward European creative-knowledge city-regions. *Urban Geography, 32*(1), 80–104.

Boros, L., Fabula, S., Horváth, D., & Kovács, Z. (2016). Urban diversity and the production of public space in Budapest. *Hungarian Geographical Bulletin, 65*(3), 209–224.

Boyd, D., & Crawford, K. (2012). Critical questions for big data: Provocations for a cultural, technological, and scholarly phenomenon. *Information, Communication, & Society, 15*(5), 662–679.

Brade, I., Herfert, G., & Wiest, K. (2009). Recent trends and future prospects of sociospatial differentiation in urban regions of Central and East Europe: A lull before the storm? *Cities, 26*, 233–244.

Cócola Gant, A. (2016). Holiday rentals: The new gentrification battlefront. *Sociological Research Online, 21*(3), 10. Retrieved from http://www.socresonline.org.uk/21/3/10.html

Colomb, C., & Novy, J. (Eds.). (2017). *Protest and resistance in the tourist city.* London: Routledge.

Csanádi, G., & Csizmady, A. (2002). Szuburbanizáció és társadalom [Suburbanisation and Society]. *Tér és társadalom [Space and Society], 3,* 27–55.

Csanádi, G., Csizmady, A., Kocsis, J., Kőszeghy, L., & Tomay, K. (2010). *Város-Tervező-Társadalom* [City-planner-society]. Budapest: Sík Kiadó.

Csanádi, G., Csizmady, A., & Olt, G. (2012). *Átváltozóban* [Transformation]. Budapest: Eötvös Kiadó.

CSO (2016). Central statistical office: Information database. Budapest: Hungarian Central Statistical Office. Retrieved from https://www.ksh.hu/tourism_catering

Czirfusz, M., Horváth, V., Jelinek, C., Pósfai, Z., & Szabó, L. (2015). Gentrification and rescaling urban governance in Budapest-Józsefváros. *Intersections, EEJSP, 1*(4), 55–77.

Daily News Hungary (2015, September 23). The Hungarian party tourism is unbeatable. Retrieved from https://dailynewshungary.com/the-hungarian-party-tourism-is-unbeatable

Dervojeda, K., Verzijl, D., Nagtegaal, F., Lengton, M., Rouwmaat, E., Monfardini, E., & Frideres, L. (2013). *The sharing economy: Accessibility based business models for peer-to-peer markets.* Brussels: Directorate-General for Enterprise and Industry, European Commission.

Egedy, T. (2010). Current strategies and socioeconomic implications of urban regeneration in Hungary. *Open House International, 35*(4), 29–38.

Einav, L., Farronato, C., & Levin, J. (2015). *Peer-to-Peer Markets* (National Bureau of Economic Research Working Paper Series No. 21496). Cambridge, MA: National Bureau of Economic Research. Retrieved from http://www.nber.org/papers/w21496

Eldridge, A. (2010). The urban renaissance and the night-time economy: Who belongs to the city at night. In T. Manzi, K. Lucas, T. L. Jones, & J. Allen (Eds.), *Social sustainability in urban areas, communities, connectivity and the urban fabric* (pp. 712–726). London: Earthscan.

Fabula, Sz., Boros, L., Kovács, Z., Horváth, D., & Pál, V. (2017). Studentification, diversity and social cohesion in post-socialist Budapest. *Hungarian Geographical Bulletin, 66*(2), 157–173.

Földi, Z. (2006). Neighbourhood dynamics in inner-Budapest: A realist approach. *Geography, 33*(6), 829–849.

Grubbauer, M., & Kusiak, J. (Eds.). (2012). *Chasing Warsaw. Socio-material dynamics of urban change since 1990* (pp. 35–60). Frankfurt: Campus Verlag.

Iwanicki, G., Dłużewska, A., & Smith, M.K. (2016). Assessing the level of popularity of European stag tourism destinations. *Quaestiones Geographicae, 35*(3), 15–29.

Jelinek, C. (2010). The phenomena of displacement and relocation during the process of gentrification in Budapest. *Studia Universitatis Babeş–Bolyai – Sociologia, 60*(2), 105–116.

Judd, D. R., & Fainstein, S. S. (1999). *The tourist city.* New Haven, CT: Yale University Press.

Kauko, T. (2012, December). An institutional analysis of property development, good governance and urban sustainability. *European Planning Studies, 20*(12), 1–19.

Keresztély, K. (2007). Cultural policies and urban rehabilitation in Budapest. In N. Svob-Dokic (Ed.), *Cultural transition in Southeastern Europe: The creative city - crossing visions and new realities in the region* (pp. 95–117). (Culturelink Joint Publication Series 11). Zagreb: Institute for International Relations.

Keresztély, K., & Scott, J.W. (2012, July). Urban regeneration in the post-socialist context: Budapest and the search for a social dimension. *European Planning Studies, 20*(7), 1111–1134. Retrieved from https://doi.org/10.1080/09654313.2012.674346

Kovács, Z. (1998). Ghettoization or gentrification? Post-socialist scenarios for Budapest. *Netherlands Journal of Housing and the Built Environment, 13*(1), 63–81.

Kovács, Z., Wiessner, R., & Zischner, R. (2013). Urban renewal in the inner city of Budapest: Gentrification from a post-socialist perspective. *Urban Studies, 50*(1), 22–38.

Kovacs, Z., Wiessner, R., & Zischner, R. (2015). Beyond gentrification: Diversified neighbourhood upgrading in the inner city of Budapest. *Geografie, 120*(2), 250–273.

Ladányi, J. (2008). *Lakóhelyi szegregáció Budapesten* [Residential segregation in Budapest]. Budapest: Új Mandátum Könyvkiadó.

Lugosi, P., Bell, D., & Lugosi, K. (2010). Hospitality, culture and regeneration: Urban decay, entrepreneurship and the 'ruin' bars of Budapest. *Urban Studies, 47*(14), 3079–3101.

Marcińczak, S., & Sagan, I. (2011). The socio-spatial restructuring of Łódź, Poland. *Urban Studies, 48*(9), 1789–1809.

Marques, L., & Richards, G. (Eds.). (2014). *Creative districts around the World*. Breda: NTV.

Mayer-Schonberger, V., & Cukier, K. (2013). *BIG DATA: A revolution that will transform how we live, work, and think*. Eamon Dolan/Houghton Mifflin Harcourt.

Michalkó, G. (2001). Social and geographical aspects of tourism in Budapest. *European Spatial Research and Policy, 8*(1), 105–118.

Michalkó, G., & Rátz, T. (2006). The Mediterranean Tourist Milieu. *Anatolia: An International Journal of Tourism and Hospitality Research, 17*(1), 93–109.

Nagy, E., & Timár, J. (2012). Urban restructuring in the grip of capital and politics: Gentrification in East-Central Europe. In T. Csapó & A. Balogh (Eds.), *Development of the settlement network in the central European countries* (pp. 121–135). Berlin Heidelberg: Springer-Verlag.

Novy, J. (2017). The selling (out) of Berlin and the de- and re-politicization of urban tourism in Europe's 'Capital of Cool'. In C. Colomb & J. Novy (Eds.), *Protest and resistance in the tourist city* (pp. 52–72). London: Routledge.

Olmedilla, M., Martínez-Torres, M. R., & Toral, S. L. (2016). Harvesting big data in social science: A methodological approach for collecting online user-generated content. *Computer Standards & Interfaces, 46*, 79–87.

Palonen, E. (2013). Millennial politics of architecture: Myths and nationhood in Budapest. *Nationalities Papers, 41*(4), 536–551.

Pap, Á., & Boros, L. (2015). Épített örökség és helyi identitás – az érdekek és konfliktusok földrajzi vizsgálata budapesti mintaterületeken [Built heritage and local identity – A geographical analysis of interests and conflicts in Budapest]. I: J. Unger & E. Pál-Molnár (szerk.), *Geoszférák 2014.* (pp. 109–131.) Szeged: SZTE TTIK Földrajzi és Földtani Tanszékcsoport.

Pappalepore, I., Maitland, R., & Smith, A. (2014). Prosuming creative urban areas. Evidence from East London. *Annals of Tourism Research, 44*, 227–240.

Perczel, A. (2007). Pest régi zsidó negyedének sorsa, jelenlegi helyzet [The fate of the old Jewish quarter of pest and the current situation]. *Múlt és Jövő, 18*(2), 100–131. Retrieved from http://www.multesjovo.hu/hu/2007-2.html

Pixová, M., & Sládek, J. (2017). Touristification and awakening civil society in post-socialist Prague. In C. Colomb & J. Novy (Eds.), *Protest and resistance in the tourist city* (pp.73–89). London: Routledge.

Rátz, T., Smith, M., & Michalkó, G. (2008). New places in old spaces: Mapping tourism and regeneration in Budapest. *Tourism Geographies, 10*(4), 429–451.

Roberts, M. (2009). Planning, urban design and the night-time city: Still at the margins? *Criminology and Criminal Justice, 9*, 487–507.

Roberts, M., Turner, C., Greenfield, S., & Osborn, G. (2006). A continental ambience? Lessons in managing alcohol-related evening and night-time entertainment from four European capitals. *Urban Studies, 43*(7), 1105–1125.

Román, A. (1998). "*Madách Imre, avagy egy sugárút tragédiája*" Budapesti Negyed 18-19 [Imre Madách or a tragedy of a promenade]. Budapesti Negyed 5–6(18–19). Retrieved from http://epa.niif.hu/00000/00003/00015/roman.htm

Sipos, A., & Zolnay, J. (2009). Ingatlanpanama a régi pesti zsidónegyed elpusztítása [Real-estate corruption the destruction of the old Jewish Quarter]. *Beszélő, 14*(5). Retrieved from http://beszelo.c3.hu/cikkek/ingatlanpanama

Smith, M. K., & Puczkó, L. (2010). Out with the old, in with the new? 20 years of post-socialist marketing in Budapest. *Journal of Town and City Management, 1*(3), 288–299.

Smith, M. K., & Puczkó, L. (2012). Budapest: From socialist heritage to cultural capital? *Current Issues in Tourism, 15*(1–2), 107–119.

Smith, M. K., Puczkó, T., & Rátz, T. (2009). Twenty-three districts in search of a city: Budapest – The capitaless capital? In R. Maitland & B. Ritchie (Eds.), *City tourism: National capital perspectives* (pp. 201–213). Wallingford: CABI.

Smith, N. (1996). *The new urban frontier – Gentrification and the revanchist city*. London: Routledge.

Sykora, L. (2005). Gentrification in post-communist cities. In R. Atkinson & G. Bridge (Eds.), *Gentrification in a global context the new urban colonialism* (pp. 91–106). London and New York, NY: Routledge.

Szelényi, I. (2015). Capitalisms after Communism. *New Left Review, 96*, 1–13.

Tóth, A., Keszei, B., & Dúll, A. (2014). From Jewish quarter into a creative district. In L. Marques & G. Richards (Eds.), *Creative districts around the World* (pp. 111–118). Breda: NHTV.

Vigvári, A. (2008). Szubszidiaritás nélküli decentralizáció: Néhány adalék az önkormányzati rendszer Magyar modelljének a korszerűsítéséhez [Decentralization without subsidiarity: Some additions to modernization of Hungarian Model of Local Government System]. *Tér és Társadalom [Space and Society], 22*(1), 141–167.

Wiest, K. (2012). Comparative debates in post-socialist urban studies. *Urban Geography, 33*(6), 829–849.

Zukin, S. (1987). Gentrification culture and capital in the urban core. *Annual Review of Sociology, 13*, 129–147.

Zukin, S. (1995). *The culture of cities.* Malden, MA: Blackwell.

Hotel development through centralized to liberalized planning procedures: Prague lost in transition

Bálint Kádár

ABSTRACT

Scholars argued for the need of better urban planning procedures in post-socialist Prague in the 1990s. But a society liberated from an oppressive political system where five-year plans defined every aspect of life did not believe in the beneficial power of regulations. Prague just started to profit from the large wave of foreign tourists arriving, and did not want to control the liberal market, trusted to upgrade the obsolete hotel infrastructure created by central planning. Literature documents well this era of transition, bringing into focus more and more the conflicts of tourism development in the historic city, often described as a tourist ghetto. This study demonstrates direct links between the extremities in tourism planning procedures and the criticized touristification process. Prague's hotel development patterns are compared with similar tourist-historic destinations: Budapest and Vienna. The building age and typology was included in the geographical analysis of hotels, revealing more of the extreme consequences of both the era of centralized planning procedures, and of the era of uncontrolled liberalization multiplied by the effects of in-kind restitution. Vienna has a totally balanced spatial distribution of hotels showing a linear development through the ages. Budapest faced the same communist period followed by a liberalization process, but the sensibility of the communist regime towards tourism demands and the avoided in-kind type of restitution during privatization in the new era kept the hotel development patterns and the tourist space system more balanced. The results of this study contribute to the general understanding of the needs and tools of tourism planning in urban tourism development.

Introduction

Visiting tourist-historic cities is an ever growing phenomenon since pioneers of urban tourism studies began to theorize and research this field (Ashworth & Turnbridge, 1990; Law, 1994; Pearce, 1998). Cities like Prague, Budapest or Vienna doubled their visitor numbers in the past 20 years, and the growth is still linear for all three (TourMIS, 2016). The development of hotels and other services follows the growth of visitor numbers; therefore an evident question must be posed: what level of planning does the expansion of tourism infrastructures need? It is assumed that a continuous development and re-development of a tourist city is needed to keep tourism sustainable as a system (Butler, 1980; Garay & Cànoves, 2011); resilience planning and policy research therefore became a more important part of urban tourism research (Lew, 2013). Singular case studies did reveal the cases when cities cannot bear tourism pressure without larger conflicts (Russo, 2002), but it is hard to theorize the causes of such conflicts if analysed separately; another problem with individual case studies is the fact that these focus on anomalies and conflicts, while the *best practices* of sustainable urban tourism systems remain undocumented, depriving from possible good planning solutions also the conflicting cases.

A city in need of more effective policy and planning for tourism is Prague. Tourism bought economic benefits for the capital of post-socialist Czech Republic, but Johnson (1995) already saw the signs of tourist concentration in the central core in 1995. At the end of the century, scholars started to describe conflicts deriving from tourist overcrowding (Simpson, 1999), environmental impacts (Deichmann, 2002) and the commercialization effects of tourism (Hoffman & Musil, 1999; Sykora, 1999). A higher awareness of the negative effects of touristification can only be seen in recent years. The measurement of the satisfaction of elderly people living in the centre showed some dissatisfaction with lowered feeling of security and increased prices in Prague 1 (Temelová & Dvořáková, 2012). Dumbrovska (2017) described the culmination of many of the abovementioned conflicts in the 'tourist ghetto' of Prague. She demonstrated that local residents are aware of these negative effects, but are willing to bear their consequences for the benefits of living in the centre. Locals have found other spaces near the centre for their local activities, therefore only few are the critical voices from the public. Prague residents are generally not against tourism, perceiving the negative impacts of touristification as a consequence of mismanagement by the local authorities. In recent years, the municipal government has been under increasing pressure from the civil society to face the challenges of tourism related development in the historical centre of Prague with more regulation and strategic planning (Pixová & Sládek, 2016). Most of the above-mentioned authors agreed that the municipality of Prague need to be more proactive in policy-making and planning to compensate the negative effects of tourism.

In a paper from 1994 analysing the problematic environment for strategic planning in the newly formed Czech Republic, Lily Hoffman expressed a desire born from the controversies of two radically different planning attitudes experienced in the period of transition:

> Although it is too soon to predict any outcomes, there is a reasonable hope that planning will neither be entirely part of the technocratic machine nor purely an economic instrument. (Hoffman, 1994, p. 701)

This paper wishes to prove the importance of her vision for balanced planning procedures, as the two extreme planning experiences contributed largely to a phenomena that Hoffman herself studied later on: Prague's unplanned touristification process (Hoffman & Musil, 1999, 2009).

The objective of this study is to demonstrate some negative effects of systematic deviations from standard planning and policy procedures affecting tourism. Such deviations were in part the cause of a distorted tourist space system in Prague's centre, resulting in negative spatial segregation (Kádár, 2013). Planning and policy implications affect indirectly such phenomena, but have a direct influence on the development of the hotel industry. Therefore, in this paper deviations from standard models of hotel placement in tourist-historic cities are examined, seeking for the procedures in planning and policy that lead to some anomalies in Prague's model. The method of a comparative study of hotel placement was selected between Prague, Vienna and Budapest. The three cities are often compared in urban tourism studies (Dolnicar, Grabler, & Mazanec, 2000; Dumbrovská & Fialová, 2014; Kádár, 2013, 2014; Puczkó & Rátz, 2000); therefore the findings of this research can contribute to a wider theorization of tourism development and planning in European tourist-historic cities.

The most interesting question from a planning perspective is not the conflicting nature of Prague's tourism per se, but the question: why the same number of tourists causes conflicts in Prague's urban space but not in Vienna? And also: why similar post-socialist urban destinations faced different tourism development trajectories? First, it is important to clarify the historical differences in tourism related planning and tourism development among these destinations.

Historical background of tourism development in three central European capital cities

Differences in the development of the tourism industries

Prague and Budapest faced a different tourism development trajectory than Vienna since the post-war period. Russian troops left Austria in 1955 without major impact; the whole economy and the tourism industry could continue to perform in a market-economy with efficient regulatory and planning procedures helping to put tourism on a sustainable trajectory.

The neutral state quickly re-joined the international tourism market, visitor numbers to Vienna increased almost linearly since 1960 (WienTourismus, 2005). Hotel development was continuous; besides the many historic hotels new facilities were constantly developed. The Austrian capital could later also profit from the fall of the Iron Curtain, positioning itself from periphery to centre.

Prague and Budapest remained under the Soviet influence after the Second World War, operating with a nationalized market and property ownership under communism. Still their tourism industries took different trajectories after the *'Prague Spring'* of 1968, when an attempt to liberalize the communist state was broken down by soviet allies. This event bought stricter centralization and more ideological governance after a period of liberalization in Czechoslovakia. In contrast, the liberalization of the Hungarian tourist market was partly a consequence of the normalization process after the revolution of 1956 was suppressed; therefore Hungary could develop its tourism industry much more freely than Czechoslovakia (Johnson, 1997). Budapest developed for itself an exceptional position between the eastern and the western world before 1989. The state consciously developed its tourism infrastructure since the early 1960s, also introducing simplified visa procedures for western tourists. At the end of the 1980s, Hungary became the fifth most visited country in the world, and Budapest the most visited destination in Central Europe (Böröcz, 1990). But after 1990, Budapest had lost half of its visitors, being deprived of its uniqueness previously manifested in the mixture of eastern and western worlds. Exactly the opposite had happened in Prague.

Prague was closed for many western tourists until 1989. Czechoslovak statistics showed an increasing number of visitors, going up to 19 million for the country in 1986, but more than 90% of these were from Eastern Bloc countries (Johnson, 1995). Just as in Hungary, the hotel industry was nationalized after the communist coup d'état of 1948; some were transformed for other uses, others kept being operational, but few new hotel developments happened until the 1970s. Prague then started to develop new hotels to host visitors from other socialist countries on organized tours and congress tourism, while in the 1980s the economic benefits of tourism became evident also to the Czechoslovak government; therefore investments in hotels compatible with western standards began. After the Velvet Revolution of 1989, the borders opened up, and new tourists from western countries started to explore the beauties of a previously closed city. Visitor numbers have boomed, posing much pressure on the existing hotel infrastructure in need of new developments to be able to host higher standard visitors (Hoffman & Musil, 1999). Since then the hotel industry could grow up to the demand of tourism, making Prague a mature destination (Dumbrovská & Fialová, 2014). Besides the evident advantages tourism bought to Prague, today it is among the problematic destinations facing extreme touristification together with cities like Venice, Barcelona, Berlin or Amsterdam (Colomb & Novy, 2016).

Differences in planning and policy affecting the development of tourism infrastructures

Prague and Budapest faced radical changes in their political and socio-economic systems during the twentieth century. From the late 1940s, an oppressive communist system bought the nationalization of property and industries, and a centralized planning system controlling every aspect of the economy, including land use and tourism. Czechoslovakia and Hungary liberated themselves not only form oppressive regimes in 1989, but also from centralized planning procedures to follow a neoliberal development of western influences. The extent of the transition is well explained by the regulations affecting the hotel industry: while in communism the placement and capacity of hotels was decided in central regulation plans, after 1989 hotels were allowed in most central zones according to the zoning plans, and permitting became responsibility of the local level of governance, not prepared and not interested in regulating the new private investors willing to develop hotels. Vienna in contrast could benefit from half a century of stability in a neutral country developing a system carefully balancing between liberal economy and centralized planning. Therefore, a centralized regional/municipal planning system defined both Vienna's urban development and its tourism system in the past half century (Paal, 2003). In 1955, a special *'Vienna's Promotion of Tourism Act'* law was accepted, providing an efficient tax collection and redistribution system for the hotel industry, and establishing the independent professional management and regulation of Vienna's tourism industry (WienTourismus, 2005). The tourist board had a budget of 25 million euros in 2014, its *Strategic Destination Development Office* keeps creating and implementing strategic documents every five years, such as the *'Turismus-konzept 2015'* to determine the tasks, and the recent *'Turismus strategie 2020'* responsible for the medium-term planning of the tourist system of Vienna (WienTourismus, 2014); this was born as an open process with the active participation of 2500 stakeholders giving 551 relevant strategic contributions. There is a reciprocal attention between tourism planning and urban planning in Vienna, as the 2001 Strategy Plan for Vienna states (Municipal Department 18 2001, p. 39):

> As tourism has become a key economic factor in Vienna, these needs have to be met within the framework of the general objectives of urban planning.

Such coherence between urban planning, urban strategy and tourism management does not exist in Prague or in Budapest (Nedović-Budić, 2001). The liberalization and decentralization of the political and economic systems followed the same trajectory – described hereafter on the case of Prague – however the Hungarian capital gained some time to develop its planning procedures (Rátz, Smith, & Michalkó, 2008), as it had a period of regression in its tourism in the 1990s, as opposed to the tourist boom of Prague (Kádár, 2012).

In Prague, the fast development of the tourism industry left no time for comprehensive planning in a country that wanted to liberate itself from the all that symbolized centralized communist governance, like the state-hold ownership of property, or the five-year plans in economy and spatial development (Cooper & Morpeth, 1998; Maier, 1998). Administrative power for regulation was given from the state to municipalities. The district structure of Prague was reorganized, giving more power to local councils of the 57 boroughs, which also had to cope with planning and regulation (Sýkora, 1994). This caused difficulties in implementing city-wide strategic planning. The major planning agency at all levels was the *City Architect's office* (Reiner & Strong, 1995), replaced by the *Prague City Development Authority*, which would have to pass strategic policies through the borough councils with significant local authorities and constant conflicts of role (Simpson & Chapman, 1999). The change from central planning to local planning was not soft in a time when the planning profession was in a legitimization- and professional crisis (Hoffman, 1994). After a somewhat chaotic period in planning, the 1996 *Strategic Plan for Prague* gave long awaited vision for the city, focusing also on the questions related to tourist use of the historical parts of the city, wishing to extend the tourist gaze to external heritage sites to relieve pressure from the centre. Still, nor the general public, nor the planning profession, local policy-makers, institutions, or other stakeholders have understood the importance of the regulation of market forces in the historic centre of Prague (Simpson & Chapman, 1999).

Privatization reordered property ownership and development possibilities in Prague in the middle of this this planning crisis. After 1948, most private property was expropriated also in Czechoslovakia, affecting not only businesses and land, but also housing. Instead of house-ownership most people gained a *right of use* of their apartments, having to pay a minimal rent as sitting tenants. But after the Velvet Revolution of 1989, original owners were compensated for the unjust deprivation of their property. Federal Assembly of the Czech and Slovak Federal Republic enacted the so-called *Small Restitution Law* in 1990, enabling in-kind property restitution to natural persons and their heirs (Crowder, 1994). This policy structure of the restitution process was not over-theorized. This was a period when most had a belief that having a free market without regulations would manage better all urban developments than central planning (Lux & Mikeszova, 2012). Restitution began in April 1991 and in the following three years most of the property transfers were completed. In Prague 1 district, 1178 houses were claimed for restitution between 1991 and 1992, 70% of the entire housing stock in this tourist-historic core had been restituted in the 1990s to the original owners or their heirs. Out of these approximately, 2500 apartment buildings were on sale on the real estate market between 1992 and 1993, mostly in the historic inner city (Sykora & Simonickova, 1994). These intensive real estate transitions were fuelled by the fact that leasing property to commercial uses instead of maintaining these as residential could generate as much as 50 times higher revenues, as housing rents were kept being regulated administratively (Sykora, 1999). Such allowance programme intended to protect sitting tenants from landlords seeking a profit, but it also impeded the maintenance of the physical state of property in lack of revenues. The controversies of restitution and privatization initially drew back foreign investors from investing in property which could be given back to previous owners (Crowder, 1994), but later the new owners themselves speeded up foreign development by selling their regained property. Foreign investors have had the capital to relocate tenants to other properties, renovate the historic buildings, and utilize these as rental flats for foreigners or convert them into hotels, or to office spaces. This process resolved the issue of physical conservation, but it lead to over-commercialization of the centre of Prague (Hammersley & Westlake, 1996). Cooper and Morpeth (1998) calculated that there were 20,000 apartments lost every year as a result of this process in the Czech Republic of the 1990s. The transformation of the functional structure of the centre was irreversible, also helped by the *Small Privatization* of businesses like shops started in 1991 (Sýkora, 1994).

Such in-kind restitution was not general in post-socialist countries (Hegedüs & Teller, 2005); Hungary for example opted for a voucher compensation, and housing was privatized at heavily subsidized prices to sitting tenants, resulting in a fragmented ownership of housing, impeding commercialization processes (Hegedüs, Horváth, & Tosics, 2014). The differences between the planning and policy procedures and the changes in property ownership in Prague, Budapest and Vienna are evident in a historical perspective. But more evidence is needed to determine whether the extremities in these procedures have had significantly contributed to the over-touristification of Prague. Comparing the spatial distribution of the development of tourism infrastructures in these three cities could reveal anomalies related to these historical planning and policy procedures.

Comparative studies of hotel geographies: theory and literature review

Comparative, or 'multiple city studies' (Henderson, 2002; Russo & van der Borg, 2002) are still rare in the field of urban tourism (Ashworth & Page, 2011; Pearce, 2001). The case of Prague shows that there is progress in this field. First, the conflicting nature of processes tied to urban tourism were revealed in important case studies (Hoffman & Musil, 1999; Johnson, 1995; Pixová & Sládek, 2016; Simpson, 1999), but soon comparative studies appeared theorising the problems with Prague's tourism comparing it with its regional rivals. Dumbrovská and Fialová (2014) demonstrated that tourist penetration rate and defert function is much higher in Prague than in Vienna, more than double than in Budapest, while tourist density rates are even lower than in the Austrian capital. This means that the same number of tourists in these cities of similar size have much more presence if compared to the local population. Kádár (2013, 2014) showed how the spatial distribution of tourists in the public spaces of Prague and Vienna differ radically, as the pedestrian tourist space system of Prague has lower complexity and is partly responsible for the overcrowding in the central areas of the tourist-historic city. Such comparative studies are capable to identify precisely the locations or procedures that show extreme deviation in the case of one of the compared cities, therefore they are useful to develop theoretical tools that help sustainable tourism planning.

Planning and policy can have a direct effect on the tangible infrastructures of tourism. Hotel development is much influenced by planning procedures and property ownership, and as the main infrastructure of tourism supply, its spatial distribution influences the whole tourist consumption in a city (Arbel & Pizam, 1977; McNeill, 2008). Hotel development itself has an effect on the development of the built environment of the neighbourhood (Li, Fang, Huang, & Goh, 2015). Correlating hotel locations in a city with standard models can reveal the anomalies deriving from special planning and policy cases.

Hotel location research is one of the most published fields among geographical studies on tourism (Yang, Luo, & Law, 2014), delivering many case studies (Bégin, 2000; Kot & Kowalczyk, 1997; Rogerson, 2013, 2014; Yang, Wong, & Wang, 2012a). It is not easy to theorize the urban hotel industry, as it adopts fast to the changing demands, even if recently peer-to-peer businesses of accommodation like Airbnb delivers even more adaptable forms of accommodation (Gutierrez, Garcia-Palomares, Romanillos, & Salas-Olmedo, 2016). Such contemporary studies show a concentration of accommodations in the core of historic cities, while until the 1980's examples of historic cities showed that central hotels either gather in city gate/marketplace locations, or in transition zones to the CBD, but not in the historic residential fabric of cities. Therefore, Ashworth's tourist-historic model, the first comprehensive model of hotel placement in historic cities had no categories for these hotels inside the historic core (Ashworth, 1989; Ashworth & Turnbridge, 1990). Other relevant geographical models for the multifunctional historic city derive from Alonso (1964) introducing a bid-rent model, and Egan and Nield (2000) developing this to a potential revenue-based model for hotel placement, stating that central locations are preferred by tourists, having higher average room rates. Shoval (2006) introduced a new variable to these models, stating that organized tourism takes advantage of peripheral hotel locations as tour operators can take advantage of lower prices organizing easily the movement of large groups to the centre. The usefulness of such models in is evident in planning; hotel developments following the patterns imposed by the model should have more stable profitability, while ill-advised decisions lower such profitability. The same logic makes these models useful for post-development evaluation, as deviances are easy to spot (Shoval, 2006). There is a great quantity of papers on hotel location connected to the topic of this study, location choice analysis were made for many multifunctional cities (Urtasun & Gutiérrez, 2006; Yang, Wong, & Wang, 2012b). A study from Hong Kong reveals some correlation between hotel location of visitors and their activity patterns among the city's sights (Shoval, McKercher, Ng, & Birenboim, 2011). Nearest to the goals of this study is a research by Shoval and Cohen-HatTable (2001), who analyses the historic patterns of tourism accommodation in Jerusalem, giving evidence on the effects of geopolitical changes on the locations of hotel developments. Similarly to the case of Jerusalem, it is worth analysing the hotel developments of Central European cities in chronological periods defined by the great geopolitical changes of the Second World War and of the fall of the Iron Curtain.

In fact Prague's hotel location model was already studied before. Kot and Kowalczyk (1997) described Prague's hotel location development until 1997, and demonstrated that western models are not adequate to describe the situation in Prague or other post-socialist cities. Still, this study only compared Prague's situation with generic models, and focused on newly developed hotels, therefore more data are needed to find evidence that centralized planning in communism and the unique policies tied to the restitution process during the privatization of property had a direct effect on the present spatial system of tourism and on the conflicts it generated.

Methods

Geographical, historical and architectural data were collected on hotels from Prague, as well as from similar urban destinations differing only in certain well controllable parameters. Budapest was selected, because it is the second largest post-socialist urban destination after Prague, which has had a different privatization process in the 1990s. Vienna was selected, because it hosts the same number of tourists since years now, therefore it was assumed that its hotel industry is on the same level of supply today.

Statistical data exist for the hotel industry of Prague and its two rivals. The Czech Statistical Office collects data on hotels by Prague's districts, listing all hotels by category and number of rooms (CSO, 2015). Only hotels were mapped, as only policies regulating hotels were studied in all three cities; in many cases less strict rules apply on pensions or private and other forms of accommodations. Processes tied to planning and policies on property development were to be analysed, therefore only entire buildings functioning as hotels were evaluated. This necessitated the removal of hotels below 20 rooms, as many of such venues fill only a part of a larger building (in Prague around 80 such hotels having around 1000 rooms were discarded, and around 7500 rooms in other forms of accommodation were also discarded, while the total room number remaining in the database is ∼34,000).

A GIS database was created for the three cities reflecting their state of November 2016. This contained the following information:

- geographical position respect to the tourist-historic, historic and suburban zones of the city;
- number of rooms;

- period (age) of construction/conversion;
- building typology: new construction or previously existing building converted to hotel.

The geographical typology of hotels had to be defined in a comparable method.

Tourist-historic core: The central historic area of the city developed mainly before the nineteenth century, where pedestrian tourist movements between places of tourists' interest form a continuously interconnected area. The mapping method of geo-tagged tourist photographs of Kádár (2014) was used, as this database delivers a comparable result, and was already published for all three cities. In Prague and in Vienna, the continuous area of pedestrian tourist use coincides with the districts called first in both cities.

Historic belt: These are the historic districts developed mostly in the nineteenth century until the First World War around the historic core, drawn in this study according to the historic urban typologies and to historic maps between the two world wars. In Vienna, this area was limited inside the *Gürtel* a main ring road.

New suburban belt: New residential zones and housing estates, but also the suburban garden city areas and many industrial areas fall into this largest zone outside the historic belt mostly developed in the twentieth century after the Second World War.

The building typology together with the period of construction or date of conversion needed an individual evaluation model.

Historic hotels operational since before 1945: This category was created by comparing hotel lists and descriptions from historic guide-books with the present lists of hotels.

New hotels from 1945 to 1989: Hotels operational in 1989 were listed browsing all hotel data from historic guidebooks from the 1980s and from telephone directories for the cities; those operational since before 1945 were subtracted to determine this category for Prague and Budapest. In Vienna, hotels converted from residential buildings from previous historic periods had to be subtracted into a new category, while no such conversions had happened in the other two cities during communism.

Converted hotels from 1945 to 1989: The previous category could be clearly separated analysing the architectural styles of Viennese hotels from this period.

New hotels from 1990 to 2016: Such category could be easily created, as these were the new constructions not listed before. The construction years of new hotels are generally well communicated, but also the architectural style clearly separated this category from the converted hotels.

Hotels converted between 1990 and 2016: Every hotel not fitting the previous categories and having a historical architectural construction from before the World Wars automatically fitted this category, but the possibility that the given building was already operational as a hotel before 1989 was double-checked. Difficulties were encountered with buildings built after 1945, but not as hotels. The date of conversion was determined with personal communication with the hotel if no other data were available. All hotels not having the abovementioned information were discarded from the database (larger hotels were always verified).

Results and discussion

Hotels were mapped in Prague (Figure 1), Vienna (Figure 2) and Budapest (Figure 3). There are significant differences in the geographical distribution of hotels in the three cities compared. The largest number of hotels can be found in Prague (326), almost double than in Budapest (169), which can be explained by the much higher number of bed-nights spent in Prague. The statistical figures of Vienna and Prague do not differ much; still there is a significant difference in hotel numbers. While both have a similar number of large hotels (16 in Prague and 15 in Vienna have more than 300 rooms), Prague has much more small venues (20 to 50 rooms) than Vienna. Most of these are hotels converted form

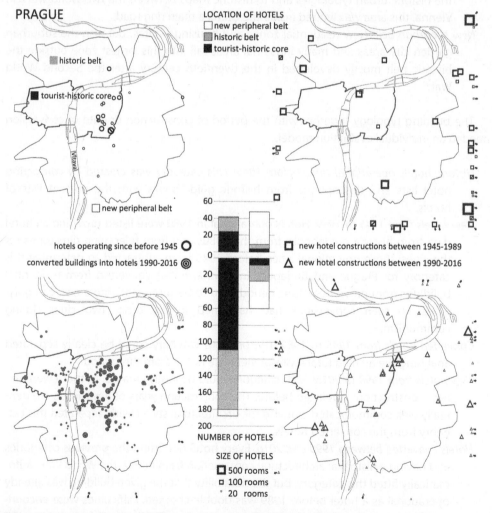

Figure 1. Location of hotels of different building age typologies in Prague.

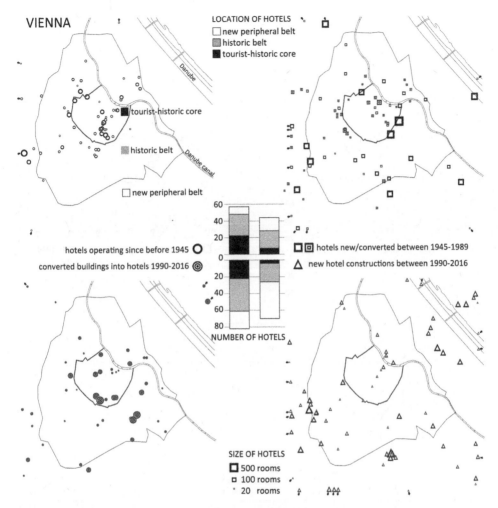

Figure 2. Location of hotels of different building age typologies in Vienna.

residential buildings, forming an extremely high percentage of Prague's hotel inventory (Figure 1). Another extremity revealed by the results is the intense hotel development of the communist era in the peripheral belts of both Prague and Budapest respect to Vienna (Figure 4). These two extremities tied to the centralized and liberalized planning procedures had some well definable negative effects on the tourism system of Prague.

Extreme peripheral locations of hotels in cities developed by central planning in state socialism

In the communist era, after many historic hotels were closed, large capacity hotels were developed in Budapest since the 1960s and in Prague since the 1970s to accommodate the growing visitor numbers. 79.5% of the 48 new hotels in Prague (Figure 1), and 74.5% of the 51 new hotels in Budapest (Figure 3) were developed outside their historic belts until 1989. In contrast, Vienna had an even distribution of post-war hotels between the various zones of the city (Figure 2).

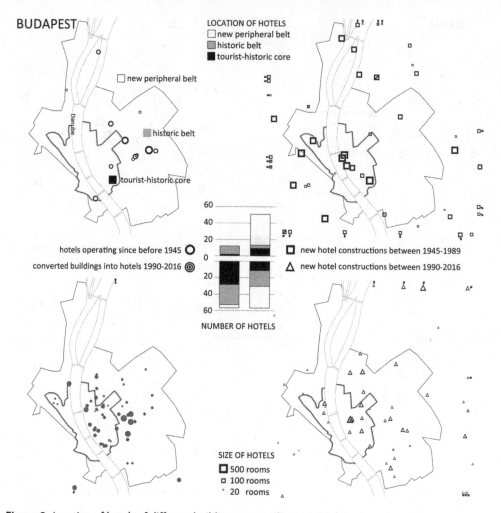

Figure 3. Location of hotels of different building age typologies in Budapest.

The inequities in the spatial distribution of new hotels constructed in the 40 year long communist era deviate from general models assuming free markets for the tourism industry. Just as other areas of urban development, tourism infrastructures of these cities were created following the five-year-plans elaborated by the nationalized planning institutions. Central planning went hand-in-hand by central tourism management, most tourist visiting these cities were using the services of the state-owned tourist agencies (CEDOC in Prague and IBUSZ in Budapest). Therefore, most visitors took part of organized tours, and were moved in groups mainly with tourist buses. The location of hotels reflects such form of organized tourism, in fact the only previously theorized model that can be applied to hotel placement of this era is the one described by Shoval (2006) that separates hotel demand according to the individual (central locations) or organized (peripheral locations) nature of tourism.

In both cities, large hotels were built by the exposition sites (Parkhotel Prague and Hotel Expo Budapest), by the roads connecting to the airports (Hotel Krystal Prague and Hotel Aereo Budapest) or built to complement new congress centres (Corinthia Hotel

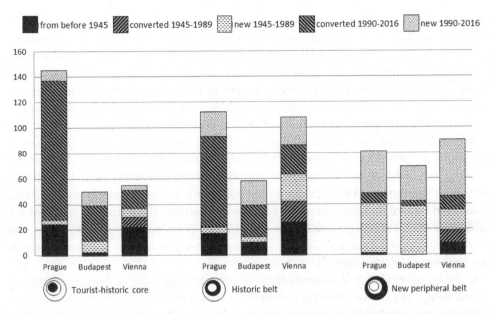

Figure 4. Quantity and location of hotels of four different building age typologies in Prague, Budapest and Vienna.

Prague and Novotel Budapest) and sport facilities (Hotel Stadion Budapest and Hotel Olympic beside the never finished Olympic village). The rest of the large new hotel developments of the communist era were placed around the historic city by the main artillery roads (for example Hotel International and Panorama in Prague, or Hotel Buda Penta, Sport and Volga in Budapest), but in Prague there is an even more external belt of hotels, developed as integral parts of the housing estates of new satellite towns (like the current Hotel Duo, Dum, Rhea, Juno, Kupa, Twin Opatov and Top Hotel Prague). It must be noted, that these hotels were so much out of the logic of tourism that they were in many cases used as accommodation for different groups of foreign and domestic workers. The great boom of visitor numbers in the 1990s made them operational as normal hotels, usually gaining three or less stars. These peripheral hotels could have contributed to the intense touristification of Prague, as they provided cheap accommodation for many tourists not willing to pay for high class inner city locations. The development of Prague's tourism industry was fuelled by foreign capital after 1990, and most of the new hotel developments aimed to create four and five start hotels which resulted to be more profitable. The lack of lower price range accommodation could have slowed down the touristification process, raising the overall prices of accommodation in Prague. As these large peripheral hotels already existed, these could operate with much lower profit margins than newly constructed lower category accommodations. This could have contributed to the overall low price level of Prague's hotel industry and an ideal model of cost/distance (Yokeno's model verified by Shoval, 2006), where tourists willing to spend more could find excellent central locations while those on a budget can find cheap accommodation more distant from the centre. As these tourists had to take the effective public transport (or organized bus tours) to reach the centre of Prague from these distant venues, no tourists walked through the historic belt, and the tourist core could separate and segregate even more.

Only in recent years the growing numbers of hotel developments and the phenomena of Airbnb initiated the tourist use of the historic belt, lowering the demand for the cheaper mass accommodations in the periphery to an extent that some were forced to close (Hotel Dum, Kupa, Twin Opatov). The same process is observable in Budapest, but at a smaller extent. Peripheral hotels built according to the spatial logics of mass tourism closed recently (like Hotel Wien on the main highway, Hotel Olimpia in a pleasant hillside environment or Hotel Volga on the northern artillery of Pest near the centre).

Budapest showed more balanced patterns of hotel development during communism as extreme peripheral locations were missing, while many hotels were built in very central locations, free for development because of World War bombings (Figure 2). Large hotels built using western capital were placed by the river Danube (former Intercontinental, Atrium and Forum), and the Hilton was carefully inserted into the historical context of the Castle District. In Prague, no hotels were built in such prominent historical locations, the InterContinental and President formed the only cluster placed near the tourist-historic city, by the river Vltava (Figure 1).

It can be concluded that Prague's hotel development practice in the communist era show the logic of a central planning system that had no connections with the market-logic of the tourism industry. Many decisions to place large hotels were made in order to give more importance to satellite towns and newly developed areas, trying to balance the mono-centric urban heritage to achieve a well distributed polycentric city. Priorities of urban planning many times outranked the demand for good locations of the tourism sector. This was not the case for Budapest, as since the 1960s the economic benefits of foreign tourism became so important that these could outrank technocratic or ideological priorities in urban planning (Johnson, 1997). A thoughtful comparison can be made between the Budapest Hilton Hotel and Prague's Four Seasons Hotel. Both luxury hotels built by American companies are placed in prominent sites of the tourist-historic core, both were built converting important national heritage buildings integrated with new wings, the architectural intervention and the commercialization of heritage was criticizes in both cases (Sykora, 1999). The only difference lies in their age, Hilton Budapest was built in 1975, while Four Seasons Prague in 1998. Communist Hungary let in foreign investors and tourists after the consolidation of the 1960, and its tourism industry followed western patterns. Czechoslovakia closed itself more from western influences after the Prague Spring of 1968, therefore a somewhat more ideological planning defined its economy and spatial structures, and tourism became prioritized only in the late 1980s. This led to a more euphoric advent of the liberalization of the country after the Velvet Revolution of 1989, also meaning that most values and procedures of the former regime were instantly refused. Protest against Hilton was unimaginable in communist Budapest. Protest against Four Seasons did not happen in Prague, as more strict regulation of private interest against the commercialization of the centre was still regarded with bad feelings towards the past era.

Extreme amount of hotel conversions from residential buildings in the centre of Prague in the era of intensive liberalization

While between 1945 and 1989 only a small portion of hotel developments took place in the historic city (18.8% in Prague and 25.5% in Budapest), this trend reversed totally after

1990, as in this contemporary period a similarly small portion of hotel developments took place outside the historic belt (16.5% in Prague and 27.2% in Budapest). In contrast, in Vienna the development of the hotel industry gradually moved outward. Before 1945, only 15.8% of hotels were placed outside the historic centre, between 1945 and 1989 this increased to 33.3%, further increasing to 46.6% after 1990 (Figure 4). Vienna gradually expanded the benefits of tourism to its peripheries.

Nothing like this can be told of the two post-socialist cities, which preformed twice radical turns in their development directions in the second half of the twentieth century, well measurable in the geography of their hotel developments. The study of Shoval and Cohen-HatTable (2001) demonstrated with a similar method how political shifts can change the development patterns of the hotel industry. The political changes in the past of post-socialist countries are among the more radical ones, resulting in the abovementioned changes.

The importance of the radical changes in Prague's hotel industry lies first in its extent, second in its role in creating conflicts of urban space usage and third in the assumption that it could have been shifted in less radical directions with proper policies.

The data-sets of this study clearly show the extremity of the commercialization and touristification pressure on Prague's tourist-historic core. At first sight this process is not evident, as only 27 out of the 207 new hotels of the historic areas are newly built, a number that is very similar to the figures of Budapest (30 new buildings) and of Vienna (26 new buildings). The rest is invisible at first glance, as the exterior appearance of the 188 hotels converted form historic buildings – in large part from residential housing – did not change at all. 109 of these hotels (plus the discarded smaller historical buildings where less than 20 rooms could fit) are in Prague 1 district, the tourist-historic core (Figure 1). 59.9% of all hotels in Prague, while 76.2% of all hotels in this central area are hotels converted from residential buildings. In comparison, Budapest has only 53 converted hotels in its tourist-historic and historic zones, only 28 in the tourist areas. 33.7% of all hotels and 49.1% of tourist area hotels are converted from an existing building (Figure 3). In Prague and in Budapest, all of the hotels that are converted from residential buildings date from after 1990; before nor was the property market, nor the hotel industry liberalized, while the state had no intention to make such delicate conversions since housing shortage was a constant problem. Therefore, Vienna has a much longer history of converted hotels (Figure 2): 34 of the 82 venues date from before 1990. Since then only 48 buildings have been converted to hotels (19% of all hotels), 37 in historic zones and only 14 in the tourist-historic city (25.5% of hotels in this area).

The fact that Prague developed more than three times more hotels than Budapest and almost seven times more hotels than Vienna in its already compact tourist-historic core shows part of the great pressure posed by tourism on Prague. This process is even more alarming when compared with the de-population trends of Prague, realizing that most of these newly converted hotels served as residential housing before. The reason why Prague's centre went through a more violent commercialization lays in the abovementioned restitution policies lacking any strategic planning. After the Velvet Revolution, tourism was one of the few prospering sectors in the urban economy, but the tourist infrastructure of the country was in need of new investments to keep up with the growing tourist numbers, and the historic centre also needed severe renovation works. With careful planning the financial resources of the tourism sector could have contributed to an even growth and gradual upgrade of the city, but this happened only partially. The decentralized municipal system and planning profession could not control the liberalized economic processes in the tourism sector, but neither the post-socialist society had any trust that any form of central planning could handle any market oriented issues. In this delicate situation, the in-kind restitution of the building stock of the centre and the small privatization of commerce intervened radically in the development of the functional system and tourist space system of the inner city. To protect the original tenants, the state also imposed fixed rents in the newly restituted properties; few of the compensated new owners kept such residential housings among such conditions, therefore many of these buildings ended up in the liberalized property market. A booming tourism sector created a demand for accommodation, and investors could select from a large market of historical buildings nearest to the flows of tourists. Foreign investors had the capital to compensate tenants; therefore these buildings were rapidly emptied out, ready for redevelopment. The tourist-historic city loose local inhabitants and services fast, but at least the physical rehabilitation also speeded up. As tourists were served where they liked to be the most – in the most attractive parts of the historic city – a well delimited area segregated functionally from local areas could consolidate rapidly.

It is probable that no other city had simultaneously such a boom in tourism demand and such abundant and in-place possibilities to build supply infrastructures. In Hungary, voucher compensation was introduced instead of in-kind restitution, and former tenants could become owners of their apartments at a heavily subsidized price. This policy made difficult enough the privatization of entire buildings, as investors had to negotiate with all separate owners of the singular apartments. This property structure still slows down hotel development in Budapest, where the new constructions on the very few empty infill plots were many times more profitable and fast than a hotel conversion project.

Conclusions

This paper gave some evidence on how extreme planning and policy procedures helped to boost a very intense and concentrated form of urban touristification. It can be concluded, that in a post-socialist situation a double effort in planning and policy-making would have been needed first to compensate the limiting givens of an obsolete tourist infrastructure inherited from communism, and second to compensate the profit-maximizing attitude of the actors of a freshly liberated market economy.

The limitations of this study lay in the fact that it still focuses on the deviations from good practices that caused problems, and not on the good practices itself that lead to a sustainable destination management.

Still, the results help the planning profession to be more aware of the cause and effect relation between urban planning and tourist consumption in tourist-historic cities. There is still little awareness on the need to regulate tourism in cities, and little knowledge on how to regulate it through policies and planning procedures. The uninterrupted planning traditions of the Austrian capital made possible the balanced regulation of the hotel industry in a liberal economy, acknowledging since 1955 the importance to integrate urban planning and tourism policies. The exact procedures of the good practice of Vienna were not fully revealed in this paper, as the main recipe is not in some special planning measures but in the long-term policy practice of balancing the needs of housing, tourism and urban development, making large structural changes (like the development area of the new Hauptbahnhof) only by following careful planning processes.

The deviation of such standard procedures delivers much more measurable impacts; therefore these were examined more deeply. The example of Budapest showed how a different kind of privatization of the housing market made commercialization of living neighbourhoods much more difficult than in Prague. While the policy of regulated rents after an in-kind restitution process favoured commercialization – therefore the appearance of hotels in the historic centre of Prague – a similar policy favouring long term tenants slowed down this process in the Viennese situation with a traditionally established property ownership. No rent regulation was needed to keep predominantly residential central Budapest as the micro-privatization process in itself impeded commercialization.

The other deviation analysed came from the central planning procedures of socialism. The liberalized tourism industry took advantage of the obsolete peripheral placement of large hotels in Prague, but this contributed to the over-touristification of the centre. The buffer zone of the historic belt around the centre remained without hotels or tourist, as budget travellers commuted by motorized transport from the periphery to the centre, while wealthier tourists could stay in the many hotels of the central core developed form privatized residential buildings.

Contemporary trends like Airbnb bring new challenges to the planning profession involved in tourism management. New forms of accommodation might change the spatial structure of tourism for good or for bad in these cities, and the methods used in this study will be usable only to give a follow-up of the processes to come. Still, if these cities learn the lesson of how the mismanagement of Prague's hotel development history lead to spatial problems of tourism consumption, they might be more capable to use good planning procedures to manage these contemporary challenges.

Disclosure statement

No potential conflict of interest was reported by the author.

References

Alonso, W. (1964). *Location and land use. Toward a general theory of land rent.* Cambridge, MA: Harvard University Press.

Arbel, A., & Pizam, A. (1977). Some determinants of urban hotel location: The tourists' inclinations. *Journal of Travel Research, 15*(3), 18–22.

Ashworth, G. J. (1989). Accommodation and the historic city. *Built Environment, 15*(2), 92–100.

Ashworth, G. J., & Page, S. J. (2011). Urban tourism research: Recent progress and current paradoxes. *Tourism Management, 32*(1), 1–15.

Ashworth, G. J., & Turnbridge, J. E. (1990). *The tourist-historic city*. London: Belhaven Press.

Bégin, S. (2000). The geography of a tourist business: Hotel distribution and urban development in Xiamen, China. *Tourism Geographies, 2*(4), 448–471.

Böröcz, J. (1990). Hungary as a destination 1960–1984. *Annals of Tourism Research, 17,* 19–35.

Butler, R. W. (1980). The concept of the tourist area life-cycle of evolution: Implications for management of resources. *Canadian Geographer, 24*(1), 5–12.

Colomb, C., & Novy, J. (Eds.) (2016). *Protest and resistance in the tourist city*. London: Routledge.

Cooper, C., & Morpeth, N. (1998). The impact of tourism on residential experience in central-eastern Europe: The development of a new legitimation crisis in the Czech Republic. *Urban Studies, 35* (12), 2253–2275.

Crowder, R. W. (1994). Restitution in the Czech Republic: Problems and Prague-nosis. *Indiana International & Comparative Law Review, 5*(1), 237–265.

CSO (Czech Statistical Office). (2015). *Tourism*. Retrieved from https://www.czso.cz/csu/czso/cestovni_ruch

Deichmann, J. I. (2002). International tourism and the sensitivities of central Prague's residents. *Journal of Tourism Studies, 13*(2), 41–52.

Dolnicar, S., Grabler, K., & Mazanec, J. A. (2000). Analyzing destination images: A perceptual charting approach. *Journal of Travel & Tourism Marketing, 8*(4), 43–57.

Dumbrovska, V. (2017). Urban tourism development in Prague: From tourist Mecca to tourist Ghetto. In N. Bellini & C. Pasquinelli (Eds.), *Tourism in the city* (pp. 275–283). Basel: Springer International Publishing.

Dumbrovská, V., & Fialová, D. (2014). Tourist intensity in capital cities in central Europe: Comparative analysis of tourism in Prague, Vienna and Budapest. *Czech Journal of Tourism, 3*(1), 5–26.

Egan, D. J., & Nield, K. (2000). Towards a theory of intraurban hotel location. *Urban Studies, 37*(3), 611–621.

Garay, L., & Cànoves, G. (2011). Life cycles, stages and tourism history: The Catalonia (Spain) experience. *Annals of Tourism Research, 38*(2), 651–671.

Gutierrez, J., Garcia-Palomares, J. C., Romanillos, G., & Salas-Olmedo, M. H. (2016). Airbnb in touristic cities: Comparing spatial patterns of hotels and peer-to-peer accommodations. *arXiv, 62,* 1–17.

Hammersley, R., & Westlake, T. (1996). Planning in the Prague region – Past, present and future. *Cities, 13*(4), 247–256.

Hegedüs, J., Horváth, V., & Tosics, N. (2014). Economic and legal conflicts between landlords and tenants in the Hungarian private rental sector. *International Journal of Housing Policy, 14*(2), 141–163.

Hegedüs, J., & Teller, N. (2005). Development of the housing allowance programmes in Hungary in the context of CEE transitional countries. *European Journal of Housing Policy, 5*(2), 187–209.

Henderson, J. C. (2002). Heritage attractions and tourism development in Asia: A comparative study of Hong Kong and Singapore. *International Journal of Tourism Research, 4,* 337–344.

Hoffman, L. M. (1994). After the fall – Crisis and renewal in urban-planning in the Czech-Republic. *International Journal of Urban and Regional Research, 18*(4), 691–702.

Hoffman, L. M., & Musil, J. (1999). Culture meets commerce: Tourism in postcommunist Prague. In D. Judd & S. Fainstein (Eds.), *The tourist city* (pp. 179–197). New Haven, CT: Yale University Press.

Hoffman, L. M., & Musil, J. (2009). *Prague, tourism and the post-industrial city* . A Great Cities Institute College of Urban Planning and Public Affairs Working Paper. No. GCP-09-05. Chicago: University of Illinois.

Johnson, M. (1995). Czech and Slovak tourism patterns – Problems and prospects. *Tourism Management, 16*(1), 21–28.

Johnson, M. (1997). Hungary's hotel industry in transition, 1960–1996. *Tourism Management, 18*(7), 441–452.

Kádár, B. (2012). Spatial patterns of urban tourism in Vienna, Prague and Budapest. In V. Szirmai & H. Fassmann (Eds.), *Metropolitan regions in Europe* (pp. 277–312). Budapest: Austrian-Hungarian Action Found.

Kádár, B. (2013). Differences in the spatial patterns of urban tourism in Vienna and Prague. *Urbani Izziv, 24*(2), 96–111.

Kádár, B. (2014). Measuring tourist activities in cities using geotagged photography. *Tourism Geographies, 16*(1), 88–104.

Kot, A., & Kowalczyk, A. (1997). The model of hotel location in Prague. *Acta Universitatis Carolinae Geographica, XXXII*(Supplementum), 349–356.

Law, C. M. (1994). *Urban tourism – Attracting visitors to large cities.* London: Mansell.

Lew, A. A. (2013). Scale, change and resilience in community tourism planning. *Tourism Geographies, 16*(1), 14–22.

Li, M., Fang, L., Huang, X., & Goh, C. (2015). A spatial-temporal analysis of hotels in urban tourism destination. *International Journal of Hospitality Management, 45*, 34–43.

Lux, M., & Mikeszova, M. (2012). Property restitution and private rental housing in transition: The case of the Czech Republic. *Housing Studies, 27*(1), 77–96.

Maier, K. (1998). Czech planning in transition: Assets and deficiencies. *International Planning Studies, 3*(3), 351–365.

McNeill, D. (2008). The hotel and the city. *Progress in Human Geography, 32*(3), 383–398.

Municipal Department 18. (2001). *Strategy Plan for Vienna.* Wien: Municipal Department 18. Retrieved from https://www.wien.gv.at/stadtentwicklung/dienststellen/ma18/

Nedović-Budić, Z. (2001). Adjustment of planning practice to the new eastern and central European context. *Journal of the American Planning Association, 67*(1), 38–52.

Paal, M. (2003). Metropolitan governance and regional planning in Vienna. In W. Salet, A. Thornley, & A. Kreukels (Eds.), *Metropolitan governance and spatial planning* (pp. 230–243). London and New York: Spon Press.

Pearce, D. G. (1998). Tourist districts in Paris: Structure and functions. *Tourism Management, 19*(1), 49–65.

Pearce, D. G. (2001). An integrative framework for urban tourism research. *Annals of Tourism Research, 28*(4), 926–946.

Pixová, M., & Sládek, J. (2016). Touristification and awakening civil society in post-socialist Prague. In J. Novy & C. Colomb (Eds.), *Protest and resistance in the tourist city, contemporary geographies of leisure, tourism and mobility* (pp. 73–89). London: Routledge.

Puczkó, L., & Rátz, T. (2000). The three forming one: Destination BPV. In J. Ruddy & S. Flanagan (Eds.), *Tourism destination marketing. Gaining the competitive edge* (pp. 367–377). Dublin: Tourism Research Centre – Dublin Institute of Technology.

Rátz, T., Smith, M., & Michalkó, G. (2008). New places in old spaces: Mapping tourism and regeneration in Budapest. *Tourism Geographies, 10*(4), 429–451.

Reiner, T. A., & Strong, A. L. (1995). Formation of land and housing markets in the Czech-Republic. *Journal of the American Planning Association, 61*(2), 200–209.

Rogerson, J. M. (2013). Reconfiguring South Africa's hotel industry 1990–2010: Structure, segmentation, and spatial transformation. *Applied Geography, 36*, 59–68.

Rogerson, J. M. (2014). Hotel Location in Africa's world class city: The case of Johannesburg, South Africa. *Bulletin of Geography, 25*(25), 181–196.

Russo, A. P. (2002). The "Vicious Circle" of tourism development in heritage cities. *Annals of Tourism Research, 29*(1), 165–182.

Russo, A. P., & van der Borg, J. (2002). Planning considerations for cultural tourism: A case study of four European cities. *Tourism Management, 23*(6), 631–637.

Shoval, N. (2006). The geography of hotels in cities: An empirical validation of a forgotten model. *Tourism Geographies, 8*, 56–75.

Shoval, N., & Cohen-Hattab, K. (2001). Urban hotel development patterns in the face of political shifts. *Annals of Tourism Research, 28*(4), 908–925.

Shoval, N., McKercher, B., Ng, E., & Birenboim, A. (2011). Hotel location and tourist activity in cities. *Annals of Tourism Research, 38*(4), 1594–1612.

Simpson, F. (1999). Tourist impact in the historic centre of Prague: Resident and visitor perceptions of the historic built environment. *The Geographical Journal, 165*(2), 173–183.

Simpson, F., & Chapman, M. (1999). Comparison of urban governance and planning policy – East looking West. *Cities, 16*(5), 353–364.

Sykora, L. (1999). Changes in the internal spatial structure of post-communist Prague. *GeoJournal, 49* (1), 79–89.

Sýkora, L. (1994). Local urban restructuring as a mirror of globalisation processes: Prague in the 1990s. *Urban Studies, 31*(7), 1149–1166.

Sykora, L., & Simonickova, I. (1994). From totalitarian urban managerialism to a liberalized real estate market: Prague's transformations in the early 1990s. In M. Barlow, P. Dostal, & M. Hampl (Eds.), *Development and administration of Prague* (pp. 47–72). Amsterdam: University of Amsterdam.

Temelová, J., & Dvořáková, N. (2012). Residential satisfaction of elderly in the city centre: The case of revitalizing neighbourhoods in Prague. *Cities, 29*(5), 310–317.

TourMIS. (2016). City tourism in Europe. Retrieved from http://www.tourmis.info

Urtasun, A., & Gutiérrez, I. (2006). Hotel location in tourism cities: Madrid 1936–1998. *Annals of Tourism Research, 33*(2), 382–402.

WienTourismus. (2005). *Wien-Tourismus 50 Jahre & die Zukunft 1955–2005*. Wien: Wiener Tourismusverband.

WienTourismus. (2014). *Tourismus Strategie 2020*. Wien: WienTourismus. Retrieved from http://tourismusstrategie2020.wien.info/downloads/WT-Tourismusstrategie-2020.pdf

Yang, Y., Luo, H., & Law, R. (2014). Theoretical, empirical, and operational models in hotel location research. *International Journal of Hospitality Management, 36*, 209–220.

Yang, Y., Wong, K. K. F., & Wang, T. (2012a). How do hotels choose their location? Evidence from hotels in Beijing. *International Journal of Hospitality Management, 31*(3), 675–685.

Yang, Y., Wong, K. K. F., & Wang, T. (2012b). How do hotels choose their location? Evidence from hotels in Beijing. *International Journal of Hospitality Management, 31*(3), 675–685.

Final reflections: Whither tourism research in the era of (post-)post-communism?

PIOTR NIEWIADOMSKI

When in 2004 Stenning and Bradshaw (2004, p. 254) reflected on the usefulness of the category of post-socialism and concluded that "only time will tell how long such a category is useful, but its time is not yet up", not many scholars or commentators were able to predict that these words would still hold true two decades later (i.e. over 30 years after the collapse of communism). While the predictions may have differed in terms of the level of optimism, there was a common expectation that sooner or later the transition would be over and that the period of post-socialism would be naturally superseded by an era where the influence of the communist past on the CEE economies and the daily lives of the CEE societies recedes into insignificance (Stenning and Bradshaw, 2004). With the European Union (EU) serving as "a model of democratic and economic stability to be pursued by the new or newly democratic countries of Europe" (Smith, 1996, p. 6), and the European Commission actively guiding many CEE states' transition from central planning to market (Dunford and Smith, 2004), the ongoing European integration played a key role in fostering this process (see Hudson, 2000, 2002, 2003 for a series of reflections and comments). Indeed, the admission of eight formerly communist states to the EU in 2004 (followed by three more between 2007 and 2013) and ten formerly communist countries (including six former members of the Warsaw Pact and three former Soviet republics!) to NATO between 1999 and 2004 (followed by four more between 2009 and 2020) not only fully attested to the changes made by these countries, but, to many of them, also symbolically marked an end of the transition, i.e. an end of post-socialism/post-communism (Pickles, 2010).

However, the shocking events in Ukraine are pungent evidence that the category of post-communism has not yet lost its analytical weight. Although expected by some as early as the annexation of Crimea in 2014, the invasion of Ukraine came as a shock and left Europe and the rest of the world in disbelief – how is it possible that after everything CEE has been through the region has to experience another destructive conflict and how is it possible that over 30 years after most CEE countries embarked on a transition from state socialism to capitalism and democracy the longing to rebuild the Soviet order in some parts of CEE can be still so strong? Indeed, apart from causing many personal tragedies and bringing a significant political, social, and economic turmoil to Europe, the invasion of Ukraine has resurrected the ghost of communism, thus reminding the world that the communist legacies continue to shape the reality of the CEE region and that post-communism is not yet over.

The events in Ukraine, however, are not the only element that attests to the incessant influence of the communist past on the presence. The rise of different populist, semi-authoritarian regimes across CEE (e.g. in Hungary and Poland), which rely on and cultivate anti-European and anti-Western sentiments, not only undermine the many successes of post-socialist transformations but also seem to push parts of CEE away from the West in political, economic, social, and geopolitical terms. Thus, instead of bringing post-communism to an end, the CEE region has entered a bizarre (and rather unexpected) era of "post-post-communism" where the trajectories of CEE countries are even more diverse than before. Because of the new wave of clashes between those looking to the West and those driven by a nostalgia for the preceding era (and led, arguably, by the last generation of politicians who obtained their education and upbringing in the communist period), the states of CEE no longer share a common objective as they did in the 1990s and throughout the first stages of transition (albeit with exceptions). While some of them have long integrated with the West, successfully developed a non-communist identity, and minimised (or suppressed) any potential influence of the communist past on the presence, others have either changed very little or are subject to a re-emergence of authoritarian tendencies that are directly or indirectly rooted in the practices inherited from the communist system. While in the 1990s and 2000s there was something "uniquely post-socialist" about CEE (Stenning and Bradshaw, 2004, p. 254), it is justifiable to infer that CEE is now uniquely and chaotically "post-post-socialist".

In this respect, the most pertinent question that needs to be asked to conclude this volume is how the (post)-post-communist reality of CEE is shaping tourism development in the region and what impacts on this new reality tourism has. Just like 20–30 years ago the task for geographers was to account for the post-socialist uniqueness of CEE and to ask what difference post-socialism makes (Stenning and Bradshaw, 2004), the challenge for geographers nowadays is to take stock of this new set of processes to make better sense of the constantly evolving diversity across CEE and offer a fuller understanding of how post-communism has moulded the region in political, social, and economic terms. To analyse the interrelationships between all these processes and tourism is, by extension, the main challenge for tourism geographers. However, given that research on tourism in the era of (post-)post-communism will be a natural continuation of the work on tourism and post-communist transformations, accounting for the scholarship on tourism development in post-communist states to date is essential groundwork if tourism geographers are to rise to this challenge. The aim of this volume is thus to lay foundations for further work on tourism in CEE and help set this process in motion.

Although it is always risky to speculate about future developments on the ground, a few key research themes that are likely to emerge in the near future can be easily identified with a degree of certainty. Given that warfare and any forms of civil unrest or political instability in tourist destinations are very strong factors deterring visitation (Suntikul, 2019; Williams, 2009), rather unsurprisingly (at least in the short term), the impacts of the events in Ukraine on the real and perceived safety of travelling to CEE will be likely at the top of this agenda. As the World Tourism Organization (UNWTO) (2022) reported, apart from Ukraine (because of the war) and Russia (because of the restrictions imposed by other states), whose tourism industries have been affected the most, in the first three months after the invasion most CEE states (mainly those neighbouring with Ukraine) noted a sudden drop in inbound flights – from 69% (Moldova), 42% (Slovenia), and 38% (Latvia) to approximately 20% in Hungary and Slovakia. The rising costs of fuel (and, hence, of transport) and the overall economic crisis caused by the war are just further consequences of the events in Ukraine that are affecting visitation to CEE (UNWTO, 2022). However, the invasion of Ukraine is also seen to have a major impact on non-CEE tourist destinations – another major theme for tourism geographers to explore in the short and medium term. Apart from the fact that the war in Ukraine has affected the overall level of confidence to global travel (UNWTO, 2022) and that the economic consequences of the invasion (including, importantly, the related energy crisis) are also seen outside CEE, international tourist markets are suffering from the shortage of Ukrainian and Russian visitors who, before the invasion, accounted altogether for 4% of international tourist arrivals and 3% of global spending on international tourism (UNWTO, 2022). Although famous European and non-European sun-and-sea destinations are hit most strongly, some Western European markets also noted a significant decrease in inbound flights in the aftermath of the invasion – from 36% and 34% in Finland and Sweden, respectively (both non-NATO members at the time of invasion, although their applications to join NATO are now under way!), to 28% in the UK and 24% in Germany (UNWTO, 2022).

In the longer term, in turn, research on tourism in (post)-post-communist states will likely unfold in multiple diverse directions, largely reflecting the avenues followed by tourism geographers after the fall of communism and thus directly building on that scholarship (although new research themes will also surely emerge). Assuming that Ukraine remains independent and regains its territorial integrity, bulk research will quite naturally concentrate on Ukraine, especially that its geopolitical situation will likely remain challenging (see Berryman, 2017, and Doan and Kiptenko, 2017, for a more in-depth discussion of Ukraine's geopolitical situation). The long-term impacts of the invasion on Ukraine as a tourist destination will also become one of the dominant themes. Much will depend in this respect on the trajectory which the country will follow, i.e. will it join the EU and NATO as it intended before the invasion or will it remain politically and socially divided, with some territories and social groups looking to the West, with others associating themselves with Russia? The important decisions which Ukrainian political leaders will have to make, and which will determine the position of Ukraine as a tourist market, will by themselves become a critical research agenda. In this respect, many parallels will be drawn to the Balkans in the 1990s and the many general dilemmas and problems which CEE countries faced after 1989 – from questions surrounding the (re-)organisation of the tourism industry and re-building the essential tourism infrastructure (see Chapters 2 and 4 in this volume) to questions about a (new?) post-war identity of the Ukrainian nation and a cultural meaning of the physical and non-physical legacies of the invasion (see Chapter 3 in this volume). Quite likely, assuming that safety will no longer be a concern, Ukraine will become a new, intriguing dark tourism destination, although reasons for engaging in such an activity may differ widely and new contributions to the ethical debates surrounding dark tourism may be made (Robinson et al., 2020; Sharpley and Stone, 2009; Williams, 2009). In turn, if Ukraine wins the war and if the post-war geopolitical circumstances (e.g. its future relations with Russia) allow Ukraine to align closer with the West and join the EU, the effects of this integration on tourism (re-) development in Ukraine (like in the case of Estonia – see Chapter 8 in this volume) will also be a key topic to explore.

At the same time, much research will likely focus on the role of tourism in re-building, re-developing, and re-structuring the Ukrainian economy after the war, mirroring the research on tourism as a force fostering post-communist transformations in the 1990s and 2000s (see Part II in this volume). Rather undoubtedly, if Ukraine again opens up to international tourism, the role of tourism in reconstructing the destroyed cities and (re-)positioning them as tourist destinations will be a particularly important research topic because of its applied value for planners and policy-makers (see Chapters 9, 10, 13, and 14 in this volume). As a substantial source of employment (Niewiadomski, 2017; Sharpley and Telfer, 2002; Williams, 2009), tourism will also be crucial to numerous livelihoods and the survival of many households in the post-war Ukraine – in urban and rural contexts. The contribution of transnational tourism corporations (e.g. hotels or travel agents) to the economic (re-)development of Ukraine (e.g. through foreign direct investment or different non-equity contracts like franchising) will also attract scholarly work (see Chapter 12 in this volume). Finally, from a purely geographical point of view, one of the key topics to address will be the role of tourism in mitigating (or deepening?) the regional economic disparities across Ukraine (see Mykhnenko and Swain, 2010), which – given the political and social differences between the various parts of the country – may be a much more complex and challenging research agenda than it would be otherwise.

The long-term effects of the invasion of Ukraine on tourism in the CEE region will also be naturally seen and researched in other CEE countries. These will range from the general perception of CEE as a tourist region to various more specific themes such as the contribution of Ukrainian refugee workers to the tourism industries in the countries where they have been offered shelter. Suffice to say, within the first two months after the invasion, 1.6 million Ukrainian refugees escaped to Poland, 0.6 million entered Germany, 0.4 million went to the Czech Republic, and over 0.3 million fled to Romania, with services being one of the key industries where Ukrainian refugees found employment (OECD, 2022). As Chapter 6 in this volume showed with regard to Hungary after 1989, Ukrainian refugees who do not return to Ukraine after the war will likely foster new forms of tourist flows between Ukraine and CEE (such as VF&R – visiting friends and relatives) and new forms of transnational, tourism-related relations between Ukraine and the rest of Europe – especially if they make investments in their home country through buying or developing tourism-related facilities and real estate. Also, one of the main research themes to emerge will focus on the position of Russia in the global tourism nexus, especially if the restrictions imposed on Russia by the West remain and the political, economic, and social line of division between Russia (and its allies) and the rest of the world persists. As Brexit demonstrated (Chen et al., 2018; Giles, 2021; Kelly, 2022), disentangling a whole country from the global economy or any part of it (voluntary or not) is not easy, if possible at all, and it will always have repercussions for every party involved. The aforementioned decrease in the volumes of Russian outbound tourists, the expected drop in Russian investments in tourism abroad, the effective closure of Russia as a tourist destination, and the cancellation of various international events in Russia will undoubtedly necessitate numerous adjustments in global tourism and give rise to new (global) tourism patterns, many of which may prove permanent and irreversible.

The renewed awareness of the CEE region's communist past may also refresh international tourists' interest in the legacies of the communist period. This will likely include the legacies of the Cold War – the tensions between Russia (then the Soviet Union) and the rest of the communist bloc on the one hand and the Western world on the other, which the current situation resembles very strongly, even though many countries have since changed sides. The rise of various far-right and semi-authoritarian tendencies across CEE, most of which cultivate nationalistic and anti-Western attitudes and views, and which are, as such, a fertile ground for some of the pre-1989 practices to re-emerge, will also be now likely looked at in a different, more informed, and more historically aware way. The threat which they pose to the democratic systems of post-communist countries and, therefore, their reputations as tourist destinations and their respective tourism industries is therefore realistic and cannot be ignored in academic work on tourism in the (post-)post-communist reality.

Finally, the revived attention to the legacies of communism and the risk that the communist past may re-surface in various forms may also need to be factored in in research on those aspects of tourism in CEE, which at first sight have very little to do with the communist history of the region. The ongoing post-COVID-19 recovery of tourism across CEE, which is being slowed down in economic terms by the current events, can serve here as one of the examples. Another example is the global sustainability agenda where tourism has its own natural place (see e.g. UNWTO and UNDP, 2017, for the relations between tourism and the UN Sustainable Development Goals). Given that environmental protection had not been a priority for communist governments, it will be pertinent to investigate to what extent any legacies of this environmental negligence are hampering sustainable tourism development in CEE nowadays.

The research on tourism in post-communist states, some of which this volume has brought together, will undoubtedly require a continuation if the general understanding of tourism in CEE as a formerly communist region (rather than as a mere geographical location) is to be developed in response to the new circumstances such as the events in Ukraine. Indeed, the war in Ukraine as well as the conflicting development agendas across CEE that attest to the political, social, and economic complexity of the region and which are likely to determine tourism development in CEE in the years to come warrant a need to study the region further. Although scholarly interest in tourism in CEE has not disappeared (see e.g. the volumes edited by Hall, 2017, and Janta et al., 2022), the recognition that the legacies of communism continue to push CEE states in various divergent directions has waned over time. Since many of the topics discussed in this volume need follow-up research, the aim of this book is to lay foundations for this new emerging agenda and help tourism geographers (and other scholars) make a first step towards addressing it.

References

Berryman, J. (2017) Crimea: geopolitics and tourism, in: D. Hall (ed.) *Tourism and Geopolitics: Issues and Concepts from Central and Eastern Europe*, Wallingford: CABI, pp. 57–70

Chen, J., Ebeke, C., Lin, L., Qu, H., Siminitz, J. (2022) Brexit: the long-term impact of Brexit on the European Union, *IMF Blog*, 10 Aug 2018, available at: www.imf.org (accessed on 7th October 2022)

Doan, P., Kiptenko, V. (2017) The geopolitical trial of tourism in modern Ukraine, in: D. Hall (ed.) *Tourism and Geopolitics: Issues and Concepts from Central and Eastern Europe*, Wallingford: CABI, pp. 71–86

Dunford, M., Smith, A. (2004) Economic restructuring and employment change, in: M. Bradshaw, A. Stenning (eds.) *East Central Europe and the Former Soviet Union*, Harlow: Pearson, pp. 33–58

Giles, C. (2021) Brexit one year on: the impact on the UK economy, *Financial Times*, 23 Dec 2021, available at: www.ft.com (accessed on 4th October 2022)

Hall, D. (ed.) (2017) *Tourism and Geopolitics: Issues and Concepts from Central and Eastern Europe*, Wallingford: CABI

Hudson, R. (2000) One Europe or many? Reflections on becoming European, *Transactions of the Institute of British Geographers*, 25, pp. 409–426

Hudson, R. (2002), Changing industrial production systems and regional development in the New Europe, *Transactions of the Institute of British Geographers*, 27, pp. 262–281

Hudson, R. (2003) European integration and new forms of uneven development (but not the end of territorially distinctive capitalisms in Europe), *European Urban and Regional Studies*, 10, pp. 49–67

Janta, H., Andriotis, K., Stylidis, D. (eds) (2022) *Tourism and Planning in Eastern Europe*, Wallingford: CABI

Kelly, M. (2022) Brexit effect comes into focus, *Financial Times*, 20 June, 2022, available at: www.ft.com (accessed on 4th October 2022)

Mykhnenko, V., Swain, A. (2010) Ukraine's diverging space-economy: The Orange Revolution, post-soviet development models and regional trajectories, *European Urban and Regional Studies*, 17, pp. 141–165

Niewiadomski, P. (2017) Economics of tourism, in: Lowry, L. (ed.) *The SAGE International Encyclopedia of Travel and Tourism*, Thousand Oaks: SAGE Publications, pp. 392–396

OECD (Organisation for Economic Co-operation and Development) (2022) The potential contribution of Ukrainian refugees to the labour force in European host countries, OECD, 27 July 2022, available at: www.oecd.org (accessed on 29th September 2022)

Pickles, J. (2010) The spirit of post-socialism: common spaces and the production of diversity, *European Urban and Regional Studies*, 17, pp. 127–140

Robinson, P., Luck, M., Smith, S. (2020) *Tourism*, 2nd edition, Wallingford: CABI

Sharpley, R., Stone, P. (eds) (2009) *The Darker Side of Travel: The Theory and Practice of Dark Tourism*, Aspects of Tourism Series, Bristol: Channel View Publications

Sharpley, R., Telfer, D. (eds) (2002) *Tourism and Development: Concepts and Issues*, Clevedon: Channel View Publications

Smith, A. (1996) The European Union and a changing Europe: establishing the boundaries of order, *Journal of Common Market Studies*, 34, pp. 5–28

Stenning, A., Bradshaw, M. (2004) Conclusions: facing the future?, in: M. Bradshaw, A. Stenning (eds) *East Central Europe and the Former Soviet Union*, Harlow: Pearson, pp. 247–256

Suntikul, W. (2019) Tourism and war: global perspectives, in: T. Dallen (ed.) *Handbook of Globalisation and Tourism*, Edward Elgar: Cheltenham, pp. 139–148

UNWTO (World Tourism Organization) (2022) *Impact of the Russian Offensive in Ukraine on International Tourism*, UNWTO 2022, available at: www.unwto.org (accessed on 29th September 2022)

UNWTO and UNDP (World Tourism Organization & United Nations Development Programme) (2017) *Tourism and the Sustainable Development Goals – Journey to 2030*, World Tourism Organization, 2017, retrieved from www.unwto.org in June 2020

Williams, S. (2009) *Tourism Geography: A New Synthesis*, 2nd edition, Abingdon: Routledge

Index